Vagueness
A Reader

Contents

Vagueness
A Reader

1   Introduction: theories of vagueness

Rosanna Keefe and Peter Smith

After this introductory essay, the papers in the volume fall into four groups.[1]

Papers 2 to 6. This selection of historically notable pieces starts with some brief passages from ancient sources. These engagingly illustrate the sorites paradox, one of the most striking problems to which vagueness gives rise. But although there was interest in the paradox in antiquity, there seems to have been relatively little further discussion of vagueness before Bertrand Russell's seminal paper, included here. A shortened version of a paper by Max Black follows, together with an excerpt from Carl Hempel's reply to Black, and a brief account of vagueness by Henryk Mehlberg.

Papers 7 to 11. Around the 1970s there was an explosion of interest in the topic; a range of detailed theories emerged which are represented in this group of classic papers. James Cargile motivates the epistemic view of vagueness; Kit Fine's contribution is the prime source of the supervaluationist theory (which is prefigured in Mehlberg); and Kenton Machina develops one version of a degree theory. Michael Dummett's and Crispin Wright's rich papers have also been the starting point for much subsequent debate.

Papers 12 to 16. Papers in the third group are more recent, but are also likely to become lasting contributions. The second piece by Crispin Wright develops and extends his earlier work. R. M. Sainsbury calls for a radical rethink of the assumptions that he claims are shared by the standard theories. In contrast, Timothy Williamson offers a detailed defense of the epistemic view, and Michael Tye develops a three-valued logic of vagueness. And in her contribution newly written for this volume, Dorothy Edgington offers an original form of degree theory.

Papers 17 to 19. The final papers form part of a clearly separable debate about vague objects and vague identity. Gareth Evans's short but much-discussed article presents an argument which purports to

---

This introduction is closely based on material from Rosanna Keefe's Cambridge University doctoral thesis.

1.   Throughout this Reader, citations given by author name alone refer to selections in this volume (where necessary, we use "Wright (I)" and "Wright (II)" to distinguish the two contributions by this author). Citations in author–date form refer to other items listed in the bibliography.

show that there can be no vague objects. David Lewis clarifies what he takes to be the intended argument, while Terence Parsons and Peter Woodruff criticize Evans's reasoning and defend the notion of indeterminate identity.

In the rest of this introduction, we look at main themes from the collected papers and at some other discussions in the literature. §1 is a general overview of the issues. In §§2 to 4, we focus on three major theories of vagueness, explaining their motivations and outlining some potential objections. Finally, in §5, we survey some of the continuing debate on vague objects and vagueness in the world.

1 Overview

The predicates "tall", "red", "bald", "heap", "tadpole" and "child" are paradigmatically vague. We begin by noting three interrelated features of such predicates—features that intuitively are closely bound up with their vagueness.

First, our sample predicates have *borderline cases*. These are, roughly, cases where it is unclear whether or not the predicate applies. Some people are borderline tall: not clearly tall and not clearly not tall. Certain reddish-orange patches are borderline red. And during a creature's transition from tadpole to frog, there will be stages at which it is a borderline case of a tadpole.

Suppose Tek is borderline tall. It seems that the unclarity about whether he is tall is not merely epistemic. For a start, no amount of further information about his exact height (and the heights of others) could help us decide whether he *is* tall. Plausibly, there is no fact of the matter here about which we are ignorant: rather, it is *indeterminate* whether Tek is tall. And arguably this indeterminacy amounts to the sentence "Tek is tall" being neither true nor false, which violates the classical principle of bivalence. The law of excluded middle similarly comes into question: "either Tek is tall or he is not" seems untrue (indeed, as Dummett p. 106 points out, we sometimes assert an instance of the law—e.g. "either he's your brother or he isn't"—in order to convey the *non*-vagueness of a sentence).

A second characteristic of vague predicates is that they apparently lack well-defined extensions. On a scale of heights, there is *no sharp boundary* between the tall people and the rest; nor is there an exact point at which our growing creature ceases to be a tadpole.[2] More generally,

---

2. It is occasionally argued that e.g. "bald" and "heap" do in fact have sharp boundaries—no one is bald unless they have absolutely no hair, and four grains can suffice to make a heap. But even if we accept there are sharp boundaries in these cases, no parallels seem available for "nearly bald", "tall", "clever" or, indeed, for most candidate vague predicates.

if we imagine candidates for satisfying some vague *F* to be arranged with spatial closeness indicating similarity, no sharp line can be drawn round the cases to which *F* applies. Instead, vague predicates are naturally described as having fuzzy boundaries. (Wright p. 154 cites Frege's conception of vague predicates as "dividing logical space as a blurred shadow divides the background on which it is reflected".) But according to classical logic and semantics, all predicates have well-defined extensions: they cannot have fuzzy boundaries. So again this suggests that a departure from classical conceptions is needed to accommodate vagueness.[3]

Third, our vague predicates are *susceptible to sorites paradoxes*. Intuitively, a hundredth of an inch cannot make a difference to whether a man counts as tall. Such tiny variations, which cannot be discriminated by the naked eye or even by everyday measurements, are just too small to matter: this seems part of what it is for "tall" to be a *vague* height term lacking sharp boundaries. So we have the principle $[S_1]$ if X is tall, and Y is only a hundredth of an inch shorter than X, then Y is also tall. But imagine a line of men, starting with someone seven foot tall, and each of the rest a hundredth of an inch shorter than the man in front of him. Repeated applications of $[S_1]$ as we move down the line imply that each man we encounter is tall, however far we continue. And this yields a conclusion which is clearly false, namely that a man less than five foot high, reached after three thousand steps along the line, still counts as tall.

Similarly there is the ancient example of the heap (Greek *soros*, from which the paradox derives its name). Plausibly, $[S_2]$ if X is a heap of sand, then the result Y of removing one grain will still be a heap. So take a heap and remove grains one by one; repeated applications of $[S_2]$ imply absurdly that even a solitary last grain must still count as a heap. (The paradox was supposedly first devised/discovered by Eubulides, to whom the liar paradox is also attributed. For other ancient examples see our initial selections "On the sorites", and for detailed discussion see Barnes 1982 and Burnyeat 1982.)

Arguments with a sorites structure are not mere curiosities: they feature, for example, in some familiar ethical "slippery slope" arguments (see e.g. Walton 1992 and Williams 1995). Consider the principle $[S_3]$ if it is wrong to kill something at time T after conception,

---

3. Clearly, having fuzzy boundaries is closely related to having borderline cases. It might be argued, for example, that for there to be no sharp boundary between the *F*s and not-*F*s just *is* for there to be a region of borderline cases of *F*. Our "two features" would then be better thought of as the same central feature of vague predicates seen from two different slants. Later, however, we shall question whether predicates with borderline cases must always lack sharp boundaries.

then it would be wrong to kill it at time *T* minus one second. And suppose we agree that it is wrong to kill a baby nine months after conception. Repeated applications of [S₃] would lead to the conclusion that abortion even immediately after conception would be wrong. The need to assess such practical argumentation increases the urgency of examining reasoning with vague predicates.

Prima facie, then, vague predicates have borderline cases, have fuzzy boundaries, and are susceptible to sorites paradoxes. And there are good reasons why such predicates are pervasive in our language.

Wright (p. 156) coins the phrase *tolerant* to describe predicates for which there is "a notion of degree of change too small to make any difference" to their applicability. For example, "tall" plausibly counts as tolerant since (as we have noted) a change of one hundredth of an inch never affects its applicability. A tolerant predicate must lack sharp boundaries: if *F* has sharp boundaries, then a boundary-crossing change, however small, will always make a difference to whether *F* applies. Moreover, a statement of the tolerance of *F* can characteristically serve as the inductive premiss of a sorites paradox for *F* (as in the example of "tall" again). Arguments that predicates of a given class are tolerant are thus arguments for their vagueness.

Wright (I) develops, in detail, a series of considerations which seem to support the thesis that many of our predicates *are* tolerant. As Russell also notes (p. 64), when the application of a word (e.g. a color predicate) is paradigmatically based on unaided sense perception, then it surely cannot be applicable to only one of an indiscriminable pair. So such "observational" predicates will be tolerant with respect to changes below the threshold of discriminability. Wright also argues that consideration of the role of ostension and memory in mastering the use of such predicates appears to undermine the thought that they have sharp boundaries which could not be shown by the teacher or remembered by the learner. Arguments of this kind are widely regarded as persuasive: we shall refer to them below as "typical arguments for tolerance".

Such arguments explain why vague predicates are actually so common; but they also seem to cast doubt on any suggestion that we *could* operate with a language free of vagueness. They make it difficult to see vagueness as a merely optional or eliminable feature of language, —a point that Dummett (p. 109) emphasizes, attributing to Wittgenstein the thought that natural language is essentially vague. Contrast this with the view of vagueness as a defect of language found, for example, in Frege (1903, §56) and perhaps in Russell's implication (p. 61) that language is vague because we have not bothered to make our predicates precise. We need not, however, debate the eliminability of vagueness: in natural language vague predicates are ubiquitous, and this motivates study of the phenomenon irrespective of whether there could be usable languages entirely free of vagueness. Even if "heap" could be replaced by some term "heap*" with perfectly sharp boundaries and for which no sorites paradox would arise, the paradox for our actual vague term would remain.[4]

So far, we have focused on a single dimension of variation associated with a vague predicate—e.g. height for "tall", number of grains for "heap". But many vague predicates are multi-dimensional. "Big", used to describe people, depends for its application on both height and volume; while "nice", for example, does not even have a clear-cut set of associated dimensions. Even whether something counts as a "heap" depends not only on the number of grains but also on their arrangement. The central features of vague predicates are shared by multi-dimensional instances. For example, there are borderline nice people: indeed, some are borderline *because* of the multi-dimensionality of "nice", by scoring well in some relevant respects but not in others.

Furthermore, not just *predicates* are vague. Adverbs like "quickly", quantifiers like "many" and modifiers like "very" are vague. The singular term "the grandest mountain in Scotland" is also vague, as are many terms with plural reference like "the high mountains of Scotland". Russell argues (controversially) that *all* natural language expressions are vague, including even the familiar logical connectives. For introductory purposes, however, we shall continue to concentrate on the central case of vague predicates, which is also the main focus of discussions in the literature.

We need to make three clarificatory distinctions. (a) The remark "Someone said something" would naturally be described as vague (who said what?). Similarly, "X is an integer greater than thirty" would often count as an unhelpfully vague hint about the value of X. Vagueness in this sense is underspecificity, a matter of being less than adequately informative for the purposes in hand. This seems to have nothing to do with borderline cases or with the lack of sharp boundaries—"is an integer greater than thirty" has sharp boundaries, has no borderline cases, and is not susceptible to sorites paradoxes. And it is not because of any possibility of borderline people or borderline cases of saying something that "someone said something" counts as vague in the alternative sense. The papers in this collection are representative in largely ignoring

---

4. See Carnap 1950 ch. 1, Haack 1974 ch. 6 and Quine 1981 for discussion of the replacement of vague expressions by precise ones. And see e.g. Grim 1982 on difficulties with the idea of such precise replacements.

the idea of vagueness as underspecificity.[5]

(b) Likewise, we should distinguish vagueness from paradigm context-dependence (i.e. having a different extension in different contexts), even though many terms have both features (e.g. "tall"). Fix on a context which can be made as definite as you like (in particular, choose a specific comparison class): "tall" will remain vague, with borderline cases and fuzzy boundaries, and the sorites paradox will retain its force. This indicates that we are unlikely to understand vagueness or solve the paradox by concentrating on context-dependence.[6]

(c) We might also distinguish vagueness from ambiguity. Certainly, terms can be ambiguous *and* vague: "bank" for example has two quite different main senses (concerning financial institutions or sloping river edges), both of which are vague. But "tadpole", we may suppose, has a univocal sense, though that sense does not determine a sharp, well-defined extension. Certain theories, however, do attempt to close the gap between vagueness and a form of ambiguity. Describing his super-valuationist proposals, Fine writes "vagueness is ambiguity on a grand and systematic scale" (p. 136)—for, in his view, to speak vaguely means leaving unsettled the choice between certain precise concepts.

We turn now to introducing the main theories of vagueness. Any theory needs to provide an account of borderline cases and apparently fuzzy boundaries; and this is closely tied up with the task of identifying the logic and semantics for a vague language. A theory must also tackle the sorites paradox. In addition we may expect it to deliver a criterion of vagueness.

The logic and semantics of vagueness. The simplest approach here is to retain classical logic and semantics. Borderline case predications *are* either true or false after all, but they are cases in which we do not and cannot know which. Similarly, despite appearances, vague predicates have well-defined extensions: there is, for example, a sharp boundary between the tall people and the rest, and between the red shades of the spectrum and the other colors. We are, however, ignorant of where such boundaries lie. On this *epistemic view*, vagueness is to be accounted for in terms of ignorance (see Cargile, Williamson and our §2).

---

5. See Burns 1995 for discussion of the exact relation between our original sense of vagueness and vagueness as underspecificity. Black (p. 72) complains that Russell's official definition (p. 66) confuses vagueness with generality or underspecificity. However, elsewhere in his article (e.g. p. 65) Russell seems to recognize the distinction.

6. Though see Raffman 1994 for an attempt to solve the sorites paradox by appealing to a distinctive kind of context-dependence. See also Goldstein 1988.

An alternative strategy is to say instead that when, for example, *a* is a borderline case of redness the truth-value of "*a* is red" is, as Machina puts it, "in some way peculiar, or indeterminate, or lacking entirely" (p. 175). This generates a number of non-classical options.

Note that a borderline case of the predicate *F* is equally a borderline case of not-*F*: it is unclear *whether or not* the candidate is *F*. This symmetry prevents us from simply counting a borderline *F* as not-*F*. But there are several ways of respecting this symmetry. Black takes the line that a predication in a borderline case is both true *and* false: there is a truth-value glut. A more popular position admits truth-value *gaps*: borderline predications are neither true nor false.[7]

One elegant development of the gap approach is Fine's *supervaluationism*. The basic idea is that a proposition involving, for example, the vague predicate "tall" is true (false) if it comes out true (false) on all the ways in which we can make "tall" precise (ways, that is, which preserve the truth-values of uncontentious cases of "*a* is tall"). A borderline case, "Tek is tall", will thus be neither true nor false, for it is true on some ways of making "tall" precise and false on others. But a classical tautology like "either Tek is tall or he is not tall" *will* still come out true because it remains true wherever a sharp boundary for "tall" is drawn. In this way, the supervaluationist adopts a non-classical *semantics* while aiming to minimize divergence from classical *logic* (see Mehlberg, Fine and §3).

Rather than holding that predications in borderline cases lack a truth-value, another option is to hold that they have a third value—"neutral", "indeterminate" or "indefinite"—leading to a three-valued logic (see Tye and §4). Alternatively, *degree theories* countenance degrees of truth, introducing a whole spectrum of truth-values from 0 to 1, with complete falsity as degree 0 and complete truth as degree 1. Borderline cases each take some value between 0 and 1, with "*x* is red" gradually increasing in truth-value as we move along the color spectrum from orange to red. This calls for an infinite-valued logic or a so-called "fuzzy logic", and there have been a variety of different versions (see Machina and §4; see Edgington for a non-standard degree theory).

In addition to considering the truth-values of borderline predications, we may seek to express in the object-language the fact that a given predication is, or that it is not, of borderline status. A common strategy is to introduce sentence operators "*D*" and "*I*" such that *Dp* holds when

---

7. As Fine points out, the differences between the "gap" and "glut" approaches need not be large: truth on the gap view could just be truth-and-the-absence-of-falsity on the glut view. A glut interpretation could be adopted within the context of a paraconsistent logic—a logic that admits true contradictions (see Priest and Routley 1989, p. 389).

p is determinately or definitely true and Ip (equivalent to $\neg Dp$ & $\neg D\neg p$) holds when p is indeterminate or borderline. Plausibly, no sentence can be true without being determinately true: Dp and p should be true in exactly the same situations. The operator is not, however, redundant: $\neg Dp$ will be true, for example, in a borderline case, when $\neg p$ is indeterminate. (The terms "determinately" and "definitely" are both used in the literature, but marking no agreed distinction. Some authors use "Δ" and "∇" in place of "D" and "I" respectively; others use "Def" or "Det" for "D".)

Wright claims that "when dealing with vague expressions, it is essential to have the expressive resources afforded by an operator expressing *definiteness* or *determinacy*" (p. 229). Arguably we can then assert that there is a gap between definite truth and definite falsity, without being committed to any gap between truth and falsity (and a confusion between these gaps might explain our non-classical intuitions about borderline cases). Wright also suggests that we need to use the D operator to say what it is for a predicate to lack sharp boundaries. Consider a series of objects x_i which form a suitable sorites series for F (e.g., for "bald", take a row of men with progressively less hair). Wright proposes (p. 229)

(W) "F" lacks sharp boundaries when there is no i for which DFx_i & $D\neg Fx_{i+1}$.

This can be contrasted with the suggestion that a predicate lacks sharp boundaries when it is tolerant—i.e. when there is no i such that Fx_i & $\neg Fx_{i+1}$. Tolerance gives rise to paradox; but lacking sharp boundaries in the sense of (W) does *not* lead straight to paradox. In particular, suppose that there are some instances that are indefinitely F between the definitely F cases and the definitely not-F cases. Then, as (W) requires, there will be no immediate leap from DFx_i to $D\neg Fx_{i+1}$. (See also Campbell 1974).

The D operator will be interpreted in different ways on different theories. For example, a supervaluationist will say that Dp is true just in case p is true on all ways of making it precise and is false otherwise (so if p is borderline, p itself will be neither true nor false, but Dp will be false); while the degree theorist can say that Dp is true if p is true to degree 1 and is false if p is true to any lesser degree. Alternatively the D operator could be taken as primitive, as Wright suggests. This would call for explanatory work on the logic and semantics of D, and for further clarification of its significance for the semantics of statements which do not contain this operator (for example, can using a D operator illuminate the semantics of the vague "a is red" itself?).[8]

---

8. See e.g. Wright II and Heck 1993 on the logic of the operator.

The positions sketched so far at least agree that there is *some* positive account to be given of the logic and semantics of vagueness. Other writers have taken a more pessimistic line. Dummett, as we shall see, argues that there can be no coherent logic of vague expressions. Russell takes it that logic assumes precision, and since natural language is not precise it cannot be in the province of logic at all. If Russell's "no logic" thesis requires wholesale rejection of reasoning with vague predicates—and hence of most reasoning in natural language—it would certainly seem extreme. Are there no distinctions to be drawn between good and bad arguments couched in a vague language? If not, it would seem e.g. that we would have no reason to trust the very arguments, themselves expressed in vague terms, that Russell and others present to support their "no logic" thesis. And as Cargile notes, there appear to be entirely unproblematic arguments involving vague predicates, for example, "anyone with less than 500 hairs on his head is bald; Fred has less than 500 hairs on his head; therefore Fred is bald".

With this rich variety of options available, how are we to choose between them and either identify an adequate logic of vagueness or else conclude that there cannot be one? What should we regard as showing that classical logic is inapplicable, or as justifying the adoption of some other logical system? Similar questions are raised in the selected excerpt from Hempel's paper. Black, for example, emphasizes conflicts between different speakers (and between the same speaker at different times) over the application of a vague predicate in borderline cases. But is this enough to show that the laws of classical logic do not apply? Hempel suggests not: he notes that the study of a language's semantics and associated logic proceeds at some level of abstraction from speech behavior—compare how the codification of the rules of some game may proceed at a level of abstraction from the fallible practices of players. And just as the fact that people cheat at chess does not show that the rules are not as they are standardly stated, so, for example, assertions (perhaps by different people) of both a sentence and its negation in a borderline case need not show that the law of non-contradiction fails. The general methodological issue raised by Hempel demands rather more careful discussion than it has received in much of the literature on vagueness.

The sorites paradox. A paradigm sorites set-up for the predicate F is a sequence of objects x_i, such that the two premisses

(1) Fx_1
(2) For all i, if Fx_i then Fx_{i+1}

both appear true, but, for some suitably large n, the putative conclusion

(3)　Fx_n

seems false. For example, in the case of "tall", the x_i might be our series of men, each a hundredth of an inch shorter than the previous one and where x_1 is seven foot tall. (1) "x_1 is tall" is then true. Plausibly, as we noted before, so is the inductive premiss (2), "for all i, if x_i is tall, so is x_{i+1}". But it is surely false that (3) x_{3000}—who is only 4′ 6″—is tall.

A second form of sorites paradox can be constructed when, instead of the quantified inductive premiss (2), we start with a collection of particular conditional premisses, (2C$_i$), each of the form "if Fx_i then Fx_{i+1}". For example,

(2C$_1$) if x_1 is tall, so is x_2
(2C$_2$) if x_2 is tall, so is x_3

and so on. Even the use of conditionals is not strictly essential: Diogenes Laertius (p. 58) uses a sequence of premisses of the form $\neg(Fx_i \ \& \ \neg Fx_{i+1})$.

Responses to a sorites paradox can (a little artificially) be divided into four types. We can

(a) deny the validity of the argument—refusing to grant that the conclusion does indeed follow from the given premisses;

(b) question the strict truth of the general inductive premiss (2) or of at least one of the conditionals (2C$_i$);

(c) accept the validity of the argument and the truth of its inductive premiss (or of all the conditional premisses) but contest the supposed truth of premiss (1) or the supposed falsity of the conclusion (3); or

(d) grant that there are compelling reasons both to take the argument form as valid, and to accept the premisses and deny the conclusion—concluding that this demonstrates the incoherence of the sorites predicate.

We shall survey each of these options in turn, ignoring here the question whether we should expect a uniform solution to all sorites paradoxes whatever their form and whatever the predicate is involved. (Wright (II) argues that different responses could be required depending on the reasons that support the premisses of a sorites.)

(a) Denying the validity of the sorites argument seems to require giving up absolutely fundamental rules of inference. This can be seen most clearly when the argument takes the second form involving a series of conditionals. The only rule of inference needed for this argument is modus ponens. Dummett argues that this rule cannot be given up, as it is constitutive of the meaning of "if" that modus ponens is valid (p. 103).

To derive the conclusion in the first form of sorites, we only need universal instantiation in addition to modus ponens; but, as Dummett again argues, universal instantiation seems too central to the meaning of "all" to be reasonably challenged (p. 103).

There is, however, a different way of rejecting the validity of the many-conditionals form of the sorites. Even though each step is acceptable on its own, it might be suggested that chaining too many steps does not guarantee the preservation of truth if, e.g., what counts as preserving truth is itself a vague matter. (And then the first form of sorites could perhaps be rejected on the grounds that it is in effect shorthand for a multi-conditional argument.) But as Dummett notes, this is to deny the transitivity of validity, which again looks a drastic move given that chaining inferences is normally taken to be essential to the very enterprise of logical proof.

Rather than questioning particular inference rules or the ways they can be combined, Russell's global rejection of logic for vague natural language leads him to dismiss "the old puzzle about the man who went bald", simply on the grounds that "bald" is vague (p. 62). The sorites arguments, on his view, cannot be valid because, containing vague expressions, they are just not the kind of thing that can be, or can fail to be, valid.

(b) Within a classical framework, denying the premiss (2), or one of the conditionals ($2C_i$), commits you to there being an i such that "Fx_i and not-Fx_{i+1}" is true. This implies the existence of sharp boundaries and requires rejecting the typical arguments for tolerance. The epistemic theorist, who takes this classical line, will explain why vague predicates appear not to draw sharp boundaries by reference to ignorance (see §2).

In a non-classical framework there is a wider variety of ways of developing option (b), and it is not so clear that these entail a commitment to sharp boundaries. For example, the supervaluationist will hold that the generalized premiss (2) "for all i, if Fx_i then Fx_{i+1}" is false: for each F^* which constitutes a way of making F precise, there will be *some* x_i or other which is the last F^* and is followed by an x_{i+1} which is not-F^*. Though since there is no particular i for which "Fx_i and not-Fx_{i+1}" is true—i.e. true however F is made precise—supervaluationists claim that their denial of (2) does not mean accepting that F is sharply bounded (see §3).

Other non-classical frameworks may allow that (2) is not true, while not accepting that it is *false*. Tye, for example, maintains that the inductive premiss and its negation both take his intermediate truth-value, "indefinite". And using a different framework with a primitive D operator, Wright II (p. 234) also suggests that the inductive premisses of some (but not all) sorites paradoxes may be of indeterminate status.[9]

Degree theorists offer another non-classical version of option (b): they can deny that premisses are strictly true while maintaining that they are *nearly* true. The essence of their account is to hold that the predications Fx_i take degrees of truth that encompass a gradually decreasing series from complete truth (degree 1) to complete falsity (degree 0). There is never a substantial drop in degree of truth between consecutive Fx_i; so, given a natural interpretation of the conditional, the particular premisses "if Fx_i then Fx_{i+1}" can all come out at least very nearly true, though some are not completely true. If the sorites argument based on many conditionals is to count as strictly valid, then an account of validity is needed that allows a valid argument to have nearly true premisses but a false conclusions (see Edgington for such an account). But with some degree theoretic accounts of validity, the sorites fails to be valid—thus a degree theorist can combine responses (a) and (b) (see §4).

(c) Take the sorites (H+) with the premisses "one grain of sand is not a heap" and "adding a single grain to a non-heap will not turn it into a heap". If we accept these premisses and the validity of the argument, it follows that there will never be a heap no matter how many grains are piled up: so there are no heaps. Similarly, sorites paradoxes for "bald", "tall" and "person" could be taken to show that there are no bald people, no tall people and indeed no people at all. Peter Unger bites the bullet and takes this line, which he summarizes in the title of one of his papers: "There are no ordinary things" (Unger 1979; see also Wheeler 1975, 1979 and Heller 1988).

The response of accepting the *conclusion* of every sorites paradox cannot be consistently sustained. For in addition to (H+), there is the argument (H–) with the premisses "ten thousand grains make a heap" and "removing one grain from a heap still leaves a heap", leading to the conclusion that a single grain of sand is a heap, which is incompatible with the conclusion of (H+). Such reversibility is typical; given a sorites series of items, the argument can be run either way through them. Unger's response to (H–) would be to deny the initial *premiss*:

---

9. Intuitionistic logic gives another non-classical position that can respond to the sorites by denying the inductive premiss (2), while not accepting the classical equivalent of this denial, $(\exists x)(Fx_i \& \neg Fx_{i+1})$, which is the unwanted assertion of sharp boundaries Putnam 1983 suggests this strategy. But Cargile, for one, argues that the move to intuitionism is not enough to meet certain other formulations of the sorites paradox Debate about Putnam's position is pursued in e g. Read and Wright 1985, Putnam 1985, Wright p. 228 fn 12, and Williamson 1996.

there are no heaps—as (H+) supposedly shows us—so it is not true that ten thousand grains make a heap.

In a slogan, the thesis is that all vague predicates lack application (Williamson 1994 calls this position "nihilism"). Classical logic can be retained in its entirety, but sharp boundaries are avoided by denying that vague predicates succeed in drawing any boundaries, fuzzy or otherwise. There will be no borderline cases: for vague *F*, everything is not *F*, and thus nothing is either *F* or borderline *F*.

Unger is driven to such an extreme position by the strength of the arguments in support of the inductive premises of sorites paradoxes. If our words determined sharp boundaries, Unger claims, our understanding of them would be a miracle of conceptual comprehension. The inductive premiss, guaranteeing this lack of sharp boundaries, reflects a semantic rule central to the meaning of the vague *F*. But can the tolerance principle expressed in the inductive premiss for e.g. "tall" really be more certain than the truth of the simple predication of "is tall" to a seven-foot man? Is it plausible to suppose that the expression "tall" is meaningful and consistent but that there could not be any tall people, when learning the term typically involves ostension and hence confrontation with alleged examples? (A different miracle of conceptual comprehension would be needed here.) It may be more plausible to suppose that if there are any rules governing the application of "tall", then, in addition to tolerance rules, there are rules dictating that "tall" applies to various paradigmatic cases and does not apply to various paradigmatically short people. Sorites paradoxes could then demonstrate the inconsistency of such a set of rules—which is option (d).

Responses (c) and (d) are not always clearly distinguished. Writers like Unger are primarily concerned with drawing ontological conclusions. It is enough for them to emphasize the tolerance of a predicate like "tall" which already guarantees, they claim, that the world contains nothing that strictly answers to that description: they are not so concerned to examine what further rules might govern the predicate and perhaps render it incoherent. But other writers, for example Dummett, explore these conceptual questions.

(d) Having argued in detail against alternative responses to the paradox, Dummett maintains that there is no choice but to accept that a sorites paradox for *F* exemplifies an undeniably valid form of argument from what the semantic rules for *F* dictate to be true premises to what they dictate to be a false conclusion. The paradoxes thus reveal the incoherence of the rules governing vague terms: by simply following those rules, speakers could be led to contradict themselves. This inconsistency means that there can be no coherent logic governing vague language (see also Rolf 1981, 1984).[10]

Wright (I and II) examines in detail the assumptions needed for such arguments for incoherence, and in particular those used to support the inductive premisses of sorites paradoxes. The assumptions he uncovers are prima facie very compelling: he calls their combination the "governing view". First, there is the thesis that language is governed by a definite set of semantic rules which are implicitly known by speakers who understand the language. The second thesis, in summary form, holds that features of those implicitly known rules "may be discerned by reflection on our practical limitations, the ways the application of an expression would be defended if challenged, the interest which we attach to the classification effected by it, the way it is standardly taught, and the criteria for someone's misunderstanding it" (Wright, p. 210). Typical arguments for tolerance essentially depend on such considerations.

Wright suggests that the inconsistency revealed by sorites paradoxes should be taken as a reductio of the assumptions of the governing view. Communication using vague language is overwhelmingly successful and we are never in practice driven to incoherence. It looks unlikely that such success and coherence could be explained by reference to our grasp of inconsistent rules. We should seek an explanation of our classificatory behavior which is *not* presented in terms of knowledge of semantic rules.[11]

Criteria of vagueness and higher-order vagueness. We began by giving paradigm cases of vague predicates and illustrating their typical features without offering a criterion of vagueness—for suggested criteria often fail to be neutral between the competing theories of vagueness.

The most common type of criterion takes borderline cases to be of the essence. Peirce 1902 (endorsed by Black, p. 71) writes, "a proposition is vague when there are possible states of things concerning which it is intrinsically uncertain whether, had they been contemplated by the speaker, he would have regarded them as excluded or allowed by the proposition"—where the uncertainty, Peirce and Black agree, is not a

---

10. Once (d)-theorists have concluded that vague predicates are incoherent, they may agree with Russell that such predicates cannot appear in valid arguments. So option (d) can be developed in such a way that makes it compatible with option (a), though this route to the denial of validity seems very different from Russell's.

11. Wright's discussion is designed to undermine typical motivations for accepting the inductive premisses of sorites paradoxes and can be, but need not be, combined with his positive theses—e.g. that some of the paradoxes have indeterminate inductive premisses, and that the condition for the lack of sharp boundaries must instead be expressed using a D operator.

matter of ignorance. Similarly, it is said that a *predicate* is vague if it can have borderline cases.[12]

But imagine a hypothetical predicate G that has a sharply-bounded set of clear positive cases, a sharply-bounded set of clear negative cases, and a sharply-bounded set of cases falling in between. Although G is stipulated to have borderline cases in the sense of instances which are neither clearly G nor clearly not-G, it is not vague—at least not in the standard way. "Tall", "red", "chair" etc. do not yield a three-fold sharp classification of this sort. The familiar arguments that there is no sharp boundary between the positive and negative extensions of "tall" would equally count against any suggestion that there is a sharp boundary between the positive extension and the borderline cases (for example, one hundredth of an inch should not make the difference to whether someone counts as borderline tall). So the case of G, with its pattern of sharp boundaries, seems to show that merely having borderline cases is not sufficient for vagueness: rather, with a genuinely vague predicate, the sets of clearly positive, clearly negative and borderline cases will each be fuzzily bounded.

It is widely recognized in the selected papers from Russell onwards that the borderline cases of a vague predicate are not sharply bounded. This is often taken to imply that there is a hierarchy of borderline cases—a phenomenon known as *higher-order vagueness*. For consider the following argument. The lack of sharp boundaries between the Fs and the not-Fs shows that there are values of x for which it is indeterminate whether x is F and equally indeterminate whether it is not-F. So similarly, the lack of a sharp boundary between the clear Fs and the borderline Fs must imply that there are borderline borderline cases— values of x for which it is indeterminate whether Fx is borderline. Hence the characteristic lack of sharp boundaries to the borderline cases commits us to second-order borderline cases. But this argument looks as though it should now iterate: if F is to be genuinely vague, there should also be no sharp boundaries to the borderline borderline Fs (yielding borderline borderline borderline Fs), and so on.[13]

Any putative theory of vagueness must accommodate the apparent lack of sharp boundaries to the borderline cases and address the issue

---

12. Clarification will be needed if we are to avoid declaring a predicate of the form "is exactly x square meters" vague just because its application to Mount Everest is of borderline status (assuming that the area of Mount Everest is indeterminate).

13. Burgess 1990, however, argues that higher-order vagueness terminates at a "rather low finite level" (p. 431)—at least for secondary-quality predicates. And Wright (II, §5) argues that the supposition that there is higher-order vagueness may lead unavoidably to paradox (while he claims, in contrast, that first-order vagueness is not paradoxical). He uses a D operator to formulate a statement that F lacks

of higher-order vagueness. Arguably this will require vagueness in the metalanguage—the language in which we frame our theory and e.g. report the borderline status of some predications. For suppose that *F* has borderline borderline cases. Then consider the metalanguage predicate which is used to report that something is a borderline *F*: this must itself have borderline cases and hence be vague. Worries about the implications of using precise metalanguages in the representation of vagueness are discussed in Sainsbury's paper.

The issue of higher-order vagueness will also have implications for our choice of criteria of vagueness. For example, Peirce's 'criterion in terms of merely first-order borderline cases is brought into question. It might be an improvement to require for genuine vagueness, not just borderline cases, but borderline cases of all orders. But it seems extravagant to suppose that there is an unlimited hierarchy of this sort associated with every vague predicate. Moreover, even admitting the hierarchy may not be enough: in particular, there could still be an unwanted sharp boundary between the cases that are borderline at some order or other and the absolutely definitely *F* things.

Perhaps a better criterion of vagueness would focus directly on the lack of any sharp boundaries rather than on borderline cases. Sainsbury develops this line of thought. Claiming that there is no such thing as an unsharp boundary, he identifies the defining feature of vagueness as "boundarylessness". And he argues that recognizing this feature is essential for a genuine understanding of vagueness and an account of its semantics.

Finally, note that almost all of the discussion so far has been about vagueness as a characteristic of language (and, by implication, of thought). But we might also ask: could the world itself be vague as well as our descriptions of it? For example, could there be vague *properties* as well as vague predicates? And could there be vague *objects* in addition to vague singular terms? Mount Everest, for example, is often said to be a vague object because it has fuzzy spatio-temporal boundaries.

Many of the selections in this Reader deal exclusively with linguistic vagueness, and several of the authors dismiss the notion of vagueness in the world, maintaining that it does not even make sense. Thus Russell: "Vagueness and precision alike are characteristics which can only belong to a representation, of which language is an example" (p. 62).

---

sharp boundaries at the second level, but he argues that a contradiction can be derived from such a statement together with certain principles which he takes to govern the *D* operator (see also Wright 1992). Wright's reasoning and his claims about the logic of the *D* operator have been criticized by Sainsbury 1991, Edgington 1993 and Heck 1993.

And Dummett writes "... the notion that things might actually *be* vague, as well as being vaguely described, is not properly intelligible" (p. 111). Tye, in contrast, believes that there are vague objects (including mountains and clouds, but also sets) and that this is crucial to his own theory of the linguistic phenomenon, which uses vague sets. Sainsbury also suggests that taking the notion of vague object as basic could be the key to providing the logic of vagueness.

Even allowing the intelligibility of the question whether the world is vague, the answer remains highly controversial. One issue which has been at the focus of the debate is represented in the final three papers reprinted here. We shall return to this issue, and to a general discussion of vagueness in the world, in §5.

First we take in turn what might be regarded as the most influential accounts of vagueness: the epistemic view (§2), supervaluationism (§3) and many-valued approaches and degree theories (§4).

2 The epistemic view

According to the epistemic view, vagueness is a type of ignorance. Classical logic and semantics can be retained because vague predicates have well-defined extensions with sharp boundaries: we just do not know where those boundaries lie. The Stoics supposedly held a position of this type,[14] and it has recently been revived by Cargile (who labels the position "realist") and by Williamson (further developed in his book, 1994). See also Campbell 1974 and work by Sorensen, e.g. his 1988.

The epistemic view does not deny that vagueness is a real and ubiquitous phenomenon: the claim that predicates have sharply bounded classical extensions must not be taken by definition to preclude vagueness. Rather, the feature of a vague predicate loosely described as its having a fuzzy boundary is to be characterized in terms of our ignorance about where the limits of the predicate's extension fall. Similarly the view admits borderline cases, again characterizing them epistemically. Although there *is* a fact of the matter about whether borderline Tek is tall—bivalence holds, so either Tek is tall, or he is not tall—we do not, and perhaps cannot, know which.

By appealing to the vagueness of predicates such as "knows that p" and "is ignorant about whether p" the epistemic view can also explain higher-order vagueness in terms of ignorance. The boundaries to the borderline cases of F appear fuzzy because of our ignorance of the

---

14. Associated in particular with Chrysippus, whose own writings on the topic do not survive, though he is reported in e.g. Cicero, this volume, pp. 59–60. Williamson 1994, ch. 1, provides a speculative reconstruction of the Stoic position; see also Barnes 1982 and Burnyeat 1982.

exact boundary to the cases in which we are ignorant about whether *F* applies.

Much of the support for the epistemic view comes from emphasizing the problems facing the non-classical alternatives. For a start, there seem to be considerable costs in giving up classical logic and semantics. Williamson urges that they "are vastly superior to the alternatives in simplicity, power, past success, and integration with theories in other domains" (p. 279). Cargile shows how much of classical logic would have to be abandoned to cope with sorites paradoxes if the epistemic view is to be rejected: it would not be enough to modify or drop just one or two disputable principles. And Williamson takes a thesis apparently central to most non-classical views—that borderline cases violate bivalence—and seeks to undermine that thesis by deriving a contradiction from it (pp. 265–66).[15] In addition, he stresses that calling borderline cases "indeterminate" is, by itself, empty unless supplemented by an illuminating interpretation of that indeterminacy, and he claims that no coherent non-epistemic interpretation has been given. Further arguments aim to show that various rival views do not, in fact, avoid the supposedly unacceptable features of the epistemic view: in particular, they are each committed to sharp boundaries of *some* sort.[16]

The epistemic view is often met by an incredulous stare. Many consider the thesis that our vague predicates have sharp boundaries to be unworthy of serious consideration, judging it absurd to think that there is a precise point on the spectrum where red turns to orange, or that the loss of a single hair can turn Fred bald. But defenders of the epistemic view are sensitive to this charge of implausibility; they have sought to make the approach more palatable and to answer articulations of the implied criticisms.

To take one form of objection. It is undeniable that meaning is intimately connected to use; intuitively, as Williamson puts it, "words mean what they do because we use them as we do" (p. 272). Now, nature does not privilege a particular sharp division in the world for our expression "tall" to latch onto: the sharp boundary, if there is one, must be drawn entirely in virtue of how we use that predicate. But we do not seem to use "tall" as if one hundredth of an inch could make a

---

15. Simons 1992 rejects this argument. Wright 1995 raises further objections to it as well as addressing a number of Williamson's and Sorensen's other arguments for the existence of sharp cut-off points. Sorensen 1995 and Williamson 1996 reply to some of Wright's objections.

16. See especially Williamson 1994 and Sorensen 1988. For more arguments in defense of the epistemic view, see Williamson 1994 and Sorensen 1988 and 1994.

difference to its applicability. More generally, we do not seem to use vague predicates as if they are sharply bounded. Thus, the objection continues, a theory that maintains a commitment to sharp boundaries must sever the connection between meaning and use. In response, Williamson argues that the connection *can* be preserved: meaning supervenes on use—there is no difference in meaning without a difference in use. But we do not know the details of how use fixes meaning. The supervenience relation may be "unsurveyably chaotic": even if we could examine use in sufficient detail, this might not reveal the boundaries of meaning.

A key question remains for the epistemic view: *why* are we ignorant of the facts about where the boundaries of vague predicates lie? Cargile suggests that it is "absurd to make an effort to find out" those facts (p. 96).[17] Certainly, we would still be ignorant of whether borderline Tek is tall even if we had all the accessible evidence about, for example, his exact height and the heights of everyone else in the world. Thus, at least in this natural sense, it seems that we *could not* know the cut-offs of vague predicates (Sorensen 1988 describes borderline case predications as unknowable "blindspots"). But it seems reasonable to ask why such knowledge is impossible.

Some defenders of the epistemic view (e.g. Sorensen 1988) have suggested that opponents who pursue an objection to unknowable sharp boundaries betray a residual verificationist antipathy to unknowable facts in general. It has also been suggested that ignorance is our default state—lack of knowledge does not stand in need of explanation. Such very general responses will strike many as unsatisfactory. Williamson, by contrast, offers a detailed explanation of the source of our ignorance (this volume; see also his 1992a and 1994, ch. 8).

Williamson's account employs the notion of a margin for error. If your true belief that *p* is to count as knowledge, your belief should not be true just by luck. But if *p* would have been false in comparable situations that you could not discriminate in the relevant respects from the actual case, it seems that you are lucky to have a true belief. So for your belief to count as knowledge, *p* should also be true in such similar cases falling within a "margin for error". Take an example not dependent on vagueness. Suppose that, on the basis merely of a rough estimate, you come to believe that there are at least *n* words in this book. And suppose that there are exactly *n* words in this book, so your belief

---

17. Campbell is reluctant to call the uncertainty distinctive of vagueness *epistemic*, since there is nothing we could find out that would allow us to have knowledge of the matter; instead he calls it "semantic uncertainty". But he still acknowledges a commitment to sharp boundaries, accepts the falsity of the sorites inductive premiss, etc.

is in fact true. Applying the same error-prone method of estimation, you could still have reached the same belief even if there had been a dozen fewer words in the book; your belief would then have been false. This prevents your actual true belief counting as knowledge, for the way you formed it does not allow the necessary margin for error.

Now consider the application of the vague predicate "tall", whose extension has a sharp boundary according to the epistemic view. And suppose that Tek is a borderline case of tallness who *is* tall, but who is only *just* on that side of the supposed sharp boundary. Then, even if you believe him to be tall, this will not count as knowledge; for if he had been marginally shorter (on the other side of the boundary and so no longer tall) you could still have formed the same belief, though it would then have been false. The requirement that you leave a margin for error would prevent your original belief about the borderline case counting as knowledge.

This neatly explains our ignorance about the application of vague predicates to particular borderline cases. But Williamson also needs to explain our ignorance of true generalizations such as (G) "*n* grains (optimally arranged) form a heap", where *n* is *just* greater than the supposed sharp minimum needed for a heap. Plausibly, facts about whether some grains form a heap supervene on facts about the number (and arrangement) of those grains; and this implies that (G), if true, is *necessarily* true. So there are no possible situations (similar to the actual one or otherwise) in which (G) is false; and a margin for error principle referring to such situations cannot help to explain our ignorance. Williamson draws instead on other margin for error principles, where the slightly different situations in the margin differ over exactly how the relevant predicate is used. Were "heap" to have been used differently, it could have had a different meaning and extension (for example, using it with stricter standards for its application would have set the boundary at a larger number of grains). And in a very similar case to the actual one where the predicate is used just slightly differently, an arrangement of *n* grains might not have correctly been called a "heap". So, if you are to know that *n* grains form a heap, then those grains must count as a "heap" in situations involving undetectable (or very small) differences in the linguistic usage of "heap". Similar arguments about the use and meaning of "tall" explain why we cannot know propositions like "anyone of height *h* is tall" (where *h* is the height of borderline Tek).[18]

---

18. Williamson 1994 maintains that it is applications of this type of margin for error principles, referring to slight differences in use, that are distinctive of vagueness and he thus employs them in his criterion of vagueness. This allows him to distinguish vagueness from other epistemic phenomena, and to meet the potential worry that

Considerations about margins for error yield principles such as:

.(K) If x_{i+1} is 0.01 inches shorter than x_i, and x_i is known to be tall, then x_{i+1} is also tall.

But unlike the tolerance principle obtained by replacing "x_i is known to be tall" with "x_i is tall", (K) does not generate paradox. And on the epistemic view, the tolerance principle itself is false. We wrongly think it true because we know of no falsifying instance. Knowing such an instance—a truth of the form "x_i is tall & x_{i+1} is not tall"—would mean that x_i was known to be tall, though x_{i+1} was not tall, and this would violate (K).

The epistemic view proves notoriously resilient to refutation, but the incredulous stare often remains fixed. We finish this section by outlining a couple of lines of attack, suggesting why we might reasonably continue to feel particularly uncomfortable with the view and its commitments.

The epistemic view apparently must say that if you coin a word, then sharp boundaries are inevitably fixed. In southern France, shutters are often painted a certain sort of blue (with, of course, some variation): let us hereby coin "shutter-blue" for that color. Is it plausible that we thereby immediately and unknowingly give "shutter-blue" sharp boundaries, and that no areas of indefiniteness remain? Moreover, predicates could be coined with the express intention of leaving their application to some cases unsettled. For example, Tappenden 1995 envisages a situation where the US Supreme Court coins the phrase "brownrate" to mean "with all deliberate speed" *intending* to avoid specifying an exact required speed (see also Sainsbury 1995). Such a practice of incomplete stipulation would have the advantage of allowing the extension to become progressively more complete as new circumstances come to light, rather than requiring the exhaustive classification to be fixed immediately. According to the epistemic view such incomplete stipulation is impossible and this too might seem an implausible consequence.

---

the epistemic view cannot explain the difference between vague predicates and predicates which, for other reasons, we often do not know when to apply.

It may, however, be disputed whether margin for error principles of this second form are as compelling as the original versions. We can supposedly be prevented from knowing a given fact, not because that fact would not have obtained in suitably similar cases, but because the sentence we actually use to describe the fact would have been false in circumstances where it would have shifted in sense. Is this reasonable? Sainsbury 1995 raises some worries about Williamson's principles and the work they are employed to do.

Another worry: what could determine the location of the sharp lines which bound the extensions of our vague predicates? It seems there are no privileged natural boundaries to the tall people or to the red things and, moreover, we do not stipulate where their boundaries lie.[19] Williamson appeals to his meaning–use supervenience claim, replying that it is our use of a predicate which determines its extension, and hence fixes its boundaries. But this does not answer the question: *how* do those unique boundary lines come to be singled out? The fact that there can be no difference in meaning without a difference in use does not fix the boundaries of extensions any more than a pass–fail divide is fixed by the fact that qualitatively the same exam scripts should receive the same score.

To illustrate: on the epistemic view there is a—possibly chaotic—function that takes us from the uses of predicates to the sets which are their precise extensions. But now consider a different function that maps the same uses to sets that are in some cases slightly different—a function that differs only in being marginally more strict over the membership of one or two particular extensions. Call its values the extensions* of the predicates in question. This function will determine sharp extensions* and these too will supervene on use. Then the question is: why is it extensions rather than extensions* that play the roles we associate with meanings in, for example, determining the truth-conditions of sentences? What could it possibly be that singles out the uniquely correct extension-determining function? An epistemic theorist can deny responsibility for answering this question (no one has a complete account of how extensions are fixed), but is this a satisfactory response?

To summarize: the main objections to the epistemic view center on its commitment to sharp boundaries (and, relatedly, on its treatment of borderline cases); while its main advantage is that it retains classical logic. A theory avoiding the objections while preserving the simplicity of classical logic might seem ideal. It has been claimed that supervaluationism is exactly such a theory, and it is this account of vagueness to which we turn next.

---

19. Williamson suggests (p. 274) that sometimes a sharply bounded property corresponding to a vague predicate may be singled out by the causal role it plays in producing our judgements. But this does not seem to be a promising account of boundary-fixing for all cases. Take e.g. Dummett's "… is a small number". There may also be problems if we take the view that causation requires laws which strictly involve only an elite category of natural properties, those that science is aiming to discover (see Lewis 1983a). For it seems unlikely that there will be precise natural properties suitably corresponding to e.g. "chair" and "nice".

3 Supervaluationism

The central ideas. A vague predicate apparently fails to divide things neatly and without remainder into two sets, its positive and negative extensions. Arguably, *pace* the epistemic view, borderline cases yield predications which are neither true nor false: there are truth-value gaps. According to Fine, these gaps reveal a deficiency in the meaning of a vague predicate. Removing the deficiency and replacing vagueness by precision would involve fixing a sharp boundary between the positive and negative extensions and thereby deciding which way to classify each of the borderline cases. However, adopting any *one* of these ways of making a vague predicate precise—any one "precisification" or "sharpening"—would be arbitrary. For there are *many*, equally good, sharpenings. According to supervaluationism, our treatment of vague predicates should take account of *all* of them. It is proposed that a sentence is true iff it is true on all precisifications, false iff false on all precisifications, and neither true nor false otherwise.

Suppose someone is over seven foot: he counts as "tall" on any precisification of that predicate, so it is true simpliciter that he is tall. But if Tek is 5'10", then he is a borderline case of tallness. Some precisifications will place Tek in the positive extension of "tall", and others will place him in its negative extension: "Tek is tall" is neither true on all precisifications nor false on all of them, hence it counts as neither true nor false. The principle of bivalence fails.

Supervaluationists claim that they can accommodate the lack of sharp boundaries to the extensions of vague predicates. There would be a sharp boundary to the tall people, they maintain, if there were a height *h* which satisfied "people of height *h* are tall but anyone shorter is not tall". But they deny that there is any such *h*. Different precisifications of "tall" draw boundaries to the tall people at different heights; and so for no *h* is it the case that on *all* precisifications people of height *h* are tall and anyone shorter is not. So no height is truly identified as marking the boundary.

Precisifications must meet certain constraints: in particular, sentences that are unproblematically true (false) before precisification should stay true (false) afterwards. This applies not just to simple predications like "Arnie is tall", but also to general statements such as "anyone taller than a tall person is also tall" and "no one who is tall is short". These statements certainly seem to be true. To preserve the first, there can be no acceptable precisification of "tall" according to which (say) people who are 5'10" are tall but people who are 5'11" are not. To preserve the second we cannot sharpen "tall" so that someone of 5'10" counts as tall, while simultaneously sharpening "short" so that someone of that height also counts as short. These two examples illustrate what Fine calls "penumbral connections", which constrain how boundaries can be drawn among the borderline cases of predicates on precisification. Such penumbral connections may be "internal", concerning instances of the same predicate (as in our first example) or "external", involving several related predicates (as in the second example).

If we take all predicates together, making them absolutely precise while respecting their manifold penumbral connections, then we get a complete precisification of the whole language (ignoring here the possible vagueness of non-predicates). All predicates will have been given classical extensions and there will be a corresponding classical assignment of a truth-value to every sentence. We can then assign values to vague sentences by a *supervaluation* quantifying over these classical valuations according to the rule that a sentence is super-true (super-false) iff true (false) on all of them. Truth simpliciter is identified with super-truth.[20]

Now consider the disjunctive sentence, "the book is green or it is blue" said of a book which is borderline between green and blue. On the supervaluationist view, this comes out true (since it is true wherever the sharp boundary between blue and green is drawn). But neither "the book is green" nor "the book is blue" is itself true: hence a disjunction can be true though neither disjunct is true. As Mehlberg notes, we must abandon "the ordinary connection between the truth-value of a disjunction and the truth-values of its members" (p. 88).

A similar result applies to the existential quantification "something is *F*", which can be true though no substitution instance is true. In particular, although there is no h for which it is true that "people of height h are tall while people 0.01 inches shorter are not tall", the existentially quantified sentence formed from it, (H) "there is a height h such that people of height h are tall while people 0.01 inches shorter are not tall", *is* true (since on each precisification, some h or other makes it true). Similarly, we have the dual result that a universally quantified proposition can be false, even though no substitution instance is false. This feature of the supervaluationist framework is central to the treatment of the sorites paradox: the negation of (H) is equivalent to "for any

---

20. The technique of supervaluationism was formally expounded, and the expression "supervaluation" coined, in the influential work of van Fraassen (1966, 1968 and 1969). He developed the technique for applications other than vagueness, in particular for the treatment of non-referring singular terms and of the liar paradox. More generally, where there are putative truth-value gaps, supervaluationism can be, and often is, wheeled in for the semantics. In each case, there will be some appropriate notion of a complete admissible valuation which keeps all actually true (false) sentences true (false), but fills in truth-value gaps, and where the supervaluation captures what is common to all of those valuations.

height h if someone of height h is tall, so is someone 0.01 inches shorter", which is the quantified inductive premiss of a sorites paradox for "tall". And this premiss is false on the supervaluationist theory (even though none of its substitution instances is false).[21]

Next, take the sentence "either Tek is tall or he is not tall": this too is true, since it is true on all precisifications (even if Tek is actually border-line tall when, again, neither disjunct is true). More generally, "$p \vee \neg p$" is true whatever the substitution for p and whatever value (or lack of value) p takes: the logical truth of the law of excluded middle is maintained. Equally, all other classical theorems are retained, for if a sentence is logically true according to classical logic, then it will be true on every complete precisification (since they each obey classical logic) and thus, by supervaluationary principles, it will count as true simpliciter.

In summary, the supervaluationist approach lays claim to conserving classical logic and respecting penumbral connections, while successfully accommodating the borderline cases and the lack of sharp boundaries distinctive of vagueness and also avoiding the sorites paradox.

Mehlberg gave what seems to be the earliest informal presentation of an essentially supervaluationist account of vagueness (in the reprinted excerpt from his 1958).[22] His account of vagueness originally seemed to draw little attention.[23] But the basic ideas later occurred to a number of different philosophers, apparently independently of Mehlberg and largely independently of each other. Dummett gives a clear, informal description of the position and its attractions, though he goes on to reject it (pp. 107–8; his paper was written in 1970 though published in 1975). And Lewis, at the end of this 1970 paper "General semantics", defends such an account, albeit briefly. Elsewhere Lewis summarizes: "I regard vagueness as semantic indecision: where we speak vaguely, we have not troubled to settle which of some range of precise meanings our words are meant to express" (1986, p. 244).[24] In 1975, Kamp

---

21. When the sorites paradox is expressed in terms of a series of conditionals, there will be no one conditional which is false, but there will be some that are neither true nor false (and on every precisification there will be one that is false).

22. Mehlberg cites a principle of verifiability as his reason for regarding vague sentences as neither true nor false since they are unverifiable. But his account of vagueness is compatible with any reason for regarding borderline case predications as neither true nor false.

23. Though it was endorsed in Przełecki 1969; see also his 1976.

24. Lewis's account is presented within his general semantic framework. A central role is played by *indices*—sequences of co-ordinates (e.g. for time, place, possible

proposed another version of supervaluationism in the context of a wider discussion of adjectives. The same year saw the publication of Fine's detailed treatment reprinted here, which is generally taken as the *locus classicus* of the supervaluationist theory of vagueness.

Some further details of Fine's theory. Fine's paper is rich and technically complex, and ranges widely over possible formal treatments of vagueness. His own account is built on the notion of a *specification space*, i.e. a set of points—specification-points—at which some or all sentences in a language L are assigned truth-values; he terms the valuations themselves "specifications". An appropriate specification space for L will consist of specification-points that each correspond to permissible precisifications of its vague expressions. Some specification points are *complete*: these are associated with ways of making all vague terms completely precise. But other points are *partial*: these correspond to partial precisifications where some or all expressions are left somewhat vague and some sentences remain truth-valueless.

Each space has an "appropriate specification-point" or *base-point*; intuitively this is the point at which the non-compound sentences of L receive their original valuation as assigned before any of the vagueness has been resolved (leaving truth-value gaps for all borderline cases). There is an *extends* relation on the space, where a specification-point b is said to extend another point a if, intuitively, b corresponds to a (possibly partial) precisification of a. All points in the space extend the base-point. And a sequence of points where each extends the previous one (giving more and more precisification) can always be further extended to reach a complete specification-point where there are no truth-value gaps left. In other words, there is always at least one way of making sentences completely precise, though this does not require that we could actually specify in some language the nature of the completion

---

world, etc.) at which the truth-value of a sentence is evaluated (and on which that truth-value might depend). Lewis 1970 suggests building into the index what he calls a "delineation co-ordinate", which specifies the way in which the relevant expressions are made precise by giving a sequence of boundary-specifying numbers (e.g. one specifying the lower boundary height of tallness, one for the maximum heat for coldness, etc.). These delineations are usually quantified over: we aim to assert statements true on all of those delineations.

In his 1969 and 1975, Lewis suggests that vagueness could alternatively be treated as a pragmatic matter—a feature of language-use rather than of languages themselves. The idea behind this approach is that languages (taken as formal abstract structures or functions from strings of symbols to meanings) are themselves precise, but there is a slackness over which of them we are using. He does not develop this pragmatic account in any detail—nor does he discuss its relation to the semantic supervaluationary theory—though Burns 1991 adopts and defends it.

(we may not be able to spell out *any* precisification of "nice", let alone all of them).

Fine formalizes certain restrictions on his specification spaces to reflect their intended use. For example, his *Stability* requirement rules that the sentences true at a specification-point must remain true at any point which extends it (i.e. truth-value gaps may be filled, but previously settled values are never changed by further precisification). This ensures that the uncontroversially true (false) predications of a vague predicate at the base-point keep their value through all later precisifications. The *Completability* condition requires that every specification-point can be extended to a complete specification-point. And the requirement of *Fidelity* formalizes the fact that the elimination of all truth-value gaps at these complete specification-points must result in a classical valuation.

Additional conditions need to be placed on specification spaces if we are to constrain further the values which are taken at partial specification-points. Stability ensures that if a sentence is true at a partial specification-point a, then it is true at all complete points that extend a. Fine's chosen account of truth-conditions, the super-truth account, additionally asserts the converse, so a sentence is true at a if and only if it is true at all complete specification-points which extend a. Truth simpliciter is truth at the base-point, and since all complete points extend the base-point, a sentence is true there iff it is true on *all* complete specifications— "truth is super-truth".

There are other ways of developing a specification space account, which differ over how truth-values are assigned to partial specifications and as a result, over the exact truth-definitions of compound statements. For example, it would be compatible with the conditions of Stability, Completability and Fidelity to take a disjunction always to be indefinite at a partial specification-point if both of its disjuncts were indefinite there. Fine outlines one alternative set of truth-definitions, which he calls "a bastard intuitionistic account". He also indicates another possibility which minimizes truth and falsity (leaving more truth-value gaps for compound sentences).[25] But these alternatives cannot respect all penumbral connections, he argues. Take again the sentence "the book is green or it is blue" asserted of a borderline blue–green book; this does not come out true on either of the alternative

---

25. Burgess and Humberstone 1987 defend a system with different truth-definitions which basically falls within the specification space approach. They share Fine's treatment of conjunctions, which accounts for the truth of the law of non-contradiction, but they diverge from Fine with regard to the sufficient conditions of truth for disjunctions in such a way that—advantageously, they claim—the law of excluded middle is no longer true.

accounts as it does on the super-truth theory and as Fine claims it should. So, the super-truth account he adopts has the merits of both simplicity and a plausible motivation.

In presenting his own theory, Fine also draws comparisons with accounts which fall outside the specification space approach. The truth-value approach—introduced in his §1 and discussed again in the light of various issues later in the paper—yields theories of vagueness which preserve truth-functionality for the logical connectives (Fine considers, in particular, three-valued accounts; see our §4). By contrast, super-valuationism rejects truth-functionality: for example, suppose p and q are both borderline (so neither true nor false). If there are no penumbral connections between them, then "$p \lor \neg q$" will also be neither true nor false, though "$p \lor \neg p$" will always be true. So, on the supervaluationist theory, molecular propositions can differ in truth-value though composed of constituents that have the same values. Fine argues that this is positive advantage of his approach and that it is a necessary feature of a theory of vagueness if penumbral connections are to be accommodated.

Fine elaborates his account by introducing a "definitely" operator, D, into the object language. A sentence is to be definitely true if it is true before any permissible sharpening of any vague expression it contains. In the specification space framework, the semantic rule for D is, in essence, that DA is true at a specification-point of a space iff A is true at the base-point. Consequently, DA is true at all specification-points of an appropriate space iff it is true at any. D is thus closely related to the metalinguistic truth predicate (since truth simpliciter *is* truth at the base-point). Given D, an "indefinitely" operator can also be defined, where $Ip \equiv \neg Dp \;\&\; \neg D\neg p$. This allows us to express in the object-language the borderline case status of certain predications, e.g. IFa holds when Fa is neither true nor false. Fine introduces such operators partly in order to pursue the issue of higher-order vagueness. This requires complicating his original story about the operator to allow, for instance, for the possibility of cases in which $IIFa$ is true, i.e. second-order borderline cases of F. In his §5 he pursues this discussion (again comparing his treatment with that of competing approaches).

Some developments of the supervaluationary approach. Lewis 1970 and Kamp 1975 describe some possible developments of the basic super-valuationist framework. They show how the framework could illuminate the semantics of a number of locutions other than simple vague predications. One of Lewis's examples is the idiom "in some sense": he suggests that "in some sense p" can be taken to be true just if p is true on some specification or other. And Lewis and Kamp both hope to explain the connection between an adjective, such as "red" and its associated comparative, "redder", proposing that "*a* is redder than *b*" is true iff the set of specifications on which "*b* is red" is true is a proper subset of those on which "*a* is red" is true.

Additionally, both propose that we add to the basic framework some measure over the specification space. We might then say that a sentence is true to a degree depending on the measure of the set of specification-points at which it comes out true (so, speaking loosely, predications true on most precisifications will come out true to a high degree). In this way we can discriminate among sentences which are neither true nor false, rather than merely clumping them all together in an undifferentiated way. Kamp emphasizes how, on this approach, the degree assigned to a compound sentence can depend not only on the degrees of its component sentences, but also on the relation between those components (compare Edgington's approach to degrees of truth).

Kamp and Lewis suggest that their notion of degrees of truth can be put to a number of other uses (though these will generally also be available to alternative theories that admit degrees of truth—see §4). We can give a semantics for various modifiers by rules that appeal to these degrees; for example, "*a* is slightly *F*" is true if "*a* is *F*" is true to some low (but non-zero) degree, while "*a* is rather *F*" requires that "*a* is *F*" is true to a higher degree. And Lewis notes how the assertibility of a vague sentence can vary with the contextually appropriate standard of precision, and that this standard can be interpreted in terms of the degree of truth required for assertion. For example, the standard for assessment of "France is hexagonal" and hence the degree of truth to which it must be true to justify assertion, would be higher in the context of a geography conference than when describing country shapes to a child (see also Lewis 1979).

Logic. Supervaluationism claims to retain classical logic. But to what extent would such conservatism be an advantage for a theory? Adhering to classical logic has the benefits of simplicity and familiarity, and avoids worries about the arbitrariness of any proposed alternative. Opponents may object, however, that classical logic, of its very nature, can never accommodate vagueness. For example, they may insist that the law of excluded middle *should* fail in the presence of vagueness: it is not enough to allow that *Fa* is neither true nor false in a borderline case, "*Fa* ∨ ¬*Fa*" must also fail to be true. Fine disagrees and defends the classical law: but such a debate may well be seen, as Machina suggests, as no more than "a battle of raw intuitions" (p. 178).

Is the logic yielded by supervaluationism really classical logic? The question is not entirely straightforward. Consider first a language with the usual connectives but lacking the "definitely" operator. If its logic is to be genuinely classical, the supervaluationist consequence relation must be classical: for any set of premises Γ and proposition B, $\Gamma \vDash_{sv} B$ iff $\Gamma \vDash_{CL} B$. Standardly, B is a consequence of Γ iff for all classical models where all members of Γ are true, B is also true. With the supervaluationary account of truth, the definition becomes: $\Gamma \vDash_{sv} B$ iff for any specification space, if all members of Γ are true (i.e. true on all complete specifications of the space), B is true (i.e. true on all the same specifications). This is, indeed, Fine's condition for consequence.

First, we show that

(i) If $\Gamma \vDash_{CL} B$ then $\Gamma \vDash_{sv} B$.

Suppose that $\Gamma \vDash_{CL} B$, so any classical valuation which makes all members of Γ true makes B true. Hence, in a specification space, if every member of Γ is true at a complete specification-point (which, by Fidelity, is classical) then B must be true there. So if every member of Γ is true at *all* the complete points, B will be true at all these complete points too. So $\Gamma \vDash_{sv} B$.

Another argument establishes the converse:

(ii) If $\Gamma \vDash_{sv} B$ then $\Gamma \vDash_{CL} B$.

If $\Gamma \vDash_{sv} B$, then in every specification space in which all the members of Γ are true, B is true. But any single classical model is a one-point degenerate case of a specification space (trivially satisfying the requirements of Stability etc.). So B is true in all classical models in which the members of Γ are all true, i.e. $\Gamma \vDash_{CL} B$.

This pair of results shows that—at least in the absence of the D operator—the supervaluationary consequence relation coincides with its classical counterpart. And since logical truths are just those instances of the consequence relation with an empty set of premises, the (D-free) logical truths of supervaluationism coincide with those of classical logic. The situation changes, however, when the D operator is introduced.

A number of commentators have emphasized how supervaluationist logic (now with the D operator) fails to preserve certain classical principles about consequence and rules of inference. For example, Machina (p. 179) questions the rule of reductio ad absurdum.[26] And contraposition, the deduction theorem, and argument by cases can be added to the list of rules that fail (see e.g. Williamson 1994, pp. 151–52). To illustrate,

---

26. Machina's argument is formulated in the supervaluationary framework with "truth" imported into the object-language. Given the close relation between truth and "definitely" that we noted above, we can run this result together with that in the body of the text.

contraposition, i.e. if $\{A\} \vDash B$ then $\{\neg B\} \vDash \neg A$, fails—since $\{A\} \vDash_{sv} DA$, but it is not typically the case that $\{\neg DA\} \vDash_{sv} \neg A$ (in a specification space where A is true on some specifications and false in others, then $\neg DA$ is super-true, while $\neg A$ is not). Similarly, as Fine himself notes, the deduction theorem fails: $\{A\} \vDash_{sv} DA$, but it is not usually the case that $\vDash_{sv} A \supset DA$ (for typical A, there can be complete specifications on which A is true and DA false).

Two kinds of question arise. First, how is the failure of classical principles possible given the arguments outlined above which apparently show that supervaluationism's logic is classical? Do those arguments fail once a "definitely" operator is introduced? And if so, why? And second, how important is their failure—what damage to supervaluationism is caused, if any? We outline some technical points in response to the first group of questions.

To compare the supervaluationist and classical logic consequence relation when sentences involve the "definitely" operator, we must consider how D is to be added to classical logic. The minimal option is to keep the logic purely classical and to treat "DA" as in effect a new atom for any A. Then (i) will still hold: truth in all classical models still entails truth in all specification spaces—for example, introducing the D operator cannot invalidate substitution instances of tautologies. But (ii) will no longer hold; for example $\vDash_{sv} DA \supset A$ but it is not the case that $\vDash_{CL} DA \supset A$. And the previous argument for (ii) fails because it is no longer the case that all classical models are (degenerate) appropriate specification spaces—a model in which DA is true and A is false is classically acceptable but not an appropriate specification space.

There is a more natural way of adding D to a classical framework. Consider a classical valuation as a one-point degenerate specification space, and take classical* logic to be classical logic plus D interpreted as it would be according to supervaluationism in this degenerate space. So DA is true in the classical* model iff A is true (D is therefore a redundant operator here). On this interpretation, if $\Gamma \vDash_{sv} B$ then it *will* be the case that $\Gamma \vDash_{CL^*} B$; the original argument for (ii) will be reinstated, for the classical* models are all degenerate specification spaces. But this time, (i) is false: it will *not* be the case that if $\Gamma \vDash_{CL^*} B$ then $\Gamma \vDash_{sv} B$. For example, $\vDash_{CL^*} A \supset DA$, but it is not the case that $\vDash_{sv} A \supset DA$. The original argument for (i) fails because if B is a consequence of Γ in all of the classical* models, this does not guarantee that there are no specifications in which the members of Γ are true and B false, for there are specifications that are not classical* models (e.g. specifications in which A is true and DA is not). To summarize: neither classical consequence nor classical* consequence coincides with supervaluationist consequence in the presence of the D operator.

So, some classical principles governing logical consequence do not apply in a supervaluationary framework that includes the "definitely" operator. If highly natural rules of reasoning such as contraposition fail, perhaps this should count strongly against supervaluationism. On the other hand, as Fine and Dummett both say, D is a non-classical notion. Rather than being a criticism, arguably it is a *requirement* of any plausible regimentation of a "definitely" operator that, for example, contraposition should fail ($\neg DA$ must not entail $\neg A$, though A entails DA).

Semantics. Whether or not the logic counts as classical, it is uncontroversial that the semantics is *not* classical. Most strikingly, a disjunction can be true without either of its disjuncts being true, and an existential quantification can be true without any of its substitution instances being true. In Fine's phrase, there can be "truth-value shifts", whereby the disjunct which renders the disjunction true can shift from one to the other on different specifications, and similarly the truth-making instance of an existentially quantified statement can be different on different specifications. These aspects of the interpretations of "or" and "there is" have been a common source of objection to supervaluationism, which is accused of distorting or misinterpreting those logical constants.[27] Fine, of course, bites the bullet and defends his interpretations. This dispute threatens to become another battle of intuitions; but further related objections to supervaluationary semantics have been pursued.

Is the supervaluationist claim to have avoided sharp boundaries justified? The semantics for the existential quantifier dictates the truth of "there's a hair that makes all the difference to baldness", and arguably this is enough to commit supervaluationism to a sharp boundary to the bald people, irrespective of the supposed lack of true substitution instances. And the fact that we assent to the inductive premisses of sorites paradoxes so naturally and confidently could be taken to be strong evidence against Fine's truth-conditions for the universal

---

27. See e.g. Sanford 1976 for objections to the interpretation of the existential quantifier; Kamp 1981 rejects supervaluationism (including his own 1975 account) for similar reasons. And Sorensen 1988 illustrates how supervaluationism is committed to comparable odd behavior of the identity relation.

One aspect of Fine's defense draws an analogy with ambiguity as ordinarily conceived. He claims (though Tye 1989 objects) that an ambiguous statement is true if it is true for each of its disambiguations, so that, again, "$p \lor \neg p$" can be true, through neither disjunct is true, each having a false disambiguation. Dummett suggests a different analogy. If statements of set-theory are called true when true in all models, then some disjunctive set-theoretic statements (including ones of the form "$p \lor \neg p$") could be true though different disjuncts are true in different models.

quantifier which guarantee the falsity of these premises.[28] Moreover, this confident assent to the inductive premises (and the closely related tolerance principles) might suggest that they too should be given the status of penumbral connections which must be respected, so that, *pace* supervaluationism, they should be true on all specifications. For example [S_1], if X is tall and Y is 0.01 shorter then Y is tall, looks compelling, and implies a relationship between penumbral cases of tallness.[29]

Many commentators challenge more directly the basic appeal to precisifications. Why should we think that we can give a successful account of our vague language by considering how things *would* be if it were made precise? Various general considerations, including the typical arguments for tolerance, seem to show that tolerance is essential to the whole *point* of our vague predicates, which, in Dummett's phrase, are "ineradicably vague". Arguably, in dealing only with precise structures, supervaluationism thus badly misrepresents our vague expressions, treating them as if they are vague only because we have not bothered to make them precise.[30]

The supervaluationary treatment of truth has also been subject to criticism on the ground that super-truth lacks features constitutive of truth. In particular, the supervaluationist must reject the Tarski schema

(T) "p" is true if and only if p.

"'p' is true" (like "Dp") counts as true if "p" is true at all specification-points and (again like "Dp") is thus itself true at all specification-points

---

28. Rolf 1981, 1984 makes this point, suggesting that supervaluationism should be taken as a proposal for reform of our language rather than an account of how it actually is. e g. recommending that we could, and perhaps should, change the meaning of the quantifier so that it obeys the supervaluationist semantics (thereby avoiding paradox).

29. See e.g. Burns 1991, Tappenden 1993. Tappenden examines some candidate penumbral connections, including tolerance rules, with a view to assigning them a different semantic status (e.g never false rather than always true).

30 See e.g. Dummett, Sanford 1976 and Sainsbury 1988.

Field 1973 proposes what is effectively a supervaluationary semantics in his treatment of "indeterminate reference" It is indeterminate, he argues, which of two relativistic quantities should be identified with the Newtonian conception of mass. Sentences about Newtonian mass should, he proposes, be true iff true for both relativistic conceptions. In this type of case, there are just two alternative denotations of "mass", and (through ignorance) we had not (on the Newtonian scheme) chosen between them The semantics could be more appropriate here than in the standard vagueness case when there are supposedly huge numbers of alternative denotations between which we would never seek to choose

if true at any. But suppose that *"p"* is true at some but not all points, so that *"'p'* is true" is true at no points. At those points where *"p"* *is* true, the conditional "if *p*, then *'p'* is true" is false, since its antecedent is true and its consequent is false (compare the argument, p. 31, that $A \supset DA$ is not always true). Consequently the biconditional (T) is also false at those points, and thus is not true simpliciter.

Another reason why supervaluationists cannot endorse (T) is that, combined with the law of excluded middle, which they accept, it entails the principle of bivalence, which they reject (see e.g. Williamson pp. 265–66; see also Machina pp. 178–79). However, it remains the case that *p* entails and is entailed by *Dp* (the truth of *p* at the base-point guarantees the truth of *Dp* there, and vice versa). So, even in the supervaluationist framework, we can retain the following version of Tarski's principle reconstructed as an inference rule:

(T*) from *p* we can infer *"p"* is true, and vice versa

(a point noted in van Fraassen 1966). And the supervaluationist might reasonably argue that preserving (T*) is all that our Tarskian intuitions require.[31]

Higher-order vagueness. In §1 we noted that a theory of vagueness should recognize that there may be no sharp boundaries between the cases where a predicate clearly applies and the borderline cases (or between the borderline cases and the borderline borderline cases, and so on). Can supervaluationism accommodate this phenomenon?[32]

One quick argument suggesting not runs as follows. According to supervaluationism, a sentence is true simpliciter iff it is true on all specifications. But, for any sentence, either it *is* true on all specifications (hence true simpliciter) or not (hence borderline or false)—so there is no scope for borderline borderline cases.

This initial argument, popular though it is, is too quick as it stands and it certainly does not do justice to Fine's detailed treatment of the issue. It apparently assumes that the set of admissible specifications is precise and unique. A natural starting point for a supervaluationist

---

31 McGee and McLaughlin 1995 identify a conflict between the disquotational feature of truth captured by the Tarski schema, and the correspondence conception of truth on which *p* is true iff "the facts about our thoughts and practices and about the world" determine that *p*. They recommend separating "truth" into two concepts, the disquotational one and "definite truth" which reflects the correspondence requirement They go on to give a supervaluationary semantics for definite truth See also McGee 1991.

32 Sainsbury (this volume), Burns 1991 and Williamson 1994 are among those who argue that considerations of higher-order vagueness defeat supervaluationism

response would be to deny this assumption. Could the notion of an "admissible specification" itself be vague? Dummett, for one, suggests that it is: plausibly, there will be vagueness over the boundary of what counts as an acceptable way to make precise and hence over the boundary to the borderline cases. This could lead to iteration of the supervaluationary technique: assessment of whether a sentence is "true on all admissible specifications" would require taking into account all precisifications of "admissible specification". We would then have to draw on a set of sets of specifications whose members are candidate precisifications of "admissible specification". Third-order vagueness would require taking sets of sets of sets of specifications and so on for still higher orders, mirroring the iterative structure of higher-order vagueness.

But retaining the identification of truth with truth on all specifications no longer seems viable given such a series of iterations, for there is no longer a unique set of "all specifications" (compare the original reason for not identifying truth with truth on a single complete specification, namely because there is no uniquely correct specification). Instead, Fine constructs a notion of an "admissible boundary", in which specifications, sets of specifications and higher-order sets figure. Truth on all admissible boundaries, he suggests, could capture the required generalization of truth on all admissible specifications. It is not clear, however, whether this complex apparatus plausibly solves the problem of modelling higher-order vagueness, and Fine's involved discussion is not intended to provide a definitive solution. Fine also moots the alternative suggestion that the set of admissible specifications is intrinsically vague, though he does not clarify what this amounts to. How supervaluationism stands with regard to higher-order vagueness remains an open question.

4 Many-valued logic and degree theories

When *a* is a borderline case of *F*, arguably "*a* is *F*" is neither true nor false: but rather than falling into a truth-value gap, perhaps this predication takes an intermediate non-classical truth-value. In this section, we consider theories of vagueness that introduce one or more new truth-values and adopt a many-valued logic.[33] Such theories can vary greatly along a number of different dimensions: to introduce them and bring out this variation we focus on a series of central questions.

---

33 Many-valued logics had previously been developed for applications other than the treatment of vagueness (e g probability and future contingents) See Rescher 1969 for a survey of different logics and some of their applications

(1) *How many values should we admit? How are these values to be understood?*

Many-valued theories usually take one of two options. Either they assign all borderline predications the same intermediate value, to be interpreted as "indeterminate" or "indefinite": this yields a three-valued logic. Or they adopt an infinite-valued logic, with the set of values typically represented by the real numbers in the closed interval [0, 1], where 0 corresponds to complete falsity and 1 to complete truth: these values are naturally interpreted as degrees of truth (hence "degree theories").

(2) *Are the sentential connectives truth-functional?*

According to classical logic and semantics, the logical connectives ¬, &, ∨ and ⊃ are truth-functional. A many-valued system can share this feature, agreeing that the value of a sentence (whether truth, falsity or a new value) is determined by the values of its component sentences. Most of the proposed many-valued theories of vagueness have been truth-functional, though detailed reasons for retaining this feature are rarely given. Advocates might appeal to considerations of simplicity or claim that the resulting accounts generalize classical logic in the right sort of way. And it might be argued that truth-functionality is of the essence of at least some of the logical connectives in question—it is a feature that cannot be given up without distorting the meaning of the expressions themselves.[34] (Compare the objections to supervaluationism's acceptance of true disjunctions without true disjuncts.) Critics of truth-functionality, on the other hand, produce cases aiming to show that there is no satisfactory choice of truth-function for a given connective; some theorists go on to produce degree theories without truth-functionality.

(3) *What is the detailed semantics of the connectives?*

Suppose we maintain truth-functionality. There are many possible truth-functional systems, but only some will be serious candidates for the job in hand. In particular, any logic for vagueness must surely meet a *normality* constraint: if a compound sentence has components that are each either completely true or completely false, then its value must coincide with the value it would receive in the classical framework (compare Fine's Fidelity condition). This restriction seems reasonable. Classical logic is supposedly inadequate to deal with the borderline cases characteristic of vague predicates because it has no intermediate

---

34. Special worries about the truth-functionality of the conditional should be set aside here as they seem generally independent of the issue of vagueness

truth-values. But this contention should not yield any challenge to classical logic when that inadequacy is irrelevant, namely when there is no departure from definiteness and all values are classical.

Consider negation: normality dictates that ¬p is false when p is true, and that ¬p is true when p is false. For a truth-functional three-valued logic, the most natural option is to add that when p is indefinite, ¬p is also indefinite. Generalizing for infinite-valued logics, it is usually agreed that negation "flips" values:

$|¬p| = 1 - |p|$ (where "$|p|$" denotes the value of p).

There is more room for variation in the treatment of conjunction and disjunction and still more in the generalization of the classical material conditional, but perhaps the most common treatments are given by the following:

$|p \ \& \ q| = \min(|p|, |q|)$ [i.e. the minimum of the values of the conjuncts]

$|p \lor q| = \max(|p|, |q|)$ [i.e. the maximum of the values of the disjuncts]

$|p \supset q| = 1$ when $|p|$ is less than or equal to $|q|$
or $= (1 - |p| + |q|)$ otherwise.

These are the truth-definitions of Łukasiewicz's many-valued systems (originally formulated for other purposes; see his 1930).

The choice of truth-definitions for the connectives will be affected by considerations about the resulting valid formulae (should these include e.g. "$p \supset p$" and "$p \lor ¬p$"?). But what formulae we count as valid will depend on whether e.g. we require them to be always true, or just never false. And this will depend on how the next question is answered.

(4) *What is validity? How is the classical notion to be generalized?*

A classically valid argument is truth-preserving: every valuation which makes the premisses true also makes the conclusion true. One way of generalizing this definition to the many-valued case is to select certain "truth-like" values as *designated*, and to equate validity with preservation of designated value: i.e. an argument is valid iff, whenever the premisses take designated values, so does the conclusion. With a three-valued logic, the designated values could be either truth alone, or both truth and indefiniteness (when validity would be preservation of non-falsity). And even given the same answers to questions (2) and (3) above, the choice between these alternatives will yield different consequence relations (e.g. the same argument with true premisses and an indefinite conclusion could be invalid or valid given different choices). In the infinite-valued case, designated values could, for example, be just degree 1 or all values greater than some threshold.

But not all treatments of validity for a many-valued logic are instances of the designated value approach. Some focus on preservation of degree of truth in a more general sense which does not privilege any particular values: for example, an argument may be deemed valid iff, necessarily, the conclusion is at least as true as the least true premiss.

(5) *What sub-sentential semantics can be given?*

As well as investigating the sentential connectives, we can ask about sub-sentential semantics. Given the standard connections between & and ∀ and between ∨ and ∃—connections that seem no less compelling in the presence of vagueness—the semantics of the universal and existential quantifiers will be fixed once we have decided the truth-definitions for & and ∨. Thus, for finite domains, the value of "(∀x)Fx" should coincide with the value of the conjunction of all the instances of Fx, and "(∃x)Fx" with the disjunction of those instances. For example, with the Łukasiewicz interpretation of "p & q", "(∀x)Fx" would take the value of the least true instance of Fx, or (to accommodate infinite domains) the greatest lower bound of the values of Fx. Similarly, "(∃x)Fx" would take the least upper bound of those instances.

What about the interpretation of predicates that come in degrees? According to Fregean semantics, a first-level predicate takes as its semantic value the function which maps the objects which satisfy the predicate to the truth-value T and all other objects to F. In a many-valued framework, the natural generalization assigns predicates functions from objects into the new, larger set of truth-values. So on a degree theory, predicates are assigned functions from objects to real numbers in the interval $[0, 1]$—e.g. "red" is assigned the function which maps objects to the numbers representing the degrees to which they are red. Such functions correspond to "fuzzy sets", where an object o belongs to a fuzzy set to degree d if the defining function maps o onto the number d.

Fuzzy-set theory is usually attributed to Zadeh (1965) who developed the fuzzy analogues of notions central to standard set-theory. But though fuzzy-set theory (and the so-called "fuzzy logic") has sometimes been portrayed as a revolutionary break-through, it is very unclear how radical a departure from classical set-theory is really involved. Fuzzy sets can be modelled by classical sets, e.g. by sets of ordered pairs of objects and numbers from the interval $[0, 1]$.

The answers given to questions (1) to (5) will serve to fix most of the central features of a many-valued theory. But a theory of vagueness must also face a cluster of further questions, (6), relating to higher-order vagueness. We shall turn to these after surveying some detailed sets of answers to the first five questions.

Tye and three-valued logics. (1) Tye employs three truth-values: true, false and indefinite (other proponents of three-valued logics of vagueness have included Halldén 1949 and Kòrner 1960). (2) His semantics is truth-functional. (3) Tye endorses the normality constraint, and offers some further considerations regarding the specific connectives which serve to isolate a logic that he claims is uniquely appropriate to capture vagueness—Kleene's three-valued system (truth-tables are given in Tye, p. 282).[35] Tye reflects that his account yields no tautologies. For example the law of excluded middle is not a tautology since "$p \vee \neg p$" is indefinite when p is indefinite. The classical tautology "$p \supset p$" is also indefinite when p is indefinite—though assuming "$\supset$" is still to be a candidate for regimenting "if", it is less obvious that the logical truth of "if p, then p" should be brought into question just because p is vague.[36] Tye notes, however, that these and other classical laws are at least never false.

(4) Tye endorses a notion of validity for which preservation of truth is of the essence—i.e. where truth is taken as the sole designated value (see p. 283, fn. 3). He takes the sorites argument to be valid, but holds that the falsity of its conclusion indicates only that one of the premises is not true, i.e. is false *or* indefinite. He goes on to claim that the inductive premiss of the argument is in fact indefinite (since the instance "if Fx_i then Fx_{i+1}" will be indefinite when x_i and x_{i+1} are borderline Fs).

In response to the questions so far, Tye diverges very little from certain earlier proponents of a three-valued treatment of vagueness. His response to (5) is novel in invoking vague sets (to be distinguished from Zadeh's fuzzy sets) as the extensions of vague predicates. But the relevance of this move is best seen in the light of (6) the issue of higher-order vagueness. We shall return to Tye's discussion of these matters later.

Difficulties arising in connection with higher-order vagueness can in fact be seen as a major reason to move from a three-valued logic (at least without Tye's modifications) to an infinite-valued one. For the standard three-valued approach formulated with a precise meta-language replaces the classical true/false sharp boundary by *two* sharp boundaries—one between the true and the indefinite cases, and another between the indefinite and the false cases. So there are still abrupt changes along the sorites series; for example, there would be a single hair whose removal makes the difference between being bald and being borderline bald. And the fact that the borderline cases are sharply

---

35 Kleene 1952, pp. 332–40 Korner 1966 chooses the same logic

36 Note that on the three-valued version of the Łukasiewicz logic "$p \supset p$" is always true.

bounded means that there is no room for the borderline borderline cases of second-order vagueness. A borderline borderline case—which ought to fall between the borderline cases and the others—cannot be slotted into a *three*-fold classification any more easily than borderline cases can within a classical *two*-valued logic.

These problems for a three-valued logic have parallels for other finite-valued logics: each will yield new sharp boundaries and abrupt changes in truth-value. Perhaps continuity would be better achieved by introducing a continuum of truth-values—which suggests that what is required is an infinite-valued logic.

Infinite-valued logics and degrees of truth. Advocates of infinite-valued treatments of vagueness include Machina, Goguen 1969, Lakoff 1973, King 1979 and Forbes 1983. Allowing a continuous range of semantic values can reflect, for example, the continuity of heights determining degrees of tallness. And the fuzzy boundary of "tall" is supposedly accommodated by the gradual changes in truth-value of predications as height smoothly varies through borderline cases.

Earlier, Black recognized the connection between vagueness and the idea of something coming in degrees. He observes that a given predication "*a* is *F*" will not command uniform assent or uniform dissent among competent speakers when *a* is a borderline case of *F*. And moreover, the proportion of such speakers who assent to an instance of "*x* is *F*" will differ for different borderline cases. Hence he suggests a measure of degree reflecting that proportion, namely the ratio of those that would assent to the prediction to those that would dissent from it. This account may seem, at best, unacceptably crude in simply calculating semantic status on the basis of a head-count.[37] Degrees of truth can be, and usually are, employed without the assumption that they can be calculated in the way that Black contends.[38]

But should we admit that truth is the kind of thing that can come in degrees? After assessing the linguistic evidence and metaphysical and methodological considerations, Haack 1980 argues not. On the other hand, attempts to defend degrees of truth could proceed in a number of ways, for example by explaining the idea of degrees of correspondence. And Sainsbury 1986 defends the notion by reference to degrees of belief

---

37 The thesis could also be undermined by the apparent possibility that x_i is taller than x_{i+1}, though "x_i is tall", as it happens, commands *less* assent than "x_{i+1} is tall".

38 Machina (p. 187) does, however, suggest that a measure of a similar sort involving "the common man's classifications" could be utilized in assigning truth-values to propositions while not determining those values uniquely The question exactly what *does* determine degrees of application will be raised in connection with question (6) below.

(measurable by betting quotients). Intermediate degrees of belief need not, he claims, always reflect epistemic uncertainty but may sometimes be the best or "right" degree of belief to have (perhaps that which a rational agent would have in epistemically ideal circumstances). Arguably, if such an intermediate degree of belief best reflects the facts, then the proposition believed is itself true to that intermediate degree.

A common type of argument that we must acknowledge degrees of truth runs as follows. If F is a typical vague predicate, then one thing can be more F than another, indicating that F-ness comes in degrees. And if things can be F to different degrees, then "x is F" can be *true* to different degrees too: if, say, a is F to degree 0.5, then neither "a is F" nor "a is not-F" can be true, rather both will be true to degree 0.5.[39] But we cannot always conclude from the fact that a is more F than b that a is F to a greater degree than b in any sense that supports the claim that "a is F" is *more true* than "b is F". For example, suppose a is 6'9" and b is 6'8": though one is taller than the other, a and b are both unquestionably *tall*, and it seems that "a is tall" and "b is tall" should both count as completely true. The degree theorist might claim that it is only for borderline cases that comparatives track differences in degrees of truth; but then we will need a new argument for adopting this apparently ad hoc position.

Other arguments for the adoption of theories invoking degrees of truth can be found in Lakoff 1973 and Zadeh 1975. They consider locutions known as "hedges"—including "very", "rather", "technically", "strictly speaking"—as well as the comparative "F-er", and claim that the representation of predicates by functions from objects to an infinite range of truth-values permits a successful account of hedges as operators on those functions. For example, "very" might work as follows: if the value of "a is F" is n, the value of "a is very F" is n^2.

Often, arguments for degrees of truth are taken to establish that we need a truth-functional many-valued semantics. However, these arguments at best show that *some* notion of degree of truth is needed, and the semantics may be non-truth-functional. Compare the idea of supplementing supervaluationism with a measure of degree of truth; within this non-truth-functional framework, Lewis and Kamp offer similar analyses of hedges to Lakoff and Zadeh (see p. 29).

---

39 Is the move from degrees of F-ness to degrees of truth undermined by the suggestion that two-place predicates of the form " ___ is F to degree ___" could be used to report degrees of F-ness without commitment to degrees of truth? Arguably not. for the introduction of these new predicates does not remove the need to ask about predications using the old one-place predicates, and it is *these* which, if F-ness comes in degrees, seem to require degrees of truth

Machina's degree theory. (1) Machina admits infinitely many truth-values which correspond to degrees of truth, and are represented by the set of real numbers in the interval [0,1]. (2) His chosen semantics *is* truth functional; and (3) he defends Łukasiewicz's truth-conditions for the connectives (given above, p. 37).[40]

(4) Machina's preferred definition construes validity as preservation of degree of truth in the following way: an argument is valid iff the conclusion must be at least as true as the least true premiss. Machina also explains how this notion can be generalized so that arguments which fail to be valid in his sense can still be judged according to the *extent* to which they preserve degree of truth—the smaller the possible drop in value between the least true premiss and the conclusion, the more nearly valid the argument.

With this notion of validity in place, Machina turns to the sorites paradox. Consider a version with a series of conditional premisses of the form "if Fx_i then Fx_{i+1}" (though Machina himself discusses the paradox in a more complex version). In borderline cases, the value of Fx_{i+1} will be lower than that of Fx_i. But, for a decent sorites series with small enough differences between consecutive members, the difference in those truth-values will only ever be small and, given Machina's truth-definition for conditionals, "if Fx_i then Fx_{i+1}" will be at least nearly true for each i. Thus, since the first premiss of the form Fx_0 is true to degree 1, all premisses will be (at least) nearly true. Since the sorites takes us from nearly true premisses to a conclusion Fx_{1000} which is, we can assume, completely false, the argument is about as far from being valid as an argument can be. Each step of the argument is an application of modus ponens which, on Machina's account, is less than fully valid (for if $|p| = 0.5$ and $|q| = 0$, then $|p \supset q| = 0.5$ and the step from p and $p \supset q$ to q takes us from half-truth to falsehood).

Next, consider the sorites with a universally quantified inductive premiss of the form "for all i, if Fx_i then Fx_{i+1}". According to Machina, "for all x, Φx" takes the greatest lower bound of the instances Φx, and so the quantified premiss will be nearly true given that all its instances are (at least) nearly true. So again, the premisses of the sorites are nearly true and the argument is invalid. Contrast the sorites argument using a series of negated conjunctions of the form "$\neg(Fx_i \& \neg Fx_{i+1})$". As Machina notes, in this case some of the premisses are only slightly more than 0.5 degrees true (for example, when $|Fx_i|$ is around 0.5, then

---

40. Although these are the most popular truth-definitions, others have been offered For example, Goguen 1969 suggests that $|p \& q|$ could be taken as the product of $|p|$ and $|q|$, considering it advantageous that $|p \& q|$ should always depend on both $|p|$ and $|q|$ and not just the smaller (note, though, that $|p \& p|$ will no longer equal $|p|$, unless $|p|$ is 0 or 1)

$|\neg Fx_{t+1}|$ and $|\neg(Fx_t \ \& \ \neg Fx_{t+1})|$ will also be around 0.5).[41]

(5) Machina adopts Zadeh's fuzzy set theory, but elaborates the basic account on which vague predicates are each assigned a single fuzzy set; for he allows a predicate to be associated with several such sets. This device can be used to capture the phenomenon that he labels "conflict vagueness", where the application of F can be a vague matter because there are several relevant factors which are in conflict. But Machina's valuation function still ensures that any predication receives a single, final value from the original truth-value set (e.g. by balancing the contribution of the different factors).

Alternative truth-value sets. Machina's truth-value set, represented by the real numbers in the interval [0, 1], establishes a complete ordering of degrees—for any pair of things, a and b, and any predicate F, either they are equally F (F to the same degree), a is more F than b, or b is more F than a. And correspondingly, comparatives like "F-er" will always be precise (all instances being true to degree 0 or 1). But when several dimensions are relevant to the applicability of F, as they are for "chair" or "nice", such assumptions seem misplaced: there is, for example, no complete ordering of people by their niceness, and two people could both be fairly nice, nice to intermediate degrees, while there is no fact of the matter about who is nicer. And while the complete ordering of degrees of truth dictates that there is always an answer to questions such as "Is 'Tek is nice' more true than 'that object is a chair'?", this too may seem implausible. So Peacocke (1981, p. 135), for example, recommends that "we must not naively take the degree to which objects may have some property as always totally ordered".

This kind of consideration leads Goguen to suggest various generalizations to the basic degree-theoretic story. First, for multi-dimensional predicates, the truth-value set may sometimes be better considered as an n-tuple of real numbers, where there is a value corresponding to each dimension relevant to applicability. To illustrate: for "big", there may be a value for volume and one for height. If there were a unique correct way to weight different dimensions, then a single value could still be assigned, but if not, the n-tuple may provide a better semantic representation. Yet even using n-tuples may not be sufficient for representing those multi-dimensional predicates where the dimensions are not themselves clear-cut. Goguen seeks maximum flexibility over appropriate

---

41. Wright (II), in the section omitted in this volume, accuses Peacocke's 1981 account and other truth-functional degree theories of being unable to treat sorites paradoxes with the premisses in this conjunctive form in a way comparable to the version with conditionals. But Machina defends the asymmetry.

truth-value sets by specifying some general features of any set that could play the role, and conducting further technical discussion at an abstract level, where the exact truth-value set is not fixed.

Differences of these kinds in the truth-value set call for other modifications to the semantics. To accommodate his generalization of the truth-value set, Goguen allows fuzzy sets to be functions from objects into any candidate truth-value set. Similarly, the appendix to Peacocke's 1981 paper gives a semantics in terms of what he calls "seas" (in effect fuzzy sets) such that objects are members of seas to different degrees. He allows that seas are not uniform—that the set of truth-values/ degrees need not be the same for different predicates—thereby allowing for incomparability of degrees.[42] These modifications made in order to model multi-dimensionality seem, however, to be of minor overall significance and to leave the resulting theories still vulnerable to other objections to degree theories.

Zadeh 1975 defends a different modification to the truth-value set and introduces fuzzy truth-values corresponding to vague expressions such as "very true", "quite false", etc. The new values are themselves fuzzy sets: sentences can be members of them to different degrees (e.g. a sentence that is true to degree n might be a member of the truth-value "quite true" to degree m and a member of "not very false" to some other degree). These fuzzy truth-values are, however, fixed on the basis of an assignment of numerical degrees of truth. Thus Zadeh's approach may not in fact depart very substantially from other infinite-valued theories. (See e.g. Haack 1979 for criticisms of the approach. Note that the expression "fuzzy logic" is used in two different ways in the literature— sometimes to refer to many-valued logics in general, especially when employed with fuzzy-set semantics, and other times to refer just to those logics employing fuzzy linguistic truth-values.)

Edgington's degree theory. The theories we have examined so far in this section all retain truth-functionality, but this feature is controversial. Suppose Tim is borderline tall (say, tall to degree 0.4) and Tek is taller (tall to degree 0.5); and assume negation flips values so that "Tek is not tall" is as true as "Tek is tall". Then consider (a) "Tim is tall and Tek is not tall" and (b) "Tim is tall and Tek is tall". Truth-functionality would imply that (a) and (b) must have the same value. But it seems that (a) must be false: if Tim is shorter than Tek, then it cannot be that Tim is tall and Tek is not. And (b) is surely *not* false for a degree-theorist, but is true

---

42. Peacocke maintains that *A* is a consequence of *B* iff all assignments of seas to predicates which make the premisses true also make the conclusion true This is a designated value approach, with truth as the only designated value

to some positive degree. (See Edgington pp. 304–5 and Fine pp. 123–24 for a range of further such examples.) An account of vagueness which uses the resources of degrees of truth while dropping truth-functionality could thus seem attractive.

Edgington offers such an account. She pursues an analogy between assignments of "verities" (her term for degrees of truth) and assignments of probability. Just as the probability of p & q is not determined by the probabilities of p and q alone—it depends on other factors such as the logical relations between p and q—so the verity of p & q is not determined simply by the verities of p and q. So (1) her truth-values are represented by the interval [0, 1] (though she also has a role for a notion of truth that does not come in degrees). And (2) the connectives are not truth-functional, with the exception of negation which has the standard truth-definition.

(3) The definitions of the two-place connectives invoke the idea of conditional verity (an analogue of conditional probability), where the verity of q conditional on p is the verity which would be assigned to q if we were to decide to count p as true. Suppose a and b are both borderline cases of redness, but b is redder than a: then deciding that a counts as red would commit us to accepting that b is red too, so the conditional verity of "b is red" given "a is red" is 1. On the other hand, assuming b's baldness is unconnected to a's redness, the conditional verity of "b is bald" given "a is red" is equal to the verity of "b is bald". The verities of conjunctions and disjunctions are calculated on the basis of such conditional verities by analogues of the familiar probabilistic formulae, e.g. the verity of p & q is the conditional verity of q given p multiplied by the verity of p (see p. 306). And in her 1992, Edgington identifies the verity of the conditional "if p, then q" with the conditional verity of q given p.

One model of Edgington's non-truth-functional verities builds on supervaluationist ideas, where verities are assigned on the basis of a measure over admissible valuations. The conditional verity of q given p could then be given by taking the valuations in which p is true, and measuring the proportion of *those* valuations in which q is also true (see p. 315 and Edgington 1992). With this supervaluationist interpretation, Edgington's account can be thought of as developing the Lewis–Kamp suggestion outlined in §3.[43]

(4) Edgington's account of validity interprets the notion of "preserving degrees of truth" in a way different from Machina. She proposes

---

43 Sanford also both admits an infinite truth-value set and uses supervaluationary techniques But, instead of classical admissible valuations, he draws on infinite-valued admissible valuations and assigns to a sentence a *range* of values according to the range of values across the different specifications. See Sanford 1976, 1979, though he only explicitly endorses this link to supervaluationism in his 1993, pp 225–26

that an argument is valid iff the unverity of the conclusion (1 minus its verity) cannot be greater than the sum of the unverities of the premisses. The unverity of each premiss of a valid argument can then be transmitted to the conclusion. This conception of validity allows Edgington to say that sorites arguments are valid. Take versions which have a series of conditional premisses. Since many of these premisses will be slightly less than completely true, and the conclusion can inherit a little unverity from each of them, the conclusion can be completely false even though the argument is valid. And, unlike Machina, Edgington can give the same account of paradoxes stated with a series of conjunctive premisses of the form "$\neg(Fx_i \& \neg Fx_{i+1})$", for her account of conjunction again renders all of these premisses at least nearly true.

(5) Edgington's semantics for statements involving the universal quantifier implies that "everything is Φ" can inherit unverity from each of its less than totally true instances, again contrasting with Machina. So the quantified sorites premiss ("for all i, if Fx_i then Fx_{i+1}") could be false, since the quantification inherits unverity from each of its instances. A version of the sorites formulated with this premiss is still valid but this time it has a false premiss.

Higher-order vagueness and exact values. Whatever answers are given to (1) to (5), a further cluster of questions needs to be addressed—questions that are the focus for a number of criticisms raised against many-valued theories of vagueness.

(6) *Can the theory deal with higher-order vagueness? Are all sharp boundaries avoided? Is the assumption that all sentences take exact values necessary? Is it acceptable?*

We shall survey the issues and consider some responses, concentrating on degree theories (though the discussion is, in general, applicable to other many-valued logics).

Although many-valued theories avoid sharp boundaries between complete truth and complete falsity, it is far from clear that all sharp boundaries have been avoided. In particular, there seems to remain a sharp divide between sentences taking truth-value 1 and those taking a value less than 1. Consequently, there is still, for example, a last man in our sorites series who counts as completely tall. Generalizing, there will be sharp boundaries to those qualifying as "tall" to degree greater than n, for all n. Objections to boundaries of this kind are raised in Wright (I), by Sainsbury, and elsewhere.

Closely related objections complain that degree theories cannot accommodate the phenomenon of higher-order vagueness. We have seen how this type of problem arises in the three-valued case which seemed to be committed to sharply bounded borderline cases. And perhaps infinite-valued logics do not, in fact, avoid the problem either. First-order vagueness was supposedly accommodated by allowing sentences to be true to intermediate degrees. But there apparently remain sharp boundaries to these intermediate cases (at the degree 1 boundary and the degree 0 boundary) which leave no room for higher-order vagueness.

These worries may seem to depend upon the assignment of exact values to all sentences.[44] But do not such assignments impose precision in a form that is just as unacceptable as a classical true/false assignment? Insofar as a degree theory avoids determinacy over whether a is F, it threatens to do so by enforcing determinacy over the *degree* to which a is F. For example "this coat is red" may be true to degree 0.322, and "he is clever" to degree 0.9265. Yet it seems inappropriate to associate our vague predicate "red" with any particular exact function from objects to degrees of truth. For a start, what could determine which is the correct function, settling that my coat is red to degree 0.322 rather than 0.321? (Compare the question asked of the epistemic view in §2 about what determines the sharp boundaries and hence the extensions of predicates.) But if the semantics for a many-valued logic is described using a precise metalanguage, then sentences will always be assigned exact values, since sentences of the metalanguage ascribing degrees of truth will themselves be true or false simpliciter.

The cluster of questions (6) has not always been directly confronted, but we outline several types of responses, which have been either defended or at least alluded to in the literature.

(a) *Biting the bullet.* First, we could accept that sentences do take unique exact values, that there are sharp boundaries to the degree 1 sentences, that there is no higher-order vagueness, and that precise metalanguages are acceptable as they stand. It could then be said that any apparent problem is simply due to the fact that we do not know what values sentences receive, a response which highlights similarities with the epistemic view and implies that second-order vagueness is a form of ignorance.[45] But this would yield a severely heterogeneous account of borderline cases (being a borderline case would be a matter of intermediate degrees of truth at the first-order level, but of ignorance at higher levels) and it calls for an urgent answer to the question: what has been gained over the classical epistemic view? Moreover, questions about what determines the unique values remain pressing.

---

44. Note that assigning a range of values instead of a unique one (as Sanford 1976 does) will be of no help if it is an exact range.

45 Simons 1992, p. 167, speculates that second-order vagueness might be due "in part" to ignorance

(b) *Vague metalanguages and iterated degrees of truth.* It might be suggested that a degree theory should employ a metalanguage whose distinctive elements (namely the predications of truth-value) are vague. Since supposedly a predicate is vague if it comes in degrees, this proposal amounts to allowing truth-value ascriptions themselves to hold to intermediate degrees. This might relieve worries about predications always taking exact values. And it follows that it could then sometimes be true to an intermediate degree that a sentence takes a value strictly less than 1, or strictly greater than 0. This serves to "fuzzify" the boundary between value 1 and values less than 1 and the boundary between value 0 and values greater than 0, which would seem to make room for second-order vagueness. To accommodate higher orders of vagueness perhaps further iteration is required: "'p is true to degree n' is true to degree m" might itself hold to an intermediate degree, and so on.

No such theory has been worked out in detail and it is unclear to what extent the approach is viable. There could be worries, for example, that the assignment of *more* numbers—degrees of truth for ascriptions of degrees of truth, then degrees for those degrees etc.—cannot defuse the objections raised above regarding the assignment of exact values to sentences. How plausible is it to suppose that the meanings of our vague expressions (together with the facts) could determine values at all orders for any predication?

(c) *Tye's response and his treatment of vague metalanguages.* Tye argues that the extensions of predicates are genuinely vague sets, and that the metalanguage in which the extensions of those predicates can be described is essentially vague. These vague sets are not to be identified with Zadeh's fuzzy sets: objects are members of fuzzy sets to specific degrees, which Tye takes to impose unwanted precision. In contrast, for Tye's vague sets, certain questions about their membership have no answers, not even in terms of degrees of membership.

So Tye admits that some metalinguistic statements about truth-value assignments are themselves indefinite. But in contrast with a three-valued analogues of the proposals considered in (b), he is wary of acknowledging that sentences of the form "p is indefinite" can themselves be indefinite and he seeks to avoid repeated iteration of indefiniteness at all orders. Among the metalinguistic sentences he *does* declare indefinite are generalizations such as "every sentence is true, indefinite or false". If true this, he claims, would commit us to sharp boundaries between the true sentences and the indefinite ones; by declaring it indefinite he claims to avoid such sharp boundaries.

(d) *Not taking too seriously the assignment of degrees.* Perhaps we should see the assignments of numbers in degree theories merely as a useful modelling device rather than taking a realist attitude to them. If it turns out that by assigning numbers to sentences we can model vague predicates without paradox while respecting certain truths (e.g. about the gradations of F-ness among borderline Fs), then this could justify employing that apparatus. It may be that the exact choice of values does not affect a number of the most important matters, such as whether a given argument is deemed valid. This accounts for a theory that assigns numbers being explanatory, even though there is nothing privileged about the numbers chosen.

Such an approach to the issue is apparent in the writing of many degree theorists, e.g. in Machina's suggestion (p. 188) that the exact numbers assigned do not matter for most purposes, and it is explicitly endorsed by Edgington (e.g. p. 297). It may seem, however, to demand something of a reconception of what a theory of vagueness should be aiming to achieve and how candidates should be assessed and compared (e.g. if the target is utility, uniqueness should not be assumed—perhaps different ways to model vagueness are useful for different purposes and none is ideal for all). And we may still wonder about the project as originally conceived. What are we to say about the real truth-value status of borderline case predications? How does it help to be told that for some purposes it is useful to treat them in such-and-such a way?

5 Ontic vagueness

The claim that it is only language and not the world itself which is vague—that there is no "ontic vagueness"—seems compatible with most of the theories considered in §§2–4. On the epistemic view, vagueness in language reflects our ignorance of the location of the real boundaries between e.g. the tall and the not-tall. For the supervaluationist, vagueness arises from our semantic indecision about e.g. which exact height boundary a predicate like "tall" should mark. And degree theorists could maintain that there are precise height properties, and that the degree of applicability of our vague predicate "tall" depends on how they are instantiated. By contrast, Tye claims that his three-valued account of linguistic vagueness does require the world to be vague, in particular requiring the existence of vague sets; and he maintains that recognition of this ontic vagueness is a key to understanding linguistic vagueness.

Even if we adopt the majority view that acknowledging linguistic vagueness does not commit you to ontic vagueness, we may still want to ask: can there be vagueness in the world? And a large part of the ensuing debate focuses on the analysis of what it could be for the world to be vague.

Parsons and Woodruff discuss the possibility of vagueness in *states of affairs*. States of affairs consist in the having of properties by objects, and if it is indeterminate whether some object has a given property, that amounts to there being an indeterminate state of affairs. Parsons and Woodruff seek to show that this type of indeterminacy is a coherent possibility. An alternative line of enquiry centers on the putative vagueness of the objects and properties that figure in states of affairs. But although discussion of linguistic vagueness has focused on the semantics of vague predicates, discussions of ontic vagueness have said little about *properties*, the worldly counterparts of predicates. The debate has very largely concentrated on the possibility of vague *objects*.[46]

Perhaps the most common intuition is that a vague object is an object with indeterminate, or fuzzy, spatio-temporal boundaries— consider, for example, the indeterminate edges of a cloud or the indeterminacy of the exact temporal span of my life.[47] And it seems that most of the macroscopic objects that we talk about are vague in this sense. Take Mount Everest: any sharp spatio-temporal boundaries drawn around the mountain would be arbitrarily placed, and fail to reflect a natural boundary. So it seems that Mount Everest must have fuzzy boundaries.[48]

One potential difficulty with acknowledging vague objects with fuzzy boundaries is that we can again construct sorites paradoxes (see e.g. Unger 1979, who considers the case of removing molecules one at a time from a table). There is also Unger's "problem of the many" (Unger 1980) and Geach's "paradox of the 1001 cats" (Geach 1980). Take Barney, the cat on the mat, and assume he has hairs that are in the process of being shed, being at present neither definitely part of him nor definitely not part of him. There are many precise groupings of molecules—call them the p-cats—each of which includes all of Barney's definite parts plus some combination of the penumbral hairs. It may seem that the p-cats are each cats (after all, they are cat-like in shape, size etc.); but then there would be many cats on the mat when, by normal cat-counting,

---

46. For one illuminating discussion of vagueness in the world, see Williamson 1994, ch 9.

47 See e g Sainsbury 1989, who suggests that x is compositionally vague if there is something, y, such that it is indeterminate whether y is a part of x Other writers regard indeterminacy over the location of an object's boundaries as just one feature that can make the object vague—indeterminacy over whether it has various other properties may suffice. E g. Zemach 1991 adopts the very liberal criterion that an object is vague iff it is a borderline case of *any* property (assuming that there is a property of redness, for example, this has the surprising consequence that something can count as a vague object just because its color is borderline red)

48 See e g Parsons 1987, Tye 1990 and Zemach 1991 for arguments that there are vague objects

only one is there.[49] The response to this problem will depend on the stand taken on various general ontological questions. Should we allow unrestricted composition and maintain that any collection of molecules constitutes an object (and in particular that all of the p-cats do)? And do all of the p-cats really qualify as cats? One option is to hold that all of the p-cats count as objects but that there is no fuzzy-boundaried object (the cat) over and above them. Using supervaluationary ideas, it can then be argued that it is nonetheless true that there is just one cat present, though there is semantic indecision over which of the p-cats it is. On any resolution of the indecision, that cat is Barney, and it is true that "Barney is the only cat on the mat" (see especially Lewis 1993).

The most discussed strand of the ontic vagueness debate, however, seems somewhat removed from such general ontological issues. It focuses instead on Gareth Evans's formal argument which aims to establish a negative answer to his question "Can there be vague objects?". His strategy is to argue that it can never be indeterminate whether a is identical to b. So we start by examining the relation between the supposed impossibility of indeterminate identity and the impossibility of vague objects.

Consider Barney again, who is a vague object in the sense of having fuzzy boundaries, and take one of the associated p-cats, P. P has as parts some of Barney's penumbral parts, and since it is indeterminate whether these parts are parts of Barney himself, and hence indeterminate whether there *is* any difference between him and P, arguably it is indeterminate whether Barney is identical to P. The argument generalizes, suggesting that vague objects will always enter into relations of indeterminate identity.

On the other hand, some authors have disputed this. For example, it can be argued that if b (determinately) lacks some of a's indeterminate parts then "$a=b$" will be *false* (and not indeterminate). The suggestion is that a is (determinately) not identical to b unless they share boundaries exactly, including the extent of fuzziness. On such a view, there could be vague objects, though they would never be indeterminately identical to anything. Evans's argument, even if successful in showing the impossibility of indeterminate identity, would then be taken to fail as an attempted proof that there could be no vague objects.

Irrespective of the link with vague objects, Evans's argument that

49 Were Barney to have precise boundaries, we could still consider p-cats lacking one or other of the hairs that are definitely among his parts, so is the problem here really one of vagueness? Arguably, in the precise case, the p-cats are *not* cats because a cat is a *maximal* lump of cat-stuff—no cat can have another cat as a proper part. But this response does not solve the problem in the fuzzy boundary case for there is then no unique maximal lump which is Barney.

there can be no indeterminate identities is still of considerable interest. For there are a range of puzzle cases about identity where we may feel compelled to conclude that there is no fact of the matter about whether we are confronted with the same thing twice over. For example, the original ship of Theseus may be indeterminately identical to a later construction containing many replacement planks. Parsons and Woodruff also remind us of familiar puzzle cases about personal identity involving e.g. partial brain transplants, where again it may seem neither right to say that the post-disruption person is definitely the same person as the original pre-disruption person, nor that he definitely is not. And there are putative examples in quantum mechanics where it can be indeterminate whether an electron which has been emitted by an atom is the same electron as one previously absorbed (see Lowe 1994).

Evans's Argument. The argument can be informally stated as follows. Suppose (1) it is indeterminate whether b is identical to a. Then (2) b is such that it is indeterminate whether it is identical to a. But (3) it is not indeterminate whether a is identical to a. So (4) a is *not* such that it is indeterminate whether it is identical to a. So, from (2) and (4) by Leibniz's Law, (5) b is not identical to a. But (5), the claim of non-identity, contradicts (1), the supposition that the identity is indeterminate. So something of the form (1) can never be true.

As Lewis (for one) notes, the conclusion is far too strong to be plausible. Suppose "b" is a vague description that indeterminately refers (for example "the nicest cat"). Indeterminate identity statements can be constructed trading on such indeterminacies of reference, e.g. "Barney = the nicest cat". But Evans's argument is fallacious as applied to such cases; the inference from (1) to (2) is not valid. For (ignoring here irrelevant worries about p-cats) there need be no one thing, the nicest cat, which is such that it is indeterminately identical to Barney, as (2) requires. Rather, of the things "the nicest cat" might refer to (i.e. Barney and his competitor cats) it could be that each is either determinately identical to Barney or determinately not.

So perhaps we should restrict the application of Evans's argument to those putative instances of indeterminate identity where there is no indeterminate reference.[50] Someone who accepts that the argument shows such cases of indeterminate identity to be impossible could then attribute all indeterminate identity to semantic indeterminacy. For example, the indeterminacy of the identity statement "Barney = P"

---

50 A variant of the Evans's argument, found in Salmon 1981, uses variables (suppose there are a pair of entities, x and y such that it is vague whether $x = y$ etc.); arguably this avoids the need for these qualifications about reference.

(where P is an associated p-cat) could be taken to show that it is indeterminate to which of the precise p-cats "Barney" refers. There is, then, no vague object that is Barney—indeed there is *no* unique object which is determinately the cat of that name.[51]

But should we in fact accept Evans's argument, even limiting its application as just suggested? We shall focus on two closely related issues. (a) How should we formulate the principle needed to infer (5) from (2) and (4)? Is there in fact an acceptable principle that validates the argument? And (b), does Evans's conclusion (5) really contradict (1)?

(a) Note that, although Evans appeals to Leibniz's Law (identicals have identical properties), he actually requires its contrapositive—he infers $\neg(a=b)$ from $\neg Ea$ and Eb, where "E" abbreviates "is such that it is indeterminate whether it is identical to a". Can we assume, however, that we are entitled to contrapose Leibniz's Law (even if we accept that law itself)? Parsons and Woodruff are among those who question the assumption, noting that contraposition, though classically valid, is not always acceptable in contexts involving an indeterminacy operator (compare p. 31 above).

Putting the issue about contraposition to one side, let us directly consider the actual principle Evans needs, which can be called the Diversity of the Dissimilar. There are a number of alternative ways of formulating such a principle. For example

(DD$_1$) if the object a has a property that b lacks, then you can infer $\neg(a=b)$.

By stating the principle in terms of objects and properties (instead, e.g., of names and predicates), we might hope to rule out a spurious proof of the non-identity of Cicero and Tully that appeals to the fact that "Tek believes that ... was an orator" yields a truth when the name "Cicero" is inserted but not the name "Tully"—for it can be denied that "Tek believes that ... was an orator" denotes a property. However, one problem with (DD$_1$) for the purpose in hand is that it is then disputable whether the predicate E succeeds in denoting a property in the sense required for the application of (DD$_1$). The indeterminacy operator plays the role of indicating that it is indeterminate whether something has a given property, and arguably expression of this should not be taken to be the (determinate) ascription of another property. But it is only if we do assume that

---

51. See Noonan 1984, Stalnaker 1988. Some authors have gone on to draw further conclusions, e g claiming that Evans's argument applied to vague diachronic identities supports an ontology of temporal parts because only this view of persistence will yield the plurality of candidates between which reference is indeterminate (Noonan 1982).

E expresses a genuine property, that we can use (DD$_1$) to infer (5) from (2) and (4).

We might try to avoid the question whether *E*-type predicates denote properties by explicitly using the "definitely" operator *D* in formulating the required principle of the Diversity of the Dissimilar. But should we specify the antecedent of the law as (*DFa* & ¬*DFb*) or as (*DFa* & *D*¬*Fb*)? Similarly, should we assume that from the chosen antecedent we can infer ¬*D*(*a*=*b*), or rather *D*¬(*a*=*b*)? Broome's 1984 and Noonan's 1990 discussions show how our assessment of Evans's inference from (2) and (4) to (5) will depend on the choices made. E.g. consider

(DD$_2$) from *DFa* and ¬*DFb*, you can infer that ¬*D*(*a*=*b*).

Although (2) and (4) give a predicate satisfying the antecedent, using (DD$_2$) would only allow us to conclude that the identity statement is not definitely true, which is weaker than Evans's conclusion that the identity statement is false (see Broome 1984). Noonan 1990, on the other hand, defends a principle which amounts to:

(DD$_3$) from (*DFa* & *D*¬*Fb*), you can infer *D*¬(*a*=*b*).

He argues that *E* fulfils the antecedent (i.e. that it is definitely applicable to *a* and definitely not to *b*) and that (DD$_3$) thus validates Evans's inference.[52]

There are other possible (DD) principles. Adopting any particular version will require detailed defense; and the availability of a variety of alternatives makes it at least as important to give reasons for isolating a chosen formulation as to show whether or not it validates Evans's argument. To make further progress, more would need to be said about the interpretation of the *D* and *I* operators, a matter also crucial to issue (b), to which we now turn.

(b) Evans claims that the conclusion of his argument, (5) *a* is not identical to *b*, contradicts the initial assumption, (1) it is indeterminate whether *a* is identical to *b*. But this is not yet an explicit contradiction of the form *p* & ¬*p*. Could we reject Evans's argument by denying that (1) does in fact contradict (5)? Consider, for example, the following compatibility argument. If it is indefinite whether *a* is identical to *b*, then it is *not true* that they are identical. And since this seems to be exactly what the conclusion asserts, rather than yielding a contradiction, the truth of (1) automatically guarantees the truth of (5).

A number of commentators have interpreted "indefinitely" as "neither true nor false", assigning *p* a third truth-value when *p* is

---

indeterminate and therefore endorsing a three-valued logic.[53] In this three-valued framework, the assessment of the compatibility argument will depend on how negation is interpreted. We can distinguish a weak and a strong negation, where the weak negation of p is true iff p is not true (false or indefinite) and the strong negation is true iff p is false. If weak negation is used in (5), then the compatibility argument is sound—contrary to Evans, (1) and (5) are consistent. On the other hand, if (5) is read with a strong negation, it is indeed incompatible with (1); but then the question whether we are licensed to infer (5) from (2) and (4) becomes particularly pressing again.

However, the adoption of a many-valued logic to meet Evans's argument is only as good as such a theory of vagueness in general. The writers who adopt this strategy rarely provide much argument for the need for a many-valued logic or confront the problems the theory faces (see §4).

Evans suggests that his determinacy and indeterminacy operators— "Δ" and "∇"—are governed by an S5 logic.[54] He maintains that (1) to (4) and the required (DD) principle can be taken to be definitely true, and he claims that S5 principles allow us to infer the definitization of (5), i.e. $\Delta\neg(a=b)$. This, by the duality of Δ and ∇, implies $\neg\nabla(a=b)$ which straightforwardly contradicts the supposition (1). But is an S5 logic for vagueness viable?

We have used "Dp" to mean "it is determinate *that* p". But Evans's remarks about duality cast doubt on this as a reading of his "Δp". For on this reading, Δp is not equivalent to $\neg\nabla\neg p$, since when p is false, Δp is false but $\neg\nabla\neg p$ is true. An alternative reading of Evans's "Δp" might be "it is determinate *whether* p" (in other words, $\Delta p \equiv Dp \vee D\neg p$). On this interpretation, while Δ and ∇ are duals, it would strictly be D rather than Δ that satisfied the S5 axiom "if Δp then p".

A more substantial worry about using an S5 logic for vagueness concerns second-order vagueness. For S5 collapses iterated modalities ($\Diamond\Box=\Box$, $\Diamond\Diamond=\Diamond$ etc.) so if indeterminacy has an S5-type logic we would analogously have $\nabla\Delta=\Delta$, $\nabla\nabla=\nabla$ etc., and this leaves no room for second-order borderline cases which would need to be characterized by $\nabla\Delta p$ and $\nabla\nabla p$. More generally, it is open to question whether any of the

53 E g Broome 1984, Garrett 1988, Johnsen 1989, Pelletier 1989 and Cowles and White 1991 Authors differ over the semantics of the connectives (e g. Johnsen selects Kleene's tables and argues against Broome's alternative) and choose different versions of Leibniz's Law (Cowles and White are unusual in adopting a version which validates Evans's argument). Some commentators (e g Broome 1984, Copeland 1995) have also considered Evans's argument from the standpoint of infinite-valued logics

54 See Hughes and Cresswell 1996, chs 2 and 3, for an introduction to S5 and other systems of modal logic

familiar modal systems can be reinterpreted to deal with vagueness as easily as Evans hoped.[55]

In sum, Evans's influential argument cannot be assessed without confronting a range of wider questions about the logic of indeterminacy.[56]

Vagueness in the world. Even if, *pace* Evans, there can be vague objects in the sense of objects with fuzzy boundaries, it can still be disputed whether this is enough for the world to count as genuinely vague.

Suppose our world is constituted by fundamental particles and fundamental properties both of which are entirely determinate: for an object a and property P in this catalogue of "base level" items, it will either be a fact that a has P, or a fact that it does not. There will be no indeterminacy and no borderline cases at this base level, which is then naturally described as being completely precise. Suppose additionally that the totality of these base-level facts fixes everything else. We would still have reason, for everyday purposes, to pick out and talk about various large collections of atoms (e.g. clouds or mountains) whose boundaries are left fuzzy. But what is true, false and left indeterminate about them would supervene on how things stand at the precise base level. Arguably, on this picture, any apparent ontic vagueness of the fuzzy-boundaried mountains etc. is merely superficial (compare the ontological framework of Lewis 1993).

This suggests that to get a substantive thesis about ontic vagueness, we need to consider a contrasting picture of a world containing non-superficial vagueness, where the vagueness "goes all the way down". In this scenario, there would be no base of determinate facts on which everything else supervened.[57] So, if there were still a level which could reasonably be called the base level, there would be at least some object a and property P at that level for which it is indeterminate whether a is P.

---

55. On worries about using an S5 logic of indeterminacy, see Rolf 1981, Gibbins 1982, Rasmussen 1986, Over 1989 and Garrett 1991 Away from the context of Evans's argument, Dummett (p 108) claims, for reasons of higher-order vagueness, that the logic of indeterminacy must be weaker than S4 to allow for enough distinct modalities Fine (p. 146) proposes the modal system T for the task (see also Williamson 1994, Appendix)

56. Rolf 1981, Broome 1984 and Parsons 1987 illustrate ways in which arguments parallel to Evans's could be turned against indeterminate cases of any predicate and hence against borderline cases in general

57 Burgess 1990 contests this picture of what is required for vagueness in the world and maintains that if there were still macroscopic vague objects, then, even if facts about them supervened on some precise facts, this would be enough to declare the world vague.

Approaching the issue linguistically, the idea of non-superficial vagueness is reflected in Evans's claim that if the world were vague, vagueness would be a necessary feature of any adequate description of it. For arguably, if there were a precise base level, there could in principle be a precise language in which a complete description of the world could be given. Similarly, Peacocke proposes that there is vagueness in the world if it "has to be described by (inter alia) vague expressions, where this need is not in some way a result of limitations on our capacities" (1981, p.132).

On such conceptions of what non-superficial vagueness in the world amounts to, the question whether the world *is* vague seems to be left—perhaps unsurprisingly—as a broadly empirical matter.[58]

---

58. For very helpful comments on an earlier draft of this introduction, we are extremely grateful to Chris Daly, Dorothy Edgington, O R. Jones, Alex Oliver, Timothy Smiley, Timothy Williamson and an anonymous reader for MIT Press.

2 On the sorites

Diogenes Laertius, Galen and Cicero

1 Diogenes Laertius, *Lives of the Philosophers* 7.44[1]

⟨A sorites is like this⟩: It is not the case that two are few and three are not also. It is not the case that these are and four are not also (and so on up to ten thousand). But two are few: therefore ten thousand are also.

2 Galen, *On Medical Experience* 16.1–17.3[2]

According to what is demanded by the analogy, there must not be such a thing in the world as a heap of grain, a mass or satiety, neither a mountain nor strong love, nor a row, nor strong wind, nor city, nor anything else which is known from its name and idea to have a measure of extent or multitude, such as the wave, the open sea, a flock of sheep and herd of cattle, the nation and the crowd. And the doubt and confusion introduced by the analogy leads to contradiction of fact in the transition of man from one stage of his life to another, and in the changes of time, and the changes of seasons. For in the case of the boy one is uncertain and doubtful as to when the actual moment arrives for his transition from boyhood to adolescence, and in the case of the youth when he enters the period of manhood, also in the case of the man in his prime when he begins to be an old man. And so it is with the seasons of the year when winter begins to change and merges into spring, and spring into summer, and summer into autumn. By the same reasoning, doubt and confusion enter into many other things which relate to the doings of men in spite of the fact that knowledge of these things is obvious and plain. There are some dogmatists and logicians who call the argument expressing this doubt "sorites" after the matter which first gave rise to this question, I mean the heap. Other people call it the "little-by-little argument". They have only named it thus in accordance with its

Galen and Cicero translations from A. A Long and D N. Sedley, *The Hellenistic Philosophers* (1987), pp. 222–25. Cambridge. Cambridge University Press © Cambridge University Press Galen translation based on R Walzer, *Galen, On Medical Experience* (1944) Oxford. Oxford University Press. © The Wellcome Trust Reprinted by permission

1 Diogenes Laertius, third century AD. The translation follows Barnes 1982, p. 28

2 Galen, later second century AD. Greek doctor and writer on medical subjects *On Medical Experience* survives only in Arabic

method which leads to doubt and confusion. ... Wherefore I say: tell me, do you think that a single grain of wheat is a heap? Thereupon you say No. Then I say: what do you say about 2 grains? For it is my purpose to ask you questions in succession, and if you do not admit that 2 grains are a heap then I shall ask you about 3 grains. Then I shall proceed to interrogate you further with respect to 4 grains, then 5 and 6 and 7 and 8; and I think you will say that none of these makes a heap. Also 9 and 10 and 11 are not a heap. For the conception of a heap which is formed in the soul and is conjured up in the imagination is that, besides being single particles in juxtaposition, it has quantity and mass of some considerable size. ... I for my part shall not cease from continuing to add one to the number in like manner, nor desist from asking you without ceasing if you admit that the quantity of each single one of these numbers constitutes a heap. It is not possible for you to say with regard to any one of these numbers that it constitutes a heap. I shall proceed to explain the cause of this. If you do not say with respect to any of the numbers, as in the case of the 100 grains of wheat for example, that it now constitutes a heap, but afterwards when a grain is added to it, you say that a heap has now been formed, consequently this quantity of corn becomes a heap by the addition of the single grain of wheat, and if the grain is taken away the heap is eliminated. And I know of nothing worse and more absurd than that the being and not-being of a heap is determined by a grain of corn. And to prevent this absurdity from adhering to you, you will not cease from denying, and will never admit at any time that the sum of this is a heap, even if the number of grains reaches infinity by the constant and gradual addition of more. And by reason of this denial the heap is proved to be non-existent, because of this pretty sophism.

3   Cicero, *Academica* 2.92–94[3]

[Speaker: Cicero on behalf of the New Academy] But since you place so much weight on that science [dialectic], see that it does not in its entirety prove to be your natural foe. It starts out by cheerfully imparting the elements of discourse, an understanding of ambiguities, and the principles of deduction. But it then, by a few increments, gets to sorites arguments, a slippery and hazardous area, which you earlier described as a fallacious kind of questioning. What of that? Is the fallaciousness you speak of our fault? Nature has permitted us no knowledge of limits such as would enable us to determine, in any case, how far to go. Nor

3   Cicero, 106–43 BC   Roman orator, politician and philosopher   Wrote extensively in Latin, presenting Hellenistic philosophy from the point of view of the New Academy.

is it so just with a heap of corn, from which the name (sorites) is derived: there is no matter whatever concerning which, if questioned by gradual progression, we can tell how much must be added or subtracted before we can give a definite answer—rich or poor, famous or unknown, many or few, large or small, long or short, broad or narrow. "But sorites arguments are fallacious." Well demolish them then, if you can, to stop them bothering you—for they will bother you if you don't take precautions. "Precautions have been taken", comes the answer. "For Chrysippus' policy[4] when being asked by gradual progression whether, say, 3 is few or many, is to become quiescent (*hēsuchazein*, as they term it) some time before reaching many." To which Carneades' reply is:[5] "For all I care you can snore, not just become quiescent. But what's the point? In time there'll be someone to wake you up and question you in the same fashion: 'If I add one to the number at which you fell silent, will it be many?' And so on you will go, as far as you think fit." Why say more? For what you're admitting is that you cannot answer which is the last of "few" or the first of "many". Error of this kind spreads so easily that I do not see where it might not reach. "That doesn't harm me", he says, "for like a skilled driver I shall restrain my horses before I reach the edge, all the more so if what they're heading towards is a precipice. In like manner I restrain myself in advance and stop replying to sophistical questions." If you have a clear answer but do not give it, that is arrogant behaviour. If you do not have one, then you too do not know. If it is because the matter is non-evident, I grant that. But in fact you say that you do not proceed as far as the non-evident cases, and hence you are stopping at cases which are clear-cut. If that is just a device for staying silent, you achieve nothing, for why should your pursuer care whether he traps you silent or speaking? If, on the other hand, you reply "few" up to, say, 9, without hesitation, but stop on 10, you are actually withholding your assent from what is certain and clear-cut—the very move which you deny me in non-evident cases. Hence this science of yours gives you no help against sorites arguments: it does not teach what is the lower or upper limit of increase or decrease.

---

4. Chrysippus, *c*. 280–207 BC. Leading Stoic philosopher and third head of the Stoic school Cicero in *On Fate* says that Chrysippus "strains every nerve to persuade us that every proposition is either true or false" It seems that the Stoic view was that it is e.g either true or false that a man is rich, but in borderline cases we do not know which, and so should fall silent when asked to judge.

5. Carneades, *c* 214–129 BC Fourth head of the New Academy and its most famous critic of the Stoics.

3   Vagueness

Bertrand Russell

Reflection on philosophical problems has convinced me that a much larger number than I used to think, or than is generally thought, are connected with the principles of symbolism, that is to say, with the relation between what means and what is meant. In dealing with highly abstract matters it is much easier to grasp the symbols (usually words) than it is to grasp what they stand for. The result of this is that almost all thinking that purports to be philosophical or logical consists in attributing to the world the properties of language. Since language really occurs, it obviously has all the properties common to all occurrences, and to that extent the metaphysic based upon linguistic considerations may not be erroneous. But language has many properties which are not shared by things in general, and when these properties intrude into our metaphysic it becomes altogether misleading. I do not think that the study of the principles of symbolism will yield any *positive* results in metaphysics, but I do think it will yield a great many negative results by enabling us to avoid fallacious inferences from symbols to things. The influence of symbolism on philosophy is mainly unconscious; if it were conscious it would do less harm. By studying the principles of symbolism we can learn not to be unconsciously influenced by language, and in this way can escape a host of erroneous notions.

Vagueness, which is my topic tonight,[1] illustrates these remarks. You will no doubt think that, in the words of the poet: "Who speaks of vagueness should himself be vague." I propose to prove that all language is vague and that therefore my language is vague, but I do not wish this conclusion to be one that you could derive without the help of the syllogism. I shall be as little vague as I know how to be if I am to employ the English language. You all know that I invented a special language with a view to avoiding vagueness, but unfortunately it is unsuited for public occasions. I shall therefore, though regretfully, address you in English, and whatever vagueness is to be found in my words must be attributed to our ancestors for not having been predominantly interested in logic.

From *Australasian Journal of Philosophy and Psychology* 1 (1923) pp. 84–92 © Bertrand Russell Peace Foundation Reprinted by permission

1. Read before the Jowett Society, Oxford (22 November 1922).

There is a certain tendency in those who have realized that words are vague to infer that things also are vague. We hear a great deal about the flux and the continuum and the unanalysability of the Universe, and it is often suggested that as our language becomes more precise, it becomes less adapted to represent the primitive chaos out of which man is supposed to have evolved the cosmos. This seems to me precisely a case of the fallacy of verbalism—the fallacy that consists in mistaking the properties of words for the properties of things. Vagueness and precision alike are characteristics which can only belong to a representation, of which language is an example. They have to do with the relation between a representation and that which it represents. Apart from representation, whether cognitive or mechanical, there can be no such thing as vagueness or precision; things are what they are, and there is an end of it. Nothing is more or less what it is, or to a certain extent possessed of the properties which it possesses. Idealism has produced habits of confusion even in the minds of those who think that they have rejected it. Ever since Kant there has been a tendency in philosophy to confuse knowledge with what is known. It is thought that there must be some kind of identity between the knower and the known, and hence the knower infers that the known also is muddle-headed. All this identity of knower and known, and all this supposed intimacy of the relation of knowing, seems to me a delusion. Knowing is an occurrence having a certain relation to some other occurrence, or groups of occurrences, or characteristic of a group of occurrences, which constitutes what is said to be known. When knowledge is vague, this does not apply to the knowing as an occurrence; as an occurrence it is incapable of being either vague or precise, just as all other occurrences are. Vagueness in a cognitive occurrence is a characteristic of its relation to that which is known, not a characteristic of the occurrence in itself.

Let us consider the various ways in which common words are vague, and let us begin with such a word as "red". It is perfectly obvious, since colours form a continuum, that there are shades of colour concerning which we shall be in doubt whether to call them red or not, not because we are ignorant of the meaning of the word "red", but because it is a word the extent of whose application is essentially doubtful. This, of course, is the answer to the old puzzle about the man who went bald. It is supposed that at first he was not bald, that he lost his hairs one by one, and that in the end he was bald; therefore, it is argued, there must have been one hair the loss of which converted him into a bald man. This, of course, is absurd. Baldness is a vague conception; some men are certainly bald, some are certainly not bald, while between them there are men of whom it is not true to say they must either be bald or not bald. The law of excluded middle is true when precise symbols are employed, but it is not true when symbols are vague, as, in fact, all symbols are. All words describing sensible qualities have the same kind of vagueness which belongs to the word "red". This vagueness exists also, though in a lesser degree, in the quantitative words which science has tried hardest to make precise, such as a metre or a second. I am not going to invoke Einstein for the purpose of making these words vague. The metre, for example, is defined as the distance between two marks on a certain rod in Paris, when that rod is at a certain temperature. Now the marks are not points, but patches of a finite size, so that the distance between them is not a precise conception. Moreover, temperature cannot be measured with more than a certain degree of accuracy, and the temperature of a rod is never quite uniform. For all these reasons the conception of a metre is lacking in precision. The same applies to a second. The second is defined by relation to the rotation of the earth, but the earth is not a rigid body, and two parts of the earth's surface do not take exactly the same time to rotate; moreover all observations have a margin of error. There are some occurrences of which we can say that they take less than a second to happen, and others of which we can say that they take more, but between the two there will be a number of occurrences of which we believe that they do not all last equally long, but of none of which we can say whether they last more or less than a second. Therefore, when we say an occurrence lasts a second, all that it is worth while to mean is that no possible accuracy of observation will show whether it lasts more or less than a second.

Now let us take proper names. I pass by the irrelevant fact that the same proper name often belongs to many people. I once knew a man called Ebenezer Wilkes Smith, and I decline to believe that anybody else ever had this name. You might say, therefore, that here at last we have discovered an unambiguous symbol. This, however, would be a mistake. Mr. Ebenezer Wilkes Smith was born, and being born is a gradual process. It would seem natural to suppose that the name was not attributable before birth; if so, there was doubt, while birth was taking place, whether the name was attributable or not. If it be said that the name was attributable before birth, the ambiguity is even more obvious, since no one can decide how long before birth the name became attributable. Death also is a process: even when it is what is called instantaneous, death must occupy a finite time. If you continue to apply the name to the corpse, there must gradually come a stage in decomposition when the name ceases to be attributable, but no one can say precisely when this stage has been reached. The fact is that all words are attributable without doubt over a certain area, but become questionable within a penumbra, outside which they are again certainly not attributable. Someone might seek to obtain precision in the use of words by saying that no word is to be applied in the penumbra, but unfortunately the penumbra itself is not accurately definable, and all the vaguenesses which apply to the primary use of words apply also when we try to fix a limit to their indubitable applicability. This has a reason in our physiological constitution. Stimuli which for various reasons we believe to be different produce in us indistinguishable sensations. It is not clear whether the sensations are really different like their stimuli and only our power to discriminate between sensations is deficient, or whether the sensations themselves are sometimes identical in relevant respects even when the stimuli differ in relevant respects. This is a kind of question which the theory of quanta at some much later stage in its development may be able to answer, but for the present it may be left in doubt. For our purpose it is not the vital question. What is clear is that the knowledge that we can obtain through our sensations is not as fine-grained as the stimuli to those sensations. We cannot see with the naked eye the difference between two glasses of water of which one is wholesome while the other is full of typhoid bacilli. In this case a microscope enables us to see the difference, but in the absence of a microscope the difference is only inferred from the differing effects of things which are sensibly indistinguishable. It is this fact that things which our senses do not distinguish produce different effects—as, for example, one glass of water gives you typhoid while the other does not—that has led us to regard the knowledge derived from the senses as vague. And the vagueness of the knowledge derived from the senses infects all words in the definition of which there is a sensible element. This includes all words which contain geographical or chronological constituents, such as "Julius Caesar", "the twentieth century", or "the solar system".

There remains a more abstract class of words: first, words which apply to all parts of time and space, such as "matter" or "causality"; secondly, the words of pure logic. I shall leave out of discussion the first class of words, since all of them raise great difficulties, and I can scarcely imagine a human being who would deny that they are all more or less vague. I come therefore to the words of pure logic, words such as "or" and "not". Are these words also vague or have they a precise meaning?

Words such as "or" and "not" might seem, at first sight, to have a perfectly precise meaning: "p or q" is true when p is true, true when q is true, and false when both are false. But the trouble is that this involves the notions of "true" and "false"; and it will be found, I think, that all the concepts of logic involve these notions, directly or indirectly. Now "true" and "false" can only have a *precise* meaning when the symbols employed—words, perceptions, images, or what not—are themselves precise. We have seen that, in practice, this is not the case. It follows that every proposition that can be framed in practice has a certain degree of vagueness; that is to say, there is not one definite fact necessary and sufficient for its truth, but a certain region of possible facts, any one of which would make it true. And this region is itself ill-defined: we cannot assign to it a definite boundary. This is the difference between vagueness and generality. A proposition involving a general concept—e.g. "This is a man"—will be verified by a number of facts, such as "This" being Brown or Jones or Robinson. But if "man" were a precise idea, the set of possible facts that would verify "this is a man" would be quite definite. Since, however, the conception "man" is more or less vague, it is possible to discover prehistoric specimens concerning which there is not, even in theory, a definite answer to the question, "Is this a man?" As applied to such specimens, the proposition "this is a man" is neither definitely true nor definitely false. Since all non-logical words have this kind of vagueness, it follows that the conceptions of truth and falsehood, as applied to propositions composed of or containing non-logical words, are themselves more or less vague. Since propositions containing non-logical words are the substructure on which logical propositions are built, it follows that logical propositions also, so far as we can know them, become vague through the vagueness of "truth" and "falsehood". We can see an ideal of precision, to which we can approximate indefinitely; but we cannot attain this ideal. Logical words, like the rest, when used by human beings, share the vagueness of all other words. There is, however, less vagueness about logical words than about the words of daily life, because logical words apply essentially to symbols, and may be conceived as applying rather to possible than to actual symbols. We are capable of imagining what a precise symbolism would be, though we cannot actually construct such a symbolism. Hence we are able to *imagine* a precise meaning for such words as "or" and "not". We can, in fact, see precisely what they would mean if our symbolism were precise. All traditional logic habitually assumes that precise symbols are being employed. It is therefore not applicable to this terrestrial life, but only to an imagined celestial existence. Where, however, this celestial existence would differ from ours, so far as logic is concerned, would be not in the nature of what is known, but only in the accuracy of our knowledge. Therefore, if the hypothesis of a precise symbolism enables us to draw any inferences as to what is symbolized, there is no reason to distrust such inferences merely on the ground that our actual symbolism is not precise. We are able to conceive precision; indeed, if we could not do so, we could not conceive vagueness, which is merely the contrary of precision. This is one reason why logic takes us nearer to heaven than most other studies. On this point I agree with Plato. But those who dislike logic will, I fear, find my heaven disappointing.

It is now time to tackle the definition of vagueness. Vagueness, though it applies primarily to what is cognitive, is a conception applicable to every kind of representation—for example, a photograph, or a barograph. But before defining vagueness it is necessary to define accuracy. One of the most easily intelligible definitions of accuracy is as follows: one structure is an accurate representation of another when the words describing the one will also describe the other by being given new meanings. For example, "Brutus killed Caesar" has the same structure as "Plato loved Socrates", because both can be represented by the symbol "xRy", by giving suitable meanings to x and R and y. But this definition, though easy to understand, does not give the essence of the matter, since the introduction of words describing the two systems is irrelevant. The exact definition is as follows: one system of terms related in various ways is an accurate representation of another system of terms related in various other ways if there is a one-one relation of the terms of the one to the terms of the other, and likewise a one-one relation of the relations of the one to the relations of the other, such that, when two or more terms in the one system have a relation belonging to that system, the corresponding terms of the other system have the corresponding relation belonging to the other system. Maps, charts, photographs, catalogues, etc. all come within this definition in so far as they are accurate.

Per contra, a representation is *vague* when the relation of the representing system to the represented system is not one-one, but one-many. For example, a photograph which is so smudged that it might equally represent Brown or Jones or Robinson is vague. A small-scale map is usually vaguer than a large-scale map, because it does not show all the turns and twists of the roads, rivers, etc. so that various slightly different courses are compatible with the representation that it gives. Vagueness, clearly, is a matter of degree, depending upon the extent of the possible differences between different systems represented by the same representation. Accuracy, on the contrary, is an ideal limit.

Passing from representation in general to the kinds of representation that are specially interesting to the logician, the representing system will consist of words, perceptions, thoughts, or something of the kind, and the would-be one-one relation between the representing system and the represented system will be *meaning*. In an accurate language, meaning would be a one-one relation; no word would have two meanings, and no two words would have the same meaning. In actual languages, as we have seen, meaning is one-many. (It happens often that two words have the same meaning, but this is easily avoided, and can be assumed not to happen without injuring the argument.) That is to say, there is not only one object that a word means, and not only one possible fact that will verify a proposition. The fact that meaning is a one-many relation is the precise statement of the fact that all language is more or less vague. There is, however, a complication about language as a method of representing a system, namely that words which mean relations are not themselves relations, but just as substantial or unsubstantial as other words.[2] In this respect a map, for instance, is superior to language, since the fact that one place is to the west of another is represented by the fact that the corresponding place on the map is to the left of the other; that is to say, a relation is represented by a relation. But in language this is not the case. Certain relations of higher order are represented by relations, in accordance with the rules of syntax. For example, "*A* precedes *B*" and "*B* precedes *A*" have different meanings, because the order of the words is an essential part of the meaning of the sentence. But this does not hold of elementary relations; the word "precedes", though it means a relation, is not a relation. I believe that this simple fact is at the bottom of the hopeless muddle which has prevailed in all schools of philosophy as to the nature of relations. It would, however, take me too far from my present theme to pursue this line of thought.

It may be said: How do you know that all knowledge is vague, and what does it matter if it is? The case which I took before, of two glasses of water, one of which is wholesome while the other gives you typhoid, will illustrate both points. Without calling in the microscope, it is obvious that you cannot distinguish the wholesome glass of water from the one that will give you typhoid, just as, without calling in the telescope, it is obvious that what you see of a man who is 200 yards away is vague compared to what you see of a man who is 2 feet away; that is to say, many men who look quite different when seen close at hand look indistinguishable at a distance, while men who look different at a distance never look indistinguishable when seen close at hand. Therefore, according to the definition, there is less vagueness in the near appearance than in the distant one. There is still less vagueness about the appearance under the microscope. It is perfectly ordinary facts of this kind that prove the vagueness of most of our knowledge, and lead us to infer the vagueness of all of it.

It would be a great mistake to suppose that vague knowledge must be false. On the contrary, a vague belief has a much better chance of being true than a precise one, because there are more possible facts that would verify it. If I believe that so-and-so is tall, I am more likely to be right than if I believe that his height is between 6 ft. 2 in. and 6 ft. 3 in. In regard to beliefs and propositions, though not in regard to single words, we can distinguish between accuracy and precision. A belief is

---

2. A word is a class of series, and both classes and series are logical fictions. See Russell 1920, ch 10; Russell 1919, ch 17

precise when only one fact would verify it; it is *accurate* when it is both precise and true. Precision diminishes the likelihood of truth, but often increases the pragmatic value of a belief if it is true—for example, in the case of the water that contained the typhoid bacilli. Science is perpetually trying to substitute more precise beliefs for vague ones; this makes it harder for a scientific proposition to be true than for the vague beliefs of uneducated persons to be true, but makes scientific truth better worth having if it can be obtained.

Vagueness in our knowledge is, I believe, merely a particular case of a general law of physics, namely the law that what may be called the appearances of a thing at different places are less and less differentiated as we get further away from the thing. When I speak of "appearances" I am speaking of something purely physical—the sort of thing, in fact, that, if it is visual, can be photographed. From a close-up photograph it is possible to infer a photograph of the same object at a distance, while the contrary inference is much more precarious. That is to say, there is a one-many relation between distant and close-up appearances. Therefore the distant appearance, regarded as a representation of the close-up appearance, is vague according to our definition. I think all vagueness in language and thought is essentially analogous to this vagueness which may exist in a photograph. My own belief is that most of the problems of epistemology, in so far as they are genuine, are really problems of physics and physiology; moreover, I believe that physiology is only a complicated branch of physics. The habit of treating knowledge as something mysterious and wonderful seems to me unfortunate. People do not say that a barometer "knows" when it is going to rain; but I doubt if there is any essential difference in this respect between the barometer and the meteorologist who observes it. There is only one philosophical theory which seems to me in a position to ignore physics, and that is solipsism. If you are willing to believe that nothing exists except what you directly experience, no other person can prove that you are wrong, and probably no valid arguments exist against your view. But if you are going to allow any inferences from what you directly experience to other entities, then physics supplies the safest form of such inferences. And I believe that (apart from illegitimate problems derived from misunderstood symbolism) physics, in its modern forms, supplies materials for answers to all philosophical problems that are capable of being answered, except the one problem raised by solipsism, namely: Is there any valid inference ever from an entity experienced to one inferred? On this problem, I see no refutation of the sceptical position. But the sceptical philosophy is so short as to be uninteresting; therefore it is natural for a person who has learnt to philosophize to work out other alternatives, even if there is no very good ground for regarding them as preferable.

4   Vagueness: an exercise in logical analysis

Max Black

1   Introduction

It is a paradox, whose importance familiarity fails to diminish, that the
most highly developed and useful scientific theories are ostensibly
expressed in terms of objects never encountered in experience. The line
traced by a draughtsman, no matter how accurate, is seen beneath the
microscope as a kind of corrugated trench, far removed from the ideal
line of pure geometry. And the "point-planet" of astronomy, the
"perfect gas" of thermodynamics, or the "pure species" of genetics are
equally remote from exact realization. Indeed the unintelligibility at
the atomic or sub-atomic level of the notion of a rigidly demarcated
boundary shows that such objects not merely are not but could not be
encountered. While the mathematician constructs a theory in terms of
"perfect" objects, the experimental scientist observes objects of which
the properties demanded by theory are and can, in the very nature of
measurement, be only approximately true. As Duhem remarks,
mathematical deduction is not useful to the physicist if interpreted
rigorously. It is necessary to know that its validity is unaltered when the
premiss and conclusion are only "approximately true" (Duhem 1906,
p. 231). But the indeterminacy thus introduced, it is necessary to add in
criticism, will invalidate the deduction unless the permissible limits of
variation are specified. To do so, however, replaces the original mathematical deduction by a more complicated mathematical theory in
respect of whose interpretation the same problem arises, and whose
exact nature is in any case unknown.

This lack of exact correlation between a scientific theory and its
empirical interpretation can be blamed either upon the world or upon
the theory. We can regard the shape of an orange or a tennis ball as
imperfect copies of an ideal form of which perfect knowledge is to be
had in pure geometry or we can regard the geometry of spheres as a
simplified and imperfect version of the spatial relations between the

From *Philosophy of Science* 4 (1937) pp. 427–55 This selection comprises, with some
cuts, §§1, 3 and 4, part of §5, and §6 of Black's original paper A number of footnotes
giving citations have been absorbed into the text, and some other footnotes omitted
© Williams and Wilkins. Reprinted by permission

members of a certain class of physical objects. On either view there remains a gap between scientific theory and its application, which ought to be, but is not, bridged. To say that all language (symbolism, or thought) is vague is a favorite method for evading the problems involved and lack of analysis has the disadvantage of tempting even the most eminent thinkers into the appearance of absurdity. Duhem (1906, p. 280) claims that "for the strict logician," a physical law is neither true nor false. For Einstein (1922, p. 28) mathematics is either uncertain or inapplicable, and Russell (p. 65) cheerfully sacrifices logic as well.

The aim of this paper is to avoid such wholesale destruction of the formal sciences by supplying in greater detail than has hitherto been attempted an analysis and symbolism for the "vagueness" or "lack of precision" of a language.

We shall not assume that "laws" of logic or mathematics prescribe modes of existence to which intelligible discourse must necessarily conform. It will be argued, on the contrary, that deviations from the logical or mathematical standards of precision are all pervasive in symbolism; that to label them as subjective aberrations sets an impassable gulf between formal laws and experience and leaves the *usefulness* of the formal sciences an insoluble mystery. And it is the purpose of the constructive part of the paper to indicate in outline an appropriate symbolism for vagueness by means of which deviations from a standard can be absorbed by a re-interpretation of the same standards in such a way that the laws of logic in their usual absolutistic interpretation appear as a point of departure for more elaborate laws of which they now appear as special or limiting cases. The method yields a process by which deviations, when recognized as such, can be absorbed into the formal system. At every stage the mathematics we already employ will provide the material for the increasing accuracy of the next stage.

It is one of the paper's main contentions that with the provision of an adequate symbolism the need is removed for regarding vagueness as a defect of language. The ideal standard of precision which those have in mind who use vagueness as a term of reproach, when it is not a shifting standard of a relatively less vague symbol, is the standard of scientific precision. But the indeterminacy which is characteristic of vagueness is present also in all scientific measurement. "There is no experimental method of assigning numerals in a manner which is free from error. If we limit ourselves strictly to experimental facts we recognize that there is no such thing as true measurement, and therefore no such thing as an error involved in a departure from it." (Campbell 1928, p. 131) Vagueness is a feature of scientific as of other discourse.

The impressionist painting of a London street in a fog is not a vague representation of what the artist sees, since his skill largely consists in the accuracy with which the visual impression is transcribed. But the picture is called vague in relation to a hypothetical laboratory record of the wave lengths and positions of the various objects in the street, while it is forgotten that that record, in supplying additional detail, obliterates just those large scale relations in which the artist or another observer may be interested. This paper is written to show that while the vague symbol has a part to play in language which cannot be equally well performed by more accurate symbols from another level (wave lengths as a substitute for names of colors) the transition to levels of higher accuracy can always in principle be made.

2 Vagueness described

The vagueness of a term is shown by producing "borderline cases", i.e., individuals to which it seems impossible either to apply or not to apply the term. Thus a word's vagueness is usually indicated, more or less explicitly, by some statement that situations are conceivable in which its application is "doubtful" or "ill-defined", in which "nobody would know how to use it" or in which it is "impossible" either to assert or deny its application.

Peirce's definition is admirably clear (Peirce 1902, p. 748): "a proposition[1] is vague when there are possible states of things concerning which it is *intrinsically uncertain* whether, had they been contemplated by the speaker, he would have regarded them as excluded or allowed by the proposition. By intrinsically uncertain we mean not uncertain in consequence of any ignorance of the interpreter, but because the speaker's habits of language were indeterminate."[2] An example will now be discussed in more detail.

Let us consider the word *chair*, say. On reflection, one is impressed by the extraordinary variety of objects to which the same name is applied: "… think of arm chairs and reading chairs and dining-room chairs, and

---

1. In this paper reference will always be made to the vagueness of a word or symbol, but no important difference is involved in speaking of a proposition's vagueness The proposition can be regarded as a complex symbol and its vagueness defined in terms of that of its constituents, or vice versa.

2 In the remainder of the passage Peirce explains that by an indeterminacy of habits he means the hypothetical variation by the speaker in the application of the proposition, "so that one day he would regard the proposition as excluding, another as admitting, those states of things " But the knowledge of such variation could only be "*deduced* from a perfect knowledge of his state of mind, for it is precisely because these questions never did, or did not frequently, present themselves, that his habit remained indeterminate "

kitchen chairs, chairs that pass into benches, chairs that cross the boundary and become settees, dentist's chairs, thrones, opera stalls, seats of all sorts, those miraculous fungoid growths that cumber the floor of the arts and crafts exhibitions, and you will perceive what a lax bundle in fact is this simple straightforward term. In co-operation with an intelligent joiner I would undertake to defeat any definition of chair or chairishness that you gave me." (Wells 1908, p. 16)

It is important in such a case that the variety of application to objects differing in size, shape and material should not be confused with the vagueness of the word. The variety of application no doubt arises from the fact that chairs are defined by the need to be satisfied. ... Being "a separate seat for one", as the dictionary puts it, is compatible with much variation in form and material.

But in speaking of the vagueness of the word chair, attention is directed only to the fact that objects can be presented whose membership of the class of chairs is incurably "uncertain" or "doubtful". It is the indeterminacy of the usage, not its extension, which is important for the purpose of the argument. The finite area of the field of application of the word is a sign of its *generality*, while its vagueness is indicated by the finite area and lack of specification of its boundary.[3] It is because *small* variations in character are unimportant to success in serving the purpose of being "a separate seat for one" that it is possible, by successive small variations in any respect, ultimately to produce "borderline cases". The cumulative action of such variation in producing large additive effects is at the root of the felt inability either to withhold or to apply a general term to the unusual and the extreme case.

One can imagine an exhibition in some unlikely museum of applied logic of a series of "chairs" differing in quality by least noticeable amounts.[4] At one end of a long line, containing perhaps thousands of exhibits, might be a Chippendale chair: at the other, a small nondescript

---

3   Cf B A. W. Russell. "A vague word is not to be identified with a general word" (Russell 1920, p 184) He adds, however, "that in practice the distinction is apt to be blurred" and blurs it himself in saying "a memory is vague when it is appropriate to *many* occurrences" (Russell 1920, p 182). This confusion between generality and vagueness invalidates his neat definition "the fact that meaning is a one-many relation is the precise statement of the fact that all language is more or less vague." (Russell, this volume, pp. 66–67)

The confusion may ultimately be traced to a certain uneasy nominalism in Russell's philosophy which tends to treat generality and vagueness indifferently as imperfections of symbolism in relation to the attempt to describe a universe composed exclusively of absolutely specific or atomic facts

4   The variation of this amount with the choice of the observer, and with conditions affecting the same observer, strengthens the subsequent argument by introducing further indeterminacy into the operation of "drawing the line "

lump of wood. Any "normal"[5] observer inspecting the series finds extreme difficulty in "drawing the line" between chair and not-chair. Indeed the demand to perform this operation is felt to be inappropriate *in principle*: "*chair* is not the kind of word which admits of this sharp distinction" is the kind of reply which is made, "and if it were, if we were forbidden to use it for any object which varied in the slightest way from the limiting term, it would not be as useful to us as it is." This is the sensible attitude but it raises difficulties for logic.

In order to circumvent these difficulties, we shall make use of the fact that the uncertainty of a single normal observer, or the variation in the decisions made by a number of such observers, either of which can be taken as the definition of vagueness, is a matter of degree, varying quantitatively, though not regularly, with the position of an object in the series. At the extremities of the series little or no uncertainty is felt, but the observer grows increasingly doubtful when the borderline cases in the center are approached; "everybody" agrees that the Chippendale chair *is* a chair, "nobody" wants to sit upon, still less to call a chair, a shapeless lump of wood, but in intermediate cases personal uncertainty is a reflection of objective lack of agreement.

We have used alternative but correlated definitions of vagueness in order not to prejudge the issue whether vagueness is subjective or objective. On the one hand we can use an observer's feelings or report of his feelings; on the other, the set of divisions made by a set of independent observers who are given sufficient inducement to make a unique division in the series irrespective of their feelings of uncertainty.

The vagueness of the word *chair* is typical of all terms whose application involves the use of the senses. In all such cases "borderline cases" or "doubtful objects" are easily found to which we are unable to say either that the class name does or does not apply. The case of a color name, whose relative simplicity is unobscured by the variation in application of such "artificial" names as chairs, is specially striking. If a series of colored cards of uniform saturation and intensity are arranged according to shades ranging by least perceptible differences from reds through oranges to yellows, the "uncertainty" which is typical of vagueness is at once demonstrated. "The changes of color in the spectrum are throughout so continuous that *it is not possible to find the exact point at which the changes of direction begin.*"[6] It would be easy, but

5 This is, in part, a definition of the "normal" observer; we shall reject the testimony of an observer who claimed to have discovered *the* point at which the division was to be made

6 Stout 1898, p 148 This manner of phrasing the situation suggests of course that the fault is in the language or in imperfect perception· there *is* an "exact point" where the transition occurs but we are unable to find it

uninstructive, to multiply examples. Reserving the terms of logic and mathematics for separate consideration, we can say that all "material" terms, all whose application requires the recognition of the presence of sensible qualities, are vague in the sense described.

3 Location of the fringe

The quantitative variation in the degree of uncertainty felt by a typical observer, or the equivalent variation in the divisions made by a number of observers, will be used later as the basis of a method for symbolizing vagueness. But before doing this it is necessary to dispose of a plausible but mistaken view which seeks to solve the problem of borderline cases by allocating them to a region of "doubtful application", a kind of no man's land lying between the regions when a term applies and does not apply. For even if it is granted that all material terms are vague in the sense described it might still be said that the existence of borderline cases is unimportant. Such cases occur so infrequently, it might be argued, that consideration can always be restricted to objects concerning which the "doubt" does not arise. To such objects difficulties concerning the indeterminacy of the boundary will not be relevant; for these cases will remain unproblematic whichever separation is made in the field of application, and since we do not choose to argue about borderline cases no difficulty remains.

An objection of this sort misses the point: we do not claim to have discovered a serious practical difficulty, but are trying to achieve the accommodation of an unduly simple conception of logic to the undoubted practical efficacy of formally invalid classificatory procedure. The presupposition of the existence of a class of "doubtful" objects will involve the assumption either of an exact boundary or of a doubtful region (of the second order)[7] between the fringe and the class of unproblematic objects.

Either assumption will be shown to be incompatible with the usual definition of negation, and thus indirectly incompatible with the strict application of logical principles. The exposition will be simplified by using a set of constant symbols to illustrate the features of vagueness described in the last section. Let L then be a typical example of a vague symbol. It has been seen that the vagueness of L consists in the impossibility of applying L to certain numbers of a series. Let the series S, say, be linear, and composed of a finite number,[8] ten say, of terms x, let the

---

7 Russell assumes an infinite series of doubtful regions, each fringe having a fringe of higher order at its boundary, but does not pursue the consequences of this assumption

8. The hypothesis of an infinite series is considered later in this section

rank of each term in the series be used as its name (so that the constant values of the variable x are the integers one to ten inclusive). Finally let the region of "doubtful application" or "fringe" be supposed to consist of the terms whose numbers are five and six respectively. There is, of course, no special significance in the choice of the numbers, ten, five, six, which are taken simply for the convenience of having definite numbers to which to refer.

In the usual notation of the propositional calculus Lx will mean *L applies to x* and $\sim Lx$ *will mean L does not apply to x or Lx is false* (synonymous expressions).

Suppose now that $L1$, $L2$, $L3$, $L4$ are true, while $L5$ and $L6$ are "doubtful". It can only follow that to assert Lx of any x is positively to exclude it only from the range 7 to 10, since we cannot be sure, when Lx is asserted, that x does not perhaps occur in the range 5, 6. Thus to assert Lx is tantamount to confining x to the range 1 to 6.

Having obtained this result, it is easy to construct a similar argument in respect of $\sim Lx$. The assertion of $\sim Lx$ can, no more than the assertion of Lx, positively exclude x from the fringe 5, 6. It follows that to assert $\sim Lx$ is tantamount to excluding x from the range 1 to 4 and confining it to the range 5 to 10.

In short, inability to find a logical interpretation of doubtful and perhaps in terms of the two truth values, truth and falsehood, forces us to admit that the ranges of application of Lx, 1 to 6, and of $\sim Lx$, 5 to 10, overlap in the fringe, 5, 6.

On the other hand, the statement $\sim Lx$ is, by definition of the logical operation of negation, true only when Lx is false, and false only when Lx is true. If, as we have assumed, asserting Lx confines x to the range 1 to 6, Lx is false only when x belongs to the range 7 to 10. Thus in contradiction to our previous result that $\sim Lx$ is true when and only when x belong to the range 5 to 10, $\sim Lx$ should be true when and only when x belongs to the range 7 to 10. The formal properties of logical negation are incompatible with an interpretation which allows the domain and the complementary domain of a propositional function to overlap.

We can clinch the argument by attempting to translate the definition of L's vagueness, in some such form as *there is at least one term to which neither L nor its contradictory applies*, into the symbolism of the propositional calculus. Translating the italicized phrase in the last sentence gives

$$(\exists x)(\sim Lx \ \& \ \sim\sim Lx)$$

which is at once transformed, by the rule of double negation, into

$$(\exists x)(\sim Lx \ \& \ Lx)$$

which is a contradiction. Such a contradiction is only to be evaded by denying the equivalence of $\sim\sim Lx$ and Lx, i.e. by refusing to identify the

operation ~ when prefixed to a vague symbol with the ordinary operation of negation. This point of view will be incomplete and unplausible
unless it is possible to define the new sense of ~, i.e. to give the rules
according to which the sign is to be used. ...

This part of the discussion should be completed by showing that we
are bound to reach the same overlapping of domains and hence the same
contradiction, if we were to allow the fringe to be itself bounded by a
fringe of higher order and that in turn by another and so on ad infinitum.[9]

It will be sufficient to consider the case of a linear continuum e.g. the
set of all geometrical points from a point a upon a straight line to a point
b on the same straight line. If there is a series of fringes each limited by
a subsidiary fringe (all composed of points between a and b) there must
be two points c and d, which may be identical with a and b respectively,
beyond which *no* fringe extends. If we choose c and d to be as close
together as possible,[10] the assertion of Lx will assign x to the interval a
to d, and the assertion of $\sim Lx$ to the interval c to b, these ranges overlapping as in the argument for the finite case. In either case, whether the
number of terms in the field of reference is finite or infinite, denial of the
existence of a unique boundary between the domains of Lx and $\sim Lx$
leads to contradiction. Thus it is impossible to accept Russell's suggestion that the fringe itself is ill-defined (Russell, p. 65). Ill-defined can
only mean undefined—there is no place for a *tertium quid* in traditional
logic. But an undefined fringe means absence of all specification of
boundary between the fields of application of a term and its contradictory—and this is in flagrant contradiction with the facts of the ordinary
use of language. *Red* and *yellow* are used as distinct, not identical,
symbols in a way which is not seriously affected by the existence of
continuous gradations between the two colors.

On the other hand, the awkwardness of assuming a well defined
boundary to the fringe is shown clearly in the classical paradox of the
heap. ... What is essentially the same argument sometimes appears in
modern dress as the paradox of the bald man. Plucking a single hair
from a man's head cannot make him bald if he is not so before. But the
plucking of all his hair will make him bald and this can be accomplished by the successive pluckings of single hairs.

Both forms of the paradox are associated with the emergence of
qualities as a result of successive small alterations in respect of some
other (quantitative) characteristic, none of which, except the last,
produce any change in quality. The repugnance felt towards this type of

9 This is Russell's assumption in Russell (this volume).

10 The argument would need trivial adjustments if the field of reference, while
having an infinite number of terms, did not constitute a continuum

discontinuity may be merely a prejudice but it seems to be more, and I am unaware of any satisfactory discussion of it. So long as this type of argument is held to apply to a few vague terms the matter is not serious, but if we admit *all* terms are vague its application will invalidate any deductive argument into which it is inserted, and is as awkward for logic as the notorious mathematical antinomies are for mathematics.

The difficulty is serious enough. If we are right in our claim that all material terms are vague, the formal apparatus of logic (and indirectly of mathematics, though this has not been shown) seems to break down. We are unable even to assume that Lx is incompatible with $\sim Lx$, without the assurance that x is not in the fringe, and we are unable to say when the fringe begins and ends. The attempt to assert that x does not belong to L's fringe, say $A('Lx')$ leads us into an infinite regress

$$A('A('Lx')'), A('A('A('Lx')')'), \text{etc.}$$

and does not evade the difficulty. To say, as Russell does, that "all traditional logic habitually assumes that precise symbols are being employed. It is therefore not applicable to this terrestial life, but only to an imagined celestial existence" is to abandon "traditional logic" (Russell, p. 65). If we can "imagine" precise symbols we can construct them—and if "*all* symbols are vague" we cannot even imagine precise ones.

4 Is vagueness subjective?

Subjective is here taken to mean whatever belongs to the processes of cognition, feeling or willing as distinct from whatever belongs to the notion of their object. ...

Are the variations in the boundary decisions made by various members of a set of observers analogous to the errors of a scientific instrument or to the variations in the readings of an instrument in accordance with objective variations in the situation measured? We have assumed that the variations are not purely random and that the variant decisions exhibit some statistical regularity. If this is a justified assumption (and without it we are unable to account for the success with which vague symbols are used) vagueness is clearly an objective feature of the series to which the vague symbol is applied.[11] And it will be shown in the next

---

11 It needs therefore, to be clearly distinguished from such features of symbolism as ambiguity The latter is constituted by inability to decide between a finite number of alternative meanings having the same phonetic form (homonyms). The fact that ambiguity *can be removed* shows it to be an accidental feature of the symbolism. But any attempt to remove vagueness by a translation is defeated by the over-specification of meaning thus produced. Cf. an attempt to replace *The hall was half full* by *The ratio of the number of persons in the hall to the number of seats was exactly half.* The presence of one person too many would falsify the second, but not the first of the statements

section how the vagueness of the symbolism can be made explicit in a way which ordinary language fails to do[12] and be made in this way to serve as an adequate model of those relations in the field of application from which it arises.

5 Definition of the consistency-profile

We propose to replace the crude and untenable distinction between fringe and region of certain application by a quantitative differentiation, admitting of degrees, and correlated with the indeterminacy in the divisions made by a group of observers.

The definition involves three fundamental notions: *language* (or *users of a language*), *a situation in which a user of a language is trying to apply a symbol L to an object x*, and *the consistency of application of L to x*. It is impossible to define them in independence of each other, for the first, which is clearly involved in the second and third, is in turn based upon the last. Thus the three notions must be defined in terms of a single process of interpretation, assigning a meaning to any context in which they are used. For the present we shall define a "language" as the vocabulary and syntax abstracted from the laws expressing the uniformity of linguistic habits of a certain group of persons; and that group of persons we call the users of the language.[13] ... We proceed to explain the notion of consistency of application. The method is based on the assumption that while the vagueness of a word involves variations in its application by the users of the language in which it occurs, such variations must themselves be systematic and obey statistical laws if one symbol is to be distinguished from another. It will be necessary to

---

12 In ordinary language, vagueness is shown explicitly by the use of adverbs of degree or number such as *many, rather, almost*, etc. These serve as a set of pseudo-quantifiers, generalisations as it were of the "respectable" quantifiers *all* and *any*, forming a sliding scale which can be attached to any adjective The method of the next section, which reduces to the conversion of propositional functions into propositional functions of an extra variable by the addition of a numerical parameter is thus the generalisation of a device already present in ordinary discourse

13 The "set of conventions" determining the vocabulary and syntax of such a language are the simplified expressions, in the imperative mood, of the empirically discoverable rules of usage While the existence of such a language presupposes, by definition, *some* uniformity in the linguistic habits of its users, the empirical laws expressing the partial uniformity of such habits are complex, in process of variation, and heterogeneous in character It is necessary to distinguish between rules of logic, grammar and good taste The neglect of certain distinctions and discriminations habitually made by users of the language provides a simplified or "model" language bearing some, but not too much, resemblance to their actual habits Then the first crude analysis can be corrected by a supplement which considers the facts neglected Thus the definition proceeds by a series of successive approximations

refer to situations in which a user of the language makes a decision whether to apply L or $\sim L$ to an object x. (Such a situation arises, for instance, when an engine driver on a foggy night is trying to decide whether the light in the signal box is really a red or a green light.) Let us call such a situation a *discrimination of x with respect to L*, or a DxL for short. (Then a DxL will be identical with a $Dx\sim L$, by definition.)

For some x's, the result of a DxL is almost independent of the observer; most users of the language, and the same user on most occasions, decide either that L applies or that $\sim L$ applies. In either case there is practical unanimity among competent observers as to the correct judgement. For other x's (in the "fringe") there is no such unanimity.

In any number of DxL involving the same x but not necessarily the same observer, let m be the number which issue in a judgment that L applies and n the number which issue in the judgment that $\sim L$ applies. We define *the consistency of application of L to x* as the limit to which the ratio m/n tends when the number of DxL and the number of observers increase indefinitely. (The second number is of course limited to the total number of the users of the language.) Since the consistency of the application, C, is clearly a function of both of L and x, it can be written in the form $C(L,x)$.

In a previous section we claimed certain systematic features in the variation of application of a vague but unambiguous symbol. It is now possible to specify these features more exactly. As we pass from left to right along the series S of terms x, the corresponding values of $C(L,x)$ will have large values at the outset (region of "certain" application of L), decrease until values near to one are reached (fringe), and decrease again until values near to zero are reached (region of "certain" application of $\sim L$). A list of the exact values of $C(L,x)$ corresponding to each member x of S will be an exact description of L's vagueness. In the figure below, a typical set of consistencies is shown in graphical form.

The numbers along the horizontal axis denote the position of terms in the series S, while the height of a point above a number vertically beneath it represents the consistency of application of the symbol in question for the corresponding term of the series. The points marking the values of the consistencies associated with each member of the series have been joined to form an open polygonal line. It will be convenient to call the curve thus obtained a *consistency profile* for the application of L to the series S. In practice the number of terms in S will usually be very much greater than 10 (e.g. there are said to be something like 700 distinguishable shades of gray) and the consistency curve will approximate to a smooth curve having a continuous gradient.

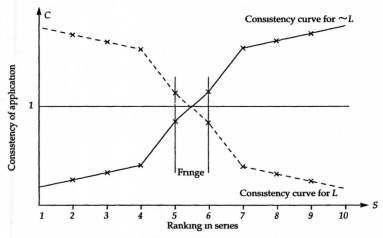

Consistency of application of a typically vague symbol

The exact shape of the consistency curve will, of course, vary according to·the symbol considered. It has been assumed that the typical symbol, *L*, is unambiguous, but an ambiguous symbol will be easily detected by the presence of more than one fringe in its consistency curve. In other words the steady decrease of consistency as we move from left to right is taken as a definition of unambiguity. Further, the introduction of consistency profiles allows us to define the relative vagueness of symbols on the basis of a classification of their corresponding consistency profile. Thus the very precise symbol would have a consistency curve made up of a straight line almost parallel to the horizontal axis, and at a great distance from it, followed by a steep drop to another line almost parallel to the horizontal axis and very close to it, i.e. the curve is marked by the narrowness of the fringe and lack of variation in the symbol's application elsewhere.

The very vague but unambiguous, symbol, on the other hand would have a consistency profile approximating to a straight line of constant negative gradient, i.e. the fringe merges into the whole field and there is continuous variation in the symbol's application. ...

It is to be noticed that the existence of a series of relatively less vague symbols does not imply the existence of a symbol of zero vagueness[14] any more than the existence of greater lengths implies the existence of a greatest or least length. The limits to the application of the term *length*

---

14 Cp Russell p 65 "we are able to conceive precision, indeed if we could not do so we could not conceive of vagueness which is merely the contrary of precision "

are of exactly the same kind as the limits to the application of *red* or *chair* or any other vague word. It is not possible to set any upper limit to the application of the term *length*, but its application becomes less consistent as very large lengths are reached. It is unnecessary in this context to follow the details of the mathematical treatment of vagueness beyond this sketch of a possible procedure.

We have seen that the relations exhibited in the consistency profile can be regarded as equivalent to a numerical function correlating a numerical value of the consistency to each member x in L's field of application. The consistency curves of L and $\sim L$, or the equivalent numerical functions, constitute the complete analysis of the implications of L and $\sim L$ so far as concerns this vagueness. We eliminate the difficulties due to the inadequacy of the dichotomy of Lx and $\sim Lx$ by providing a more adequate symbolism in which explicit account is taken of those quantitative relations in the field of reference of which the difficulties in interpretation of the dichotomy are a sign.

If the analysis of L (i.e. the specific consistency profile) be denoted as L', an alternative mode of formulation would be to regard the consistency distribution as indication of the degree to which L', the more explicit symbol is applicable to the corresponding terms of the series S. We then regard L in its analysed form as the incomplete expression of a propositional function having *two* arguments, reading $L'(x,C)$ as L' *is present in x with degree C*. In this form of expression attention is drawn to the objective relations between L' and S which determine the consistency distribution.

To remove a possible source of misunderstanding it may be as well to add that the analysis of Lx in the manner suggested does not involve the claim that a person asserting Lx in a DxL should know the analysis, i.e. the corresponding distribution of consistencies of application, either at that or at any subsequent time. Any assumption that ability to use a symbol correctly involves extensive statistical knowledge of the behavior of other users would involve a vicious circle. But we can very well use a symbol correctly, i.e. in statistical conformity with the behavior of a certain group of users, without knowing in detail to what we are committed by the linguistic habits of the group.

5   Vagueness and logic

Carl G. Hempel

Do the principles of logic lose their general validity when vague symbols are involved?

Mr. Black raises this interesting question and answers it in the affirmative. His discussion of the problem is based on the assertion that with respect to a vague symbol, there are certain "doubtful objects" or "border-line cases" concerning which "it is intrinsically impossible to say either that the symbol in question does, or does not, apply". The main point in Mr. Black's argument may briefly be stated thus (Black p. 75). Let "L" be a vague one-place predicate, and b an object which constitutes a doubtful case with respect to "L". Then b has to be included in the class of all objects which have the property L; since, as a doubtful object, it is not positively excluded from that class. Analogously, b has also to be included in the class of all objects which have the property not-L. This is clearly "incompatible with the usual definition of negation, and thus indirectly incompatible with the strict application of logical principles" (p. 74) To overcome these difficulties, Mr. Black suggests introducing a more complex logical symbolism, replacing each vague one-place propositional function "$L(x)$" by a two-place one "$L(x,C)$", whose second argument indicates the consistency of application ... of "L" to x. "$L(x,C)$" is to be read "L applies to x with consistency C". ...

For a discussion of the questions which arise in this context, it is important to distinguish *two different ways of dealing scientifically with a given language*, and in particular with the *laws* of its logic.

The first way may be called *the behavioristic approach*: the given language—say, that of a newly discovered tribe in Borneo—is examined as an empirical phenomenon, namely as a part of the total behavior of its users. An investigation of this type would aim at determining the different expressions of the language and the modes of their combination; further, the subject matter which they serve to refer to, the conditions under which they are employed, and the psychological effects by which their use is accompanied in the users and in the persons to whom the considered utterances are addressed. The results thus arrived at can be expressed in empirical statements. They are comparable with the

From *Philosophy of Science* 6 (1939) pp 163–180 This selection is §6 of Hempel's original paper, with omissions © Williams and Wilkins Reprinted by permission

description which an observer who does not know the rules of chess might give of the playing behavior of people playing chess.

Second, the attempt may be made to abstract, from the empirical evidence thus collected, a *theoretical linguistic system* which is *governed by precise rules of syntax and semantics*. The syntax determines the terms of the language, the rules according to which they are combined into sentences, and the principles of logical inference. The semantics determines the meanings of the linguistic expressions. This may be done, for example, by defining the *relation of designation* for the given language; in other words, by indicating for each of its words its designatum, i.e. the object, property, relation or whatever else it designates, and by setting up rules which determine the meaning of the complex expressions, mainly of the sentences, in terms of the meanings of the words of which they are composed.

In abstracting such a theoretical linguistic system from the empirical data obtained in the behavioristic study of a language, one has to omit any reference to the users of the language, to their psychological reactions connected with the use of the terms, etc.; in other words, one has to disregard those features of the language which form the subject matter of what Prof. Morris calls the pragmatical rules of the language (Morris 1938, p. 35). This procedure is comparable, in the example of chess, with an attempt of the observer at abstracting a theoretical system of rules of chess from the evidence established by behavioristic observation. In doing so, the observer would dismiss many features as *inessential*, such as the fact that before moving a chessmen, a player will often frown thoughtfully, that a player, when pronouncing the words "check-mate", displays in general more signs of pleasure than his partner, etc.

In the case of a language as well as in that of a game, the theoretical system thus obtained is an *abstraction*. It is no longer properly descriptive of the way in which the language is actually used or the game is actually played by a certain group of people. Its logical character is rather that of a set of empirical statements. Though, of course, the choice of those rules and definitions is directed by the empirical evidence found in the behavioristic study, and though the theoretical system is set up in such a way as to correspond as far as possible to the results of those studies, it is no longer properly descriptive. The rules of a theoretical system of chess will sometimes be violated by people playing chess; and the rules of the theoretical syntax and grammar of an interpreted language, say of French, will often be violated by the users of that language.

Now, these rules which are usually called the logical principles of a language, form a part of the theoretical system of syntax and semantics which is established by the abstractive process which has just been discussed: the logic of a language is determined by its syntax and semantics.[1] Therefore, the last statement applies in particular to the logical principles of a language: none of them is strictly descriptive of the speaking behavior of its users; each of them will sometimes be violated in the actual use of the language, even if it is as common as the principles of excluded middle and of excluded contradiction.

The vagueness of all linguistic terms favours the occurrence of such violations (though it is not their only possible source). In fact, if, e.g., some observers apply to a certain object the term "yellow", others the term "not yellow", and if all the statements thus established are included in one common system of assertions, this system violates the principle of contradiction.

However, the last remark cannot be interpreted as proving an incompatibility between the vagueness of the terms of a language and the validity of logical principles. In fact, as has been shown above, the question of logical principles arises, strictly speaking, only on the abstract level where language is dealt with as a theoretical semantico-syntactical system; the questions concerning vagueness, on the other hand, refer to language as a form of behaviour, as a system of linguistic utterances of a group of speakers; and on this behavioristic level, any form of logic, the customary as well as any new one, will sometimes be violated by the actual speaking utterances of the users of the language under consideration.

---

1   For the connections between syntax and logic, see Carnap 1935, Carnap 1937, for semantics and logic, Tarski 1935, Carnap 1939

6 Truth and vagueness

Henryk Mehlberg

The Principle of Verifiability maintains that unverifiable statements are neither true nor false. The existence of statements having no definite truth-value, which may be called indeterminate statements, seems to be incompatible with the basic laws of logic. We shall therefore investigate the logical status of *indeterminate statements*, examining first the logical mechanism mainly responsible for the existence of such statements in ordinary language, and then ascertaining whether their presence has any bearing on the laws of logic valid in this language.

It seems obvious that the presence of statements which, ostensibly at least, are neither true nor false, is often due to the vagueness of their terms. That "life can be beautiful" cannot be shown to be true or false, because the concepts involved in this saying are too vague. Shall we nonetheless say that since, according to the Law of Excluded Middle, every statement is either true or false, this statement must also fall under one of these categories, although we never shall be able to make out under which? This would amount to assuming an occult quality of truth or falsehood residing within this statement and concealed forever from the human mind. It seems more in keeping with a sober scientific outlook to suppose that it will never be discovered whether this sentence is true or false, because it is neither. Within such an outlook, truth and falsehood are to be construed as empirically ascertainable properties of only those statements to which they are justifiably ascribable, rather than as occult qualities one of which is attributable to any and every statement.

One might argue, of course, that this saying is neither true nor false because it is not a genuine statement at all and that only genuine statements have a definite truth-value and are referred to by the Law of Excluded Middle. Such a view would be taken by the follower of the verifiability theory of meaning; since the saying is obviously unverifiable, it would have to be regarded as meaningless. Yet some verifiable statements have no definite truth-value either, unless truth and falsehood are construed as occult qualities. Consider, for example, the prediction "The first man I shall meet today will be bald". This statement is verifiable according to all the current criteria, since we

From Henryk Mehlberg, *The Reach of Science* (1958) Toronto· University of Toronto Press This selection is from §29, pp. 256–59 © University of Toronto Press Reprinted by permission

know under what possible observable circumstances we would have to admit it as true, and under what other equally possible circumstances we would have to reject it as false. If the first man I came across were like the Count of Monte Cristo just before he escaped from prison, the statement would be found to be false; if he closely resembled Picasso, the statement would have to be accepted as true. The statement is therefore verifiable in principle. Nevertheless, should the man I meet have his hair spread thinly enough to make the vagueness of the adjective "bald" apparent, we would be unable to make out whether the statement is true or false. Under such circumstances, ascribing to the statement a definite though unknowable truth-value would make an occult quality out of truth.

It goes without saying that the vagueness of the adjective "bald" would be responsible for the statement's misbehaviour. However, the responsibility would not rest entirely with the vagueness of this term, since other statements containing the same term may turn out to have a definite truth-value. Picasso is certainly bald and Monte Cristo certainly was not. Moreover, since every empirical term is vague to some extent, we would be left with no determinate statements at all, if all those which contain vague terms had to be rejected as indeterminate. In other words, the mere presence of a vague term in a statement does not automatically lead to its indeterminacy. Some additional condition must be fulfilled in those cases where the vagueness of a term in a sentence does affect its truth-value. The logical mechanism of this phenomenon depends obviously upon the nature of linguistic vagueness.

A vague term may be characterized tentatively as one the correct use of which is compatible with several distinct interpretations. The term "Toronto" is vague because there are several methods of tracing the geographical limits of the city designated by this name, all of them compatible with the way the name is used. It may be interpreted, for instance, either as including some particular tree on the outskirts of the city or as not including it. The two areas differing from each other with respect to the spot where this tree is growing are two distinct individual objects; the word "Toronto" may be interpreted as denoting either of these two objects and is 'for that reason vague. Of course the vagueness of this name is much greater than is suggested by the two areas just referred to, since there are a great number of admissible interpretations.[1]

A statement including vague terms may nevertheless be either true or false if its truth-value is not affected by the multiplicity of their

---

1   Vagueness must not be confused with ambiguity. A proper name is vague if it can be interpreted as applying to any individual of a number of overlapping individuals A proper name is ambiguous if its correct interpretation depends upon

admissible interpretations. Such a statement is true (or false, as the case may be) if it remains true (or false) under every admissible interpretation of the vague terms it contains. Thus, although both "Toronto" and "Canada" are vague terms, it is nevertheless true that Toronto is in Canada, because this statement remains true under any admissible interpretation of the two geographical terms it contains. Similarly the sentence "Toronto is in Europe" is false, because its falsehood is not altered by the choice of any admissible interpretation. The statement "The number of trees in Toronto is even" becomes true under some of the admissible interpretations of its subject, and false under the remaining interpretations; it is therefore neither true nor false. We may say that in this last statement the vagueness of the word "Toronto" becomes relevant and affects the truth-value of the statement; and this is why the statement is indeterminate. Accordingly, the presence of vague terms in a language always entails the indeterminacy of some of its statements, namely, those whose truth-value happens to be affected by the vagueness of their terms.

Let us now discuss the apparent incompatibility between the existence of indeterminate statements and the Law of Excluded Middle. Since we are prepared to acknowledge the validity of this law for ordinary language, we must square it somehow with the indubitable vagueness which prevails in the vocabulary of this language. It is important to distinguish carefully the *metalogical* Law of Excluded Middle asserting that every statement is either true or false from the *logical* Law of Excluded Middle which is exemplified in such sentences as "Either the earth is round or the earth is not round", "Either John is bald, or John is not bald". The difference between these laws is obvious. The metalogical law refers to statements, it involves the concept of truth, and it is expressible in ordinary language. The logical law involves neither the concept of truth nor a reference to sentences; moreover, although every instance of this law is expressible in ordinary language, the law itself is not so expressible, since this language lacks propositional variables. One may be tempted to minimize the difficulty connected with indeterminate statements by pointing out that their existence is incompatible with the metalogical law, but not with the logical law, so that the admission of such statements entails only the minor calamity of abandoning the metalogical law. The validity of the logical Law of Excluded Middle would not be affected by the presence of indeterminate statements.

---

its context The name "Toronto" is vague It is also ambiguous because there are several non-overlapping localities denoted by it The expression "Toronto, Ontario" is no longer ambiguous but it is still vague. To remove the ambiguity of a word, it suffices to place it in a suitable context A vague term, however, cannot cease to be vague unless it acquires another meaning and thus becomes another term

This advice is, however, of little comfort since the two laws are by no means independent of each other. Although the logical law is not expressible in ordinary language, all its instances are logically true statements of this language. According to ordinary rules, the truth of any disjunction implies the truth of at least one of its members. Since, moreover, the disjunction of any sentence and its denial is expressible in ordinary language, we must conclude that one member of any disjunction of this kind is true, hence that every statement of ordinary language is either true or false. The fact that it is logically true, for example, that "Either John is bald, or John is not bald" would compel us to admit that it is either true or false that John is bald, even if he manages to strike a troublesome balance between Picasso and Monte Cristo. There seems then to be no means of abandoning the metalogical Law of Excluded Middle without giving up, by the same token, the logical law as well. We are thus once more driven to the apparent incompatibility between the requirement of not making occult qualities out of truth and falsehood in reference to statements which are affected by the vagueness of their terms and the more imperative requirement of remaining on friendly terms with the laws of logic.

The answer seems to be that the ordinary connection between the truth-value of a disjunction and the truth-values of its members does not apply to statements with vague terms. Since a statement with vague terms is true provided it remains true under every admissible interpretation of its terms, a disjunction with vague terms may well happen to be true, even if its members are indeterminate. This will obviously be the case whenever neither member of the disjunction is true under every admissible interpretation, whereas the disjunction itself always remains true, owing to a suitable interrelatedness of its members. For instance, although neither the statement "The number of trees in Toronto is even" nor its denial remains true under every admissible interpretation of "Toronto", the disjunction itself does remain true under all such interpretations and is therefore true. Thus it seems that the indeterminacy of statements with vague terms is compatible with the validity of ordinary logic in ordinary discourse (viz., with the fact that all instances of the formulae of the propositional calculus expressible in ordinary discourse are logically true sentences), provided that the usual connection between the truth-values of compound sentences and of their components be readjusted in cases where the presence of vague terms becomes relevant.

7   The sorites paradox

James Cargile

> What mathematicians call "Mathematical Induction" is known
> outside mathematics as "The Slippery Slope Fallacy".
>
> José Benardete

Suppose that a movie camera is focused on a tadpole confined in a small
bowl of water. The camera runs continuously for three weeks, and at the
end of that time there is a frog in the bowl. At 24 frames per second we
will have, assuming that the camera works perfectly, 43,545,600
pictures. Let these be arranged in a series S in the order in which they
were taken. Then consider this property of numbers: the property of
being the number of a picture in series S which is such that the creature
shown in the picture is, at the time the picture was made, a tadpole. It
seems clear that however doubtful the ascription of this property may
be in some cases, it is correctly ascribable to 1 and not correctly ascribable to 43,545,600. That is, the first picture depicts a tadpole and the last
does not. These two apparently unquestionable facts may be expressed
symbolically, letting "P" stand for the property of numbers just
described, as follows:

A. $P(1)$
B. $\sim P(43{,}545{,}600)$.

However, from A and B, it is easy to derive, using the classical version
of the least number principle,

C. $(\exists n)(P(n)\ \&\ \sim P(n+1))$.

(The classical version of the least number principle is that if the number
1 has a certain predicate and a larger number n does not, then there is a
least number among the set of numbers between 1 and n which do not
have the predicate. See e.g. Kleene 1952, p. 190.)

Why should this be paradoxical? Well, on the meaning we have given
to "P", C means that there is some picture in the series S such that it is
a picture of a tadpole, while the very next picture, taken one twenty-
fourth of a second later, is not a picture of a tadpole. So it would seem
to follow that the creature depicted was a tadpole, and then a split

From *British Journal for the Philosophy of Science* 20 (1969) pp. 193–202. © James
Cargile. Reprinted by permission

second later, was not. And this argument is obviously independent of the speed of the camera, which could be taken right up to the theoretical limit of camera speed, so that the split second in which the thing depicted ceases to be a tadpole would be a very short time indeed. And this strikes many people as extremely counterintuitive. Many people, even many with at least some grasp of logic, would accept A and B but reject C, which follows from A and B by simple rules of logic.

This reluctance to accept C on the basis of A and B could be reinforced by considering a wide range of similar cases. For example, it is common for philosophers to point out that while there is a time when a child does not have the ability to speak English and later on a time when he does have this ability, there is no moment when a child becomes able to speak English. But if we let "*P*" stand for the property of being able to speak English and we serially order a child's life by seconds or whatever fraction of a second you please, it will follow from the fact that at the start of the series it is not the case that the child has the ability while at the end it is the case, that there is a split second such that it is true that second that the child has the ability, while a split second before, he did not. This will follow in exactly the same way that the conclusion follows in our case of the tadpole. And it should be easy to see how this procedure can be applied to any case of change in time.

I think that very many philosophers would say quite flatly that there is not a fraction of a second such that a child can speak English at that time, while it was not the case that he could speak English a fraction of a second before. And they would say the same thing in connection with our tadpole and in a great variety of other cases. That is, they would, in a great many cases, assert things like A and B while not only refusing to assert the associated C, but while even flatly asserting its negation

D. $\sim(\exists n)(P(n)\ \&\ \sim P(n+1))$.

Furthermore, I think that such philosophers, if pressed to justify asserting A, B, and D, in face of the fact that these propositions are, taken together, provably inconsistent with the classical least number principle, would reply that the predicates involved, such as "being the number of a picture in series *S* which depicts a tadpole" are *vague*, and that such principles as the classical least number principle do not hold for vague predicates.

The classical least number principle is not an axiom, but a theorem of the classical theory of numbers. So those who hold that it does not apply to vague predicates must hold the same doctrine with respect to at least some of the axioms or rules of inference involved in its derivation. The most natural candidate among these is the law of excluded middle, which could be set forth, for the present purposes, in the form

$$(\forall n)(P(n) \lor \sim P(n)).$$

The law of excluded middle is a natural target for those who want to refuse to apply the classical least number principle to vague predicates, because it is common to hold that the law of excluded middle does not apply to vague predicates. It is common to hold that vague predicates admit of "borderline cases" in which it is not correct either to apply or deny the predicate.

However, while its being common to deny the law of excluded middle application to vague predicates may indicate that it is reasonable to say this, it does not explain why it is reasonable. Furthermore, the fact that rejecting the law of excluded middle for vague predicates will allow rejecting the classical least number principle for vague predicates does not explain why it is reasonable to reject either of these laws for vague predicates.

I am unable to imagine any consideration which would justify rejecting either the law of excluded middle or the classical least number principle, with respect to any predicate whatsoever, whether vague or not. But at any rate, the important point here is that it is easy to prove, using the intuitionist version of the least number principle (see Kleene 1952, p. 190),

E. $\sim\sim(\exists n)(P(n) \ \& \ \sim P(n + 1)).$

Since the intuitionist least number principle does not rest on the law of excluded middle, this means that those who assert A, B and D will not avoid a charge of inconsistency by rejecting the law of excluded middle. They will have to reject something among the principles which allow the derivation of the intuitionist least number principle.

There is one principle involved in the derivation of the intuitionist least number principle which some might deny. The principle of contraposition might be denied by a logician attempting to formalise Strawson's notion of presupposition. But this would concern only cases of denotationless singular terms (assuming an interpretation of "singular term" on which this phrase is not contradictory). And there is nothing of that sort in the present cases.

Once we set aside the restrictions on logical principles which result from attempting to accommodate denotationless singular terms, and we recognise that the law of excluded middle need not be brought into consideration those who would assert A, B, and D must oppose principles at the very heart of logic.

However, it might be held that there is an alternative to opposing these principles. It might be held that rejecting the *application* of these principles in deriving E (or C) from A and B, is not to reject the principles, but merely to deny that A, B and E (or C) are all the sorts of things the principles are concerned with.

Thus it might be said that the application of a vague predicate to a borderline case does not result in a "statement"—where it is implied that only statements can figure as premises in logical arguments.

This is a common doctrine in connection with the law of excluded middle. For example, Strawson held that if someone says "The king of France is wise" where there is no king of France, nor even anyone called "king of France" in jest, then he has not made a statement, true or false, even if he was making a serious attempt at making a statement. And yet Strawson does not reject the law of excluded middle.[1] It is just that the law only applies to statements, and not to the less fortunate sentences involved in failure of reference. A similar attitude is common with respect to the application of vague predicates to borderline cases. For example, it is said of the sentence, "Socrates was bald when he drank the hemlock":

> ... if in fact Socrates had an amount and distribution of hair of the sort that lies within the vague boundary of application of the term "bald", the sentence has no truth-value, known or unknown, and in fact makes no statement, even though we may not know that it makes no statement. (Jeffrey 1967, p. 7.)

It seems clear that this quotation is meant to rule the application of a vague predicate to a borderline case out of logic, because such an application is held not to yield a true or false statement, and this textbook makes no provisions for arguments with premises or conclusion that are neither true nor false. The idea, as with Strawson, seems to be that logic is concerned with uses of sentences that yield statements, and not with less fortunate uses.

I do not think that either failure of reference or application of a vague predicate to a borderline case necessarily leads to failure to say something true or false. But whether or not this is right is a question which cannot be separated from the question as to the truth of the law of excluded middle. For this law, like all logical laws, is concerned with whatever can occur as premise or conclusion in a logically valid argument. And it is obvious that premises with failure of reference or

---

1. Strictly speaking, it is the law of bivalence (for every *p*, *p* is either true or false) rather than the law of excluded middle (for every *p*, either *p* or ~*p*) that is involved here In a technical investigation of the consequences of denying these laws, the distinction could be important But I assume it is not important in this paper

that represent the application of a vague predicate to a borderline case can occur in logically valid arguments. For example, the arguments:

> Anyone with less than 500 hairs on his head is bald. Socrates had less than 500 hairs on his head when he drank the hemlock. Therefore, Socrates was bald when he drank the hemlock;

and

> If there is a Queen of France, then there is a King of France. If the Queen of France is happy, then the King of France is wise. There is a Queen of France and she is happy. Therefore, the King of France is wise;

are both obviously valid arguments. Both could be seriously put forward as part of a seriously held (even if seriously mistaken) position. If their conclusions lack truth value, then the law of excluded middle must be given up[2] because this law is about the premises and conclusions of logical arguments.

To this it may be objected that the laws of logic need not be taken to apply to everything that can occur as a premise or conclusion in a valid argument. For example, such an argument as "I am hungry; therefore, I am not satiated in every respect" might be held to be valid despite the fact that the premise is surely not true or false when the "I" is not related to any specific person. And yet we equally surely do not wish to consider the isolated sentence "I am hungry", a counterexample to the law of excluded middle.

In reply to this it is only necessary to observe that "I am hungry therefore, I am not satiated in every respect" is not, strictly speaking, an argument, but is rather a form of words which could be put forward to present different (though similar) arguments, varying according to the person designated by "I". The intuition of validity is really based on the recognition that each of these arguments would be valid.

Another objection might be that if we rule that the laws of logic must apply to all things that can be premises or conclusions in valid arguments we will deprive ourselves of one of the commonest "solutions" to the semantic paradoxes; namely, the one that turns on holding that certain troublesome sentences do not convey statements. Now I confess that preserving this "solution" to the paradoxes is of no great concern to me, but at any rate, the "solution", such as it is, is not eliminated by the present ruling. For someone advocating this solution may not only say that "'Heterological' is heterological" doesn't convey a statement. He may also deny that such an argument as "'Heterological' is heterological; therefore, 'heterological' does not apply to

---

2 Subject to the technicalities mentioned in footnote 1

itself" is *valid*.[3] (Whether he will have any good reason for denying this is beside the present point.) So our ruling will not require him to count the premise or conclusion of the argument as falling under the laws of logic. Of course someone else who feels that, regardless of the question as to the truth or falsity of the premise, the argument *is* clearly valid, can then appeal to our ruling as a basis for rejecting the proposed "solution". But to defend the solution is at least consistent with accepting our ruling.

Since A, B, C, D, and E, and the instances of $P(n)$ where n is a number in series S are clearly all things that can figure as premises or conclusions in valid deductive arguments (whatever the truth values may be), and since E can be derived from A and B from an extremely conservative selection of logical laws, it is not possible to retain much general logic while asserting A, B, and D.

However, this does not mean that someone could not maintain all the usual laws of logic in restricted versions. One mathematical logician I talked with about the sorites paradox said simply that he had always assumed that logic was concerned only with mathematics. In other words the laws of logic are true with respect to arguments in mathematics, but are not true with respect to arguments outside this area.

This attitude might be considered a bit snobbish. Hard-core physical scientists might get their vocabularies included in the category to which logical laws apply, but biologists, who have occasion to speak of such things as tadpoles, would be excluded. Perhaps it would be replied that this is just an added incentive to biologists to get their discipline assimilated to some more precise one.

The attitude is very similar to Tarski's famous suggestion that ordinary language is inconsistent. This suggestion is frequently criticised on the grounds that ordinary language is not a system with axioms, rules of inference, or theorems, so that it does not make sense to say it is

---

3   This is not to deny that some philosophers who advocate the view that the paradox sentences do not convey statements do so *on the grounds* that the derivations of contradictions in which these sentences figure as premises or conclusions are valid! For example.

"h" $\in$ h $\equiv$ $\sim$("h" $\in$ h) might be called "a true contradiction" ... "The contradiction is true" means: it is proved, derived from the rules for the word "h" Its employment is, to show that "h" is one of those words which do not yield a proposition when inserted into "$\xi \in$ h" (Wittgenstein 1956, §V–22, p. 178e.)

Presumably, the point of holding that "h" $\in$ h is not a "proposition" is to preserve the laws of logic. Presumably, it is necessary to say this, so that it is not being held that "the rules for the word 'h'" are themselves contradictory (which would make it unnecessary to say that "h" $\in$ h is not a proposition) But then, where were the laws of logic when the contradiction was "proved"?

consistent or inconsistent. But if brought in line with the attitude towards the sorites paradox we are discussing, these objections would not apply. Tarski's doctrine would then be just that a certain hard core of logical laws, plus a theory of truth which must be part of any good theory of truth, do not hold for sentences in ordinary language. So if you want to work with these principles, the powers of sentence formulation of ordinary language must be restricted. And while logicians are tightening up the formation rules to prevent the formulation of sentences like:

F. The sentence labelled "F" in Cargile's paper on the sorites paradox does not convey a true statement;

they can also put a stop to sentences using "bald", "tadpole", "is able to speak English" and the like.

This position involves rejecting the laws of logic in their full generality. This might seem to threaten intellectual anarchy, and I used to think it did have some such consequence. For how could anyone deny the law of non-contradiction, for example? How could he hold that there is something which is the case but also is not the case? But it is not necessary to do this. Any derivation of any kind of paradox will involve more than one crucial logical assumption. So no one need be denied, nor could any one such assumption be reasonably denied (in my opinion). But to observe that they do not work as a group with respect to some sentences is another matter. To make such an observation it is only necessary to give up the definition of valid inference in terms of being truth-preserving in favour of the more external, "syntactic" definitions of validity favoured by nominalists.

The definition of valid inference in terms of preserving truth from premises to conclusion tends to be platonistic. Consider this familiar argument for realism. The inference:

G. All monks are bachelors;

Therefore,

H. No monk is married;

is valid. Therefore, by the truth-preserving definition of validity, it must be logically impossible for the premise to be true and the conclusion false. But then the premise and conclusion cannot be the sentences G and H, because it is always possible for one of a pair of sentences to be true and the other false, no matter what the sentences, because the fact that a sentence is true is always in part an empirical fact about the rules governing the language in which it is constructed. So something more than sentences (say, the "propositions" the sentences express) is involved in the validity of an inference.

I do not say this realistic argument cannot be answered without giving up the "truth-preserving" definition of validity. But a simpler alternative for the nominalist is simply to give up strict implication as a necessary condition for validity and rely instead on "syntactic" rules that make validity depend on the form of the premises and conclusion, or on the form of definitional equivalents (or even just of "synonyms" established by some "good" standard of synonymy) of them.

If this is done, then a paradox can be described as a case where the rules for validity give a conclusion which is wrong, either by some intuitive standard (as with the sorites paradox) or by the rules themselves, as with the Liar paradox. But the rules need not be rejected altogether because of this failure. Rather, it may be held just that they do not work for arguments which have premises or conclusions constructed in certain sorts of language. And then pains may be taken to avoid these sorts of language. Ordinary language, which allows these forms of speech will be in just this sense inconsistent—not so much in that it disobeys rules of logic as that these rules yield bad results when applied to it.

Personally, I cannot accept this position, but to criticise it adequately is at least beyond the scope of the present paper. When the doctrine that ordinary language is inconsistent is taken in this way, rather than in the way which requires finding a sense in which ordinary language forms a system with inconsistent theorems, it becomes a formidable opponent for the platonistic view of language for which such an attitude is unacceptable.

Perhaps this position might even provide a meeting ground for logicians such as Tarski and those ordinary language philosophers who say that "ordinary language has no exact logic", if this latter claim is modified so as to include the recognition that there may be a pretty exact logic that applies to ordinary language—exact, but not much of a logic.

There remain two alternatives, which might be called "realistic" and "nominalistic", respectively. The realistic account is this: it is just true that our creature (let us call him "Amphibius") ceases to be a tadpole at some instant, and at some (not earlier and probably later) instant, becomes a frog. And at some instant, a child acquires the ability to speak English, and in general, when a thing changes in time by losing or acquiring a property, it loses or acquires it instantaneously. We may not know exactly what instant it is and it may be of absolutely no practical significance that we do not know, and absurd to make an effort to find out. But still, that is how logic requires that change must be, and so it must (logically) be.

The nominalistic response would say that rather than there being some unknown instant at which Amphibius ceases to be a tadpole, it is just that, if we are making use of logic, we may be forced to choose some instant arbitrarily to be the instant when Amphibius ceases to be a tadpole, in much the same way that we may have to assume, in applying the differential calculus to a physical problem, that matter is infinitely divisible.

This attitude is that in some cases, "you have to draw the line somewhere" as university admissions offices say. They do not pretend that an examination score of 599 shows less aptitude for university work than a score of 600. And they admit that they might find room for the few more students that would qualify if the minimum were dropped from 600 to 599. It is just that they had to draw the line somewhere to prevent serious overcrowding and/or unteachable students.

This may seem a very casual attitude towards a line which logic itself requires us to draw, but then logic does leave the crucial question as to exactly where the line is to be drawn quite open. If the nominalist were got to admit that there are some stages at which it is not merely an arbitrary matter that Amphibius is a tadpole, and were then asked at which instant this comes to be an arbitrary matter, he might answer that this is an arbitrary matter and that the line might be drawn differently by different people.

Of course the opposition between nominalism and realism here need not be absolute. Someone could be a nominalist about the property of being a tadpole and a realist about some other property.

One other response to the paradox which might be worth mentioning is the idea that we should give up saying that Amphibius is, in the first picture, a tadpole, and say instead that he is 100 per cent tadpole. Then we will be able to make the changes in percentages just as small as the changes in Amphibius. He can "drop" from 87.081289 per cent to 87.081288 per cent tadpole, and so on. But the fact remains that he must eventually reach 0.0 per cent and there must be some exact first picture where this is so. And that this final disappearance of tadpoleness from Amphibius takes place at an instant is just as surprising, and the determination of this instant is just as mysterious, as in the case of the property of being a tadpole.

However, this attitude might be extended to a preference for properties which, unlike that of being a tadpole, or being able to speak English, are such that we are able, at least if we bother to pay close attention, to precisely place the time of their arrival or departure. Thus we could describe Amphibius in his change from his first picture to the last in the series, not in terms of "tadpole" and "frog", but descriptions for which we could always cite the precise first (or last) picture to which they applied.

This would only avoid the paradox if such preferences were made a basis for dropping predicates like "is a tadpole" or "is able to speak

English" altogether, at least in contexts where logical precision is maintained. This would fit the attitude already discussed, of holding that the laws of logic only apply to language more restrictive than ordinary language. But it is a great deal of trouble just to avoid such a harmless assumption as our realism.

Finally, it may be said that our realism is not so harmless, because it involves denying, for example, that it takes time to acquire the ability to speak English, or to become a frog, and this is utterly absurd.

To this I reply that the realist point need not be put in these terms, and is only put in these terms because they can be understood in the necessary way. What is essential is that there will be one instant when Amphibius is a frog, such that, an instant before, he was not. And there will be one instant when a person does have the ability to speak English, such that, an instant before, he did not. It is not being denied that, for the young tadpole, Amphibius, it will be a long time until he is a frog, or that, for the baby, it will be a long time until he is able to speak English. Learning and growing can take lots of time. But acquiring properties does not. It is like reaching the top of a mountain. We can say that it took five hours to reach the top. And yet we can also say that at the end of four hours and 59 minutes of climbing we had not yet reached the top, and at the end of five hours, we had.

8   Wang's paradox

Michael Dummett

This paper bears on three different topics: observational predicates and
phenomenal properties; vagueness; and strict finitism as a philosophy
of mathematics. Of these three, only the last requires any preliminary
comment.

Constructivist philosophies of mathematics insist that the meanings
of all terms, including logical constants, appearing in mathematical
statements must be given in relation to constructions which we are
capable of effecting, and of our capacity to recognise such constructions
as providing proofs of those statements; and, further, that the principles
of reasoning which, in assessing the cogency of such proofs, we
acknowledge as valid must be justifiable in terms of the meanings of the
logical constants and of other expressions as so given. The most powerful form of argument in favour of such a constructivist view is that
which insists that there is no other means by which we can give
meaning to mathematical expressions. We learn, and can only learn,
their meanings by a training in their use; and that means a training in
effecting mathematical constructions, and in recording them within the
language of mathematics. There is no means by which we could derive
from such a training a grasp of anything transcending it, such as a
notion of truth and falsity for mathematical statements independent of
our means of recognising their truth-values.

Traditional constructivism has allowed that the mathematical
constructions by reference to which the meanings of mathematical
terms are to be given may be ones which we are capable of effecting
only in principle. It makes no difference if they are too complex or,
simply, too lengthy for any human being, or even the whole human race
in collaboration, to effect in practice. Strict finitism rejects this concession
to traditional views, and insists, rather, that the meanings of our terms
must be given by reference to constructions which we can in practice
carry out, and to criteria of correct proof on which we are in practice
prepared to rely: and the strict finitist employs against the old-
fashioned constructivist arguments of exactly the same form as the
constructivist has been accustomed to use against the platonist; for,
after all, it is, and must necessarily be, by reference only to constructions

From *Synthese* 30 (1975) pp 301–24. © Kluwer Academic Publishers Reprinted by
permission

which we can in practice carry out that we learn the use of mathematical expressions.

Strict finitism was first suggested as a conceivable position in the philosophy of mathematics by Bernays in his article "On platonism in mathematics" (1935). It was argued for by Wittgenstein in *Remarks on the Foundations of Mathematics* (1978); but, with his staunch belief that philosophy can only interpret the world, and has no business attempting to change it, he did not propose that mathematics be reconstructed along strict finitist lines—something which evidently calls for a far more radical overhaul of mathematical practice than does traditional constructivism. The only person, so far as I know, to declare his adherence to strict finitism and attempt such a reconstruction of mathematics is Essenin-Volpin. But, even if no one were disposed to accept the arguments in favour of the strict finitist position, it would remain one of the greatest interest, not least for the question whether constructivism, as traditionally understood, is a tenable position. It can be so only if, despite the surface similarity, there is a disanalogy between the arguments which the strict finitist uses against the constructivist and those which the constructivist uses against the platonist. If strict finitism were to prove to be internally incoherent, then either such a disanalogy exists or the argument for traditional constructivism is unsound, even in the absence of any parallel incoherence in the constructivist position.

On a strict finitist view, the conception must be abandoned that the natural numbers are closed under simple arithmetical operations, such as exponentiation. For by "natural number" must be understood a number which we are in practice capable of representing. Clearly, capacity to represent a natural number is relative to the notation allowed, and so the single infinite totality of natural numbers, actual on the platonist view, potential on the traditional constructivist view, but equally unique and determinate on both, gives way to a multiplicity of totalities, each defined by a particular notation for the natural numbers. Such notations are of two kinds. As an example of the first kind, we may take the Arabic notation. The totality of natural numbers which we are capable in practice of representing by an Arabic numeral is evidently not closed under exponentiation; for instance, $10^{10^{10}}$ plainly does not belong to it. As an example of a notation of the second kind, we may take the Arabic numerals supplemented by the symbols for addition, multiplication and exponentiation. The totality of natural numbers determined by this notation evidently does contain $10^{10^{10}}$, and is closed under exponentiation. On the other hand, it does not have the property, which a totality determined by a notation of the first kind shares with the totality of natural numbers as traditionally conceived, that, for any number n, there are n numbers less than it: for, plainly, the totality does not contain as many as $10^{10^{10}}$ numbers. Since a totality determined by a notation of the second kind will still not be closed under all effective arithmetical operations definable over it, it possesses no great advantage over a totality of the first kind, and, for most purposes, it is better to take the natural numbers as forming some totality of this first kind.

Strict finitism is coherent only if the notion of totalities of this sort is itself coherent. My remarks will bear on strict finitism only at this point.

These preliminaries completed, consider the following inductive argument:

> 0 is small;
> If n is small, $n + 1$ is small:
> Therefore, every number is small.

This is Wang's paradox. It might be urged that it is not a paradox, since, on the ordinary understanding of "small", the conclusion is true. A small elephant is an elephant that is smaller than most elephants; and, since every natural number is larger than only finitely many natural numbers, and smaller than infinitely many, every natural number is small, i.e., smaller than most natural numbers.

But it is a paradox, since we can evidently find interpretations of "small" under which the conclusion is patently false and the premisses apparently true. It is, in fact, a version of the ancient Greek paradox of the heap. If you have a heap of sand, you still have a heap of sand if you remove one grain; it follows, by repeated applications, that a single grain of sand makes a heap, and, further, that, by removing even that one grain, you will still have a heap. Wang's paradox is merely the contraposition of this, where "n is small" is interpreted to mean "n grains of sand are too few to make a heap". Another interpretation which yields a paradox is "It is possible in practice to write down the Arabic numeral for n".

On either of these interpretations, the predicate "small" is vague: the word "heap" is vague, and the expression "possible in practice" is vague. In fact, on any interpretation under which the argument constitutes a paradox, the predicate "small" will be vague. Now, under any such interpretation, premiss 1 (the induction basis) is clearly true, and the conclusion as clearly false. The paradox is evidently due to the vagueness of the predicate "small": but we have to decide in what way this vagueness is responsible for the appearance of paradox. We have two choices, it appears: either premiss 2 (the induction step) is not true, or else induction is not a valid method of argument in the presence of vague predicates.

The induction step certainly seems correct, for any arbitrary n. One possibility is that, in the presence of vague predicates, the rule of universal generalisation fails, i.e., we are not entitled to pass from the truth, for any arbitrary n, of "$A(n)$", in this case of

If n is small, $n + 1$ is small,

to that of "For every n, $A(n)$", i.e., here of

For every n, if n is small, then $n + 1$ is small.

But, even if we suppose this, we should still be able to derive, for each particular value of n, the conclusion

n is small,

even though we could not establish the single proposition

For every n, n is small.

And this does not remove the paradox, since for each suitable interpretation of "small" we can easily name a specific value of n for which the proposition

n is small

is plainly false.

Let us therefore consider the possibility that induction fails of validity when applied to vague properties. Reasoning similar to that of the preceding paragraph seems to suggest that this is not an adequate solution either. If induction fails, then, again, we cannot draw the conclusion

For every n, n is small;

but it is a well-known fact that each particular instance of the conclusion of an inductive argument can be established from the premises of the induction without appeal to induction as a principle of inference. That is, for any specific value n_0 of n, the conclusion

n_0 is small

can be established from the induction basis

0 is small

and a finite number of instances

If 0 is small, 1 is small;
If 1 is small, 2 is small;
...
If m is small, $m + 1$ is small;
...

of the induction step, by means of a series of n_0 applications of modus ponens. Hence, just as in the preceding paragraph, it is not sufficient, in order to avoid the appearance of paradox, to reject induction as applied to vague properties.

It therefore appears that, in order to resolve the paradox without declining to accept the induction step as true, we must either declare the rule of universal instantiation invalid, in the presence of vague predicates, or else regard modus ponens as invalid in that context. That is, either we cannot, for each particular m, derive

> If m is small, then $m + 1$ is small

from

> For every n, if n is small, then $n + 1$ is small;

or else we cannot, at least for some values of m, derive

> $m + 1$ is small

from the premisses

> If m is small, then $m + 1$ is small

and

> m is small.

But either of these seems a desperate remedy, for the validity of these rules of inference seems absolutely constitutive of the meanings of "every" and of "if".

The only alternative left to us, short of questioning the induction step, therefore appears to be to deny that, in the presence of vague predicates, an argument each step of which is valid is necessarily itself valid. This measure seems, however, in turn, to undermine the whole notion of proof (= chain of valid arguments), and, indeed, to violate the concept of valid argument itself, and hence to be no more open to us than any of the other possibilities we have so far canvassed.

Nevertheless, this alternative is one which would be embraced by a strict finitist. For him, a proof is valid just in case it can in practice be recognised by us as valid; and, when it exceeds a certain length and complexity, that capacity fails. For this reason, a strict finitist will not allow the contention to which we earlier appealed, that an argument by induction to the truth of a statement "$A(n_0)$", for specific n_0, can always be replaced by a sequence of n_0 applications of modus ponens: for n_0 may be too large for a proof to be capable of containing n_0 separate steps.

This, of course, has nothing to do with vagueness: it would apply just as much to an induction with respect to a completely definite property. In our case, however, we may set it aside, for the following reason. Let us call n an *apodictic* number if it is possible for a proof (which we are capable of taking in, i.e. of recognising as such) to contain as many as n

steps. Then the apodictic numbers form a totality of the kind which the strict finitist must, in all cases, take the natural numbers as forming, that is to say, having the following three properties: (a) it is (apparently) closed under the successor operation; (b) for any number n belonging to the totality, there are n numbers smaller than it also in the totality; and (c) it is bounded above, that is, we can cite a number M sufficiently large that it is plainly not a member of the totality. A possible interpretation of "n is small" in Wang's paradox would now be "$n + 100$ is apodictic". Now it seems reasonable to suppose that we can find an upper bound M for the totality of apodictic numbers such that $M - 100$ is apodictic. (If this does not seem reasonable to you, substitute some larger number k for 100 such that it does seem reasonable—this is surely possible—and understand k whenever I speak of 100.) Since M is an upper bound for the totality of apodictic numbers, $M - 100$ is an upper bound for the totality of small numbers, under this interpretation of "small". Hence, since $M - 100$ is apodictic, there exists a proof (which we can in practice recognise as such) containing $M - 100$ applications of modus ponens whose conclusion is the false proposition that $M - 100$ is small. That is to say, an appeal to the contention that only a proof which we are capable of taking in really proves anything will not rescue us from Wang's paradox, since it will always be possible so to interpret "small" that we can find a number which is not small for which there apparently exists a proof, in the strict finitist's sense of "proof", that it is small, a proof not expressly appealing to induction.

We may note, before leaving this point, that the question whether Wang's paradox is a paradox for the strict finitist admits of no determinate answer. If "natural number" and "small" are so interpreted that the totality of natural numbers is an initial segment of the totality of small numbers (including the case when they coincide), then it is no paradox—its conclusion is straightforwardly true: but, since "small" and "natural number" can be so interpreted that the totality of small numbers is a proper initial segment of the totality of natural numbers, Wang's paradox can be paradoxical even for the strict finitist.

It thus seems that we have no recourse but to turn back to the alternative set aside at the very outset, namely that the second premiss of the induction, the induction step, is not after all true. What is the objection to supposition that the statement

> For every n, if n is small, then $n + 1$ is small

is not true? In its crudest form, it is of course this: that, if the statement is not true, it must be false, i.e., its negation must be true. But the negation of the statement is equivalent to:

> For some n, n is small and $n + 1$ is not small,

whereas it seems to us *a priori* that it would be absurd to specify any number as being small, but such that its successor is not small.

To the argument, as thus stated, there is the immediate objection that it is assuming at least three questionable principles of classical, two-valued, logic—questionable, that is, when we are dealing with vague statements. These are:

(1) that any statement must be either true or false;

(2) that from the negation of "For every n, $A(n)$" we can infer "For some n, not $A(n)$"; and

(3) that from the negation of "If A, then B" we can infer the truth of "A".

However, as we have seen, in order to generate the paradox, it is sufficient to consider a finite number of statements of the form

If m is small, then $m + 1$ is small.

If all of these were true, then the conclusion

n_0 is small

would follow, for some specific number n_0 for which it is evidently intuitively false. If, then, we are not to reject modus ponens, it appears that we cannot allow that each of these finitely many conditional statements is true. If we were to go through these conditionals one by one, saying of each whether or not we were prepared to accept it as true, then, if we were not to end up committed to the false conclusion that n_0 is small, there would have to be a smallest number m_0 such that we were not prepared to accept the truth of

If m_0 is small, then $m_0 + 1$ is small.

We may not be able to decide, for each conditional, whether or not it is true; and the vagueness of the predicate "small" may possibly have the effect that, for some conditionals, there is no determinate answer to the question whether they are true or not: but we must be able to say, of any given conditional, whether or not we are prepared to accept it as true. Now, since m_0 is the smallest value of m for which we are unprepared to accept the conditional as true, and since by hypothesis we accept modus ponens as valid, we must regard the antecedent

m_0 is small

as true; and, if we accept the antecedent as true, but are not prepared to accept the conditional as true, this can only be because we are not prepared to accept the consequent as true. It is, however, almost as absurd to suppose that there exists a number which we can recognise to be small, but whose successor we cannot recognise to be small, as to suppose that there exists a number which is small but whose successor is not.

Awkward as this seems, it appears from all that has been said so far that it is the only tolerable alternative. And perhaps after all it is possible to advance some considerations which will temper the wind, which will mitigate the awkwardness even of saying that there is a number n such that n is small but $n + 1$ is not. Let us approach the point by asking whether the law of excluded middle holds for vague statements. It appears at first that it does not: for we often use an instance of the law of excluded middle to express our conviction that the statement to which we apply it is not vague, as in, e.g., "Either he is your brother or he isn't". But, now, consider a vague statement, for instance "That is orange". If the object pointed to is definitely orange, then of course the statement will be definitely true; if it is definitely some other colour, then the statement will be definitely false; but the object may be a borderline case, and then the statement will be neither definitely true nor definitely false. But, in this instance at least, it is clear that, if a borderline case, the object will have to be on the borderline between being orange and being some other particular colour, say red. The statement "That is red" will then likewise be neither definitely true nor definitely false: but, since the object is on the borderline between being orange and being red— there is no other colour which is a candidate for being the colour of the object—the disjunctive statement, "That is either orange or red", will be definitely true, even though neither of its disjuncts is.

Now although we learn only a vague application for colour-words, one thing we are taught about them is that colour-words of the same level of generality— "orange" and "red", for example—are to be treated as mutually exclusive. Thus, for an object on the borderline, it would not be incorrect to say, "That is orange", and it would not be incorrect to say, "That is red": but it would be incorrect to say, "That is both orange and red" (where the object is uniform in colour), because "orange" and "red" are incompatible predicates. This is merely to say that "red" implies "not orange": so, whenever "That is either orange or red" is true, "That is either orange or not orange" is true also.

It is difficult to see how to prove it, but it seems plausible that, for any vague predicate "P", and any name "a" of an object of which "P" is neither definitely true nor definitely false, we can find a predicate "Q", incompatible with "P", such that the statement "a is either P or Q" is definitely true, and hence the statement "a is either P or not P" is definitely true also. And thus it appears plausible, more generally, that, for any vague statement "A", the law of excluded middle "A or not A" must be admitted as correct, even though neither "A" nor "Not A" may be definitely true.

If this reasoning is sound, we should note that it provides an example of what Quine once ridiculed as the "fantasy" that a disjunction might be true without either of its disjuncts being true. For, in connection with vague statements, the only possible meaning we could give to the word "true" is that of "definitely true": and, whether the general conclusion of the validity of the law of excluded middle, as applied to vague statements, be correct or not, it appears inescapable that there are definitely true disjunctions of vague statements such that neither of their disjuncts is definitely true. It is not only in connection with vagueness that instances of what Quine stigmatised as "fantasy" occur. Everyone is aware of the fact that there are set-theoretic statements which are true in some models of axiomatic set theory, as we have it, and false in others. Someone who believed that axiomatic set theory, as we now have it, incorporates all of the intuitions that we have or ever will have concerning sets could attach to the word "true", as applied to set-theoretic statements, only the sense "true in all models". Plainly he would have to agree that there exist true disjunctive set-theoretic statements neither of whose disjuncts is true.

When vague statements are involved, then, we may legitimately assert a disjunctive statement without allowing that there is any determinate answer to the question which of the disjuncts is true. And, if the argument for the validity, as applied to vague statements, of the law of excluded middle is accepted as sound, this may prompt the suspicion that all classically valid laws remain valid when applied to vague statements. Of course, the semantics in terms of which those laws are justified as applied to definite statements will have to be altered: no longer can we operate with a simple conception of two truth-values, each statement possessing a determinate one of the two. A natural idea for constructing a semantics for vague statements, which would justify the retention of all the laws of classical logic, would be this. For every vague statement, there is a certain range of acceptable ways of making it definite, that is, of associating determinate truth-conditions with it. A method of making a vague statement definite is acceptable so long as it renders the statement true in every case in which, before, it was definitely true, and false in every case in which, before, it was definitely false. Corresponding things may be said for ingredients of vague statements, such as vague predicates, relational expressions and quantifiers. Given any vague predicate, let us call any acceptable means of giving it a definite application a "sharpening" of that predicate; similarly for a vague relational expression or a vague quantifier. Then, if we suppose that all vagueness has its source in the vagueness of certain primitive predicates, relational expressions and quantifiers, we may stipulate that a statement, atomic or complex, will be definitely true just in case it is true under every sharpening of the vague expressions of these kinds which it contains. A form of inference will, correspondingly, be valid just in case, under any sharpening of the vague expressions involved, it preserves truth: in particular, an inference valid by this criterion will lead from definitely true premisses to a definitely true conclusion.

A logic for vague statements will not, therefore, differ from classical logic in respect of the laws which are valid for the ordinary logical constants. It will differ, rather, in admitting a new operator, the operator "Definitely". Of course, the foregoing remarks do not constitute a full account of a logic for vague statements—they are the merest beginning. Such a logic will have to take into account the fact that the application of the operator "Definitely", while it restricts the conditions for the (definite) truth of a statement, or the (definite) application of a predicate, does not eliminate vagueness: that is, the boundaries between which acceptable sharpenings of a statement or a predicate range are themselves indefinite. If it is possible to give a coherent account of this matter, then the result will be in effect a modal logic weaker than S4, in which each reiteration of the modal operator "Definitely" yields a strengthened statement.

But, for our purposes, it is not necessary to pursue the matter further. It is clear enough that, if this approach to the logic of vague statements is on the right lines, the same will apply to an existential statement as we have seen to apply to disjunctive ones. When "$A(x)$" is a vague predicate, the statement "For some x, $A(x)$" may be definitely true, because, on any sharpening of the primitive predicates contained in "$A(x)$", there will be some object to which "$A(x)$" applies: but there need be no determinate answer to the question to *which* object "$A(x)$" applies, since, under different sharpenings of the primitive predicates involved, there will be different objects which satisfy "$A(x)$". Thus, on this account, the statement "For some n, n is small and $n + 1$ is not small" may be true, although there just is no answer to the question *which* number this is. The statement is true because, for each possible sharpening of the predicate "small", or of the primitive notions involved in its definition, there would be a determinate number n which was small but whose successor was not small; but, just because so many different sharpenings of the predicate "small" would be acceptable, no one of them with a claim superior to the others, we need have no shame about refusing to answer the challenge to say which number in fact exemplified the truth of the existential statement.

This solution may, for the time being, allay our anxiety over identifying the source of paradox. It is, however, gained at the cost of not really taking vague predicates seriously, as if they were vague only because we had not troubled to make them precise. A satisfactory account of vagueness ought to explain two contrary feelings we have: that expressed by Frege that the presence of vague expressions in a language invests it with an intrinsic incoherence; and the opposite point of view contended for by Wittgenstein, that vagueness is an essential feature of language. The account just given, on the other hand, makes a language containing vague expressions appear perfectly in order, but at the cost of making vagueness easily eliminable. But we feel that certain concepts are ineradicably vague. Not, of course, that we could not sharpen them if we wished to; but, rather, that, by sharpening them, we should destroy their whole point. Let us, therefore, attempt to approach the whole matter anew by considering the notions involved in a theory which takes vague predicates very seriously indeed—namely, strict finitism; and begin by examining these queer totalities which strict finitism is forced to take as being the subject-matter of arithmetic.

Let us characterise a totality as "weakly infinite" if there exists a well-ordering of it with no last member. And let us characterise as "weakly finite" a totality such that, for some finite ordinal n, there exists a well-ordering of it with no nth member. Then we should normally say that a weakly finite totality could not also be weakly infinite. If we hold to this view, we cannot take vagueness seriously. A vague expression will, in other words, be one of which we have only partially specified a sense; and to a vague predicate there will therefore not correspond any specific totality as its extension, but just as many as would be the extensions of all the acceptable sharpenings of the predicate. But to take vagueness seriously is to suppose that a vague expression may have a completely specific, albeit vague, sense; and therefore there will be a single specific totality which is the extension of a vague predicate. As Essenin-Volpin in effect points out, such totalities—those characterised as the extensions of vague predicates—can be both weakly finite and weakly infinite. For instance, consider the totality of heartbeats in my childhood, ordered by temporal priority. Such a totality is weakly infinite, according to Essenin-Volpin: for every heartbeat in my childhood, I was still in my childhood when my next heartbeat occurred. On the other hand, it is also weakly finite, for it is possible to give a number N (e.g., 25×10^8), such that the totality does not contain an Nth member. Such a totality may be embedded in a larger totality, which may, like the totality of heartbeats in my youth, be of the same kind, or may, like the set of heartbeats in my whole life, be strongly finite (have a last member), or, again, may be strongly infinite (that is, not finitely bounded). Hence, if induction is attempted in respect of a vague predicate which in fact determines a proper initial segment, which is both weakly finite and weakly infinite, of a larger determinate totality, the premisses of the induction will both be true but the conclusion will be false. (By a "determinate" totality I mean here one which is either strongly finite, like the set of heartbeats in my whole life, or strongly infinite, like the set of natural numbers, as ordinarily conceived, or, possibly, the set of heartbeats of my descendants.)

Thus, on this conception of the matter, the trouble did not after all lie where we located it, in the induction step. We found ourselves, earlier, apparently forced to conclude that the induction step must be incorrect, after having eliminated all other possibilities. But, on this account, which is the account which the strict finitist is compelled to give for those cases in which, for him, Wang's paradox is truly paradoxical, the induction step is perfectly in order. The root of the trouble, on this account, is, rather, the appeal to induction—an alternative which we explored and which appeared to be untenable. Not that, on this view, induction is always unreliable. Whether it is to be relied on or not will depend upon the predicate to which it is being applied, and upon the notion of "natural number" which is being used: we have to take care that the predicate in respect of which we are performing the induction determines a totality at least as extensive as the totality of natural numbers over which the induction is being performed.

A possible interpretation of "n is small" would be "My heart has beaten at least n times and my nth heartbeat occurred in my childhood". Now clearly the picture Essenin-Volpin is appealing to is this. Imagine a line of black dots on some plane surface; there is no reason not to take this array of dots as strongly finite, i.e., as having both a leftmost and a rightmost member. The surface is coloured vivid red (except for the dots themselves) on its left-hand half; but then begins a gradual and continuous transition through purple to blue. The transition is so gradual that, if we cover over most of the surface so as to leave uncovered at most (say) ten dots, then we can discern no difference between the shade of colour at the left-hand and at the right-hand edge. On the basis of this fact, we feel forced to acknowledge the truth of the statement, "If a dot occurs against a red background, so does the dot immediately to its right". The leftmost dot is against a red background: yet not all the dots are. In fact, if the dots are considered as ordered from left to right, the dots which have a red background form a merely weakly finite proper initial segment of the strongly finite set of all the dots.

This example is important; it is not merely, as might appear at first sight, a trivial variation on the heartbeat example. In examples like the heartbeat one, it could seem that the difficulty arose merely because we had not bothered, for a vague word like "childhood", to adopt any definite convention governing its application. This is what makes it appear that the presence in our language of vague expressions is a feature of language due merely to our laziness, as it were, that is, to our not troubling in all cases to provide a sharp criterion of applicability for the terms we use; and hence a feature that is in principle eliminable. Such an explanation of vagueness is made the more tempting when the question whether the presence of vague terms in our language reflects any feature of reality is posed by asking whether it corresponds to a vagueness in reality: for the notion that things might actually *be* vague, as well as being vaguely described, is not properly intelligible. But the dot example brings out one feature of reality—or of our experience of it—which is very closely connected with our use of vague expressions, and at least in part explains the feeling we have that vagueness is an indispensable feature of language—that we could not get along with a language in which all terms were definite. This feature is, namely, the non-transitivity of the relation "not discriminably different". The dropping of one grain of sand could not make the difference between what was not and what was a heap—not just because we have not chosen to draw a sharp line between what is and what is not a heap, but because there would be no difference which could be discerned by observation (but only by actually counting the grains). What happens between one heartbeat and the next could not change a child into an adult—not merely because we have no sharp definition of "adult", but because human beings do not change so quickly. Of course, we can for a particular context—say a legal one—introduce a sharp definition of "adult", e.g., that an adult is one who has reached midnight on the morning of his 18th birthday. But not all concepts can be treated like this: consider, for instance (to combine Essenin-Volpin's example with one of Wittgenstein's), the totality of those of my heartbeats which occurred before I learned to read.

A says to B, "Stand appreciably closer to me". If B moves in A's direction a distance so small as not to be perceptibly closer at all, then plainly he has not complied with A's order. If he repeats his movement, he has, therefore, presumably still not complied with it. Yet we know that, by repeating his movement sufficiently often, he can eventually arrive at a position satisfactory to A. This is a paradox of exactly the form "All numbers are small". "n is small" is here interpreted as meaning "n movements of fixed length, that length too small to be perceptible, will not bring B appreciably closer to A". Clearly, 1 is small, under this interpretation: and it appears indisputable that, if n is small, $n + 1$ is small.

This, at any rate, provides us with a first reason for saying that vague predicates are indispensable. The non-transitivity of non-discriminable difference means, as Nelson Goodman has pointed out, that non-discriminable difference cannot be a criterion for identity of shade. By this is not meant merely that human vision fails to make distinctions which can be made by the spectroscope—e.g., between orange light and a mixture of red, orange and yellow light. It means that phenomenal agreement (matching) cannot be a criterion of identity for phenomenal shades. "*a* has the same shade of (phenomenal) colour as *b*" cannot be taken to mean "*a* is not perceived as of different shade from *b*" ("*a* matches *b* in colour"); it must mean, rather, "For every *x*, if *a* matches *x*, then *b* matches *x*". Now let us make the plausible assumption that in any continuous gradation of colours, each shade will have a distinct but not discriminably different shade on either side of it (apart of course from the terminal shades). In that case, it follows that, for any acceptable sharpening of a colour-word like "red", there would be shades of red which were not discriminably different from shades that were not red. It would follow that we could not tell by looking whether something was red or not. Hence, if we are to have terms whose application is to be determined by mere observation, these terms must necessarily be vague.

Is there more than a conceptual uneasiness about the notion of a non-transitive relation of non-discriminable difference? I look at something which is moving, but moving too slowly for me to be able to see that it is moving. After one second, it still looks to me as though it was in the same position; similarly after three seconds. After four seconds, however, I can recognise that it has moved from where it was at the start, i.e. four seconds ago. At this time, however, it does not look to me as though it is in a different position from that which it was in one, or even three, seconds before. Do I not contradict myself in the very attempt to express how it looks to me? Suppose I give the name "position *X*" to the position in which I first see it, and make an announcement every second. Then at the end of the first second, I must say, "It still looks to me to be in position *X*". And I must say the same at the end of the second and the third second. What am I to say at the end of the fourth second? It does not seem that I can say anything other than, "It no longer looks to me to be in position *X*": for position *X* was defined to be the position it was in when I first started looking at it, and, by hypothesis, at the end of four seconds it no longer looks to me to be in the same position as when I started looking. But, then, it seems that, from the fact that after three seconds I said, "It still looks to me to be in position *X*", that I am committed to the proposition, "After four seconds it looks to me to be in a different position from that it was in after three seconds". But this is precisely what I want to deny.

Here we come close to the idea which Frege had, and which one can find so hard to grasp, that the use of vague expressions is fundamentally incoherent. One may be inclined to dismiss Frege's idea as a mere prejudice if one does not reflect on examples such as these.

How can this language be incoherent? For there does not seem to be any doubt that there is such a relation as non-discriminable difference (of position, colour, etc.), and that it is non-transitive. But the incoherence, if genuine, appears to arise from expressing this relation by means of the form of words, "It looks to me as though the object's real position (colour, etc.) is the same". And if this language is incoherent, it seems that the whole notion of phenomenal qualities and relations is in jeopardy. (Perhaps there is something similar about preference. The question is sometimes raised whether preference is necessarily a transitive relation. It may be argued that a person will never do himself any good by determining his choices in accordance with a non-transitive preference scale: but it seems implausible to maintain that actual preferences are always transitive. But if, as is normally thought allowable, I express the fact that I prefer *a* to *b* by saying, "I believe *a* to be better than *b*", then I convict myself of irrationality by revealing non-transitive preferences: for, while the relation expressed by "I believe *x* to be better than *y*" may be non-transitive, that expressed by "*x* is better than *y*" is necessarily transitive, since it is a feature of our use of comparative adjectives that they always express transitive relations.)

Setting this problem on one side for a moment, let us turn back to the question whether Essenin-Volpin's idea of a weakly finite, weakly infinite totality is coherent. It appears a feature of such a totality that, while we can give up an upper bound to the number of its members, e.g. 25×10^8 in the case of heartbeats in my childhood, we cannot give the exact number of members. On second thoughts, however, that this is really a necessary feature of such totalities may seem to need some argument. Can we not conceive of quite small such totalities, with a small and determinate number of members? Suppose, for example, that the minute hand of a clock does not move continuously, but, at the end of each second, very rapidly (say in 10^{-5} seconds) moves 6 min of arc; and suppose also that the smallest discriminable rotation is 24 min of arc. Now consider the totality of intervals of an integral number of seconds from a given origin such that we cannot at the end of such an interval perceive that the minute hand has moved from its position at the origin. This totality comprises precisely four members—the null interval, and the intervals of 1, 2 and 3 seconds. The interval of 4 seconds plainly does not belong to it; it is therefore at least weakly finite. Can we argue that it is weakly infinite? Well, apparently not: because it has a last member, namely the interval of 3 seconds duration. But would it not be plausible to argue that the totality is closed under the operation of adding one second's duration to an interval belonging to the totality?

This appears to be just the same contradiction, or apparent contradiction, as that we have just set aside. It *appears* plausible to say that the totality is closed under this operation, because, from the end of one second to the end of the next, we cannot detect any difference in the position of the minute hand. Hence it appears plausible to say that, if we cannot detect that the position of the minute hand at the end of n seconds is different from its initial position, then we cannot detect at the end of $n + 1$ seconds that its position is different from its initial position. But the non-transitivity of non-discriminable difference just means that this inference is incorrect. Hence the totality of such intervals is not a genuine candidate for the status of weakly infinite totality.

In fact, from the definition of "weakly infinite totality", it appears very clear that it *is* a necessary feature of such totalities that they should not have an assignable determinate number of members, but at best an upper bound to that number. For the definition of "weakly infinite totality" specified that such a totality should not have a last member: whereas, if a totality has exactly n members, then its nth member is the last.

But this should lead us to doubt whether saying that a totality is closed under a successor-operation is really consistent with saying that it is weakly finite. It appears plausible to say that, if my nth heartbeat occurred in my childhood, then so did my $(n + 1)$th heartbeat: but is this any more than just the illusion which might lead us to say that, if the position of the minute hand appeared the same after n seconds, it must appear the same after $(n + 1)$ seconds?

The trouble now appears to be that we have shifted from cases of non-discriminable difference which give rise to vague predicates to ones which do not. That is, we assigned the non-transitivity of non-discriminable difference as one reason why vagueness is an essential feature of language, at least of any language which is to contain observational predicates. But the totality of intervals which we have been considering is specified by reference to an observational feature which is not vague (or at least, if it is, we have prescinded from this vagueness in describing the conditions of the example). The plausibility of the contention that the totality of heartbeats in my childhood is weakly infinite depends, not merely on the fact that the interval between one heartbeat and the next is too short to allow any discriminable difference in physique or behaviour by reference to which maturity is determined, but also on the fact that the criteria for determining maturity are vague. So we must re-examine more carefully the connection between vagueness and non-discriminable difference.

"Red" has to be a vague predicate if it is to be governed by the principle that, if I cannot discern any difference between the colour of a and the colour of b, and I have characterised a as red, then I am bound to accept a characterisation of b as red. And the argument was that, if "red" is to stand for a phenomenal quality in the strong sense that we can determine its application or non-application to a given object just by looking at that object, then it must be governed by this principle: for, if it is not, how could I be expected to tell, just by looking, that *b* was not red? But reflection suggests that no predicate can be consistently governed by this principle, so long as non-discriminable difference fails to be transitive. "Consistent" here means that it would be impossible to force someone, by appeal to rules of use that he acknowledged as correct, to contradict himself over whether the predicate applied to a given object. But by hypothesis, one could force someone, faced with a sufficiently long series of objects forming a gradation from red to blue, to admit that an object which was plainly blue (and therefore not red) was red, namely where the difference in shade between each object in the series and its neighbour was not discriminable. Hence it appears to follow that the use of any predicate which is taken as being governed by such a principle is potentially inconsistent: the inconsistency fails to come to light only because the principle is never sufficiently pressed. Thus Frege appears to be vindicated, and the use of vague predicates— at least when the source of the vagueness is the non-transitivity of a relation of non-discriminable difference—is intrinsically incoherent.

Let us review the conclusions we have established so far.

(1) Where non-discriminable difference is non-transitive, observational predicates are necessarily vague.

(2) Moreover, in this case, the use of such predicates is intrinsically inconsistent.

(3) Wang's paradox merely reflects this inconsistency. What is in error is not the principles of reasoning involved, nor, as on our earlier diagnosis, the induction step. The induction step is correct, according to the rules of use governing vague predicates such as "small": but these rules are themselves inconsistent, and hence the paradox. Our earlier model for the logic of vague expressions thus becomes useless: there can be no coherent such logic.

(4) The weakly infinite totalities which must underlie any strict finit- ist reconstruction of mathematics must be taken as seriously as the vague predicates of which they are defined to be the extensions. If conclusion (2), that vague predicates of this kind are fundamentally incoherent, is rejected, then the conception of a weakly infinite but weakly finite totality must be accepted as legitimate. However, on the strength of conclusion (2), weakly infinite totalities may likewise be rejected as spurious: this of course entails the repudiation of strict finitism as a viable philosophy of mathematics.

It is to be noted that conclusion (2) relates to observational *predicates* only: we have no reason to advance any similar thesis about relational expressions whose application is taken to be established by observation. In the example of the minute hand, we took the relational expression "x is not in a discriminably different position from y" as being, not merely governed by consistent rules of use, but completely definite. This may be an idealisation: but, if such an expression is vague, its vagueness evidently arises from a different source from that of a predicate like "red" or "vertical". If the application of a predicate, say "red", were to be determined by observational comparison of an object with some prototype, then it too could have a consistent use and a definite application: e.g. if we all carried around a colour-chart, as Wittgenstein suggested in one of his examples, and "red" were taken to mean "not discriminably different in colour from some shade within a given segment of the spectrum displayed on the chart", then, at least as far as any consideration to which we have so far attended is concerned, there is no reason why "red" should even be considered a vague term. It would not, however, in this case be an observational predicate, as this notion is normally understood.

What, then, of phenomenal qualities? It is not at first evident that this notion is beyond rescue. Certainly, if the foregoing conclusions are correct, we cannot take "phenomenal quality" in a strict sense, as constituting the satisfaction of an observational predicate, that is, a predicate whose application can be decided merely by the employment of our sense-organs: at least, not in any area in which non-discriminable difference is not transitive. But cannot the notion be retained in some less strict sense?

One thing is beyond question: that, within some dimension along which we can make no discriminations at all, the notion of "not phenomenally distinct" is viable and significant. For instance, light of a certain colour may be more or less pure according to the range of wavelengths into which it can be separated: if human vision is altogether incapable of discriminating between surfaces according to the purity of the light which they reflect, then here is a difference in physical colour to which no difference in phenomenal colour corresponds.

But how do things stand in respect of a dimension along which we can discern differences, but for which non-discriminable difference is not transitive? It may be thought that we know the solution to this difficulty, namely that, already mentioned, devised by Goodman. To revert to the minute-hand example: we called the position which the minute-hand appeared to occupy at the origin "position X"; and we may call the positions which it appears to occupy at the end of 3, and of 4, seconds respectively "positions Y and Z". Now an observer reports that, at the end of 3 seconds, the minute-hand does not appear to occupy a position different from that which it occupied at the origin: let us express this report, not by the words "It appears still to be in position *X*", but by the words "Position *Y* appears to be the same as position *X*". At the end of 4 seconds, however, the observer will report both, "Position *Z* appears to be different from position *X*", and, "Position *Z* appears to be the same as position *Y*". This has, as we remarked, the flavour of paradox: either we shall have to say that a contradictory state of affairs may appear to obtain, or we shall have to say that, from "It appears to be the case that *A*" and "It appears to be the case that *B*", it is illicit to infer "It appears to be the case that *A* and *B*". However, Goodman can take this apparent paradox in his stride. For him, position *Y*, considered as a phenomenal position, may appear to be identical with position *X*: it is, nevertheless, distinct, since position *Y* also appears to be identical with position *Z*, while position *X* does not. Will not Goodman's refined criterion of identity for phenomenal qualities save the notion of such qualities from the fate that appeared about to overwhelm them?

It is clear that *a* notion survives under Goodman's emendation: what is seldom observed is how unlike the notion that emerges is to the notion of phenomenal qualities as traditionally conceived. For let us suppose that space and time are continua, and let us change the example so that the minute-hand now moves at a uniform rate. Let us further suppose that whether or not the minute-hand occupies discriminably different positions at different moments depends uniformly upon whether or not the angle made by the two positions of the minute-hand is greater than a certain minimum. It will then follow that, however gross our perception of the position of the minute-hand may be, there is a continuum of distinct phenomenal positions for the minute-hand: for, for any two distinct physical positions of the minute-hand, even if they are not discriminably different, there will be a third physical position which is discriminably different from the one but not from the other.

This conclusion may not, at first, seem disturbing. After all, the visual field does appear to form a continuum: what is perplexing to us is not to be told that it is a continuum, but to be told that it is not, that, on the ground that we can only discriminate finitely many distinct positions, the structure of the visual field is in fact discrete. So perhaps Goodman's account of the matter, according to which there really is a continuum of distinct phenomenal positions, even though we can make directly only finitely many discriminations, may seem to be explanatory of the fact that the visual field impresses us as being a continuum. But a little reflection shows that the matter is not so straightforward: for the argument that the visual field must contain a continuum of distinct phenomenal positions is quite independent of the fineness of the discriminations that we can make. Imagine someone with a vision so coarse that it can directly discriminate only four distinct positions in the visual field (say right or left, up or down): that is, it is not possible to arrange more than four objects, big enough for this person to see, so that he can distinguish between their position. So long as non-discriminable difference of position remains for this person non-transitive, and discriminable difference of position depends for him on the physical angle of separation of the objects, the argument will prove, for him too, that his visual field, considered as composed of phenomenal positions distinguished by Goodman's criterion of identity, constitutes a two-dimensional continuum.

The argument has nothing to do with infinity. Let us consider difference of hue, as manifested by pure light (light of a single wavelength); and let us assume that the possible wavelengths form a discrete series, each term separated by the same interval from its neighbours, so that the series is finite. And let us suppose an observer with colour-vision so coarse that he cannot distinguish more than four colours, i.e., it is not possible to show him pure light of more than four different wavelengths so that he can discriminate directly between any two of them. If, for him, discriminable difference depends solely on the actual interval between the wavelengths of two beams, then, again, the argument will establish that, for this observer, there are just as many phenomenal colours as physical colours. In fact, we see quite generally that, within any dimension along which we can discriminate by observation at all, and within which non-discriminable difference is non-transitive (as it surely always is), the phenomenal qualities are simply going to reflect the distinct physical qualities, irrespective of the capacities of the observer to discriminate between them. There is, of course, nothing wrong with the definition of "phenomenal quality" which yields this result, considered merely as a definition: but what it defines is surely not anything which we have ever taken a phenomenal quality to be.

The upshot of our discussion is, then, this. As far as strict finitism is concerned, common sense is vindicated: there are no totalities which are both weakly finite and weakly infinite, and strict finitism is therefore an untenable position. But this vindication stands or falls with another conclusion far less agreeable to common sense: there are no phenomenal qualities, as these have been traditionally understood; and, while our language certainly contains observational predicates as well as relational expressions, the former (though not the latter) infect it with inconsistency.

9 Vagueness, truth and logic

Kit Fine

My investigation of this topic began with the question "What is the correct logic of vagueness?" This led to the further question "What are the correct truth-conditions for a vague language?" And this led, in its turn, to a more general consideration of meaning and existence.[1]

The contents of the paper are as follows. The first half contains the basic material. Section 1 expounds and criticizes one approach to the problem of specifying truth-conditions for a vague language. The approach is based upon an extension of the standard truth-tables and falls foul of something I call penumbral connection. Section 2 introduces an alternative framework, within which penumbral connection can be accommodated. The key idea is to consider not only the truth-values that sentences actually receive but also the truth-values that they might receive under different ways of making them more precise. Section 3 describes and defends the favoured account within this framework. According to this account, as roughly stated, a vague sentence is true if and only if it is true for all ways of making it completely precise. The second half of the paper then deals with consequences, complications and comparisons of the preceding half. Section 4 considers the consequences that the rival approaches have for logic. The favoured account leads to a classical logic for vague sentences; and objections to this unpopular position are met. Section 5 studies the phenomenon of higher-order vagueness: first, in its bearing upon the truth-conditions for a language that contains a definitely-operator or a hierarchy of truth-predicates; and second, in its relation to some puzzles concerning priority and eliminability.

Some of the topics tie in with technical material. I have tried to keep this at a minimum. But the reader must excuse me if the technical undercurrent produces an occasional unintelligible ripple upon the surface. Many of the more technical passages can be omitted without serious loss in continuity.

First published in *Synthese* 30 (1975) pp. 265–300 © Kluwer Academic Publishers Reprinted by permission, with corrections.

1   I should like to thank Gordon Baker for numerous stimulating conversations on the topics of this paper. My ideas would not have taken their present form without his help I should also like to thank Michael Dummett for some valuable remarks in a discussion of the paper.

Let us say, in a preliminary way, what vagueness is. I take it to be a semantic feature. Very roughly, vagueness is deficiency of meaning. As such, it is to be distinguished from generality, undecidability, and ambiguity. These other features may be described, by contrast, as a deficiency in content, possible knowledge, and univocal meaning, respectively.

These contrasts can be made very clear with the help of some artificial examples. Suppose that the meanings of the natural number predicates "nice$_1$", "nice$_2$", and "nice$_3$" are given by the following clauses:

(1) (a) n is nice$_1$ if $n > 15$
     (b) n is not nice$_1$ if $n < 13$

(2) (a) n is nice$_2$ if and only if $n > 15$
     (b) n is nice$_2$ if and only if $n > 14$

(3) n is nice$_3$ if and only if $n > 15$

Clause (1) is reminiscent of Carnap's (1952) meaning postulates; its two sub-clauses are to be taken conjunctively. Clauses (2)(a)–(b), on the other hand, are not intended to be equivalent to a single contradictory clause; they are somehow to be insulated from one another. With these understandings, "nice$_1$" is vague, its meaning is under-determined; "nice$_2$" is ambiguous, its meaning is over-determined; and "nice$_3$" is highly general or unspecific. The sentence "there are infinitely many nice$_3$ twin primes" is possibly undecidable but certainly not vague or ambiguous.

Any type of expression that is capable of meaning is also capable of being vague, whether the expression be a name, or a name-operator, a predicate, a quantifier, or even a sentence-operator. The clearest, perhaps paradigm, case of a vague expression is the vague predicate.

A further characterization of vagueness will not, I think, be theory-free; for it will rest upon an account of meaning. Whatever endows expressions with meaning will by its absence characterize vagueness. So, in particular, if meaning can have an extensional and intensional aspect, then so can vagueness. Thus extensional vagueness will be deficiency of extension, intensional vagueness deficiency of intension. Moreover, if intension is the possibility of extension, then intensional vagueness will be the possibility of extensional vagueness. By way of illustration, consider the case of predicates. A predicate is extensionally vague if it has borderline cases, intensionally vague if it could have borderline cases. Thus "bald" is extensionally vague, I presume, and remains intensionally vague in a world of hairy or hairless men. (The distinction is roughly Waismann's (1945) vagueness/open-texture one, but without the epistemological overtones.)

Extensional vagueness is closely allied to the existence of truth-value gaps. Any (extensionally) vague sentence is neither true nor false; for any vague predicate *F* there is a uniquely referring name *a* for which the sentence *Fa* is neither true nor false: and for any vague name *a* there is a uniquely referring name *b* for which the identity-sentence *a* = *b* is neither true nor false. Some have thought that a vague sentence is both true and false and that a vague predicate is both true and false of some object. However, this is part of the general confusion of under- and over-determinacy. A vague sentence can be made more precise; and this operation should preserve truth-value. But a vague sentence can be made to be either true or false and therefore the original sentence can be neither.

This battle of gluts and gaps may be innocuous, purely verbal. For truth on the gap view is simply truth-and-non-falsehood on the glut view and, similarly, falsehood is simply falsehood-and-non-truth. However, it is the gap-inducing notion that is important for philosophy. It is the one that directly ties in with the usual notions of assertion, verification and consequence. The glut-inducing notion has a split sense; for it allows truth to rest upon either correspondence with fact or absence of meaning.

Despite the connection, extensional vagueness should not be defined in terms of truth-value gaps. This is because gaps can have other sources, such as failure of reference or presupposition. What distinguishes gaps of deficiency is that they can be closed by an appropriate linguistic decision, viz. an extension, as opposed to change, in the meaning of the relevant expression.

1 The truth-value approach

It is this possibility of truth-value gaps that raises a problem for truth-conditions. For the classical conditions presuppose Bivalence, the principle that every sentence be either true or false, and so they are not directly applicable to vague sentences. In this, as in other, cases of truth-value gap, it is tempting to treat Neither-true-nor-false, or Indefinite, as a third truth-value and to model truth-value assessment along the lines of the classical truth-conditions.

The details of this and subsequent suggestions will first be geared to a first-order language. Only later will we consider the complications that arise from extending the language. Let us fix, then, upon an intuitively understood, though possibly vague, first-order language *L*. There are three possible sources of vagueness in *L*: the predicates, the names, and the quantifiers. To simplify the exposition, we shall suppose that only predicates are vague. Indeed, it might be argued that all vagueness is reducible to predicate vagueness. For conceivably one could replace, without change in truth-value, each vague name by a corresponding vague predicate and each quantifier over a vague domain by an appropriately relativised quantifier over a more inclusive but precise domain. We shall also suppose, though only to avoid talk of satisfaction, that each object in the domain has a name.

We now let a partial specification be an assignment of a truth-value —True (*T*), False (*F*) or Indefinite (*I*)—to the atomic sentences of *L*; and we call a specification *appropriate* if the assignment is in accordance with the intuitively understood meanings of the predicates. Thus an appropriate specification would assign True to "Yul Brynner is bald", False to "Mick Jagger is bald" and Indefinite to "Herbert is bald", should Herbert be a borderline case of a bald man. The present sugges- tion is that the truth-value of each sentence in *L* should be evaluated on the basis of the appropriate specification. The valuation is to be truth- functional in the sense that the truth-value of each type of compound sentence is to be a uniform function of the truth-values of its immediate sub-sentences.

The possible truth-conditions can be subject to two natural constraints. The first is that the conditions be faithful to the classical truth-conditions whenever these are applicable. Call a specification *complete* if it assigns only the definite truth-values, True and False. Then the Fidelity Condition F states that a sentence is true (or false) for a complete specification if and only if it is classically true (or false); evaluations over complete specifications are classical.

The second constraint is that definite truth-values be stable for improvements in specification. Say that one specification *u extends* another *t* if *u* assigns to an atomic sentence any definite truth-value assigned by *t*. Then the Stability Condition S states that if a sentence has a definite truth-value under a specification *t* it enjoys the same definite truth-value under any specification *u* that extends *t*; definite truth- values are preserved under extension.

The two constraints work together: definite truth-values for a partial specification must be retained upon the classical evaluation of any of its complete extensions. Indeed, if quantifiers are dropped, the two constraints are equivalent to the classical necessary conditions for truth and falsehood:

(i) $\vDash \neg B \rightarrow \dashv B$
    $\dashv \neg B \rightarrow \vDash B$

(ii) $\vDash B \,\&\, C \rightarrow \vDash B$ and $\vDash C$
    $\dashv B \,\&\, C \rightarrow \dashv B$ or $\dashv C$

Similarly for the other truth-functional connectives. (I use "$\vDash A$" for "*A* is true", "$\dashv A$" for "*A* is false", and "$\rightarrow$" for informal material implication.)

However, the constraints still allow some latitude in the formulation of truth-conditions. One can move in the direction either of minimizing or of maximizing the degree to which sentences receive definite truth-values under a given specification.[2] At the one extreme, the indefinite truth-value dominates: any sentence with an indefinite subsentence is also indefinite. Sentences are only definite under a classical guarantee. At the other extreme, the indefinite truth-value dithers: a sentence is definite if its truth-value is unchanged for any way of making definite its immediate indefinite subsentences.[3] In effect, the arrows in the clauses (i) and (ii) above are reversed so that the only divergence from the classical conditions lies in the rejection of Bivalence. To illustrate, a conjunction with indefinite and false conjuncts is indefinite on the first account, but false on the second. There are intermediate possibilities, but they are not very interesting. Indeed, clause (i) uniquely determines the conditions for negation, for the weak and strong senses are excluded, and the above alternatives are the only ones for commutative conjunction.

Is any account along truth-value lines acceptable? Any account that satisfies the constraints F and S appears to make correct allocations of definite truth-value. However, even the maximizing policy fails to make many correct allocations of indefinite truth-value. For suppose that a certain blob is on the border of pink and red and let P be the sentence "the blob is pink" and R the sentence "the blob is red". Then the conjunction $P \& R$ is false since the predicates "is pink" and "is red" are contraries. But, under the maximizing account, the conjunction $P \& R$ is indefinite since both of the conjuncts P and R are indefinite.

A more general argument applies to any three-valued approach, regardless of whether it satisfies the constraints F or S. For $P \& P$ is indefinite since it is equivalent to plain P, which is indefinite, whereas $P \& R$ is false. Thus a conjunction with indefinite conjuncts is sometimes indefinite and sometimes false and so "&" is not truth-functional with respect to the three truth-values, True, False and Indefinite.

A similar argument also applies to the other logical connectives. For example, the disjunction $P \vee P$ is indefinite since it is equivalent to plain P, which is indefinite; whereas the disjunction $P \vee R$ is true since the predicates "is pink" and "is red" are complementary over the given

---

2   Kleene's (1952, pp 329 and 332) "weak/strong" and "regular" correspond to our "minimal/maximal" and "stable", though his motivation for introducing the terms is different from ours.

3   Frege 1952 (p 63) and Hallden 1949 have adopted the minimal truth-value approach, though Frege would not be happy in regarding Indefinite as a third truth-value   Korner 1960 (p 166) and Åqvist 1962 have espoused the maximal approach

colour range. Again, the conditional $P \supset \neg P$ is presumably not true, whereas $P \supset \neg R$ is true. It is more difficult to find examples for the quantifiers. But for the universal quantifier, say, we may consider the sentences "All pretenders to the throne are the rightful monarch", and "All pretenders to the throne are bald" where the domain of quantification consists of several pretenders who are all borderline cases of the predicates "is a rightful monarch" and "is bald". Then the first sentence is false, and the second not, even though both have only indefinite instances.

Nor is there any safety in numbers. The argument can be extended to cover any finite-valued or multi-valued approach that requires a conjunction with indefinite conjuncts to be indefinite. Such approaches are common and include those that are based upon degrees of truth[4] and those that satisfy a fidelity and stability condition with respect to a trichotomy of ranges of true, false, and indefinite truth-values.

The specific examples chosen should not blind us to the general point that they illustrate. It is that logical relations may hold among predicates with borderline cases or, more generally, among indefinite sentences. Given the predicate "is red", one can understand the predicate "is non-red" to be its contradictory: the boundary of the one shifts, as it were, with the boundary of the other. Indeed, it is not even clear that convincing examples require special predicates. Surely $P \ \& \ \neg P$ is false even though P is indefinite.

Let us refer to the possibility that logical relations hold among indefinite sentences as *penumbral connection*; and let us call the truths that arise, wholly or in part, from penumbral connection, *truths on a penumbra* or *penumbral truths*. Then our argument is that no natural truth-value approach respects penumbral truths. In particular, such an approach cannot distinguish between "red" and "pink" being independent and being exclusive upon their common penumbra.

Placing the Indefinite on a par with the other truth-values is analogous to basing modal logics on the three values Necessary, Impossible and Contingent, or to basing deontic logic on the values Obligatory, Forbidden and Indifferent. For here, too, truth-functionality may be lost: a conjunction of contingent sentences is sometimes contingent, sometimes impossible; a conjunction of indifferent sentences is sometimes indifferent, sometimes forbidden. In all of these cases there appears to be a dogmatic adherence to a framework of finitely many

---

4. See the work of Zadeh 1965 and others. It is not clear that one can make much sense of degrees of truth within a closed interval for "multi-dimensional" vagueness, as in "chair" and "game" It is even less clear that any *semantical* sense can be given to the notion Possibly there is a confusion with the higher-order vagueness of Section 5

truth-values. Perhaps our understanding of sentential operators is, in some sense, finite but this is not to say that it is based upon a finite substructure of truth-values.

2 An alternative framework

How can we account for penumbral connection? Consider again the blob that is on the border of pink and red and suppose that it is also a borderline case of the predicate "small". Why do we say that the conjunction "The blob is pink and red" is false but that the conjunction "The blob is pink and small" is indefinite? Surely the answer must rest on the fact that in making the respective predicates more precise the blob cannot be made a clear case of both the predicates "pink" and "red" but can be made a clear case of both the predicates "pink" and "small". In other words, the difference in truth-value reflects a difference in how the predicates can be made more precise.

Such a suggestion can be made rigorous within the following framework. A (specification) *space* is taken to consist of a non-empty set of elements (which we can call specification-points), and a partial ordering ≥ (which we read as "extends" or "precisifies") on the set. We assume that ≥ is reflexive, transitive and antisymmetric. To each point in a specification space, thus abstractly conceived, may be assigned a specification, as previously defined. The space itself is then said to be *appropriate* if the following three conditions are satisfied: first, each of the associated specifications corresponds to a precisification, i.e. to a legitimate way of making the language more precise; second, to each precisification there corresponds an associated specification; and, third, one point extends another just in case the precisification corresponding to the one extends the precisification corresponding to the other. We regard the ways of precisifying in a generous light and, in particular, do not tie them to the expressions of any given language. Thus a specification space is the abstract counterpart to the space of all precisifications as ordered by the natural relation of extension; and, under a less abstract approach, one might simply take the specifications to be the precisifications themselves and the partial ordering to be the natural extension-relation on precisifications.

The present suggestion is that truth-valuation be based, not upon the appropriate specification, but upon an appropriate specification space, i.e. upon the specification-points that correspond to the different ways of making the language more precise. The truth-valuation is to be uniform in the sense that it only makes use of the specification-points at which the given subsentences are true or false. There may, of course, be several appropriate spaces, differing only in the identity of their points. But their differences should make no difference to the truth-valuation.

This framework could be generalized in various ways. For example, the space could contain extra points, not associated with a legitimate precisification. An expanded space of this sort would be appropriate if some subset of points determined a space that was appropriate in the old sense. Such an approach would allow the truth-definition to call upon specifications that did not correspond to precisifications. However, such generalizations appear to have little intuitive foundation and will not be considered further.

Our account of appropriacy makes use of the intensional notion of precisification. A strictly extensional account could avoid this in a variety of ways. Perhaps the simplest of these is to identify the specification-points with the specifications themselves. Thus a specification space is, in effect, a collection of specifications partially ordered by the natural extension-relation. A space is appropriate if the specifications are what one might call the *admissible* ones. Unofficially, a specification is admissible if it is appropriate for some precisification; but officially, according to the extensional account, the notion of admissibility must be taken as primitive.

There are various formal constraints that can be imposed upon a specification space. One is that it has a base-point, the appropriate specification-point. This corresponds to the precisification of which all other precisifications are extensions. Another is Completability. It states that any point can be extended to a complete point within the same space, i.e.

C $(\forall t)(\exists u \geq t)(u$ is complete)

where a point is complete if its specification is complete.

There are further constraints that can be imposed upon the truth-definition. The main ones are the appropriate modifications of the earlier fidelity and stability conditions. Fidelity will state that the truth-values at a complete point are classical, i.e.

F $t \vDash A \leftrightarrow t \vDash A$ (classically) for t complete.

Stability will state that truth-values are preserved under extensions of points within a given space, i.e.

S $t \vDash A$ and $t \leq u \rightarrow u \vDash A$
     $t \dashv A$ and $t \leq u \rightarrow u \dashv A$

As with the truth-value approach, there is the problem of how to tag truth values to the different specifications. One can tend to minimize or to maximize the amount of truth and falsehood. Minimizing gives nothing new. However, maximizing gives something altogether different: a sentence is true (or false) at a partial specification point if and only if it is true (or false) at all complete extensions. A sentence is true simpliciter if and only if it is true at the appropriate specification-point, i.e. at all complete and admissible specifications. Truth is super-truth, truth from above.[5]

In contrast to the truth-value approach, there are now many interesting intermediate truth-definitions. The most notable is the bastard intuitionistic account, which follows the intuitionistic conditions for $\neg$, &, $\vee$, $\supset$ and $\exists$, and the classical definition of $\neg \exists \neg$ for $\forall$.[6] Given that the domain of quantification is constant, the clauses run like this:

I (i) $t \vDash \neg B \leftrightarrow (\forall u \geq t)(\text{not-} \ u \vDash B)$
  (ii) $t \vDash B \& C \leftrightarrow t \vDash B$ and $t \vDash C$
  (iii) $t \vDash B \vee C \leftrightarrow t \vDash B$ or $t \vDash C$
  (iv) $t \vDash B \supset C \leftrightarrow (\forall u \geq t)(u \vDash B \rightarrow u \vDash C)$
  (v) $t \vDash (\exists x)B(x) \leftrightarrow t \vDash B(a)$ for some name a
  (vi) $t \vDash (\forall x)B(x) \leftrightarrow (\forall u \geq t)(\exists v \geq u)(v \vDash B(a))$ for each name a.

There are two common factors in all of the rival approaches to truth-conditions. One is the insistence that the procedures for truth-valuation be uniform. The other is the insistence that the appropriate form of stability be satisfied.

These factors can be made explicit within an abstract theory of extensions. The standard Fregean theory has a principle of Functionality:

(1)   The extension of a compound $\phi(A_1, \ldots, A_k)$ is a function f_ϕ of the extensions of its parts $A_1, \ldots, A_k$.

This corresponds to the appropriate form of Uniformity. We now suppose that the extensions are partially ordered by a relation of extending and add a principle of Monotonicity:

(2)   If extensions $x'_1, \ldots, x'_k$ extend extensions $x_1, \ldots, x_k$, respectively, then f_ϕ applied to $x'_1, \ldots, x'_k$ extends f_ϕ applied to $x_1, \ldots, x_k$.

This corresponds to the appropriate form of stability.

The most important of the two common factors is Monotonicity. This constraint was not argued for in the previous section, but it can be given an intensional foundation. To do this, we must first graft a theory of intensions onto the earlier theory. We shall not be too concerned with the nature of intensions. A specific model can be obtained by indexing extensions with possible worlds. (I presume that the specification-

---

5   Van Fraassen 1968 has already made much of the super-truth notion, though with different applications in mind He has also drawn out the consequences for logic and considered the possibility of minimizing and maximizing truth-value (the conservative/radical distinction of van Fraassen 1969)

6   The semantics for intuitionistic logic comes from Kripke 1965 The bastard account can be found in Fitting 1969

points remain constant from world to world.) However, such a model would suffer from familiar difficulties. For example, if the meaning of A is relevant to the meaning of $A \vee \neg A$, then the vagueness of A should be relevant to the vagueness of $A \vee \neg A$. Thus $A \vee \neg A$ should be vague for vague A, though on the super-truth account it is equally and completely precise for all A.

The pure theory of intensions should contain the analogues of Functionality and Intensionality.

(3) The intension of a compound $\phi(A_1, ..., A_k)$ is a function F_ϕ of the intensions of its parts $A_1, ..., A_k$;

(4) If intensions $X'_1, ..., X'_k$ extend intensions $X_1, ..., X_k$, respectively, then F_ϕ applied to $X'_1, ..., X'_k$ extends F_ϕ applied to $X_1, ..., X_k$.

The combined theory should link intensions to extensions. Each intension X determines an extension x; and each extension is so determined. Intensions and their corresponding extensions are constrained by the following two principles:

(5) The intension $F_\phi(X_1, ..., X_k)$ determines the extension $f_\phi(x_1, ..., x_k)$,

and

(6) X extends Y if and only if x extends y.

(5) states that a computed intension determines the correspondingly computed extension; and (6) states that one intension extends another if and only if the extension determined by the one extends the extension determined by the other.[7]

We can now derive (2), i.e. Monotonicity, from (4), (5) and (6). For simplicity, take the case of $k = 1$. Now suppose x extends y. Then X extends Y by (6); $F_\phi(X)$ extends $F_\phi(Y)$ by (4); the extension determined by $F_\phi(X)$ extends the extension determined by $F_\phi(Y)$, by (6) again; and so $f_\phi(x)$ extends $f_\phi(y)$ by (5).

The main assumptions behind this argument are (4) and (6). (4), with (3), is tantamount to the assumption that an expression is made more precise through making its simple terms more precise. This assumption is correct for the first-order language L. For the logical constants are transparent to vagueness, as it were; any precisification of a constituent

---

7   The Fregean theory and its extension have a nice algebraic formulation The usual theory states that there is a homomorphism from the word algebra into the algebra of intensions, and from the algebra of intensions into the algebra of extensions, and hence a homomorphism from the word algebra into the algebra of extensions The extended theory states that the extension and intension algebras both possess a monotonic partial ordering, which is respected by the homomorphism

shines through into the compound. Indeed, the converse of the assumption also holds; an expression is made more precise *only* through making its simple terms more precise. For the logical constants are already perfectly precise; and since the logical constants are the grammatical particles, all vagueness can be blamed on constituents as opposed to constructions.

The second assumption says, roughly, that extension does not decrease with an increase in intension. In particular, a sentence does not become indefinite upon being made more precise. This is, perhaps, partly definitional of "making more precise". For what distinguishes this operation from a mere change in meaning is that it preserves truth-value. To precisify *is* to rule out the possibility of certain truth-value gaps. In any case, it would be odd if definite truth-value could disappear upon precisification. Truth could then hold by default, in virtue of a lack of meaning. It could be a product of linguistic laziness and not be consequent upon a positive concordance of meaning and fact.

What is the rationale for these two assumptions? It lies, I think, in our desire for an enduring use of language. Under the pressure of their own use, the meanings of terms will need to change. The terms, in their old sense, will not be adequate to express the new truths, pose the next questions, make the right distinctions. Now clearly it is convenient that the changes in meaning be conservative, that the true records before the change remain true after the change. We may wish, for example, to settle a new case within a classificatory scheme without upsetting the principles of classification. But it is the two assumptions which guarantee that truth-value be preserved upon precisification of terms, that allow for the stability of recorded truth within the required instability of meaning.

These two assumptions tie in well with a dynamic conception of language. For language need not retain its identity upon arbitrary changes in meaning; or rather, any such identity is a matter of degree and dependent upon how much change there is. On the other hand, language can retain its identity upon precisification or conservative meaning change; for the two assumptions result in a natural constraint upon change. The identity of language is visible, as it were, in the permanence of recorded truth.

If language is like a tree, then penumbral connection is the seed from which the tree grows. For it provides an initial repository of truths that are to be retained throughout all growth. Some of the connections are internal. They concern the different borderline cases of a given predicate: if Herbert is to be bald, then so is the man with fewer hairs on his head. But many other of the connections are external. They concern the common borderline cases of different predicates: if the blob is to be red, it is not to be pink; if ceremonies are to be games, then so are rituals; if sociology is to be a science, then so is psychology. Thus penumbral connection results in a web that stretches across the whole of language. The language itself must grow like a balloon, with the expansion of each part pulling the other parts into shape.

The two approaches to truth-conditions agree on requirements, but differ on how the requirements are to be met. The agreement consists in their satisfying the principles of an abstract theory of extension; the disagreement consists in how they satisfy these principles. Under the truth-value approach, the extension of a sentence is a truth-value—True, False or Indefinite. Each truth-value extends itself; True and False extend Indefinite; and that is all. The extensions and extending-relation for other parts of speech are determined in a natural manner. And it is then easy to verify that the different accounts on the truth-value approach will satisfy the principles and that Monotonicity is equivalent to the appropriate form of stability.

Under the approach in terms of specification spaces, there is a slight difficulty in understanding the relevant notion of extension. For we will want to talk of the extension of an expression at different stages of precisification even though the relevant notion of extension is not relative. Somehow the original expression and a specification-point must be wrapped up into a single object. There are various more or less natural ways of achieving this result. One possibility is to regard each expression as an ordered pair (A, t), where A is an ordinary expression and t is the specification-point. Another is to imagine that, in precisifying, an expression is not endowed with a new sense but is succeeded by an expression with that sense. Thus the language expands in an orderly manner throughout the specification space; and each of the new expressions can be associated with the first point at which it is introduced. Let us opt for the first proposal. The extension of a sentence (A, t) can be taken to be an ordered pair (U, V), where $U = \{u: t \leq u\}$ and $V = \{v \in U: v \vDash A\}$. One extension (U', V') extends another (U, V) if $U' \subseteq U$ and V' is $V \cap U'$. With these definitions, it is again then easy to verify that the principles are satisfied and that Monotonicity is the appropriate form of stability.

Note that, on this approach, the extension is no longer purely non-linguistic. For each extension is a set of points, which must be understood in terms of their associated specifications. Moreover, if there are external penumbral connections, this linguistic dependency cannot be avoided. It will be part of the extension of "red", for example, that its completion never overlaps with the completion of the extension of "pink". Only for the language as a whole will extension be non-linguistic.

On the super-truth account, the definitions can be simplified. The extension of a sentence (A, t) can be taken to be an ordered pair (U, V), where $U = \{u: t \leq u$ and u is complete$\}$ and $V = \{v \in U: v \vDash A\}$. The relation of extension then has a similar definition. The partial specification-points can be recovered from the complete ones so long as two further conditions are satisfied. The first is that two points are identical if the complete specifications assigned to their successors are the same. The second is that for any non-empty set of complete points there is a point extended by exactly those points in the set. For then each partial point can be identified with a non-empty set of complete specifications. The first condition is harmless and the second can be justified. For the only constraint on admission into the appropriate space is that a point can verify all the original penumbral truths. But if they are true at all of the complete points, they are true at any point extended by a certain subset of the complete points.

The interpretation for the second approach has an important distinguishing feature. On both approaches, the extension-relation is used to formulate a constraint on extensions. But only on the second approach does this relation enter into the extensions themselves. Thus how an extension can be extended is already part of the extension. The extension of an expression at a given point uniquely determines its extension at a subsequent point.

The intensional analogue of this is that how an expression can be made more precise is already part of its meaning. Let the *actual* meaning of a simple predicate, say, be what helps determine its instances and counter-instances. Let its *potential* meaning consist of the possibilities for making it more precise. Then the point is that the meaning of an expression is a product of both its actual and potential meaning. In understanding a language one has thereby understood how it can be made more precise; one has understood, in terms of the earlier dynamic model, the possibilities for its growth.

This difference in extension (or intension) implies a corresponding difference in the notion of making more precise. On the first approach, to extend is to resolve new cases. On the second approach to extend is to resolve new cases *or* to make new penumbral connections. For to exclude ways of making more precise that would otherwise be available is itself a way of making more precise. Suppose, for example, that there were no penumbral connections between "red" and "pink". Then to require that no pink objects are red is to extend on the second approach, but not on the first. The actual extensions of "red" and "pink" remain the same, though their potential extensions differ.

3 The super-truth theory

In this section we shall argue for the super-truth theory, that a vague sentence is true if it is true for all admissible and complete specifications. An intensional version of the theory is that a sentence is true if it is true for all ways of making it completely precise (or, more generally, that an expression has a given Fregean reference if it has that reference for all ways of making it completely precise). As such, it is a sort of principle of non-pedantry: truth is secured if it does not turn upon what one means. Absence of meaning makes for absence of truth-value only if presence of meaning could make for diversity of truth-value.

The theory is a partial vindication of the classical position. For the truth-conditions are, if not classical, then classical at a remove. There is but one rule linking truth to classical truth, viz. that truth is truth in each of a set of interpretations. This rule is of general application and not dependent upon the nature of the language or interpretation. The actual work is done by the clauses for truth in a single interpretation, and these are classical.

The super-truth view is better than the others for at least two reasons. The first is that it covers all cases of penumbral connection. For example, where P is "the blob is pink" and R is "the blob is red", $P \& R$ is false and $P \vee R$ is true since one of P and R is true and the other false in any complete and admissible specification. For the bastard intuitionistic account, on the other hand, $P \& R$ is false but $P \vee R$ is indefinite.

Indeed, one can argue that the super-truth view is the only one to accommodate all penumbral truths. For consider the following clauses:

A (i) $\text{not--}t \vDash A \to (\exists u \geq t)(u \dashv A)$, for A atomic
       $\text{not--}t \dashv A \to (\exists u \geq t)(u \vDash A)$, for A atomic

  (ii) $t \vDash \neg B \leftrightarrow t \dashv B$
       $t \dashv \neg B \leftrightarrow t \vDash B$

  (iii) $t \vDash B \& C \leftrightarrow t \vDash B \text{ and } t \vDash C$
       $t \dashv B \& C \leftrightarrow (\forall u \geq t)(\exists v \geq u)(v \dashv B \text{ or } v \dashv C)$

  (iv) $t \vDash (\forall x)B(x) \leftrightarrow t \vDash B(a)$ for any name a
       $t \dashv (\forall x)B(x) \leftrightarrow (\forall u \geq t)(\exists v \geq u)(v \dashv B(a)$ for some name $a)$

Clause (i) is a Resolution Condition R for atomic sentences and states that an indefinite atomic sentence can be resolved in either way upon improvement in precision. The necessary truth and falsehood conditions are to the effect that all truth-functional pledges are to be redeemed. For example, clause (iii) for & requires that whenever $B \& C$ is false it is possible to point to a subsequent specification-point at which either B or C is false.

All of these clauses are reasonable with the possible exception of the sufficient falsehood conditions for & and ∀. But these clauses are required to account for such penumbral falsehoods as "The blob is pink and red" or "All pretenders to the throne are the rightful monarch". Similar considerations apply to the other logical constants ∨, ⊃ and ∃. Now given the ancillary conditions F, S and C, the clauses above are equivalent to the super-truth account. Thus the claims of penumbral connection force one to adopt our favoured view.

The second reason for preferring the super-truth view is that it follows an optimizing strategy: maximize one's advantage within the given constraints. The theory maximizes the extent of truth and falsehood subject to the constraints F, S and C. The argument can be put another way. The Resolution Condition R should hold for all sentences, so that it should be possible to resolve any indefinite sentence in either one of the two ways. For the value of indefinite sentences lies in the possibility of this bipolar resolution: they are born, as it were, to be true or false. There is no point in withholding truth from a sentence that can be made true by improving any improvement in precision. Now the super-truth account is the only one to satisfy the four conditions F, C, S and R. Thus placing the right value on indefiniteness also forces one to adopt our favoured view.

These arguments are essentially claims of the following form: such and such theory is the only one to satisfy the reasonable conditions X, Y and Z. Such claims are of great importance, for they provide a point or rationale for the theory in question: if you want the conditions then you must accept the theory. All too often, truth-conditions for different languages have been constructed with insufficient regard for rationale. Their basis has often been a scanty set of intuitions. Thus a great advantage of the present approach is its possession of a uniquely determining rationale.

One might object to the previous arguments on the grounds that they presuppose Completability, which is unreasonable. However, there is a perfectly a priori argument for this condition. Suppose that the "limit" of a chain of admissible specifications is also admissible. This is a slight restriction on penumbral connection: for example, it excludes the requirement that the specifications be finite (in an obvious sense) or that they verify decidable theories. Then, by Zorn's Lemma, any admissible specification can be extended to a maximally admissible specification. Now suppose that each atomic sentence can always be settled in at least one of two ways, i.e. that no atomic sentence is ever always indefinite. This is a very weak form of Resolution. Then it follows that the maximally admissible specification is complete.

Even without Completability, our arguments will still go through. In place of the super-truth theory we use an anticipatory account that makes a sentence A true if $\neg\neg A$ is true on the (bastard) intuitionistic account, i.e. if A is always going to be intuitionistically true. In effect, we mould intuitionism to the Resolution Condition: a sentence whose truth can always be anticipated is already true. This account is the maximal one to satisfy Stability and the necessary A-clauses. (The latter consist of A(i), Resolution for atomic sentences, and the left-to-right parts of A(ii)-(iv), Redemption of truth-functional pledges.) Moreover, for countable domains, anticipatory truth turns out to be a form of super-truth.[8] Say that a sequence of specification points is *complete* if

(a) each member of the sequence extends its predecessor, and

(b) any sentence is settled by some member of the sequence.

Then a sentence is true on the anticipatory account iff it is true in all generic specifications, i.e. in all limits of complete sequences.

Thus quantification over generic (complete) specifications can be eliminated in favour of quantification over partial specifications. The generic models figure as ideal points; they do not "exist", but truth-values can be calculated as if they did. This reformulation lends itself to a nominalistic interpretation. The partial specifications are identified with the corresponding precisified predicates. One requires that any borderline case be under our control in the sense that it can be settled by making the predicates more precise. But one does not require that any predicate can be made perfectly precise.

The objection to Completability may really be a question about our understanding of a vague sentence. How, it may be asked, do we *grasp* all of those complete and admissible specifications, the existence of which is necessary to determine truth-value?

There are, I think, three main possibilities. The first is that we understand each of the predicates that make the given predicate perfectly precise. We then grasp the complete and admissible specifications indirectly, as those appropriate to the perfectly precise predicates. Thus a vague sentence, say:

The blob is red

is like the scheme:

The blob is R

where "R" stands in for perfectly precise predicates that we are able to enumerate. The main objection to this account is that in understanding a vague predicate we may not understand all or, indeed, any of the predicates that make it perfectly precise.

---

8   The argument is Cohen's (1966).

The second possibility is that we directly grasp all of the admissible and complete specifications. Thus the vague sentence:

The blob is red

is like the open sentence:

The blob belongs to R,

where R is a variable that ranges over complete and admissible extensions of "red". In case of penumbral connection, there will be restrictions on how the variables relate; and in case "admissible" is vague, it will give way to a third-order variable, and so on. But in any case the principle is the same: one grasps the specifications as being sets of a certain sort. The trouble with this account is that "admissible" contains a hidden quantifier over nonextensional entities. An admissible specification is one that is appropriate for some precisification. For example, an admissible and complete extension for "red" is one that is determined by a suitable pair of sharp boundary shades; and a shade is, or corresponds to, a property as opposed to a set.

Thus the third possibility is that we grasp all of the perfect precisifications. The sentence:

The blob is red

is now like the open-sentence

The blob has R,

where R is a variable that ranges over all of the properties that perfectly precisify "red". The perfect properties are grasped, not individually, but as a whole—in one go. There are, perhaps, two main ways in which this can be done. First, they may be understood from below, as the limits of relevant imperfect properties; examples are provided by "chair" and "game". Second, they may be understood from above, in terms of some more direct condition; an example is the sliding scale for "red".

Perhaps the main objection to this account is that grasping all properties of a certain kind requires that one be able, in principle, to find a predicate for one such property. But I do not see why any but a constructivist should accept this. One can quantify over a domain without being able to specify an object from it. Surely one can understand what a precise shade is without being able to specify one.

These accounts bring out well the connection and contrast with ambiguity. Vague and ambiguous sentences are subject to similar truth conditions; a vague sentence is true if true for all complete precisifications; an ambiguous sentence is true if true for all disambiguations. Indeed, the only formal difference is that the precisifications may be infinite, even indefinite, and may be subject to penumbral connection.

Vagueness is ambiguity on a grand and systematic scale.

However, how we grasp the precisifications and disambiguations, respectively, is very different. Ambiguity is understood in accordance with the first account: disambiguations are distinguished; to assert an ambiguous sentence is to assert, severally,[9] each of its disambiguations. Vagueness is understood in accordance with the third account: precisifications are extended from a common basis and according to common constraints: to assert a vague sentence is to assert, generally, its precisifications. Ambiguity is like the super-imposition of several pictures, vagueness like an unfinished picture, with marginal notes for completion. One can say that a super-imposed picture is realistic if each of its disentanglements are; and one can say that an unfinished picture is realistic if each of its completions are. But even if disentanglements and completions match one for one, how we *see* the pictures will be quite different.

4 The logic of vagueness

This completes our discussion of the truth-conditions for the language *L*. We now turn to logic and consider how the preceding analyses affect the notions of validity and consequence.

On the truth-value approach, a formula is *valid* if it takes a designated value for every specification. If True is the sole designated value, then no formulas are valid on any account that conforms to the stability and fidelity conditions. For they require that any sentence is indefinite if all of its atomic subsentences are. If, somewhat unaccountably, True and Indefinite are the designated values, then validity is classical on any account that conforms to the conditions. For if a sentence is false for a specification, it is false for any of its complete specifications and so is not classically valid. Thus the truth-value approach leads either to classical logic or to the trivial logic, in which there are no valid formulas at all.

Formula *B* is a *consequence* of formula *A* if, for any specification, *B* takes a designated value whenever *A* does. If True is the sole designated value, then *B* is a consequence of *A* on the minimal account iff *B* is a

---

9. To assert, severally, sentences $P_1, \ldots, P_k$ is not to assert the conjunction or, for that matter, the disjunction of the sentences For the conjunctive assertion is false if one of the sentences is false, whereas the multiple assertion is false only if each of the sentences is false; and the disjunctive assertion is true if one of the sentences is true, whereas the multiple assertion is true only if each of the sentences is true. These distinctions may have a useful application to the cluster theory of names. For suppose predicates $F_1, \ldots, F_k$ underlie the name a. Then the assertion of $\phi(a)$ can be regarded as the multiple, as opposed to the conjunctive or disjunctive, assertion of $\phi(\text{the } F_1\text{-er}), \ldots, \phi(\text{the } F_k\text{-er})$. A truth-value gap results in case some of the predicates individuate and others do not

classical consequence of A and either A is contravalid or any predicate (or sentence) letter in B is also in A. The maximal account leads to a different consequence-relation with A to $B \vee \neg B$ being the characteristic non-consequence. If True and Indefinite are the designated values then B is a consequence of A on either account iff $\neg A$ is a consequence of $\neg B$ with True as sole designated value.

On the specification space approach, A is valid if it is true in all specification spaces and B is a consequence of A if, for any specification space, B is true whenever A is. This approach gives rise to numerous logics. For example, the bastard intuitionistic truth-conditions lead to a slight extension of intuitionistic logic. On the other hand, the super-truth and anticipatory accounts lead to classical logic. For if a formula is classically valid, i.e. true in all classical models, it is true for all specification spaces, since it is true for each complete specification within the space; and conversely, if a formula is true for all specification spaces, it is classically valid, since each classical model is a degenerate case of a specification space. A similar argument establishes that the consequence-relation is classical for the language at hand. Thus the super-truth theory makes a difference to truth, but not to logic.

Can we maintain that there is no special logic of vagueness? Let us consider two objections against this, one against classical validity and the other against classical consequence.

The first objection is that the Law of the Excluded Middle may fail for vague sentences. For suppose that Herbert is a borderline case of a bald man but that the disjunction "Herbert is bald $\vee \neg$(Herbert is bald)" is true. Then one of the disjuncts is true. But if the second disjunct is true the first is false. So the sentence "Herbert is bald" is either true or false, contrary to the supposition that Herbert is a borderline case of a bald man.

The argument here rests on two assumptions. The first is that the classical necessary truth-conditions for "or" and "not" are correct. From this it follows that the Law of the Excluded Middle implies the Principle of Bivalence. The second assumption is that borderline cases give rise to sentences without truth-values, i.e. to breakdowns of Bivalence. So from both assumptions it follows that LEM fails for such sentences.

It would be perverse to deny the force of this argument; both of its assumptions are very reasonable. However, I think that one can make out that the argument is a fallacy of equivocation. If truth is super-truth, i.e. relative to a space, then the necessary truth-conditions for "or" and "not" fail, though truth-value gaps can exist. If on the other hand, truth is relative to a complete specification then the truth-conditions hold but gaps cannot exist.

An analogy with ambiguity may make the equivocation more palatable. An ambiguous sentence is true if each of its disambiguations is true. Now let J be the ambiguous sentence "John went to the bank"; let J_1 and J_2 be its disambiguations, viz. "John went to the money bank" and "John went to the river bank"; and suppose that John is after fish rather than money. Then the disjunction $J \vee \neg J$ is true, for its disambiguations, $J_1 \vee \neg J_1$ and $J_2 \vee \neg J_2$. are true. However, neither disjunct is true, for each disjunct has a false disambiguation. Thus a truth-value gap exists for assertible or unequivocable truth, whereas the classical truth-conditions hold for truth as relative to a given disambiguation.

Mere ambiguity does not impugn LEM. So why should vagueness? There is, however, a good *ontological* reason for disputing LEM. Suppose I press my hand against my eyes and "see stars". Then LEM should hold for the sentence $S =$ "I see many stars", if it is taken as a vague description of a precise experience. However, LEM should fail for S if it is taken as a precise description of an intrinsically vague experience. Again, if the universal set V is taken to be vague, then the sentence "$V \in V \vee \neg V \in V$ " is, I imagine, not true. More generally, a set is vague if it is not the case of every object that it either belongs or does not belong to the set. One cannot but agree with Frege (1952, p. 159) that "the law of the excluded middle is really just another form of the requirement that the concept should have a sharp boundary".[10]

The second objection against the classical solution is that it gives rise to the sorites-type of paradox. Consider the following instance, which is said to go back to Eubulides:

> A man with no hairs on his head is bald
> If a man with n hairs on his head is bald then a man with $(n + 1)$ hairs on his head is bald.
> ∴ A man with a million hairs on his head is bald.

The conclusion follows from the premises with the help of a million applications of modus ponens and universal instantiation.

The objection now runs like this. The first premiss is true. The second premiss is true: for if not, it is false; but then there is an n such than a man with n hairs on his head is bald and a man with $(n + 1)$ hairs on his head is not bald; and so the predicate "bald" is precise after all. The conclusion is false. Therefore the reasoning, which is classical, is at fault.

---

10. Philosophers have been unduly dismissive over intrinsically vague entities This attitude may derive, in part, from the view that any piece of empirical reality is isomorphic to a mathematical structure, since the structure is precise, so is the reality Thus, the blurred outline becomes isomorphic to a set of points in Euclidean space However, I am not even sure that all mathematical entities are precise Perhaps one could develop an intuitive theory of vague sets Hopefully, it would not even be interpretable within standard set theory, so that the sceptic could not then treat vague sets on the onion-model, as a "façon de parler".

This argument contains two non-sequiturs. The first is that the non-truth of the second premiss implies its falsity; Bivalence may fail for vague sentences. The second is that the existence of the hair-splitting n implies that the predicate "bald" is precise. One need no more accept this than accept that Herbert is bald or not bald implies that Herbert is a clear case of a bald man.

In fact, on the super-truth view, the second premiss is false. This is because a hair splitting n exists for any complete and admissible specification of "is bald". I suspect that the temptation to say that the second premiss is true may have two causes. The first is that the value of a falsifying n appears to be arbitrary. This arbitrariness has nothing to do with vagueness as such. A similar case, but not involving vagueness, is: if n straws do not break a camel's back, then nor do $(n + 1)$ straws. The second cause is what one might call truth-value shift. This also lies behind LEM. Thus $A \vee \neg A$ holds in virtue of a truth that shifts from disjunct to disjunct for different complete specifications, just as the sentence "for some n, a man with n hairs is bald but a man with $(n + 1)$ hairs is not" is true for an n that shifts for different complete specifications.

It is, perhaps, worth pointing out that no special paradoxes of vagueness can arise on the super-truth view, at least for a classical language. For suppose that intuitively false B is a classical consequence of intuitively true A. Then for some complete and admissible specification, A is true and B is false, and this is a classical paradox within a second-order language. This paradox can be brought to the level of the original language if there are predicates to correspond to the complete specification.

Thus the two objections against classical logic for vague sentences cannot be sustained. I do not wish to deny that LEM is counter-intuitive. It is just that external considerations mitigate against it. In particular, an adequate account of penumbral connection appears to require that the logic be classical.

One could, of course, still attempt to construct a logic that was more faithful to unreformed intuition. However, such an attempt would soon run into internal difficulties. One is that our unreformed intuitions on validity do not enable us to decide between the various ways of avoiding LEM. For example, if LEM goes, then so does $A \supset A$ or the standard definition of $\supset$ in terms of $\vee$ and $\neg$. But which? Again, if LEM goes, then one of $\neg(A \& \neg A)$, de Morgan's Laws, or the substitutability of A for $\neg\neg A$ must go. Or again, if modus ponens holds but the logic is not classical then either the $(\supset, \vee)$ or $(\supset, \neg)$ fragment is non-classical.

Another difficulty is that it is hard to motivate a departure from classical logic. Perhaps the best that can be done is this. One interprets

"*A* or *B*" as "clearly *A* ∨ clearly *B*", "if *A* then *B*" as "clearly *A* ⊃ clearly *B*", "*A* and *B*" as "*A* & *B*", and "not *A*" as "clearly ¬*A*". The standard natural deduction rules for disjunction, implication and conjunction will then hold (with consequence as the preservation of super-truth). For example, one still has: if *B* is a consequence of *A* then "if *A* then *B*" is valid. Only negation bears the burden of non-classicality. Also, this account discriminates in a fairly plausible way between conjunction and disjunction. The conjunctions "*P* and not *P*" and "*P* and *R*" are false, while the disjunctions "*P* or not *P*" and "*P* or *R*" are not true. Shifts in the truth-values of conjuncts under different specifications are allowed, while shifts in the truth-values of disjuncts are not.

However, such an alternative does not, in any way, create a challenge for classical logic. For the connectives have merely been re-interpreted within an extension of classical logic. The underlying logic remains classical. There are, then, at least three reasons for adopting a classical solution. The first is that it is a consequence of a truth-definition for which there is strong independent evidence. The second is that it can account for wayward intuitions in an illuminating manner. And the last is that it is simple and non-arbitrary.

5 Higher-order vagueness

One distinctive feature of vagueness is penumbral connection. Another is the possibility of higher-order vagueness. The vague may itself be vague, or vaguely vague, and so on. For suppose that James has a few fewer hairs on his head then his friend Herbert. Then he may well be a borderline case of a borderline case or a borderline case of a borderline case of a borderline case of a bald man.

This feature of vagueness can be expressed with the help of the operator "*D*" for "it is definitely the case that". Let us define the operator "*I*" for "it is indefinite that" by:

$$IA =_{df} \neg DA \,\&\, \neg D\neg A.$$

This is in analogy to the definition of the contingency operator in modal logic. But note that "*D*", unlike the adjective "definite" or the truth-value designator "*I*", is biased towards the truth.

The formula $I^n Fa = \overbrace{II...IFa}^{n}$ expresses that what *a* denotes is an *n*-th order borderline case of *F*. For example, the first of the two possibilities for James is expressed by: *II* (James is bald). The same possibility can be put in terms of the truth-predicate. One says: the sentence "James is bald is neither true nor false" is neither true nor false. Thus higher-order vagueness can be expressed in the material mode, with the help of the definitely-operator, or in the formal mode, with the help of the truth-predicate.

The above notations would appear to undermine scepticism over the existence of higher-order vagueness. For if *IFa* can be true, then so surely can *IIFa*, *IIIFa*, and so on. Or again, if *a* can denote a borderline case of the predicate *F*, then surely the sentence *Fa* can be a borderline case of the predicate "is neither true nor false". In both instances higher-order vagueness is a species of first-order vagueness: in the first, the higher-order consists in the correct application of *I* to a statement of indefiniteness; and in the second, the higher-order consists in the truth-predicate possessing borderline cases. This makes a sudden discontinuity in the orders appear unreasonable.

In any case, artificial examples of higher-order vague predicates can readily be constructed. One might stipulate which borderline cases are to be clear and which not. Indeed, most, if not all, vague predicates in natural language are higher-order vague, though some, such as "red", have a higher concentration of "lateral" or first-order vagueness, whilst others, such as "few", appear to have a higher concentration of "vertical" or higher-order vagueness.

How can we characterize higher-order vagueness? We shall consider two equivalent forms of this question. The first is: what are the truth-conditions for a language with the definitely-operator? The second is: what are the truth-conditions for a language with a hierarchy of truth-predicates? To answer the first question, we let *L'* be the result of enriching the original language *L* with the operator *D*, and, to simplify the answer, we first take care of the case of mere first-order vagueness. We consider the truth-value and rival approaches in turn; though, in view of earlier criticisms, the consideration of the former is an act of generosity.

On the truth-value approach, *D* should satisfy the following clauses:

$$\vdash DA \leftrightarrow \vdash A$$
$$\dashv DA \leftrightarrow \text{not} \vdash A$$

The extended language will no longer satisfy the stability condition, for *DA* is false for *A* indefinite, but true for *A* true. Indeed, *all* three-valued truth-functions can be defined in terms of maximal &, ¬, *D* and a constant for the Indefinite, whilst all three-valued functions satisfying stability can be defined in terms of maximal &, ¬ and constants for the Indefinite and the True.[11]

On the specification space approach, *D* can receive the following clause:

$$w \vdash DA \leftrightarrow w_s \vdash A$$

where w_s is the base-point, or appropriate specification-point, of the

---

11 For references to other results on functional completeness, see Rescher 1969

specification space S. In this case, the original form of Stability will still hold for the enriched language. However, the proper form of stability is:

$w \vDash A$ (for the space S) and $w \leq v \to v \vDash A$ (for the space R),

where R is obtained from S by taking v instead of w as the base point. Now B may be indefinite at w but true at v. So $A = DB$ will be false at w (in S) but true at v (in R). Thus the original "internal" form of Stability holds, while the present "external" form of Stability does not.

The reason for this divergence between the two forms of Stability is that the clause for D ignores any improvement in specification that may have taken place; it simply takes us back to the appropriate specification-point. If the clause were oriented to the current specification-point, it would take the form:

$$w \vDash DA \leftrightarrow w \vDash A$$
$$w \dashv DA \leftrightarrow \text{not-} w \vDash A$$

The original backward-looking clause is analogous to that for the operator "Now" in tense logic (see Prior 1968) or to the reference clause for certain rigid designators as in Kaplan 1979 or Kripke 1972. In all of these cases, the reference (or truth-value) of an expression at an arbitrary point is given in terms of the reference of a simpler expression at a privileged point, be it the appropriate specification or the present time or the actual world. Reference is frozen, as it were, at the privileged point.

The intensional aspect of the present phenomenon is that the sentences of L' are not necessarily made more precise through making their predicates more precise. Suppose that "bald" is only first order vague. Then the sentence:

Definitely Herbert is bald

is not made more precise through making "bald" more precise. Indeed, the sentence is, in the relevant way, already perfectly precise. More generally, the compound sentence will suffer from n-th order vagueness only if its constituent sentence suffers from $(n + 1)$-th order vagueness.

The definitely-operator is not the only one to behave in this way. For example, the sentence:

Casanova believes that he has had many mistresses

may be a precise report of a vague belief or a vague report of a precise belief. In the latter case, the sentence can be made more precise through making "many" more precise; but in the former case, it cannot.

A compound sheds, as it were, the n-th order vagueness of its constituent and comes under the control of its $(n + 1)$-th order vagueness. The phenomenon is formally similar to that behind Frege's distinction between direct and indirect reference. Reference may depend upon indirect reference, indirect reference upon indirectly indirect reference, and so on. Similarly, zero-order vagueness may depend upon first-order vagueness, first-order vagueness upon second-order vagueness, and so on. If indirect reference is taken to be sense, and indirect sense to be itself, then the reference hierarchy has essentially only two terms. The vagueness hierarchy, on the other hand, will have as many terms as there are orders of vagueness.

The logics for D on the different accounts are all quite distinctive. Indeed, one might say that the characteristic logical feature of vagueness is not a non-classical logic but a non-classical notion. For the truth-value approach there are six logics in all, one for each independent choice of maximal or minimal and of $\{T\}$ or $\{T, I\}$ as the set of designated values. We shall not go into details. However, for all choices, the unacceptable formula $D(B \vee C) \supset (DB \vee DC)$ is valid. On the super-truth view, the set of valid formulas is given by the modal system S5. This is because a sentence is true at a complete specification-point if and only if it is true at the base specification-point, which holds if and only if the sentence is true at all of the complete points.

On all of the accounts (with the exception of truth-value accounts with T and I as designated values), the Deduction Theorem does not hold for the consequence-relation. This again distinguishes the presence of D from its absence. In particular, DA is a consequence of A but $A \supset DA$ is not valid. For the truth of A guarantees the truth of DA, but the indefiniteness of A implies the falsity of $A \supset DA$. Thus in one sense A and DA are equivalent, for to assert A is to assert DA; while, in another sense, A and DA are not equivalent, for to assert $\neg A$ is not to assert $\neg DA$. The relationship between consequence and validity is given, not by the Deduction Theorem, but by: B is a consequence of A if and only if $DA \supset B$ is valid. However, in the presence of higher-order vagueness, the relationship takes the complicated form: B is a consequence of A if and only if $A \& DA \& DDA \ldots \supset B$ is valid, i.e. if and only if the set $\{\neg B, A, DA, DDA, \ldots\}$ is not satisfiable.

It is worth noting that the truth of $DA \supset A$ is not completely straightforward. For it involves a sort of penumbral connection between orders of vagueness. Thus on the super-truth view, any complete specification for the predicates of A must be a member of the first-order space that helps to determine the truth-value of DA. This point is even clearer for the truth-predicate. If the sentence Fa is made a clear case of "true", then the denotation of a must also be made a clear case of F. There is a penumbral connection between "true" and F.

We must now consider how higher-order vagueness affects the truth-conditions for D. On the truth-value approach, we can no longer be satisfied with the trichotomy True, False and Indefinite. For example,

DA will be true if *A* is definitely true but indefinite if *A* is indefinitely true. Thus *D* will not be truth-functional with respect to the three truth-values.

In order to determine the truth-value of *DA* we need to know whether *A* is definitely, indefinitely or definitely-not true. But *DA* may itself come under the scope of a *D*-operator. So we need to know whether these qualifications apply definitely, indefinitely or definitely-not, and so on. In general, a truth-value of order $n \geq 0$ is a 3-valued truth-function f with n arguments. Thus the ordinary truth-values—*T, F* and *I*—are the 0-order functions. That sentence *A* has "truth-value" f means that for any ordinary values $x_1, ..., x_n$, the formula $O_{x_n} O_{x_{n-1}}...O_{x_1} A$ has value $y = f(x_1, ..., x_n)$. Here O_{x_i} is the operator corresponding to x_i, for $i = 1, ..., n$. Thus O_T is *D*, O_I is *I* and O_F is *D¬*.

A sentence can contain any finite number of nested *D*'s. So we must also define an infinite-order value. This may be regarded as an infinite sequence $f^0 f^1 f^2 ...$ such that:

(a) f^i is an *i*-th order value

(b) $f^{i+1}(x_0, x_1, ..., x_{i-1}, f^i(x_0, x_1, ..., x_{i-1})) \neq F$
     for any $x_0, x_1, ..., x_{i-1}, i = 0, 1, 2, ...$

(b) is a compatibility condition: if f^i says that $O_{x_{i-1}} O_{x_{i-2}}...O_{x_0} A$ has value x_i, then f^{i+1} must not say that $O_{x_i} O_{x_{i-1}}... O_{x_0} A$ has value *F*.

The truth-conditions are more involved. Suppose second-order functions f and g are assigned to *B* and *C* respectively. Then what second-order function $h = f \cap g$ should be assigned to *B & C* upon the maximal account? Let us illustrate the construction of h by putting $x_0 = I$ and $x_1 = T$. The ordinary truth-value of *DI(B & C)* is the same as that for *D[IB & (DC ∨ IC) ∨ IC & (DB ∨ IC)]*, which is the same as that for *DIB & (DDC ∨ DIC) ∨ DIC & (DDB ∨ DIC)*. So that if $f(I, T) = g(T, T) = T$ and $f(T, T) = g(I, T) = I$, say, then $h(I, T) = I$.

This calculation can be made precise as follows. Given a function f of $(n + 1)$ arguments and a 0-order truth-value z, we let f_z be the function defined by:

$$f_z(x_1, ..., x_n) = f(z, x_1, ..., x_n).$$

We now define operations $\overline{f}, f \cup g, f \cap g$ by induction on the degree n of f and g:

$$n=0. \quad \overline{T} = F, \overline{F} = T, \overline{I} = I$$
$$f \cup g = T \text{ iff } f \text{ or } g = T$$
$$\qquad = F \text{ iff } f = g = F$$
$$f \cap g = T \text{ iff } f = g = T$$
$$\qquad = F \text{ iff } f \text{ or } g = F$$

$n > 0.$ $\overline{f}_T = f_F, \overline{f}_F = f_T, \overline{f}_I = f_I$

$(f \cup g)_T = f_T \cup g_T$

$(f \cup g)_F = f_F \cap g_F$

$(f \cup g)_I = (f_I \cap (g_F \cup g_I)) \cup (g_I \cap (f_F \cup f_I))$

$(f \cap g)_T = f_T \cap g_T$

$(f \cap g)_F = f_F \cup g_F$

$(f \cap g)_I = (f_I \cap (g_T \cup g_I)) \cup (g_I \cap (f_T \cup f_I))$

There are similar definitions for the minimal account.

The semantic clauses should now go as follows. If infinite-order values $f^0 f^1$ ... and $g^0 g^1$ ... are assigned to B and C respectively, then $(f^0 \cap g^0)(f^1 \cap g^1)$ ... is assigned to $(B \ \& \ C)$, $(f^0 \cup g^0)(f^1 \cup g^1)$ ... is assigned to $(B \vee C)$, $\overline{f}^0 \overline{f}^1$... to $\neg B$, and $f_T^1 f_T^2$ ... to DB.

It is reasonable to impose several further conditions upon what functions can be values. For example, one can require that $f(x_0, ..., x_{n-1}, z) \neq F$, for some value z, or that if $f(x_0, ..., x_{n-1}, x_n) = T$ then $f(x_0, ..., x_{n-1}, z) = F$ for $z \neq x_n$. In case there is merely vagueness to order k, one should require of the infinite-order values that $f^l(x_0, x_1, ..., x_{l-1}, z) = T$ for $z = f^{l-1}(x_0, x_1, ..., x_{l-1})$ and $= F$ otherwise, for any $l > k$.

The most natural choice for the designated value is the sequence $d^0 d^1$ ..., where d^i is the i-th order value such that $d^i(x_0, x_1, ..., x_{i-1})$ is T if $x_0 = x_1 = ... = x_{i-1} = T$ and is F otherwise. However, I have not worked out the logics that result from this or other choices.

It would be a bad mistake to fit the values into a discrete linear ordering. For example, one might try to work with the truth-values T = true, I^k = indefinite to degree k, $k > 0$, and $F = I^0$ = false and declare that DB had value I^k if B had value I^{k+1} and value T (respectively F) if B had T (F). Such an account would ignore important distinctions. For suppose that we move our blob on the border of pink and red to the pink side of the colour spectrum. Then the sentence P might be indefinitely true but definitely not false, though the above ordering could express no such distinction. It would be an even worse mistake to treat the values as a continuous or densely ordered set, say the real closed interval between 0 and 1, as in Zadeh 1965. More distinctions would go. For example, one could no longer express the fact that Herbert was a clear borderline case of a bald man.

We must now consider how the rival approach fares for the language L' under conditions of higher-order vagueness. The general set-up is extremely complicated, so let us consider the special case of the super-truth theory.

To simplify further, we identify specification-points with specifications. Now suppose we pick upon an admissible complete specification for the language L. If the language suffers from first-order vagueness, this specification is not unique and we may pick upon an admissible set of complete specifications. If the language also suffers from second-order vagueness, this set is not unique and we may pick upon an admissible set of sets, and so on. After $(n + 1)$ such choices, we obtain what might be called an n-th-order boundary.

Let us be more precise. A zero-th order space is a complete specification and a $(n + 1)$-th order space is a set of n-th order spaces. A n-th order boundary is then a sequence $s^0 s^1 \ldots s^n$ such that s^i is an i-th order space, $i \leq n$, and $s^j \in s^{j+1}$, $j < n$; and an ω-order boundary is an infinite sequence $s^0 s^1 \ldots$ such that each $s^0 s^1 \ldots s^i$ is an i-order boundary, $i = 1, 2, \ldots$. A boundary is admissible if each of its terms are and we suppose that the members of an admissible $(n + 1)$-order space are also admissible.

We can now define the truth of L'-sentences relative to an ω-order boundary, or boundary for short. The clauses for the logical constants are standard. The clause for "D" is:

$$b \vDash D\phi \Leftrightarrow (\forall \text{ boundaries } c)(bRc \Leftrightarrow c \vDash \phi),$$

where $b = b_0 b_1 \ldots Rc = c_0 c_1 \ldots$ if $c_i \in b_{i+1}$, $i = 0, 1, \ldots$ The justification of the clause is this: $D\phi$ is true at b if ϕ is true for all admissible ways of drawing the boundaries; but the admissible zero-order boundaries are the $c_0 \in b_1$, the admissible first-order boundaries the $c_0 c_1$ such that $c_0 \in b_1$ and $c_1 \in b_2$, and so on. Assertible or absolute truth is, in accordance with the super-truth view, truth in all admissible boundaries.

The above clause has the form of the necessity clause in the standard relational semantics for modal logic. However, the "accessibility" relation R is not primitive but is determined from the structure of the boundary points. This structure is such that R is reflexive; and, in fact, the resulting logic is the modal system T. Further restrictions on R could be obtained by restricting the possible boundary points. For example, given any $n \geq 0$, one could require that each boundary $b = b_0 b_1 \ldots$ tapers after n, i.e. that $b_{i+1} = \{b_i\}$, for $i > n$. This corresponds to there being at most n-th order vagueness.

So much for the truth-conditions of L'. We must now consider the truth-conditions for a language with a hierarchy of truth-predicates. We let the metalanguage M^0 of level 0 be the original language L, the metalanguage M^{n+1} of level $n + 1$ be the result of adding the truth-predicate for M^n to M^n (with appropriate means for referring to the sentences of M^n), and the metalanguage M^ω of infinite level be the union, in an obvious sense, of the previous languages $M^0, M^1, M^2, \ldots$.

In one way, it is simpler to provide truth-conditions for M^ω than for L'. For each of the meta-languages is merely another first-order language. So any account for the original language L should, when properly generalized, lead to an account for each of the meta-languages.

However, the details for the general case are very complicated. For the truth predicate for L will be defined in terms of the following predicates, we may suppose: x is an admissible L-specification; x extends y; the atomic L-sentence A is true (false, indefinite) at x. So the truth-predicate for M^1 will be defined in terms of the corresponding primitives for the language M. But then, in particular, the third primitive must tell us whether it is true, false or indefinite at an M-specification that an atomic L-sentence is true, false or indefinite at an L-specification. The whole process must then be successively repeated for the other meta-languages. If we imagine that the truth-conditions for L are given in the form of a (labelled) tree, then those for M^1 are given by a tree whose nodes are trees that "grow" throughout the bigger tree, and those for M^2 by a similar such tree whose nodes are trees for M^1, and so on.

However, for particular approaches, the details may be much simpler. On the truth-value approach, the truth-predicate for L is defined solely in terms of the primitives: the atomic sentence A is *true*, is *false*, is *indefinite*. Since truth-value is determined relative to a unique appropriate specification, the admissible specifications drop out of view. The truth-predicate for M^1 is then defined in terms of the primitive: the atomic M^1-sentence A is *true, false,* or *indefinite*. But the atomic M^1-sentences will now include the atomic L-sentences and the sentences of the form:

"A" is true (false, indefinite),

where "A" is an atomic L-sentence. Similarly for the other meta-languages.

On the super-truth view, the truth-predicate for L is defined in terms of the primitive: "x is a complete and admissible L-specification". The assignments of truth-values can be regarded as internal to the specifications and so left out of view. The truth-predicate for M^1 is then defined in terms of the predicate: x is a complete and admissible M-specification. But such a specification will consist of an L-specification and an assignment of an extension to the predicate "x is a complete and admissible L-specification". Similarly for the other meta-languages.

Higher-order vagueness gives rise to two puzzles, to which it is difficult to give convincing answers. The first arises from the systematic correlation between the sentences of L' and M^ω. This is provided by the equivalence:

"A" is true $\leftrightarrow$ It is definitely the case that A.

For a sentence of L' can be converted into one of M^ω upon successively replacing innermost "DA" by "A" is true$_n$", for n an appropriate level indicator. Accordingly, there should also be a conversion of truth-conditions. Since we have already given independent truth-definitions for L' and M^ω, this conversion should provide a check on correctness. I cannot give details, but let us observe that there will also be a conversion of conditions. For example, the conditions given for no vagueness of order $(n + 1)$ in L' will correspond to the conditions which guarantee that the truth-predicate for M^{n+1} has no borderline cases.

The puzzle is: should we regard "DA" as merely elliptical for "'A' is true"? This would be to regard the definitely-operator as a device for incorporating the meta-language into the object-language. The device would, strictly speaking, be improper since it ignores use/mention and type distinctions; but it would be harmless if no quantifiable variables occurred within the scope of "D". On the semantic side, it is a matter of whether the extended spaces or truth-values have an independent status or whether they are merely fanciful formulations of the ordinary spaces or values, but for a richer language. An analogous question is whether necessity is best regarded as an operator on or a predicate of sentences.

The ellipsis view has the general advantage of replacing a non-extensional operator with an extensional predicate. It has the general disadvantage of involving an incorrect reference to language. Suppose "bald" has first-order vagueness and the borderline cases are stipulated to be just those people with 40 to 60 cranial hairs. Then "It is indefinite that Herbert is bald" is synonymous with "Herbert has between 40 and 60 cranial hairs", but this latter sentence is not synonymous with any claim about a sentence being true. The indefiniteness of vague sentences is as much a matter of fact as the truth or falsehood of precise ones.

Also, the ellipsis view has the particular disadvantage of making for a sudden discontinuity between first- and second-order vagueness. First-order vagueness is a matter of ordinary predicates having borderline cases, but second-order vagueness is a matter of the truth-predicate having borderline cases. There is, of course, a *correlation* between the second-order vagueness of ordinary predicates and the first-order vagueness of the truth-predicate. But we feel that the latter arises from the former, and not vice versa. The truth-predicate is supervenient upon the object-language; there can be no independent grounds for its having borderline cases.

Indeed, I think that "D" is a prior notion to "true" and not conversely. For let "true_T" be that notion of truth that satisfies the Tarski-equivalence, even for vague sentences:

> "A" is true_T if and only if A.

The vagueness of "true$_T$" waxes and wanes, as it were, with the vagueness of the given sentence; so that if a denotes a borderline case of F then Fa is a borderline case of "true$_T$". Then the ordinary notion of truth is given by the definition:

x is true $=_{df}$ Definitely (x is true$_T$).

Thus "true$_T$" is primary; "true" is secondary and to be defined with the help of the definitely-operator.

The second puzzle arises from the demand for a perfectly precise meta-language. So far, we have only demanded of our truth-conditions that they provide correct allocations of truth. To respect the truth-value gap, to account for penumbral connection, to yield the correct logic; these are all special cases of this more general demand. However, one may also require that the meta-language not be vague or, at least, not so vague in its proper part as the object-language. Thus it will not do to subject truth to the standard equivalences:

"A" is true if and only if A.

For then truth will be truth$_T$; the truth-conditions will be classical; and the vagueness of the truth-predicate will exactly match that of the object-language.

What we require is that the true/false/indefinite trichotomy be relatively firm. Ideally, the truth of the disjunction "A is true, false or indefinite" should imply the truth of one of its disjuncts. It is not that the infirmity of this trichotomy in any way impugns the correctness of the previous accounts. In particular, validity is still classical on the super-truth view; for classically valid A is true in all complete and admissible specifications, regardless of whether it is clear that a particular complete specification is admissible. Rather it is that the infirmity gives rise to the problem of providing truth-conditions for the meta-language.

This raises the puzzle: is there a perfectly precise meta-language? Certainly, each of the meta-languages M^n could be vague. One could take the whole construction into the transfinite and have, for each ordinal α, a meta-language M^α or strong definitely-operator D^α. But the same problem would arise anew. At no point does it seem natural to call a halt to the increasing orders of vagueness.

However, if a language has a semantics in terms of higher-order boundaries, then it also has a firm truth-predicate. For the boundaries will be based upon a set of admissible specifications and we can let truth (or falsehood) be truth (or falsehood) in all such specifications. Anything that smacks of being a borderline case is treated as a clear borderline case. The meta-languages become precise at some, but no pre-assigned, ordinal level. The only alternative to this is that the set of admissible specifications is itself intrinsically vague. There would then be a very intimate connection between vague language and reality: what language meant would be an intrinsically vague fact.

If higher-order vagueness terminates at some stage α then vagueness can, in a sense, be eliminated. For each sentence A can be replaced by a perfectly precise sentence $D^\alpha A$ that entails it. However, this method is unsatisfactory in several ways. First, one may not be able to specify the α. Second, even if one can, one may not be able to make much sense of D^α. Our intuitions seem to run out after the second or third orders of vagueness. Perhaps this is because our understanding of vague language is, to a large extent, confused. One sees blurred boundaries, not clear boundaries to boundaries. Finally, the method is too uniform to be discriminate. Penumbral connections may be lost: our blob, for example, is not definitely red or definitely pink. Indeed, the question of making predicates perfectly precise[12] is independent of whether higher-order vagueness terminates. The predicate "small", as applied to numbers, may suffer from endless higher-order vagueness; yet it can still be made perfectly precise.[13]

---

12 This question is usually settled upon covertly constructivist lines Our powers of perceptual discrimination are limited, therefore we cannot *settle* whether an object has such and such exact shade But could not a non-constructivist take "red", say, to mean the colour of *that*, where "that" refers to a perfectly uniform shade? The inability to know would not affect the ability to mean.

13 (Added in the 1975 proofs). After writing the paper, I discovered that the super-truth account of vague languages had also been espoused by the following authors H Kamp (1975), D Lewis (1970); M. Przełecki (1969), and P A Williams in Chapter 1 of his doctoral thesis The view seems to go back to H Mehlberg's 1958 (this volume)

10   Language-mastery and the sorites paradox

Crispin Wright

1 Throughout Frege's writings are scattered expressions of the conception that the vagueness of ordinary language, and especially the occurrence of predicates for which it is not always determinate whether or not they may truly be applied to an object, is a defect. His reason for such a view seems to have been that orthodox logical principles fail when applied to sentences containing expressions whose range of application has been defined only partially.[1] Thus Frege seems not to have considered, or not to have thought worth considering, the possibility that vague terms might require a *special* logic. Vagueness is rather something which can and should be expurgated from language, if it is to be suitable for "scientific purposes". The same conception is to be found in Russell's Introduction to the *Tractatus*. Ordinary language is always more or less vague, but a logically perfect language would not be vague at all; so the degree of vagueness of a natural language is a direct measure of its distance from being everything which it "logically" ought to be.

Of course, we have since learned a greater respect for language as we find it; we no longer regard the vagueness of ordinary language as a defect. But a higher-order analogue of the Frege-Russell view continues to figure in our thinking about language: even if many predicates in natural language are vague, there can still be a precise semantics for such expressions and indeed for the whole language, i.e. a theoretical model of the information assimilated in learning it as a first language or, equivalently, of the conceptual apparatus possession of which constitutes mastery of the language. There need be no imprecision, it seems, in such a model; at any rate, none occasioned purely by the vagueness of the expressions of mastery of whose senses it is to provide an account.

From *Truth and Meaning*, edited by G Evans and J McDowell (Oxford Clarendon Press, 1976), pp. 223–47 © Oxford University Press Reprinted by permission

This discussion is a synopsis of, or, better, a series of excerpts from Wright 1975

1   Excluded Middle is the obvious example But, as Frege points out, contraposition also fails (Frege 1903, p 65)

We tend to picture our use of language as something essentially *regular*. We tend to think of language-learning as ingestion of a set of rules for the combination and application of expressions. Thus the task of a philosophical theory of meaning, in one natural sense of that phrase, would be to give a systematic account of the contribution made by the constituents of a semantically complex expression to its overall sense; and the theory would be concerned especially with the epistemology of the transition from understanding of subsentential components of a new sentence to recognition of the sense of the whole. Such a philosophical theory will normally only be concerned with *types* of contribution made by constituent expressions; in just this connection arise the familiar questions concerning the nature of the distinction between proper names and other singular terms, between singular terms generally and predicative expressions, whether the notion of reference may illuminatingly be extended to predicative expressions, etc. So the completion of such a theory would only be a preliminary to what we think of as a full semantic description of a natural language; for it is not just the type of contribution but the *specific* contribution which a constituent expression makes to complex expressions containing it which we think of as determined by rule.

It is worth emphasizing that no obstacle to such a conception is posed by the fact that we cannot in general state such rules in such a way as to explain the sense of an expression to someone previously unfamiliar with it. Consider a schematic rule for a one-place predicate, *F*:

F may truly be applied to an individual, *a*, if and only if *a* satisfies the condition of being ϕ.

How should we specify ϕ if *F* is "red"? Clearly the only completion of the rule which is actually constitutive of our understanding of "red", rather than a mere extensional parallel, is to take ϕ as the condition of being red. In general we cannot expect instances of such a schematic rule to be of explanatory use if they are stated in a given language for a predicate of the same language; in consequence, it will not generally be possible to appeal to such rules to settle questions about the applicability of an expression. Nevertheless we may still legitimately regard such a rule as an exact expression of (part of) what is understood by someone who understands e.g. "red", for it states conditions recognition of which is sufficient to justify him in describing an object as "red"; the statement of the rule is uninformative only in the sense that such a capacity of recognition cannot be imparted just by stating it.

So our picture is that correct use of language is essentially nothing other than use of it which conforms with a set of instructions, a set of semantic rules, which we have learned. Of course we handle language in general in a quite automatic way. But a chess player's recognition of the moves allowed for a piece in a certain position can be similarly automatic; it remains true that an account of his knowledge is to be given by reference to the rules of chess.

If language-mastery is thought of in such terms, the question arises, what means are allowable in the attempt to discover general features of the *substantial* rules for expressions in our language, the rules which determine specific senses? The view of the matter on which this paper centres is that here we may legitimately approach our use of language from within, i.e. reflectively as self-conscious masters of it, rather than externally, equipped only with behavioural notions. Thus it is legitimate to appeal to our conception of what justifies the application of a particular expression; to our conception of what we should count as an adequate explanation of the sense of a particular expression; to the limitations imposed by our senses and memories on the kind of instruction which we can actually carry out in practice; and to the kind of consequence which we associate with the application of a particular predicate, to what we think of as the point or interest of the distinction which the predicate implements. The primary concern of this paper is with the idea, henceforward referred to as the *governing view*, that from such considerations can be derived a reflective awareness of how we understand expressions in our language, and so of the nature of the rules which determine their correct use. The governing view, then, is a conjunction of two claims: that our use of language is rightly seen, like a game, as a practice in which the admissibility of a move is determined by rule, and that general properties of the rules may be discovered by means of the sorts of consideration just described. What I am going to argue is that these theses are mutually incoherent.

The difficulty has to do with the fact that the second thesis of the governing view, concerning the means whereby general features may be discovered of the semantic rules which we actually follow, forces us to recognize *semantic incoherence* in our understanding of a whole class of predicates—elements whose full exploitation would force the application of these expressions to situations in which we should otherwise regard them as not applying. The second thesis requires us to recognize rules which, when considered in conjunction with certain general features of the situations among which their associated expressions are to be applied, issue in contradictory instructions. Nevertheless we succeed in using these expressions informatively; and it seems that to use language informatively depends on using it, in large measure, consistently. It follows that our use of these expressions cannot correctly be pictured purely as the implementation of rules of the character which the second thesis yields for them; these rules cannot be implemented by any consistent pattern of behaviour. The governing view is therefore incoherent; for if its second thesis is true, the semantic rules governing certain predicates are capable by consistent beings only of selective implementation and thus, contrary to the first thesis, are not *constitutive* of what we count as the correct use of these expressions.

The predicates in question are all vague; but their vagueness is not just a matter of the existence of situations to which it is indeterminate whether or not they apply. Rather it is something which Frege, under the guise of a favourite metaphor, constantly runs together with possession of borderline-cases, viz., the idea of lacking "sharp boundaries", of dividing logical space as a blurred shadow divides the background on which it is reflected. The conflation is natural because the figure equally exemplifies the idea of the borderline-case, a region falling neither in light nor shadow. But there is no clear reason why possession of borderline-cases should entail possession of blurred boundaries. If, following Frege, we assimilate a predicate to a *function* taking objects as arguments and yielding a truth value as value, then a predicate with borderline-cases may be seen simply as a partial such function—which is consistent with the existence of a perfectly sharp distinction between cases for which it is defined and cases for which it is not. Borderline-case vagueness of this straightforward kind presents no difficulty for the governing view; it is merely that there are situations to which no response in terms of a certain range of predicates is determined by their associated semantic rules as correct. In contrast, if the second thesis of the governing view is correct, then predicates with "blurred boundaries" are, in typical cases, rightly regarded as semantically incoherent.

This incoherence is implicit in the very nature of their vagueness. Vagueness is hardly ever, as Frege and Russell thought, merely a reflection of our not having bothered to make a predicate precise. Rather, the utility and point of the classifications expressed by many vague predicates would be frustrated if they were supplied with sharp boundaries. The sorts of argument allowed by the second thesis of the governing view will transpire to yield support for the idea that such predicates are essentially vague. The thesis equips us to argue that lack of sharp boundaries is not in general merely a superficial phenomenon, a reflection of a mere hiatus in some underlying set of semantic rules. In almost all the examples one comes across lack of sharp boundaries is not the consequence of an omission, but e.g. a product of the kind of task to which an expression is put, the kind of consequences which we attach to its application or, more deeply, the continuity of a world which we wish to describe in purely observational terms. Lack of sharp boundaries is a phenomenon of semantic depth. It is not usually a matter simply of our lacking an instruction where to "draw the line";

rather the instructions we already have determine that the line is *not* to be drawn.

This conclusion might seem a welcome contribution to our understanding of the nature of vagueness, even from the standpoint of the governing view, were it not that it comes out in the form that no sharp distinction may be drawn between cases where it is definitely correct to apply such a predicate and cases of *any* other sort. But that is obviously a paradoxical concept. Thus it is that someone who espouses the governing view simply has no coherent approach to the Frege-Russell view of vagueness. His second thesis furnishes him with conclusive reasons to reject the suggestion that vagueness is a superficial, eliminable aspect of natural language with no real impact upon its informative use. But it does so in such a way that he is constrained to regard many vague predicates as semantically incoherent—specifically, as prone to the reasoning of the sorites paradox—so that, unless the Frege-Russell view is right, he cannot maintain his first thesis with respect to such expressions. Only if their vagueness were an incidental feature could he maintain that the *essential* semantics of such expressions conformed to his first thesis.

2 Let us then consider some examples of the sorites paradox in order to be clear how the governing view cuts off traditional lines of solution, indeed, all lines of solution. To begin with the classical case: if a pile of salt is large enough to be fairly described as a heap, the subtraction of a single grain of salt cannot make a relevant difference; if $n + 1$ grains of salt constitute a heap, so do n grains. Thus one grain, and, indeed, zero grains constitute a heap. To block the paradox, it seems we have to be able to insist that, for some particular value of n, $n + 1$ grains of salt would amount to a heap while n grains would not. But that is simply not the sense of "heap". Exact boundaries for the concept of a heap, either in terms of the precise number of grains contained or, indeed, in terms of any other precise measure, simply have not been fixed. But without such boundaries, a transition from $n + 1$ grains to n grains can never be recognized as transforming a case where "heap" applies into a case where it does not. Here we gravitate towards the idea that lack of exact boundaries is, as such, an essentially incoherent semantic feature.

A second example is given by Essenin-Volpin (1961, p. 203). Consider the typical span of time between one human heartbeat and its successor. Then the concept of childhood—the sense of "child"—is such that one does not, within a single heartbeat, pass from childhood to adolescence. Not that we are children for ever; but at least childhood does not evaporate between one pulse and the next. Similarly for the transition from infancy to childhood, and from adolescence to adulthood. "Infant", "child", "adolescent", "adult" are thus all semantically incoherent expressions; for the sense of each of these predicates is such that, in a typical process of growing-up, their correct application will always survive the transition from one heartbeat to its successor or to its predecessor. So, by appropriately many steps of *modus ponens*, we may force the application of each of these predicates to cases we should otherwise regard as falling within the domain of one of the others.

As a third example, consider a series of homogeneously coloured patches, ranging from a first, red patch to a final, orange one, such that each patch is *just* discriminable in colour from those immediately next to it, and is more similar in respect of colour to its immediate neighbours than to any other patches in the series. That is, marginal changes of shade are involved in every transition from a patch to its successor, and each such transition carries us further from red and closer to orange. Now, the sense of colour predicates is such that their application always survives a very small change in shade. If one is content to call something "red", one will still be so content if its colour changes by some just discriminable amount. There is a notion of a degree of change in respect of colour too small to amount to a change *of* colour. Only if a substantial difference comes between two patches of colour shall we consider ourselves justified in ascribing to them incompatible colour predicates.

This, obviously, is to attribute semantic incoherence to colour predicates. We have an easy proof that all the patches in the example are red, or that they are all orange, or that they are all doubtfully either. Moreover any two colours can be linked by such a series of samples; so any colour predicate can be exported into the domain of application of one of its rivals.

What is involved in treating these examples as genuinely paradoxical is a certain *tolerance* in the concepts which they respectively involve, a notion of a degree of change too small to make any difference, as it were. The paradoxical interpretations postulate degrees of change in point of size, maturity and colour which are insufficient to alter the justice with which some specific predicate of size, maturity or colour is applied. This is quite palpably an incoherent feature since, granted that any case to which such a predicate applies may be linked by a series of "sufficiently small" changes with a case where it does not, it is inconsistent with there being any cases to which the predicate does not apply. More exactly, suppose ϕ to be a concept related to a predicate, F, as follows: that any object which F characterizes may be changed into one which it does not simply by sufficient change in respect of ϕ. Colour, for example, is such a concept for "red", size for "heap", degree of maturity for "child", number of hairs for "bald", etc. Then F is *tolerant* with respect to ϕ if there is also some positive degree of change in respect of

ϕ insufficient ever to affect the justice with which F applies to a particular case.

In essentials, then, the sorites paradox interprets certain vague predicates as tolerant. But this might seem a tendentious interpretation. Not that there is any doubt that the predicates in question do lack sharp boundaries; and the antiquity of the paradox bears witness to how easy it is to interpret this as involving the possession by these predicates of a principle of re-application through marginal change. But is this a correct interpretation? Because "heap" lacks sharp boundaries, it is plain that we are not entitled to single out any particular transition from n to $n-1$ grains of salt as being the decisive step in changing a heap into a non-heap; no one such step is decisive. That, however, is not to say that such a step always *preserves* application of the predicate. Would it not be better to assimilate the situation to that in which bordering states fail to agree upon a common frontier? Their failure to reach agreement does not vindicate the notion that e.g. a single pace in the direction of the other country always keeps one in the original country. For they have at least agreed that there is to be a border, that *some* such step is to be a decisive one; what they have not agreed is where. If we regard the predicates in the example in the terms of this model, we shall conclude that their vagueness is purely a reflection of our intellectual laziness. We have, as it were, decided that a disjunction is to be true—at some stage, n grains will be a heap where $n-1$ grains will not—without following up with a decision about *which* disjunct is true. On this view, the notion that these predicates are tolerant confuses a lack of instruction to count it the case that a proposition is false with the presence of an instruction to count it true. This conflation would be permissible only if the semantic rules for our language were in a certain sense complete, that is, if we possessed instructions for every conceivable situation. But for there to be vague expressions in our language is, on this view, precisely for this not to be so.

Someone who holds the governing view is bound to reject this suggestion as a deep misapprehension of the nature of the vagueness of these predicates. The lack of sharp boundaries possessed by these examples is correctly interpreted as tolerance, provided that we may discover elements of their senses in accordance with the second thesis. It would be inconsistent with elements already present in the semantics of these predicates so to refine their senses that the sorites reasoning was blocked. How is this?

"Heap" is essentially a coarse predicate, whose application is a matter of rough and ready judgement. We should have no use for a precisely demarcated analogue in contexts in which the word is typically used. It would, for example, be ridiculous to force the question of obedience to the command, "pour out a heap of sand here", to turn on a count of the grains. Our conception of the conditions which justify calling something a heap is such that the appropriateness of the description will be unaffected by any change which cannot be detected by *casual observation*.

A different argument is available for supposing colour predicates tolerant with respect to marginal changes in shade. We learn and teach our basic colour vocabulary ostensively. Evidently it is a precondition of the feasibility of so doing that we can reasonably accurately remember how things look. Imagine someone who can recognize whether simultaneously presented objects match in colour, so that he is able to use a colour-chart, but who cannot in general remember shades of colour sufficiently well to be able to handle without a chart colour predicates for which we are able to dispense with charts. Such a person might, for example, be quite unable to judge whether something yellow, which he was shown earlier, would match the orange object now before him. Thus, for such a man, an ostensive definition of "yellow" would be useless; in order to apply "yellow" as we apply it, he would have to employ a chart. We, in contrast, are able to dispense with charts for the purpose of making distinctions of colour of the degree of refinement of "yellow". Any object to which a colour predicate of this degree of refinement definitely correctly applies may be recognized as such just on the basis of our ostensive training. Plainly, then, it has to be a feature of the senses thereby bestowed upon these predicates that changes too slight for us to remember—that is, a change such that exposure to an object both before the change is undergone and afterwards leaves us uncertain whether the object *has* changed, because we cannot remember sufficiently accurately how it was before—never transform a case to which such a predicate applies into one where such is not definitely the right description. The character of our basic colour training presupposes the *total memorability* of the distinctions expressed by our basic colour predicates; only if single, unmemorable changes of shade never affect the justice of a particular basic description can the senses of these predicates be explained entirely by methods reliant upon our capacity to remember how things look.

For the tolerance of "child", etc., the governing view affords a third type of argument. The distinctions expressed by these predicates are of substantial social importance in terms of what we may appropriately expect from, and of, persons who exemplify them. Infants, for example, have rights but not duties, whereas of a child outside infancy we demand at least a rudimentary moral sense; we explain the anti-social behaviour of some adolescents in terms of their being adolescents; and we make moral and other demands of character on adults which we would not impose on the immature. Plausibly, these predicates could not endure such treatment, were they not tolerant with respect to marginal changes in degree of maturity—certainly with respect to the changes involved in the transition from one heartbeat to the next. It is *ceteris paribus* irrational and unfair to base substantial distinctions of right and duty on marginal differences; if we are forced to do so, e.g. with electoral qualifications, it is with a sense of injustice. Moreover it is only if a *substantial* change is involved in the transition from childhood to adolescence that we can appeal to this transition to explain substantial alterations in patterns of behaviour. That predicates of degree of maturity should possess tolerance is a direct consequence of their social role; very small differences cannot be permitted to generate doubt about their application without correspondingly coming to be associated with a burden of moral and explanatory distinctions which they are too slight to carry.

On the second thesis of the governing view, then, our embarrassment about where to "draw the line" with these examples is to be viewed as a consequence not of any hiatus in our semantic programme but of the tolerance of the predicates in question. If casual observation alone is to determine whether a predicate applies, then items not distinguished by casual observation must receive the same verdict.[2] So single changes too slight to be detected by casual observation cannot be permitted to generate doubt about the application of such a predicate. Similarly, if the conditions under which a predicate applies are to be generally memorable, it cannot be unseated by single changes too slight to be remembered. Finally, very slight changes cannot be permitted to generate doubt about the application of predicates of maturity without contravening their moral and explanatory role. The utility of "heap", the memorability of the conditions under which something is "red", the point of "child" impose upon the semantics of these predicates tolerance with respect to marginal change in the various relevant respects.

To allow these considerations is to concede that the vagueness of these examples is a phenomenon of semantic depth—that it is sacrificed at much more than the cost of the intellectual labour of the stipulation—and that it is a structurally incoherent feature. Two things follow. First, there is no special logic for predicates of this sort, crystallizing what is distinctive in their semantics in contrast with those of exact predicates; for what is so distinctive is their inconsistency. Second, the fashion in which we typically use these expressions needs some other model than

---

2 Not that it has to be the case that a definitely correct verdict can always be reached, but if it cannot, that in turn must be the situation with respect to each item in question

the simple implementation of rules, if these rules are to incorporate all the features of their senses which we should wish to recognize on the basis of the second thesis.

3 There is a fourth, and more profound way in which tolerance, according to the second thesis, would seem to arise. Colour predicates will again serve as an illustration. Plausibly, these predicates are in the following sense purely *observational*: if it is possible to tell at all what colour something is, it can be told just by looking. The look of an object decides its colour, as the feel of an object decides its texture, or the sound of a note its pitch. The information of one or more senses is decisive of the applicability of an observational predicate; so a distinction exemplified by a pair of sensorily-equivalent items cannot be expressed solely by means of such predicates. What is about to be illustrated is a feature of any predicate whose sense is purely observational in the fashion just adumbrated.

If colour predicates are observational, any pair of patches indistinguishable in colour must satisfy the condition that any colour predicate applicable to either is applicable to both. Suppose, then, that we build up the series of colour patches of the third example, interposing new patches to the point where every patch in the resultant series is indiscriminable in colour from those immediately adjacent to it. The possibility of doing so, of course, depends upon the non-transitivity of our colour discriminations. The observationality of "red" requires it to be tolerant with respect to the kind of change involved in passing from any patch in this series to an immediate neighbour, so we have a sorites paradox. If "red" is observational, its sense must be such that from the premisses, that x is red and that x looks just like y, it follows that y is red, no matter what objects x and y may be. Thus we are equipped to conclude that each successive patch in the series is red, given only the true premiss that the first patch is red.

The memorability, then, of the conditions of application of "red" requires that it be tolerant with respect to changes which, under favourable circumstances, we can actually directly discern. Now, however, it appears that even if our memories were to be as finely discriminating as our senses, colour predicates and others would still possess tolerance; only the changes which their application tolerated would not be changes which we could directly discern in objects which underwent them. This tolerance has nothing to do with the limitations of our memories; it is a consequence of the observationality of these predicates.

These considerations are broadly analogous to what was said of "heap": if we so fix the sense of a predicate that whether it applies has to do with nothing other than how an object seems when casually observed, then changes other than such as can be determined by casual observation cannot transform a case to which the predicate applies into one to which there is some question whether it applies. The point remains good if we omit the word "casual". But this fourth example is prima facie deeper-reaching, at any rate for someone who, like Frege, believes that language should be purified of vague expressions. The cost of eliminating predicates of casual observation would be no more than convenience; to require, however, that language should contain no expression tolerant in the manner of the fourth example would be to require that it contained no expressions of strictly observational sense. If we stipulated away the tolerance of colour predicates, we should have to forgo our whole present idea of what justifies the application of these predicates, viz. the *look* of a thing. In general, there would be no predicate whose application to an object could be decided just on the basis of how it looked, felt, sounded, etc. Might there not then be a higher price to pay, namely the jeopardizing of contact between language and empirical reality?

We shall return to the last thought. First we require to see how the governing view sustains the idea that there is a large class of predicates whose senses are purely observational. If we are to understand the scope of the fourth example, we also require to know under what circumstances we may expect our sensory discriminations to be non-transitive.

That we do intuitively regard the semantics of colour predicates as purely observational is beyond doubt; and simply illustrated by the fact that we should regard it as a criterion of lack of understanding of such a predicate if someone was doubtful whether both of a pair of objects which he could not tell apart should receive the same description in terms of it. We regard it as a criterion of understanding such a predicate that someone, presented under suitable conditions with an object to which it applies, can tell that it does so just on the basis of the object's appearance. Certainly, then, our ordinary conception of how to tell that a particular colour predicate applies, of what justifies its application, would involve that these predicates are purely observational.

In addition, it is plausible to suppose that any *ostensively definable* predicate must be observational. If an expression can be ostensively defined, it must be possible to draw to someone's attention those features in his experience which warrant its application; and if this is possible, there can be no question of the expression applying to some but not others among situations which he cannot distinguish in experience. It would be a poor joke on the recipient of an ostensive definition if the defined expression applied selectively among situations indistinguishable from one which was originally displayed to him as a paradigm.

In general the connection between an expression's being observational—its applying to both, if to either, of any pair of observationally indistinguishable situations—and its being ostensively definable is as follows. The picture of acquiring concepts by experience of cases where they do apply and cases where they do not—a picture which surely has *some* part to play in a philosophically adequate conception of the learning of a first language—cannot be wholly adequate for concepts which differentiate among situations which look, feel, taste, sound and smell exactly alike. So if that picture is wholly adequate for any concepts, they must be concepts whose range of application does not include situations which experience cannot distinguish from situations which may not definitely correctly be regarded as falling within that range. To master the sense of a predicate is, at least, to learn to differentiate cases to which it is right to apply it from cases of any other sort. If such mastery can be bestowed ostensively, a comparison of two such cases must always reveal a difference which sense-experience can detect. The notion that the whole range of application of a predicate can be made intelligible by ostensive means presupposes that it is never the case that only one of a pair of objects, which the senses cannot tell apart, is characterized by it.

This is a clear, absolutely general connection. If there is in the conditions of the correct application of a predicate nothing which is incapable of ostensive communication, then the predicate must apply to both, if to either, of any pair of indistinguishable objects. But it seems manifest that adjectives of colour, and many others, do precisely not involve any such further condition of correct application; on the contrary, ostensive training would appear fully determinant of their meaning—or, if it is not, it is the only training which we get. The governing view thus vindicates the observationality of colour predicates twice over: as a consequence both of our general conception of what justifies their application, and of the character of the training in their use which we receive.

The other question was to do with the scope of the phenomenon of non-transitive indiscriminability. Suppose that we are to construct a series of colour patches, ranging from red through to orange, among which indiscriminability is to behave transitively. We are given a supply of appropriate patches from which to make selections, an initial red patch, and the instruction that each successive patch must either match its predecessor or be more like it than is any other patch not matching it which we later use. Under these conditions it is plain that we cannot generate any change in colour by selecting successive matching patches; if indiscriminability is to be transitive, then if each patch in the first *n* selections matches its predecessor, the *n*th selection must match the first patch. The only way to generate a change in colour will be to select a non-matching patch.

When the series is complete, how will it look in comparison with the series of the fourth example? It is clear that we shall have lost what was distinctive of that series: the appearance of *continuous* change from red to orange. In the new series the shades are exemplified in discrete bands, containing perhaps no more than one patch, and all the changes take place abruptly in a transition from a patch to its successor. It thus appears that, were our judgements of indiscriminability to be universally transitive among samples of homogeneous colour, no field of colour patches could be ordered in the distinctive fashion now possible: i.e., so as to give the impression of a perfectly smooth change of colour. If matching generally behaved transitively among shades, no series of colour patches could give the impression of continuous transformation of colour; by contraposition, then, for matching to function non-transitively among a finite set of colour patches, it is sufficient that they may be arranged so as to strike us as forming a phenomenal continuum. This reasoning may obviously be generalized. Any finite series of objects, none of which involves any apparent change in respect of ϕ, may give an overall impression of continuous change in respect of ϕ only if indiscriminability functions non-transitively among its members.

The reasoning may in fact be generalized further. It can be shown (cf. Wright 1975) that the non-transitivity of our discriminations may be seen as a consequence of the continuity of change, viewed as a pervasive structural feature of our sense-experience. The general lesson of the fourth example is thus as follows. If we attempt to mark off regions of a seemingly continuous process of change in terms of predicates which are purely observational—predicates of which it is understood that ostensive definition gives their whole meaning—these expressions are bound to display tolerance in a suitable series of stages selected from the process. An analogue of the fourth example may thus in principle be constructed for any ostensively defined predicate; for absolutely anything which it characterizes might undergo seemingly continuous change to a point where it could be so characterized no longer. The fourth example indicates a basic fault, as it were, lying deep in the relation between the nature of our experience and those parts of language by means of which we attempt to give the most direct, non-theoretical expression to it.

This conclusion rests upon two assumptions: that it is right to regard the senses of colour predicates, etc., as purely observational; and that this is a very fundamental fact about their senses, whose sacrifice would be possible only at great cost. The governing view, as we have seen, yields the first assumption. For the second, however, no argument has so far been presented; I merely voiced concern that "contact" between language and the empirical world might be attenuated if the use of purely observational predicates was abandoned. Before this concern is evaluated, and the general implications assessed of stipulating away the tolerance, and so the observationality, of the relevant predicates, we must consider a general objection to the way in which all four examples have been treated.

4 If it is conceded that the vagueness of these examples is correctly interpreted as tolerance, then plainly no consistent logic does justice to the semantics of such predicates. It is natural to suggest, however, that the argument for this interpretation may have overlooked an essential feature of this sort of predicate: that they typically express distinctions of *degree*. There are degrees of redness, of childishness, and, if a smaller heap is regarded as less of a heap, of heaphood.

What is it for the distinction between being F and not being F to be one of degree? Typically, it is required that the comparatives, "is less/more F than", are in use and that iteration of one of these relations may transform something F into something not F, or vice versa. In addition, the semantic relations between the comparatives and the simple descriptions, "is F" and "is not F", are such that if a is less/more F than b, then the degree of justice with which a can be described simply as F is correlatively smaller or larger than that with which b can be so described. That is, a twofold classification of possible states of affairs into those which would justify the judgment, "a is F", and those which would not, misses what is distinctive about the predicate whose application is a matter of degree. For that to be so is exactly for there to be *degrees* of such justice.

It is thus plausible to suppose that a logic for distinctions of this sort cannot be based upon simple bivalence. With such predicates there are, as it were, degrees of truth, whose collective structure is that of the set of degrees of being F. In this sense it is arguable that the examples do require a special, non-classical logic. But how did the earlier arguments for the tolerance of these predicates overlook that they expressed distinctions of degree?

The suggestion is that the paradoxical reasoning essentially depends upon the constraints of bivalence. Consider a pair of objects one of which, a, we are happy to describe as F, while b is slightly less F than a. How is b to be described? If our admissible descriptions are restricted to "F" and "not F", if we *have* to say one or the other, then presumably we shall describe b as F. For if something is more like something F than something not *F*, to describe it as *F* is the less misleading of the two alternatives. But the justification with which "*F*" is applied in successive such cases successively decreases. We have no principle of the form: if *a* is *F*, and *b* differs sufficiently marginally from *a*, then *b* is *F*; with distinctions of degree there are no "small changes insufficient to affect the justice with which a predicate applies"; they are, on the contrary, small changes in the degree of justice with which the predicate may be applied. Of course, we do have the principle: if the judgment that *a* is *F* is justified to some large degree, and *b* is marginally less *F* than *a*, then the description of *b* as *F* will be better justified than its description as not *F*. But that is not a paradoxical principle.

Anyone who thinks he here feels the cool wind of sanity fanning his brow would do well to be clear why we do not still have *this* principle: if *b* is marginally less *F* than *a*, then if the less misleading description of *a* is "*F*", the less misleading description of *b* is "*F*". Yet if this principle is false, there must in any sorites-type series be a last case of which we are prepared to say that if we *had* to describe it either as *F* or as not *F*, the better description would be "*F*". Why, then, is it usually embarrassing to be asked to identify such a case without any sense of arbitrariness?

Let us assign to "*a* is *F*" a *designated* value just in case "*F*" is a less misleading description of *a* than "not *F*". Then our embarrassment is exactly to identify a last object to which the application of "*F*" would receive a designated value. But now the suspicion arises that tolerance is with us still; only it is no longer the *truth* of the application of "*F*" that would survive small changes but its designatedness.

Is this suspicion justified? One thing is clearly correct about the assumption of bivalence: faced with a situation and a predicate, we have only two choices—to apply or to withhold. There is not a series of distinct linguistic acts in which we can reflect every degree of justification with which a predicate may be applied. The crucial practical notion to be mastered for a predicate associated with the distinction of degree is thus that of a situation to which the application of the predicate is *on balance* justified. Without mastery of this notion no amount of information about the structure of variations in the degree with which "*F*" applies entails how the predicate is to be used. Now of this notion may it not still be a feature that it always survives sufficiently small changes?—that if *a* and *b* are dissimilar only to some very small extent, then if describing *a* as *F* is on balance justified, so is thus describing *b*?

It is clear that all the previous considerations will apply, and that the introduction of a complex structure of degrees of justification will get us no farther. For among these degrees we have still to distinguish those with which for practical purposes the application of the predicate is to be associated; otherwise we have not in repudiating bivalence done anything to replace the old connection between justified assertion and truth. But plainly, once we attempt to make such a distinction, the arguments afforded by the governing view sweep aside this proposed solution to the sorites paradox as an irrelevance. To rehearse the reasons: if we are to be able to *remember* how to apply *"F"*, then differences too slight to be remembered cannot transform a situation to which its application is on balance justified into one which is not so; if we are to be able to apply *"F"* just on the basis of *casual observation*, the same applies to differences too subtle to be detected by casual observation; if the distinction between cases to which the application of *"F"* is on balance justified and others is to be made just on the basis of how things look, or sound, etc., then any pair of indistinguishable situations must receive the same verdict; finally, if *"F"* is associated with moral or explanatory distinctions which we are unwilling to tie to very small changes, we shall likewise be unwilling to allow such changes to generate doubt about the status of a situation previously regarded as on balance justifying description as *F*. Of course the use here being made of the notion of a situation to which the application of *"F"* is "on balance" justified is quite uncritical. But this is legitimate. For, as remarked, there must be *some* such notion if a many-valued logic for distinctions of degree is to have any practical linguistic application.

5   Let us turn then to the question whether we could not eliminate, at not too heavy a cost, the tolerance of observational predicates. The resulting predicates would no longer be strictly observational; hence the initial doubt whether such a purified language could engage with the observational world at all. On reflection, though, it is clear that the dislocation of language and the world of appearance generated by such a purification would not have to be as radical as that. When three situations collectively provide a counter-example to the transitivity of indiscriminability, there is nothing occult in the circumstance that they do so. It is an observationally detectable difference between indiscriminable situations that one is distinguishable from a third situation from which the other is not; the relation, *"a* matches *b* matches *c* does not match *a"*, is an *observational relation*, i.e. one whose application to a trio of objects can be determined just by looking at them, listening to them, etc.

Observational concepts evidently require narrower criteria of reapplication than indistinguishability, if they are to be purified of tolerance. But we should not jump to the conclusion that to provide such criteria will require surrender of observationality altogether, for the phenomenon which is causing the trouble is itself observational. Indeed, the *only* kind of observationally detectable difference which there can be between indiscriminable items is that one should be distinguishable from some third item from which the other is not. So if the class of expressions in question is to remain in contact with observation, we have to look for some form of stipulation which *exploits* the non-transitivity of indistinguishability to provide a basis for describing indiscriminable situations differently. No other explanation can correspond to a distinction which sense-experience can determine to obtain, a distinction which we can simply be shown.

After such a stipulation, the question whether a pair of indiscriminable colour patches should receive the same colour description may turn on their respective relations of indiscriminability/discriminability with respect to some third patch. But now we have to take note of a striking aspect of the philosophical psychology of non-transitive matching: it does not seem to be possible to conduct experiments with non-transitively matching triads in *memory*. For suppose that a predicate, F, is defined ostensively by reference to some individual, a, which, it is noted at the time, perfectly matches another individual, c; it is understood that F is not to be applied to individuals which match a unless they also match c. Later the trainee comes across b which, so far as he can determine, matches a perfectly; the question is, does b match c? It is evident that the issue is only resoluble by direct comparison, and especially that it cannot be settled by memory, however accurate. For the most perfect memory of c can give no further information than that it looked just like a; which, when non-transitive matching is a possibility, is simply insufficient to determine whether it would match b. This, it must be emphasized, in contrast with our conclusions concerning the third example, is not a limitation imposed by the feebleness of our memories; it is a limitation of principle.

It thus appears that if we are to be able to exercise expressions whose application to matching individuals depends upon their behaviour in relation to a third, possibly differentiating individual, then we have to be able to ensure the *availability* of the third individual. Expressions of this species will be practicably applicable only in relation to a system of paradigms. So we can see, even in advance of attempting a specific stipulation to remove the tolerance of "red" as displayed in the fourth example, that the kind of semantic construction it will have to be is going to tie the application of expressions of colour to the use of a colour-chart.

Let us then consider, as a test case, how we might go about the construction of such a chart. What we require of the chart is that it should enable us to identify a last red patch in any series of the type of the fourth example. There is one obvious way to achieve this, namely to devise a single ad hoc paradigm. It is plausible to suppose that we could complete a colour-chart for the red/orange region at least in the sense that anything which we should wish to regard as falling within that region would match something on the chart. Consider, then, an arrangement of colour patches which form in this sense a complete colour-chart for the red/orange region and which are simply ordered by similarity, i.e. every patch on the chart more closely resembles its immediate neighbours than any other patches on the chart. Then a sharp red/orange distinction can be generated as follows. Select some patch towards the middle of the chart; then any colour patch matching something on the chart either matches the selected patch or it does not; if it does, it is red; if it does not, but matches a sample to the left of the selected patch, it is again red; otherwise, it is orange.

Naturally it could not be guaranteed that duplicates of this chart would always deliver the same verdict. Charts could look absolutely similar, and even satisfy the condition that the nth sample on either matched and was distinguishable from exactly the same samples on the other chart as its own nth sample, yet deliver discrepant results. But they would not often do so. Besides, the situation is not novel. Rulers, for example, sometimes give different results. A final criterion for one system is deposited in Paris; and we could do the same with a colour-chart.

Generalized, this proposal might seem quite ludicrous in practical terms. We are confronted with the spectacle of a people quite lost without their individual wheelbarrow loads of charts, tape-recordings, smell- and taste-samples and assorted sample surfaces. But this caricatures the proposal. There would be no need for all this portable semantic hardware. This is clear if we pursue the analogy with the use of rulers: it is true that, without a ruler, we can only guess at length; but after the introduction of an ad hoc paradigm for colours, the use of colour predicates will presumably be analogous not to that of expressions like "two feet long", but rather to that of expressions like "less than two feet long", i.e. expressions of a *range* of lengths. Of such expressions the criterion of application is still measurement; but unless the example is a peripheral one, we can tell *without* measuring what the outcome of measurement would be. Training in the use of paradigms might be essential if one is to grasp the sense of such expressions; but, once grasped, most cases of practical application could be decided without the use of paradigms—for most practical purposes, the wheelbarrow could be left behind.

It would appear, then, that if we adopted such stipulations as a general strategy, it would not have to affect our use of observational language very much at all. At present we can tell of anything red that it is so just by looking at it. This would still usually be true after the proposed stipulation; and if the new distinction was suitably located, cases where it was not true would in general coincide with borderline-cases of the old red/orange distinction. The use of predicates so refined could thus greatly resemble their present use; the distinctions which they expressed would be empirically decidable; and there would be one crucial disanalogy—they would be tolerance-free.

It is apparent that exactly parallel considerations may be brought to bear upon the earlier treatment of the first and third examples. Even after a precise re-definition of "heap", we would be able to learn to tell in most cases just by casual observation what verdict the new criterion would give if applied; it would seldom be necessary actually to count the grains. And the distinction between red and orange, supposing an exact distinction were drawn by means of a chart, would be unmemorable only within that small range of shades which could not by unaided memory be distinguished from the last red sample. It would thus appear that the cost of eliminating tolerance in cases of these two types need not after all be high, since we could expect to be able to tell in general just by looking at, etc., an item on which side of the dividing line it would fall.

If there need, after all, be no substantial sacrifice in endowing formerly observational predicates with exact boundaries, what has become of the alleged profound tension between phenomenal continuity and language designed to express how things seem to us? The answer, of course, is that it has simply been swept under the carpet. The possibility of our dispensing with paradigms for most practical purposes depends upon our capacity e.g. to distinguish between cases where we could tell whether or not "red" applied just by looking and cases where we could not, where we should have recourse to a chart. But if we are able to make such a distinction, there can be no objection to introducing a predicate to express it. And then, it seems, the semantics of *this* predicate will have to be observational. On what other basis should we decide whether something looks as though comparison with a chart would determine it to be red than how it looks? Of any pair of colour patches which look exactly alike, if either looks as though the chart would deliver the verdict "red", both must. So the new predicate, introduced to reflect our capacity to make this distinction, will be applicable to both members of any pair of matching colour-samples, if to either.

It is not that there is any compelling reason to have such a predicate; only that there is no reason not to. If we were sometimes able to tell without using a chart whether something was red, it would surely be possible to make intelligible to us a predicate designed to apply in just such circumstances. So it transpires that a language all of whose observational concepts were based on paradigms would avoid containing tolerant predicates only by not containing means of expression of all the observational distinctions which we are in fact able to make. The dispensability of the wheelbarrow requires the exercise of observational concepts.

It would of course be absurd to propose that the tolerance of such new predicates—"looks as though it would lie to the left of the last red shade", "looks as though it contains fewer than ten thousand grains", etc.—might in turn be stipulated away. Their meaning will not permit it; it cannot be allowed of things which look exactly alike that one may look as though it satisfies some condition which the other looks as though it does not, unless how a thing looks may not be determined by looking. The earlier discussion of the first and third examples involved an over-estimation of our interest in preserving the tolerance of the predicates involved only if we possess a coherent understanding of these new predicates; if the first and third examples do not, after all, pose a substantial problem for the governing view, it is because of our capacity to handle expressions falling within the scope of the fourth example.

6 Let us, then, finally review the character of the difficulty for the governing view which originates in the fourth example.

It is a fundamental fact about us that we can learn to classify items according to their appearance, that we are able, consistently as it seems to us, to apply or to withhold descriptions just on the basis of how things strike the senses. In a discrete phenomenal world, there would be no special difficulty—no difficulty not inherent in the idea of a semantic rule as such—in viewing our use of such expressions as essentially nothing but the following of rules of which it was a consequence that indiscriminable phenomena should receive the same description. But if mutually exclusive use is made of a pair of such predicates, and if cases to which one applies permit of continuous transformation into cases where the other applies, it cannot be correct to represent the use made of either predicate just as the doing of what is required by a set of rules with such a consequence. Yet we are forced—if the relevance is allowed of considerations to do with what we should regard as adequate explanation of such expressions, or with certain criteria which we should accept of misunderstanding such an expression—to attribute to the rules governing these predicates precisely such an implication; and *all* the phenomena which we confront in our world are in principle capable of seemingly continuous variation.

It will not quite do, though, to present the difficulty as that of the inadequacy of any inconsistent set of rules to explain a consistent pattern of behaviour. To begin with, it is unclear how far our use of e.g. the vocabulary of colours *is* consistent. The descriptions given of awkward cases may vary from occasion to occasion. Besides that, the notion of using a predicate consistently would appear to require some objective criteria for variation in relevant respects among items to be described in terms of it; but what is distinctive about observational predicates is exactly the lack of such criteria. So we may not lean too heavily, as though it were a matter of hard fact, upon the consistency of our employment of colour predicates. The point rather has to do with the fact that our use of these predicates is largely *successful*; the expectations which we form on the basis of others' ascriptions of colour are not usually disappointed. Agreement is generally possible about how colours are to be described; which is equivalent to saying that others *seem* to use colour predicates in a largely consistent way.

It is this fact of which the governing view can provide no account. A semantic rule is supposed to contribute towards determining what is an admissible use of its associated expression. The picture evoked by the first thesis of the governing view is that there is, for any particular expression in the language, a set of such rules *completely* determinant of when the expression is used correctly; such a set thus provides a model of the information of which a master of the use of the expression may be deemed to be in possession. Clearly, however, the feasibility of such a picture requires that the rules associated with an expression, about whose use we generally agree, be consistent. For if they issue conflicting verdicts upon the correctness of a particular application of the expression, it cannot be explained just by appeal to the rules why we agree that the application is e.g. correct.

The problem presented for the first thesis by the occurrence of tolerant predicates, or of any kind of semantically incoherent expression, is not that, in a clear-cut way, nothing can be done to implement an inconsistent set of instructions. Strictly, of course, anything that is done will conflict with a part of them. But we can imagine a game whose rules conflict, but which is nevertheless regularly and enjoyably played to a conclusion by members of some community because, for perhaps quite fortuitous reasons, whenever an occasion arises to appeal to the rules, the players concur about which element in the rules is to be appealed to, so that an impasse never comes about. We need not enquire whether they have noticed the inconsistency in the rules. The point of the analogy is that in practice they always agree whether a move is admissible, as we generally agree whether something is red. The analogue of the first thesis in relation to this example is the notion that the rules completely determine when a particular move is admissible. But while it may be true that the authority of the rules can be cited for any of the moves the community actually make, it is plain that the rules alone do not provide a satisfactory account of the practice of the game. For someone could master the rules yet still not be able to join in the game, because he was unable to guess what sort of eclectic application of them an opponent was likely to make in relation to any given move.

An outsider attempting to grasp our use of a tolerant predicate would presumably not encounter exactly this difficulty; it would be clear that we were not prepared to allow remote consequences of its tolerance, inferred by means of reasoning of the sorites type. The difficulty of principle for the first thesis, however, is the same. The rules of the game cannot provide an account of how the game is played, for it is possible that someone might grasp them yet be unable to participate. The semantic rules for an expression are supposed to provide an account of its correct use; they cannot do so if someone whose use of it differed radically from ours could still be thought of as in possession of exactly the same brief—as he can be, if it consists in an inconsistent set of instructions.

What, then, have we learned? The comparison of language with a game is an extremely natural one. What better explanation could there be of our ability to agree in our use of language than if, as in a game, we are playing by the same rules? We are thus attracted towards the assimilation of our situation to that of people to whom the practice of a highly ramified, complex game has been handed down via many generations, but of which the theory has been lost. Our central task, as philosophers of language, is to work towards the recovery of such a theory: a theory which will explain the mechanism of our recognition of the senses of new complex expressions by displaying them as functions of the senses of their constituents and their mode of combination, which will explicate our apprehension of valid inferences—which, in short, will explicate the overall character of our mastery of the language game. What we have learned is that we probably cannot combine this conception of what a theory of meaning should accomplish with the notion that the investigation is something which, as masters of the language in question, we are better placed to carry out than an observer of our practice. We have to avoid appeal, at any rate, to a range of considerations which it is our antecedent prejudice to consider must be relevant: considerations to do with what we should deem a proper explanation of the sense of an expression, the criteria which we should employ for determining that someone misunderstands it, what we use the expression for, i.e., what issues turn on its application, the limitations imposed by our senses and memories on the information which we can absorb from our linguistic training, and our general conception of what justifies the application of the expression. And what privilege do we enjoy in the quest for a theory of meaning which an observer of our usage does not, if all these traditionally accepted guidelines for sense are dismissed?

But we have seen that we must dismiss them if we want a coherent account of the senses of vague expressions. The methodological approach to *these* expressions, at any rate, must be more purely behaviouristic and anti-reflective, if a general theory of meaning is to be possible at all.

11   Truth, belief and vagueness

Kenton F. Machina

When Jones believes that Horatio planted petunias in the garden yesterday, and Smith shares this belief, then there is something which both Smith and Jones believe. The most convenient name I can think of for the thing which both believe is "proposition". And since I think all of us have many beliefs, I also think there are many propositions, at least some of which are believed by at least one of us. Of course, it is nothing philosophically new to cast propositions in the role of objects of belief, disbelief, and various other so-called "propositional attitudes". Moreover, if Jones, or anyone else for that matter, believes that Horatio planted petunias in the garden yesterday, it would be unreasonable for Jones to deny that Horatio planted petunias. It would be unreasonable because obviously Jones' belief logically implies that Horatio planted petunias, even though logicians may dispute about the formalities of this implication. This illustrates the point that the propositions which can serve as the objects of belief (or of propositional attitudes in general) have logical implications, and also are implied by propositions which in turn can be the objects of propositional attitudes. Thus, the very same propositions which serve as the objects for propositional attitudes *also* serve as subject matter for logic, although the preceding considerations leave open the possibility that the class of propositions dealt with in logic is wider than the class of possible objects for propositional attitudes of people. (Some propositions included in the subject matter of logic, for example, may be too complex to be believed by any person.)

Logic, then, has at least the task of providing an account of the implications of and the various other logical relations between our beliefs, our disbeliefs, and the objects of our other propositional attitudes. (In addition, if there are propositions not subject to being objects of such attitudes, logic will also deal with them.) Because the set of propositions which logic must handle includes those propositions which real people actually believe in their day-to-day lives, logic must be prepared to deal with vague propositions, for people often have vague beliefs. This is not to say that in order to fulfill its mission to handle vague propositions

From *Journal of Philosophical Logic* 5 (1976) pp 47–78 © Kluwer Academic Publishers. Reprinted by permission

logic itself must become vague. (The study of dead civilizations need not itself be dead.) But in order to deal with vague propositions, traditional logic does have to be generalized, since traditional logic is designed to handle only precise propositions; it thus cuts itself off from telling us about the logical relations between the propositions we actually believe most of the time. The purpose of this paper is to provide a philosophical discussion of the issues involved in the generalization of traditional logic. The paper is accessible to those with a background in elementary model theory.

When I say that ordinary beliefs are often vague, I do not mean the linguistic expression which may be given the belief by the believer, or an onlooker, is ambiguous—i.e., possessed of multiple senses, or characterized by indeterminacy of reference due to the existence of competing candidates to serve in the role of referents for some of the referring expressions in the linguistic expression. If I say Jones believes Horatio planted petunias in the garden yesterday, my utterance may very well be ambiguous, in that there may be more than one Horatio, or there may be several gardens of which I might be speaking. But such ambiguity does not cause any peculiar difficulties for classical theory of inference so far as I can see, although it is both interesting and difficult to handle in doing formal semantics. In any case, ambiguity is not what I mean by vagueness.

Jones' belief about Horatio might not be very specific, either. He may not have any particular belief about the tools used by Horatio, or the time of day at which the planting was done. But this lack of specific detail in Jones' belief is not vagueness, in the sense in which I mean to use the term. Again, no peculiar problems for classical logic seem to arise from the generality or lack of specificity characterizing some beliefs. So long as there is a determinate range of facts which would make the belief true or false, were any of the facts in this range to obtain, the belief is precise, for my purposes. The vagueness of belief which requires that classical logic be generalized is the vagueness which results in indeterminacy with respect to the truth conditions for the belief; so that for each vague belief (or any other vague proposition) the range of possible facts which would make that belief (or proposition) true were these facts to obtain is at least somewhat indeterminate. This means that for each vague proposition there are possible worlds in which the proposition's truth value is in some way peculiar, or indeterminate, or lacking entirely. It is this sort of vagueness which characterizes most of our beliefs, and which requires changes be made in logic in order to allow logic to deal with the properties and relations of vague propositions.

For example, classical logic insists on the principle of bivalence: any given proposition is either simply true or simply false, but not both.

However, Jones' belief that Horatio planted petunias in the garden yesterday fails to satisfy the principle of bivalence, because there are many conceivable circumstances in which the belief is neither simply true nor simply false. Suppose Horatio's idea of planting petunias is to soak the intended flower bed and then throw the baby petunia plants onto the top of the soil where they are allowed to lie untouched and unimplanted. Some of them may even survive and grow, if the next few days are cloudy and Horatio pours on the water. I for one, though, do not think it simply true under these circumstances that Horatio planted petunias in the garden yesterday. Nor simply false. The number of such peculiar but possible cases seems limited only by the power of one's imagination. Surely there does not exist a simple "yes" or "no" answer in each such case to the question, "True?", asked of Jones' belief.

The classical logician, wishing to preserve hallowed traditions, may quite naturally try to come to the rescue of bivalence, perhaps with a speech proclaiming that whether Horatio succeeded in planting petunias in our imagined case above depends on what concept of *planting* is relevant. The difficulty with this speech is that it is *Jones'* concept of planting that is relevant, and Jones' concept of planting is vague—provided Jones is like the rest of us—with the result that one probably cannot settle the question whether Horatio planted by looking at Jones' concept of planting. (Of course, the question *could* be settled that way if Jones' concept of planting definitely does or definitely does not include Horatio's actions, but then there will be other cases for which Jones' concept of planting provides no ready answer.)

In short and in sum, there is no reason to suppose that once one has gotten clear about Jones' concepts, and the context of Jones' coming to believe that Horatio would do his bit to beautify the world, and anything or everything else about Jones that could possibly be relevant, then one will always have information which will determine a unique, old-fashioned truth value for the proposition Jones believes. That proposition does not relate to the detailed facts of the world in a neat two-valued way. It cannot, therefore, be formally represented as a function from possible worlds to old-fashioned truth values. Nor can it be thought of as a fully detailed, fleshed-out "state of affairs", such as, e.g., Horatio Van Alstanwine III planted$_5$ petunias$_2$ fully within the outermost boundaries of a plot of ground located ... between 12 midnight, April 23, 1975, and 12 midnight, April 24, 1975.[1] Jones does not believe the things which can be represented in these ways, because Jones' belief is not nearly so precise. So long as logic is thought to deal

---

1. This is intended as a parody of sorts on the kind of account of propositions given by Chisholm. Cf., e.g., Chisholm 1971, pp. 24–26.

only with such precise propositions, logic will not be able to treat of many of the objects of propositional attitudes.

Since many of the propositions people believe are not bivalent, it is important to discover what becomes of such propositions when they are neither simply true nor simply false. The most elegant view would seem to be that in such a case they are lacking a truth value entirely. I say this view is elegant, because if one adopts it, one need not try making sense of the idea that there are more than two truth values.

Thomason, Fine, and van Fraassen at least have indicated sympathy for handling vague propositions in this elegant way.[2] Their move is made formally by using supervaluations.[3] Roughly, the idea is that a vague proposition's truth value is its supervaluation, which is a function of the proposition's tentative classical valuations. Each different tentative classical valuation is the ordinary classical truth value the proposition would have if it were made precise in some particular way, so as to rule out all borderline cases. For each way of making the proposition precise, we get a new tentative classical valuation for that proposition, indicating whether the proposition as newly interpreted is true or is false. If *every* way of making the proposition precise makes the proposition classically true, all the tentative classical valuations will be true, for that proposition. If every precise version of the proposition is false, all the tentative classical valuations are false. Otherwise, we get a mixture of tentative valuations. The supervaluation of the original vague proposition is then said to be truth just in case all the tentative classical valuations are true; false if and only if all the tentative valuations are false; and undefined otherwise. Thus, on this view a vague proposition is true just in case all ways of making it precise are true propositions, false just in case all precise versions of it are false, and neither true nor false otherwise. When the proposition is neither true

---

2   Thomason and van Fraassen in conversation and unpublished essays. Kit Fine in Fine, this volume Cf Lewis 1970 Fine argues that any approach such as the one I take will fail to capture the "penumbral connections" between vague predicates. By a "penumbral connection" he means a logical relation, such as contrariety I think Fine is right to say even vague predicates have logical relations to one another, and that it is important to insist, as he does, that an adequate logic of vagueness capture such relations, or at least not rule them out. But I believe it is not at all obvious that the penumbral connections on which he builds his case against the sort of theory I hold really exist E g , he claims that "red" and "pink", even though vague and admitting of borderline cases of applicability, are nevertheless logically connected so that to say of some color shade that it is both red and pink is obviously to say something false. I must confess being completely insensitive to that intuition of a penumbral connection.

3   Cf van Fraassen 1968 for an account of supervaluations in another context

nor false it has no truth value at all. On this view, Jones' belief about Horatio's petunia planting would presumably be neither true nor false under the circumstances described earlier, since some ways of making Jones' belief precise would render the belief false while others would render the belief true.

One presumed advantage of the supervaluation approach is that the theorems of classical logic remain logically true when interpreted as outlined above, since these theorems will always all be true on every tentative classical valuation. Whether this feature of the supervaluation approach is in fact an advantage or a disadvantage I suppose might be questioned. My own intuitions happen to run counter to claiming that the law of noncontradiction, for example, is always completely true. But I will not press that line here, for a battle of raw intuitions is liable to bore onlookers.

Instead, I think it more fruitful to point out that Tarski's convention (T) would appear to favor a more radical approach to vague propositions. Applying (T) to our gardening example yields what seems to be an obvious truth:

(1) "Horatio planted petunias in the garden yesterday" is true if and only if Horatio planted petunias in the garden yesterday.

(1) can be abbreviated as

(2) $T(Q)$ if and only if P

where "Q" is a name of the sentence whose quotation-name appears in (1), and "P" is an abbreviation for that sentence. If Q lacks a truth value entirely, as it may on the supervaluation approach, or on any other approach which denies truth values to vague propositions,

(3) "$T(Q)$" is (out-and-out) false

because

(4) Q has no truth value.

Treating "if and only if" in (2) and (1) as material equivalence will allow us to infer

(5) Q is false

from (2) and (3). But surely (4) and (5) are incompatible. That is, on this interpretation of (2), we cannot allow (4). It looks as if we must give up Tarski's (T) as applied in (1) if we are to allow vague propositions to lack truth value.

However, in such matters it pays to be cautious. One might read the "if and only if" in (2) and (1) to mean that the truth of "$T(Q)$" in some sense necessitates the truth of Q (i.e., the truth of "P"), and the truth of

"P" (i.e., Q) in the same way necessitates the truth of "T(Q)".[4] Then, from (2) and (3) it would follow that Q is not true (for if it were, "T(Q)" would be true as well, contrary to (3)); but proving that Q is not true does not amount to proving that Q is false (i.e., does not amount to proving (5)).

Nevertheless, there will still be trouble, even on the new reading of (2) and (1). Consider what happens if we assume (2), (3), and (4) are completely and unproblematically true, as they ought to be on the supervaluation approach. In addition, we perversely assume that Horatio planted petunias in the garden yesterday. I.e., we assume

(6)   P.

(2) under the present interpretation tells us, among other things, that if "P" is true, "T(Q)" is bound to be true as well. Hence, (2) warrants the inference from (6) to

(7) $T(Q)$

and, similarly, from (7) to

(8) $T(T(Q))$

which clearly contradicts (3). Thus, we cannot allow both (3) and (6) if we want to keep (2). This much might seem obvious, and unproblematic, since (3) and (6) are intuitively incompatible.

Operating classically, we could go on to conclude that from (2) and (3) we would obtain

(9) $\sim P$

by indirect proof. This lands us in hot water. Suppose we take the plunge. From (9) we get

(10) $T(R)$

where "R" is a name of "$\sim P$"; but (10) is presumably definitionally equivalent to (5), which is still incompatible with (4). This would show the supervaluation approach to be incompatible with Tarski's convention (T), if we were allowed to infer (9) by indirect proof. But the supervaluation approach cannot allow the validity of indirect proof in general. On that approach, a valid argument leading to a contradiction does lead to a clearly false conclusion, but that merely shows not all the premises in the argument are true. It may be the untrue premises aren't false, either, for they may lack a value entirely. If they do lack a truth value, so do their negations. Hence, one ought not infer (9) as we did.

But is this rejection of indirect proof rationally justified when dealing with vagueness? The rejection does show the supervaluation approach

<hr>

4   This reading is due to van Fraassen 1968

to be less classical than it might at first appear, for even though it preserves all the classical tautologies, it does not preserve all the classical rules of inference. I would prefer a logic of vagueness which would allow the inference to (9) once (8) and (3) are seen to be completely incompatible. I.e., it seems very desirable to adopt a view of logical consequence which has it that whenever a set of premises, S, together with some additional proposition, Φ, has as logical consequence two completely incompatible propositions, Ψ and Δ, then S has $\sim\Phi$ as a logical consequence. I can see that in a somewhat different context, when Ψ and Δ are vague propositions whose truth values are in some doubt, the inference to $\sim\Phi$ may not be warranted, since in such a context Ψ and Δ may not be completely incompatible. But in the case at hand, involving the inference from the incompatibility of (8) and (3) to the assertion (9), we have a case of *complete* incompatibility, on the supervaluation account.[5] And thus in the case at hand, the supervaluation approach (as well as any other approach which denies truth values to vague propositions) runs afoul of what seem to be reasonable requirements on what can count as valid inferences. Accordingly, I urge we search for another approach which will allow us to interpret the connective in (2) as material equivalence and which will preserve the limited version of indirect proof described above as being reasonable.

There may at this point seem to be nowhere left to go. We abandoned bivalence earlier. Now we are prohibited from denying truth values to vague propositions. There is, however, one alternative left to the stout-hearted: vague propositions must take on unusual truth values when they fail to have the usual truth or falsehood as values.

Such unusual truth values might conveniently be thought of as degrees of truth and falsehood, so that when Horatio throws the petunias on the soggy ground and floods them with water it is more true to say Horatio planted petunias than it would have been were Horatio to dump the petunias in the garbage can and go off to sun himself at the beach. This approach has been advocated by several authors—notably, the mathematicians Zadeh and Goguen—and is the one for which I am attempting to provide adequate motivation.[6]

Perhaps if one is firmly tied to a correspondence theory of truth, the notion of degrees of truth will not ring any more strangely than the notion of degrees of correspondence—the latter notion surely being at

---

5 It seems to me that even if one does not approve of the unrestricted use of reductio to draw "irrelevant" conclusions from a set of premises, one could still approve its use in the present instance where relevance is not a problem

6 Zadeh 1965 and Goguen 1969 Cf. also Machina 1972 for a fuller argument that there are vague propositions and for a modification of the Goguen semantics for a first-order logic of vagueness.

least moderately intelligible. On such a view, propositions may be formally represented as functions from possible worlds to the new, improved truth set containing as many truth values as one needs to deal with the logical phenomena. And we can represent Jones' believings in the most straightforward way as instances of the believing relation, holding between Jones and various propositions most of which are vague.

In outline, then, I want to allow for inversely variant degrees of truth and falsehood in vague propositions, with the classical truth values representing complete truth and complete falsehood. Although my inclinations in this matter are at least verbally in agreement with the common sense view that some beliefs are "truer" than others, that agreement cannot be taken at face value as an indication that the common man thinks of degrees of truth in the same way I do. The everyday assertion that P is truer than Q can in fact mean many different things. It might mean that P is more epistemically certain than Q. Or, that although P and Q are both really false, P is somewhat more accurate than Q. This probably means that the state of affairs which would make P true, were that state to obtain, is more similar to the actual state of affairs in the world than is the state of affairs which would make Q true were that state to obtain. It is important to distinguish these ordinary ways of talking about degrees of truth from the way of talking about degrees of truth which I wish to adopt. The conception of degrees of truth which is relevant in dealing with vagueness, and which could serve as a useful notion in logic when characterizing validity of argument forms, tautologous sentence forms, and the like, is *not* an *epistemic* notion like degrees of certainty; nor is it to be used to award consolation prizes to statements that really are false. E.g., since some crows are not in fact black, "All crows are black" will be considered just plain false on my view, even though *most* crows are black, and people might commonly say the statement is "nearly" true.

But if a proposition is true *only* to a degree (i.e., not fully), then it seems that it must also be *false* to at least some degree, since to whatever extent the proposition fails to correspond fully with the way the world is that proposition is false. In application to our petunia planting example, it would seem there are many actions which Horatio could perform which are not full-fledged, clear examples of petunia planting, but yet are not full-fledged, clear examples of failure to plant petunias, either. So when we say it is only to some degree true that Horatio planted petunias, we shall not mean that Horatio simply *failed* to plant petunias, but came close; we shall mean instead that to some degree he succeeded in planting petunias, and to some degree he failed. And if we say that it is true only to some degree that this color chip is red, we shall *not* mean the color chip is simply not red, but comes close to being red; we shall mean instead that the chip really is somewhat red.

The task now before us then is to discuss the foundations of a many-valued logic in which the various values are to be construed as degrees of truth or falsity as outlined above. Of course, a large number of many-valued formal logical systems already exist. But the bare many-valuedness of a system provides no guarantee the system is suitable for the purposes at hand. We need to consider what conditions ought to be met by a logical system suitable for our purposes.

One limitation on the system which may be laid down at the outset is almost dictated by the fact that vague propositions sometimes take the classical truth values (now thought of as "complete truth" and "complete falsehood"), and when they do, the usual classical treatment will be just as acceptable for them as it is for precise propositions. I have no desire to quarrel here with the classical treatment of the usual truth-functional connectives, even though there are some cases in which such connectives clearly fail to provide adequate representations of connectives in a natural language such as English. (I have in mind, e.g., the failure of classical logic to provide an adequate treatment of the non-truth-functional connective, "because".) There is no reason to suppose a generalization of classical logic adequate to deal with vagueness should also thereby become adequate to deal with connectives in natural language which are non-truth-functional even when flanked by precise propositions. Hence, I will require for the sake of simplicity that the logic of vagueness be *normal*, in the sense that the sentential connectives shall be defined in such a way that when operating on propositions with classical values they yield propositions with the usual classical values. The normality requirement rules out, for example, a negation operator which when applied to a (completely) true proposition yields a proposition which is something besides (completely) false. To this extent, anyway, the logic we want is truth-functional.

We may now go on to ask whether our desired logical system is *entirely* truth-functional with regard to its sentential connectives. I find this a very difficult question to settle decisively, although I shall argue for the truth-functional approach. In this regard, too, the system I favor differs from that advocated in the supervaluation method. From the point of view of supervaluation theory, the truth value of a complex formula in the sentential calculus is a function of the tentative classical valuations of the complex formula taken as a whole. Each tentative classical valuation is, of course, truth-functional. But the resulting supervaluations are not. E.g., "$p \vee \sim p$" is true on each tentative classical valuation; hence any proposition of this form has truth for its supervalue as well—all of this despite the possibility that the proposition substituted for "*p*" may itself lack a (super) truth value entirely, being vague. In point of truth-functionality, then, the approach I advocate is more classical than the theory generated by supervaluations, but this similarity to the classical position does not by itself constitute an argument for the appropriateness of treating the sentential connectives truth-functionally.[7]

It does not seem entirely clear at the outset whether, say, a formula of the form "*p* & *q*" should always find its value from the values of "*p*" and "*q*", even when "*p*" or "*q*" have intermediate values. For, what do we say about an expression of the form "*p* & ~*p*" when "*p*" is "half" true? After all, both conjuncts are true to a degree. Does that mean that contradictions can be "half" true, as wholes? If we take the truth-functional approach, it seems we shall be committed to the partial truth of some contradictions. On the other hand, if we were willing to give up truth-functionality, we could insist that in the case of a contradiction, even though both conjuncts are true to a degree, nevertheless the whole formula is completely false, because the conjuncts are not logically independent of one another. One might be reminded here of probability theory, in which the conjunction of two events, *A* and *B*, each having probability greater than 0 and less than 1, may nevertheless have probability 0 when *A* and *B* are mutually exclusive events.

Similar questions may be raised with respect to the law of the excluded middle, "*p* ∨ ~*p*", when neither "*p*" nor "~*p*" is completely true or completely false. In such a case, the truth-functional approach demands that "*p* ∨ ~*p*" be treated just like any other formula of the form "*p* ∨ *q*". So it would seem that the most natural sort of truth-functional definitions of the connectives "∨" and "&" in our multi-valued logic are likely to result in the loss of both the law of noncontradiction and the law of the excluded middle. Indeed, this is exactly what happens in the logic for which I shall argue. I take it that the loss of these laws may seem initially to be a sufficient ground for rejecting my approach; my strategy will be to try to make the loss seem appropriate and welcome. It happens that one can give up these laws without destroying logic; in fact in a sense it even turns out that these laws are preserved in the system to be described below—although they will not be always completely true, they will always be at least half true.

Of course, in designing a formal multi-valued logic of vague propositions there is nothing to prevent us from defining some truth-

---

7 One need not use supervaluations to ground a non-truth-functional logic of vagueness David Sanford adopts a unique approach to the development of such a system in Sanford 1975

functional connectives which we may choose capriciously to call "and", "or", etc. But what we really want is to define these connectives in such a way that they work as good symbolizations of logical functions actually employed in our vague speaking. So the issue is whether a truth-functional "and", or "or", or whatever, will be useful as a tool in adequately symbolizing complex vague propositions. And this issue is to be settled here in the same way it is settled in classical logic, by appeal to our understanding of the truth conditions for various sorts of complex propositions. But it is well-known that the classical sentential logic connectives do not all fit their English counterparts well. There are all sorts of difficulties about causal "if ... then" propositions, for example. I do not intend to solve any of these problems here. Rather, I have the more modest aim of providing the foundations for a logic of vague propositions which will handle them as well as classical first-order predicate logic handles precise propositions. My contention is that a truth-functional approach will do this job, even though in a sense we have to give up noncontradiction and the excluded middle in the process.

Consider negation first, because it seems clearest. I do not know of any reason why one would want negation to operate in anything but a truth-functional way in a logic of vagueness. There are, however, several different truth-functions which one might allow to play the role of negation. Of these the most natural have it that as "p" gets truer, "$\sim p$" gets falser, and vice versa, with the values of "p" and "$\sim p$" more or less equal when "p" is about half true. It is just such a notion of negation which caused the trouble over noncontradiction and the excluded middle above, and it is just such a notion of negation which I wish to adopt.

Consider conjunction next, taking Jones' belief about Horatio once again for an example. We want to say Jones' vague belief is not completely true, but neither is it completely false. For the same reasons I should think it natural to say the negation of Jones' belief is neither out-and-out true nor out-and-out false. If you will, Jones' belief is true to some extent and also false to some extent. Similarly, for the negation of Jones' belief. It should by now be clear that in so characterizing Jones' belief, or its negation, I am not thereby trying to say part of the proposition he believes is true and part of it is false. Nor that in some respect, or in some sense, or at some time it is true, and in some other respect, sense, or time it is false. I.e., I am carefully avoiding those common misunderstandings of the law of noncontradiction which lead people to suppose the law false for bad reasons. I am trying to indicate, instead, that Jones' belief and its negation are both neither completely true nor completely false in the same respect, in the same sense, at the same time. Ontologically, I suppose this means there is not a relation of planting, not even a determinable as opposed to a determinate one, which Jones believes Horatio to stand in with respect to the petunias. For, if there were such a relation, I should think that Horatio would either stand in it with respect to the petunias, or not, as the case might be. Rather, what is going on here is that there are *many* properties and relations having to do with Horatio's actions vis-à-vis the petunias—all of which are relevant to the truth value of Jones' belief. And that belief on this occasion is constructed in such a way that these properties and relations do not all add up to something definitely falling within, or without, Jones' concept of petunia planting. This can happen because that concept does not pick out a precisely bounded set of such properties and relations which would then constitute petunia planting. Instead, a fairly indefinite range of such properties and relations is included under the concept, so that troublesome cases like the one under consideration can arise.

Given this understanding of the truth conditions for Jones' belief, it seems quite reasonable to say that Horatio to some extent planted petunias in the garden yesterday and that to some extent he did not plant petunias in the garden yesterday, in the same respect, in the same sense, and at the same time. The most reasonable thing to say in this case, then, seems to me to be that Horatio to some extent both planted and did not plant petunias in the garden yesterday. Given our understanding of degrees of truth it then becomes reasonable to say the proposition that Horatio planted and did not plant petunias in the garden yesterday is at least partially true. To deny Horatio to some extent did both seems unreasonable. In other words, a truth-functional definition of "&" in our logic will give us just the sort of result we want, since it now seems to be an essential characteristic of a vague proposition that a contradiction consisting of the proposition and its negation can be partially true.

This argument for allowing contradictions to be at least partially true does not work at all if one supposes that "degrees of truth" merely represent degrees of epistemic certainty. If the *only* issue here were lack of certainty, one might well insist that even though no one *knows* whether Horatio planted those petunias, nevertheless he either did or did not succeed in doing the requisite planting, but not both. If that were the case the proposition that he both planted and did not plant would be plainly false, although no one would know which conjunct was true and which false. One would not want truth-functionality in a "logic" whose "truth values" represented degrees of epistemic certainty.

Similarly, one would not want truth-functionality if the "truth values" represented the truth values a proposition could have if it were made precise, as we noted earlier in the discussion of supervaluations.

It should be clear by now that the truth values which will appear in the system advocated here represent neither degrees of epistemic certainty nor the results of evaluating propositions after having made them more precise in various ways.

We turn to disjunction next. I wish to treat disjunction in the same way as conjunction—i.e., truth-functionally—for reasons quite parallel to those offered in favor of the truth-functionality of conjunction. As noted earlier, this approach immediately calls into question the law of the excluded middle, since a partially true "*p*" yields a partially true "*~p*", so that "*p* ∨ *~p*" has neither disjunct completely true in such a case, with the result that it is hard to see how "*p* ∨ *~p*" could be completely true on a truth-functional interpretation of "∨". In fact, I do want to claim that in such a case, the value of "*p* ∨ *~p*" is an intermediate, or nonclassical one. So there will be propositions of the form "*p* ∨ *~p*" which are not completely true. But as it turns out, there will not be any that are more than half-way false. So we will have a law of the more or less excluded middle.

Given the truth-functionality of negation, conjunction, and disjunction it seems pointless to argue whether we ought to include a truth-functional analog of classical material implication in our logic. We already know that material implication does not correspond well to the English "if ... then" precisely because the English is non-truth-functional whereas material implication is truth-functional. Material implication in classical logic merely represents the best truth-functional way to handle many "if ... then" propositions (ignoring the effects of vagueness). We shall try for something similar in our logic, leaving the questions of better non-truth-functional representations of "if ... then" to another time, since these questions seem to have nothing special to do with vagueness. The details will be developed below along with the precise definitions of "*~*", "*&*", and "*∨*".

I hope the preceding discussion has showed that those logical notions which are truth-functional for precise propositions as in classical logic are also truth-functional in the logic of vagueness, and that we might expect vague propositions to be just about as adequately symbolized in our logic of vagueness with its truth-functional connectives as precise propositions are in classical first-order logic.

We now have formulated two restrictions which any formal logic will have to meet in order to be suitable for our purposes: 1) normality, and 2) truth-functionality. There are of course many different systems which fulfill both 1) and 2). I wish now to consider further restrictions which ought to be placed on the system we want.

It would be nice to know something more precise about the set of truth values which our propositions can have. So far we have merely talked vaguely about "more true", "less true", and so on, and have assumed that the truth set has cardinality greater than or equal to three. Now, if we were to choose a truth set with only three elements, there would not be any chance to accurately represent situations in which a number of borderline cases arrange themselves in a natural ordering with respect to the degree to which they are F's. We would simply have to say that all the borderline cases of an F are in the same truth-boat— i.e., to say of any one of them that it is an F is to say something with the one and only nonclassical truth value. In fact it is conceivable that we shall at times have a continuum of borderline cases with respect to some predicate F, and that to identify the degree to which any one of them is an F with the degree to which any other one is an F would seem completely arbitrary. This suggests that we really want a continuum of truth values, with an ordering relation defined on it. I will use the unit interval, with 0 representing complete falsehood and 1 representing complete truth, as has become fairly common practice.[8]

This means that we may on occasion assign $1/\pi$ to some proposition, to serve as its truth value; one may well wonder what sense can be made of such assignments. I am myself unable to see how one might arrive at such an assignment with any confidence that it, and it alone out of the whole continuum of possible assignments, correctly gives the truth value of a given proposition under a given set of circumstances. However, the assignments need not be completely arbitrary. For example, if we are dealing with the classification of bald men, an empirical investigation could reveal at approximately what point people begin to feel unsure whether sample baldish men are really bald; conceivably a great many variables could be involved, such as the age of the sample man, the color of his hair, and of course its density and distribution. After lengthy investigation, however, some patterns in the common man's classification of people as bald or not bald should emerge. One could then use these patterns to assign truth values to the propositions asserting that various intermediately baldish men are bald. The result would not be completely determined by the empirical data, but neither would it be completely arbitrary. It would have something

---

8   There are other, more unfamiliar, constructs one might try out as truth sets, but the present paper is an exploration into what can be done with the unit interval However, use of the unit interval does raise questions, especially since the interval's total ordering makes the truth values of all vague propositions pairwise comparable. Some would consider this result counterintuitive and would prefer a merely partially ordered truth set. It seems to me, however, that the difficulties about comparability are really just difficulties about how to assign degrees of truth to propositions, and that in general the unit interval can serve quite well as our truth set.

of the character of a scientific hypothesis in empirical semantics. Fortunately, the assignment of exact values usually doesn't matter much for deciding on logical relations between vague propositions; what is of importance instead is the ordering relation between the values of various propositions.

We turn now to the precise definition of the connectives. As it happens, here again, as above, the problem is not to devise a new system but rather to lay down well-motivated constraints on the system we are looking for. It turns out that the Łukasiewicz system known as $L_\aleph$ satisfies them all. Thus, I am urging that Łukasiewicz' calculus is well-suited to serve as a logic of vagueness—an interpretation of the system quite different from that which Łukasiewicz himself placed on it.[9]

First of all, negation seems quite naturally defined in the usual way as follows: $|{\sim}p| = 1 - |p|$. (Here the bar-lines around a formula are read: "the value of".) This definition gives us normality, and the inverse relation between $|p|$ and $|{\sim}p|$ which we want. There are, of course, other definitions which would do the same thing, but all of them seem arbitrary by comparison.

Given our decision to have truth-functional "&" and "∨", these definitions cause no trouble: if $|p| = m$ and $|q| = n$, then $|p \& q|$ clearly ought to be no truer than the maximum of m and n. Moreover, we ought also to have $|p \& q| \geq \min(m, n)$. The only possible question here is whether we could have strict inequality in the last formula. I am inclined to think of conjunction in a fairly classical way here: when one conjunct is false, that makes the whole conjunction false, no matter how true the other conjunct might be. Accordingly, I will require $|p \& q| = \min(|p|, |q|)$.[10] After all, if one allows $|p \& q| > \min(|p|, |q|)$, then the conjunction of the premises in a given argument could be truer than the falsest premise in that argument, so that the argument from $\{p, q\}$ to r might be truth-preserving while the argument from $\{p \& q\}$ to r might not be. Such a

---

9. Cf. Rescher 1969, pp 36 ff. and bibliography; and Łukasiewicz and Tarski 1930

10. Goguen (1969, p. 347) suggests that multiplication instead of min yields the more adequate symbolization of the English "and" I fail to see this, especially in view of Goguen's own earlier definition of fuzzy set intersection (p 338) which has it that an element belongs to the intersection of two fuzzy sets to the minimal degree to which it belongs to either of the fuzzy sets taken singly. Later in his paper, Goguen proves that various formulas are tautologies, assuming that the truth set has certain properties As an example of such a truth set, Goguen mentions [0, 1], with the operation of multiplication serving as the analog of conjunction. (p 355, cf pp. 361 ff) However, the operator min will serve just as well on [0, 1], with 1 as the identity (i e. min $(a, 1) = a = $ min $(1, a)$ for any $a \in [0, 1]$), so that Goguen's theorems also go through using min instead of multiplication

result seems peculiar to me. Similarly, I will think of "$\vee$" in a somewhat classical way, requiring $|p \vee q| = \max(|p|, |q|)$.

I have proceeded here by working out definitions of "$\sim$", "$\&$" and "$\vee$" independently of one another, rather than, say, defining $|p \& q| = |\sim(\sim p \vee \sim q)|$, simply because it is not always clear which classical tautology, if any, ought to continue to link these connectives in a logic of vagueness. I prefer to derive the definitions of the connectives from a list of conditions which seem reasonable for our purposes. It does happen, though, that $|p \& q| = |\sim(\sim p \vee \sim q)|$, and $|p \vee q| = |\sim(\sim p \& \sim q)|$, all of which is very nice.

We do need to consider very carefully how to generalize material implication for our logic. Intuitions are no clear guide here. For example, it is tempting to try to take a shortcut by simply defining "$\supset$" by means of the relation $|p \supset q| = |\sim p \vee q|$. But this would be a mistake, I think, which illustrates the need for developing our definitions to satisfy reasonable conditions rather than defining the connectives directly in terms of one another by means of classically valid formulas. To see that the proposed definition is questionable, consider the formula "$p \supset p$". It seems that even in logic which admits vague instantiations for "p", all instantiations of this formula ought to be completely true, since the truth values of the antecedent and consequent are of necessity always equal. Thinking of English sentences which would be symbolized this way, we would be inclined to say they are analytically true (if we don't mind the concept of analyticity). But if we define "$\supset$" as proposed, and let $|p| = 1/2$, then $|p \supset p| = 1/2$, rather than 1.

There are further considerations which will help settle this issue. It would be nice to preserve the very important classical connection between "$\supset$" and logical inference; i.e., we want a proposition of the form "$p \supset q$" to take value 1 in all models just in case the inference from p to q is valid in the sentential calculus. Although we have not yet given a formal definition of argument validity for the multi-valued system being generated here, it is clear that validity will have to amount to something like truth-preservation in virtue of logical form. I.e., when an argument instantiates an argument form possessing the property that its conclusion must always be at least as true as the falsest premise, the argument will be fully valid. Translation of this notion of argument validity into a condition on the definition of "$\supset$" yields the result that "$\supset$" must be defined in such a way that whenever the consequent is at least as true as the antecedent, the whole conditional statement is completely true. From these considerations, we obtain the following restriction on "$\supset$":

$$\text{if } |p| < |q| \text{ and } |r \supset p| = 1, \text{ then } |r \supset q| = 1 \qquad (1)$$

We can obtain additional restrictions on "⊃" if we decide that when $|q|$ < $|p|$ and $|q| \neq |r|$, then $|p \supset q| \neq |p \supset r|$. The only reasonable alternative to such a decision would be to rule that $|p \supset q| = 0$ uniformly, for all values of $|q|$ such that $|q| < |p|$. A choice of the latter alternative, as opposed to the former, would break down the classical connection between "⊃" and logical inference, because in developing the theory of logical inference in a multi-valued calculus we shall surely want to draw some distinction between those forms of argument which are nearly truth-preserving and those which are not at all truth-preserving. If there is a form of argument such that the truth value of its conclusion must always be at least 80% of the truth value of its falsest premise, that form of argument deserves higher logical honors than a form of argument like

$$p$$
$$\underline{q}$$
$$r$$

in which there is no guarantee at all that the value of the conclusion is greater than 0 even when the premises are valued at 1. Accordingly, I believe the first alternative for defining "⊃" is more appropriate than the second. A choice of the first alternative suggests the following conditions:

If $|p| < |q| \leq |r|$, then $|r \supset p| < |r \supset q|$.   (2)

If $|r| \leq |p| < |q|$, then $|q \supset r| < |p \supset r|$.   (3)

Conditions (1), (2), and (3) jointly uniquely determine a definition for "⊃" when the set of truth values is *finite*. We can generalize the definition of "⊃" obtained from these conditions to the case of the infinite truth set.[11] To see what definition of "⊃" is implied by (1), (2), and (3) when the set of truth values is finite, suppose there are n such truth values: $0, 1/n - 1, 2/n - 1, \ldots, 1$. First, we use (2) to find the values of "$r \supset p$" when $|r| = 1$ and $|p|$ varies through n possibilities. (2) requires each such value of "$r \supset p$" be different and ordered so that as $|p|$ becomes smaller, so does $|r \supset p|$. Since there are only n different values to work with, $|r \supset p| = |p|$ must hold. A similar argument shows that (3) requires $|p \supset r| = 1 - |p|$ when $|r| = 0$, since in this case as we run through the various values for "p" we need to have $|p \supset r|$ increase as

---

11 Arto Salomaa 1959 discusses various conditions which might be placed on many-valued connectives My set (1)–(3) is equivalent to his set C_8. Most of Salomaa's sets of conditions employ the device of *designating* some subset of the truth value set and treating this designated subset as if it were the value true I find the use of designation in the semantics for many-valued logic philosophically very puzzling, despite its technical usefulness

$|p|$ decreases. We now know the values of the conditional when the antecedent has value 1 or the consequent has value 0. By exactly similar reasoning we can fill in the rest of the values for the conditional when the antecedent is at least as true as the consequent. In each case we can use (2) or (3) to establish an ordering between the various values of "$r \supset p$" (or "$p \supset r$") keeping $|r|$ fixed at some intermediate value. A rigorous proof would show by mathematical induction on n that for any finite cardinality n of the set of truth values, $|p \supset q| = 1 - |p| + |q|$ when $|p| \geq |q|$. We then use (1) to establish $|p \supset q|$ when $|p| < |q|$. This turns out to be trivial, since we already know from our earlier work that $|r \supset p| = 1$ when $|r| = |p|$, so that if we let $|q| > |p|$, $|r \supset q| = 1$, by (1). Hence $|p \supset q| = 1$ when $|q| > |p|$. Summarizing these results we obtain

$$|p \supset q| = \begin{cases} 1, & |q| > |p| \\ 1 - |p| + |q|, & |q| \leq |p|. \end{cases}$$

The degree to which the conditional is true thus amounts to an inverse measure of the degree to which the consequent fails to be as true as the antecedent. The amount by which $|p \supset q|$ falls short of complete truth is the amount by which $|q|$ fails to be as true as $|p|$. The above definition of $|p \supset q|$ can of course be used also when the set of truth values is infinite. We shall do just that.

We shall also adopt for convenience the definition

$$|p \equiv q| = |(p \supset q) \,\&\, (q \supset p)|.$$

As I noted earlier, the system proposed here is due to Łukasiewicz. I know of no place in which Łukasiewicz himself indicated any interest in thinking of his logic as a logic of vagueness. In fact he seems to have had a quite different interpretation in mind—an interpretation of the values as probabilities. In retrospect his interpretation seems doomed to failure, since probability logic ought not be truth-functional. In fact, I know of no one who has proposed that the system just described be used for capturing the logical relations between vague propositions—a use for which the logic seems eminently well-suited.

In order to provide for quantification theory in our logic and at the same time to provide a set-theoretic semantics which will accord with the definitions of the connectives already given, we can employ a generalized set theory described by Zadeh and developed by Goguen. Basically, the generalized set theory differs from ordinary set theory by dint of allowing the set membership relation to admit of degrees. Formally, this is achieved by mapping an ordinary set into an (ordinary) index set, so that the mapping function can be thought of as a so-called "fuzzy" set. An element of the domain of the function "belongs to" the fuzzy set to the degree indicated by the element of the index set which is its image under the mapping. We shall use the unit interval for our index set, in order to provide a natural connection between the present semantics and our earlier decision to use the unit interval as our truth set; however, this move is not absolutely necessary, and one should not confuse the two roles of the unit interval as index set and as truth set.

Roughly, we will follow the strategy of assigning a fuzzy set to each predicate letter in the calculus which we wish to interpret. If a given predicate letter is not vague, or if it is vague but happens not to have any problematic instances in the domain of discourse at issue, the fuzzy set which serves as its extension will presumably map the domain into {0, 1}—i.e., the fuzzy set won't have any fuzziness and will behave like an ordinary set.

However, this picture is to be modified a bit in order to provide for a formal display of various types of vagueness. It seems that there are at least three different sorts of vagueness which arise relative to predicates within a natural language, and my intention is to provide a formal mechanism for capturing these varieties of vagueness. We can name these types of vagueness with suitably descriptive phrases: (a) Conflict Vagueness, (b) Gap Vagueness, and (c) Weighting Vagueness. Briefly, Conflict Vagueness occurs when a single predicate is used in such a way that the semantical rules governing its application on the occasion in question conflict with one another. Gap Vagueness occurs when the semantical rules for a predicate fail to say anything at all about whether certain sorts of possible objects are to be included in the extension of the predicate. And Weighting Vagueness occurs when the natural semantics governing the use of the predicate provides that some one property or some combination of properties of a given object count to only a certain limited extent toward placing the object into the extension of the predicate, even though these properties are the only ones which are at all relevant in deciding the applicability of the predicate to the object. All the well-worked examples of vagueness occurring in the literature are of this latter sort.

I do not wish to argue here that all three types of vagueness actually exist in, say, English. I have given examples of these types of vagueness elsewhere (Machina 1972). The three types of vagueness mentioned above do not correspond in any neat way with the more standard classification scheme introduced by Alston in which vagueness is divided into two types: (a) that which stems from a "lack of a precise cutoff point along some dimension", and (b) that which derives from the interaction of "a number of independent conditions of application" for a predicate (Alston 1964, p. 87). I classify vagueness in the unique way described above because the formal representation of each type is distinct in what follows.

In order to represent Conflict Vagueness, I allow a given predicate letter to be assigned more than one (fuzzy) partial extension in the model. Each such partial extension is intended to represent the extension determined by one *nonconflicting* set of criteria for application of the predicate expression being abbreviated by that predicate letter. The degree to which a given element of the domain belongs to one such partial extension need not equal the degree to which that same element belongs to another such partial extension of the same predicate letter: a given object b in the domain may be clearly an F when judged by one set of criteria for F-ness, but only partially an F when judged by another, equally appropriate, set of criteria. The valuation of "Fb" will then be settled by taking some appropriately weighted average of the values one would obtain for "Fb" under each set of criteria taken separately. In order to represent Gap Vagueness, I allow the functions which set the assignment of extensions to predicate letters to remain silent as to whether a given element, say, b, of the domain of discourse is in the fuzzy extension of a given predicate letter, say, "F". In such a case, there is a question about what should be done about the truth value of "Fb". Two possibilities suggest themselves: (a) "Fb" lacks truth value. (b) "Fb" is just as true as it is false—i.e., it has value 1/2. In order to avoid the difficulties with truth-valueless propositions, I opt for the latter alternative, which has the advantage of making "$Fb \supset Fb$" a tautology. Finally, in order to represent Weighting Vagueness I allow predicate letters to have fuzzy extensions such that some members of the domain are "in" the extension of a given predicate letter only to a limited extent. In so far as mere computation of truth values is concerned, most of this complexity in assigning extensions to predicate letters could be avoided —we could have a model theory for vague predicates simply by using fuzzy extensions, without making distinctions between the three types of vagueness just described. But if our model theory is intended to reveal important semantic relationships, and is intended to be useful in some of the more formal aspects of doing semantics of a natural language, then the addition of some such detail as I have outlined may be justifiable.

Let the language to be interpreted be a first-order predicate calculus (without identity, definite descriptions, or operation constants), with a denumerable set of predicate letters for each finite number of places, and a denumerable set of individual constants. (The introduction of operation constants poses no special problems, but identity and definite descriptions are another matter.[12]) An interpretation, M, for such a language consists of the following:

---

12. The interpretations satisfying the conditions given below make reference precise. In a full treatment of vagueness, I believe vague reference would have to be

(1)   A non-empty set **D**, called the *domain* of the interpretation **M**.

(2)   The unit interval, **I**, called the *index* of the interpretation **M**.

(3)   The set **E**, called the *set of possible extensions*, consisting of all the ordered pairs whose first members are n-place predicate letters ($n \geq 1$) and whose second members are n-tuples of elements of **D** where the number of places in the predicate letter equals the number of places in the n-tuple in each case.

(4)   A finite set **F**, the set of *predicate interpretation functions*, each member of which is a function having a subset of **E** as domain and a (perhaps improper) subset of **I** as range. For each predicate letter we require that at least one member of **F** have in its domain an element of **E** having that predicate letter as first member. (We do not require that all the various elements of **F** map a given element of **E** onto the same element of **I**, nor that all the elements of **E** be in the domain of some element or other of **F**. This allows for gaps, conflicts, and weighting.)

(5)   A function **d** called the *denotation function*, which assigns to each individual constant an element of **D**. (However, for simplicity of notation we shall merely write, e.g., "a" below in those places where "**d**('a')" would strictly be required.)

(6)   A *valuation function*, **v**, such that:

   (a)   Each sentence letter is assigned a value in [0, 1] by **v**, and

   (b)   **v** assigns to each n-place predicate letter, ϕ, followed by n individual constants, $a_1, a_2, \ldots a_n$, a value in [0, 1] satisfying the following conditions:

   (b.1)   If only one element, **f**, of **F** interprets ϕ at $\langle a_1, a_2, \ldots a_n \rangle$, then $\mathbf{v}(\phi(a_1, a_2, \ldots a_n)) = \mathbf{f}(\langle \phi, \langle a_1, a_2, \ldots a_n \rangle \rangle)$.

   (b.2)   If no elements of **F** interpret ϕ at $\langle a_1, a_2, \ldots a_n \rangle$, then $\mathbf{v}(\phi(a_1, a_2, \ldots a_n)) = .5$.

   (b.3)   If more than one element of **F** interpret ϕ at $\langle a_1, a_2, \ldots a_n \rangle$, then $\mathbf{v}(\phi(a_1, a_2, \ldots a_n))$ shall be chosen so as to lie somewhere within the range of values given to $\langle \phi, \langle a_1, a_2, \ldots a_n \rangle \rangle$ by these elements of **F**.

   (c)   If a predicate letter has variables in any of its argument places, an assignment of values (in **D**) to these variables

---

taken into account as well, so that one would say "John existed on April 24" has an intermediate truth value if John was, if anything, only a partially developed fetus on April 24 In such cases the problems of vagueness are apparently connected with vague reference I hope to consider such problems in a future paper

is made in the usual way and then **v** of the whole is determined, relative to this assignment, in a manner analogous to that outlined in (b) above.

(d)   For any wffs, A and B, and a given assignment of values to variables, $\mathbf{v}(\sim A) = 1 - \mathbf{v}(A)$; $\mathbf{v}(A \,\&\, B) = \min(\mathbf{v}(A), \mathbf{v}(B))$; $\mathbf{v}(A \vee B) = \max(\mathbf{v}(A), \mathbf{v}(B))$; $\mathbf{v}(A \supset B) = 1 - \mathbf{v}(A) + \mathbf{v}(B)$ when $\mathbf{v}(B) < \mathbf{v}(A)$ and $\mathbf{v}(A \supset B) = 1$ otherwise.

(e)   For any wff, A, $\mathbf{v}((\forall x)A)$, relative to an assignment of values to variables, is the greatest lower bound of the various values of $\mathbf{v}(A)$ relative to all possible assignments which differ from one another at most with respect to the value assigned to x. (If there are no free variables in A other than x, $\mathbf{v}((\forall x)A)$ will no longer be relative to an assignment, but will instead be uniquely determined for all assignments.) Similarly, $\mathbf{v}((\exists x)A)$, relative to an assignment of values to variables, is the least upper bound of the values of $\mathbf{v}(A)$ relative to all possible assignments which differ from one another at most with respect to the value assigned to x. Let "$\mathrm{glb}_x(\mathbf{v}(A))$" denote the greatest lower bound described above; let "$\mathrm{lub}_x(\mathbf{v}(A))$" denote the least upper bound described above.

If A and B are fuzzy sets, we define $A \cup B$ to be the fuzzy set such that (1) x belongs to $A \cup B$ iff x belongs to A to some degree or x belongs to B to some degree, and (2) x belongs to $A \cup B$ to the higher of the degrees to which x belongs to A or x belongs to B. Similarly, $A \cap B$ is the fuzzy set such that x belongs to $A \cap B$ to the lower of the degrees to which it belongs to A or to B.[13] These definitions preserve the usual connection between conjunction and set intersection and between disjunction and set union.

The value of $\mathbf{v}(A)$ for any *sentence* A is to be thought of as A's truth value. (If A is not a sentence, and A contains at least one free variable, then the valuation assigned to A by **v** will be the truth value of A, but only relative to an assignment of values to variables.)

It is not hard to show that $1 - \mathrm{glb}_x(1 - \mathbf{v}(A)) = \mathrm{lub}_x(\mathbf{v}(A))$ for any wff A, and hence that the classical relation between the universal and existential quantifiers is maintained—i.e., $|\sim(\forall x)\sim A| = |(\exists x)A|$. Similarly, $|(\forall x)A| = |\sim(\exists x)\sim A|$. Moreover, the classical relations between conjunction, disjunction, and quantification in a finite **D** continue to hold: e.g., $|(\forall x)Fx| = |Fa_1 \,\&\, Fa_2 \,\&\, \ldots \,\&\, Fa_n|$ where the a_i exhaust the domain,

---

13. For a fairly full development of this sort of set theory see Goguen's work

and $|(\exists x)Fx| = |Fa_1 \vee Fa_2 \vee \ldots \vee Fa_n|$ similarly, since when the domain is finite, the glb = min and the lub = max.

Given the preceding understandings regarding quantification, sentential connectives, predication, and the truth set, there are of course an enormous number of interesting questions to explore. One might ask about axiomatizations, about natural deduction systems, and then about completeness and consistency, and about key theorems. Before doing these investigations, however, some additional concepts would need definition: the concept of a valid argument, and of a tautology or valid formula, at least. We have said nothing about these important matters yet. A brief discussion of these latter concepts will complete our sketch of the foundations of a logic of vagueness.

The most commonly used technique in multi-valued logic for defining "valid argument" and "valid formula" employs the notion of *designation*: Informally speaking, to designate an element or a set of elements of the truth set is to pick out these elements as being true-like, in some sense; so that when a formula is assigned a designated value, that formula is to be thought of as somehow true, or true-like. It has never been clear to me what understanding of truth lies behind such talk. However, designation does provide a convenient crutch on which one may lean in order to construct a notion of a valid formula or valid argument: a logically valid formula (or tautology) is one which can take on only designated truth values, no matter what consistent assignments are made to its various parts. And an argument form is valid if and only if the assignment of any designated value to its premises guarantees its conclusion will have a designated value as well.

Given our understanding of the truth set as representing degrees of truth, is there any sense in designating some of these truth values? Yes, I suppose some attention should be paid to the task of isolating those formulas which uniformly take on the value 1, and those argument forms which are constructed in such a way that the complete truth of all the premises guarantees the complete truth of the conclusion. It might also be interesting to explore these same questions with regard to the values greater than or equal to .5.[14] However, the more interesting question is the more general one of analysing argument forms with an

---

14 Richard C T. Lee and Chin-Liang Chang (1971) have proved that in the fragment of the present logic which employs only negation, conjunction, and disjunction a formula uniformly takes on values greater than or equal to 5 if and only if that formula is a classical tautology, and that a formula uniformly takes on values less than or equal to 5 if and only if that formula is a classical contradiction However, the Lee-Chang result cannot be generalized to the whole logic, for $|\sim(P \ \& \ (P \supset \sim P))| = 4$ when $|P| = .6$ (I owe this example to my colleague, Lawrence Eggan.)

eye to the *degree* to which they are truth-preserving, and analysing formulas with the goal of discovering the range of possible truth values they can take on. We really want to know for a given form of argument what constraints, if any, are placed by that form on the possible truth value of the conclusion if the premises have given truth values. For example, if all the premises have value greater than n does it not follow that the conclusion has value greater than n? Greater than $n/2$? And so on. Similarly, we may ask of individual formulas whether there is some minimum or maximum value which it is possible for them to receive. We need not restrict our attention to the formulas which uniformly take on value 1.

Hence, rather than a notion of tautology, I propose we use a notion of a *minimally n-valued formula*: a formula is minimally n-valued iff it can never have a value less than n. We can also use the parallel notion of a *maximally n-valued formula*. Then one can ask, with respect to a given formula, for the maximal n such that the formula is minimally n-valued. And instead of the notion of a designation-preserving form of argument, we want the notion of a *truth-preserving argument form*: a form of argument is truth-preserving iff its conclusion must be at least as true as its falsest premise. (We could call such argument forms "valid".) Finally, this notion can be generalized to the notion of the *degree of truth-preservation* possessed by an argument form: here what is wanted is the function which determines the minimal truth value possible for a given argument form's conclusion given the various possible values of the premises.

In this connection, we can confirm that there is an interesting and useful relationship between our definition of "⊃" and the business of truth-preservation in argument forms. (This relationship is the analog of the relation between the classical horseshoe and classically valid argument forms.) Let "Φ implies Ψ to degree n" mean roughly that $|\Psi|$ can not dip below $|\Phi|$ by more than $1 - n$, so that when n is near 1, the difference between $|\Phi|$ and $|\Psi|$ must be near 0. More precisely, let "$\Phi \vdash_n \Psi$" mean that n is the least upper bound of all the numbers m such that $(|\Phi| - |\Psi|) \leq (1 - m)$ for all possible assignments of values to Φ and Ψ, provided that at least some of those assignments result in a positive value for $(|\Phi| - |\Psi|)$; if $(|\Phi| - |\Psi|)$ is always negative or 0, then we stipulate that $n = 1$. Given this definition of "$\Phi \vdash_n \Psi$", it follows that n is the greatest lower bound of the set of possible values of the formula "$\Phi \supset \Psi$". That is, if Ψ is always at least as true as Φ, then $\Phi \vdash_1 \Psi$ and $|\Phi \supset \Psi|$ is always 1, but if Ψ can get a bit falser than Φ, then $\Phi \vdash_n \Psi$ where n is some number near 1 and $|\Phi \supset \Psi|$ will sometimes dip a bit below 1—in fact, it will dip just as far as n. And if it is possible for $|\Psi|$ to be 0 even when $|\Phi| = 1$, then $\Phi \vdash_0 \Psi$ and $|\Phi \supset \Psi|$ goes as low as 0—which is to say that Φ in this case does not imply Ψ at all.

The logical system outlined above can be used to solve the ancient *sorites* paradox. I shall consider only one of the most straightforward members of the *sorites* family of paradox-generating arguments, but I believe it fair to assume other members of the family would yield to similar analysis.[15] In English, the argument goes like this:

> Horatio the would-be petunia planter has no hair
> on his head.   (1)
> Anyone who has no hair is bald.   (2)
> Anyone who has just one more hair on his head than
> any bald man is also bald.   (3)
> _____
> Anyone who has 10^7 hairs on his head is bald.   (4)

From (1) and (2) we are to conclude Horatio is bald; from this conclusion and (3) we are to conclude that anyone who has just one more hair than Horatio is bald. From the latter conclusion and (3) we obtain the further result that anyone having just one more hair than anyone having just one more hair than Horatio is bald. And so on, until (4) is obtained.

Adopting the following scheme of abbreviation will yield a formalization of the argument sufficient for our purposes:

> Nx: x has no hair on his head
> Mxy: x has just one more hair on his head than y
> Bx: x is bald

The first steps of the argument then might be symbolized as follows:

> Nh (5)
> $(\forall x)(Nx \supset Bx)$ (6)
> _____
> Bh (7)
> $(\forall x)(\forall y)(Mxy \ \& \ By \supset Bx)$ (8)
> _____
> $(\forall x)(Mxh \supset Bx)$ (9)
> $(\forall x)(\forall y)(Mxy \ \& \ By \supset Bx)$ (8)
> _____
> $(\forall x)(\forall y)(Mxy \ \& \ Myh \supset Bx)$ (10)
> $(\forall x)(\forall y)(Mxy \ \& \ By \supset Bx)$ (8)
> _____
> $(\forall x)(\forall y)(\forall z)(Mxy \ \& \ Myz \ \& \ Mzh \supset Bx)$ (11)

Here (5), (6), and (8) are symbolizations of the original English premises, and (8) is used repeatedly to obtain further conclusions. Sufficient repetition of the pattern exhibited in the steps from (9)–(11) would ultimately yield a very long sentence equivalent to (4). In classical

---

15 For some other versions of the paradox, see James Cargile (this volume) and Max Black 1963 The solution to the paradox given below is the same in spirit as that given by Goguen

logic the argument (5)–(11) is valid; hence the paradox if (5) happens to be true, since (6) and (8) seem true a priori.

In contrast to the classical analysis of (5)–(11), our nonclassical interpretation of the logical constants in the argument shows the argument to be in trouble from the outset, for the argument from (5) and (6) to (7) is not fully valid. To be sure, when (5) and (6) have value 1, $|Bh| = 1$ also, as can be seen from clauses (d) and (e) in the definition of v. (One of the assignments of values to variables which one considers in evaluating (6) is the assignment of h to "x".) Even when (5) has value 1 and (6) is less than completely true, things still look fine. Suppose (6) has value $m < 1$. Then $|Bh|$ can differ from $|Nh|$ by at most $(1 - m)$; i.e., $||Nh| - |Bh|| \leq (1 - m)$. But we are assuming for the moment that $|Nh| = 1$. Hence $(1 - |Bh|) \leq (1 - m)$, or $|Bh| \geq m$; i.e., the value of (7), the conclusion, is at least as great as the value of the falsest premise, (6). Nevertheless, when we consider the case in which (5) is *not* fully true, the form of argument exhibited in (5)–(7) is revealed not to be fully valid. E.g., let $|Nh| = .6$ and $|(\forall x)(Nx \supset Bx)| = .4$. Then we know only that $(|Nx| - |Bx|) \leq .6$ for every assignment of values to "x". It could happen that $|Nh| - |Bh| = .6$; in this case, $|Bh| = 0$ since $|Nh| = .6$, resulting in a completely false conclusion from premises not completely false. Hence the argument form is not completely truth-preserving.

In general, if $|(5)| = n$ and $|(6)| = m$, then the best guarantee on the truth of (7) comes from the inequality $(|Nh| - |Bh|) \leq (1 - m)$ which we get from the value of (6). Putting $|Nh| = n$ in this inequality yields the guarantee that $|Bh| \geq (m + n - 1)$. It is only to this degree that the argument form is valid in general. When $(|(5)| + |(6)|) > 1$, $|Bh| > 0$. When $(|(5)| + |(6)|)$ is close to 2, $|Bh|$ is close to 1. Thus it would be unfair to say simply that the argument form of the *sorites* is invalid. That would not explain its deceptiveness. In fact, given the assumption that (5) and (6) are in reality completely true, we know from our analysis that (7) is then completely true as well, so that in a sense the *sorites* argument is quite all right down through (7). *That* is part of its deceptiveness.

The argument begins to get into more difficulty with the introduction of premise (8). The value of (8) is a function of the truth values of

$$Mxy \ \& \ By \supset Bx \qquad\qquad (12)$$

obtained from various assignments of denotation to "x" and "y". For simplicity, assume "M" is not vague. When "x" and "y" are assigned denotations not in relation M, or when "y" is assigned a completely non-bald individual $|(12)| = 1$. But we want to know the glb of the values of (12). $|(12)|$ dips below 1 when $|Mxy| = 1$ and $|Bx| < |By|$, for then $|Mxy \ \& \ By| = |By|$ and $|Mxy \ \& \ By \supset Bx| = 1 - |By| + |Bx|$. Presumably, on the intended interpretation of "B", any two individuals standing in relation M will be nearly equally B's. But at least within a certain range of such individuals, we shall want to say that a man with just one more hair is just a very, very small amount less bald. In this range, neither "Bx" nor "By" will be valued at 1, and the difference $|By| - |Bx|$ will be some very small positive number, ε, perhaps on the order of 10^{-5}. The net result is that $|(8)| = 1 - \varepsilon$, rather than 1. Here is another factor in the deceptiveness of the *sorites* argument. It is easy to suppose (8) is completely true since its instances in many cases are completely true and in all cases are at least almost completely true.

Essentially the same analysis done earlier on the argument (5)–(7) will reveal with respect to (7)–(9) that so long as $|(7)| = 1$, $|(9)| \geq |(8)|$. I.e., given that $|(5)|$ and $|(6)| = 1$, and $|(8)| = (1 - \varepsilon)$, we know $|(9)| \geq (1 - \varepsilon)$. Now, however, for the argument (9)–(10), it may be that *neither* premise (9) nor (8) is completely true. $|(8)|$ still $= (1 - \varepsilon)$ and $|(9)|$ might be the same. What guarantee do we get for $|(10)|$? Assume "x" and "y" are assigned values such that "Mxy" and "Myh" are simultaneously completely true. From $|(9)| \geq (1 - \varepsilon)$ we know $|By| \geq (1 - \varepsilon)$. Moreover, since $|(8)| = (1 - \varepsilon)$, we know $|By| - |Bx| \geq \varepsilon$ for x such that $|Mxy| = 1$. If $|Bx|$ did fall as much as ε below $|By|$, and $|By|$ took its lowest possible value, $(1 - \varepsilon)$, then $|Bx| = (1 - 2\varepsilon)$ and $|(10)| = (1 - 2\varepsilon)$. This is the worst that can happen to (10). I.e., we now know $|(10)| \geq (1 - 2\varepsilon)$.

As the pattern (9)–(10) is repeated in (10)–(11) and beyond, the guarantee of truth of each successive conclusion diminishes by ε for each repetition. Thus, the guarantee for (11) is down to $1 - 3\varepsilon$, and the guarantee for the next conclusion would be $1 - 4\varepsilon$. Clearly, if $\varepsilon = 10^{-5}$, in approximately 10^5 steps, the guarantee of truth will be $1 - 10^5(10^{-5})$; i.e., there will be no guarantee left. Each step of the argument is slightly invalid, so the truth guarantee slowly leaks away as we try to carry it along the chain. The *sorites* is thus handled in what seems to me to be a very natural way when formalized in $L_\aleph$.

Note that if we use

$$(\forall x)(\forall y)\sim(Mxy \ \& \ By \ \& \sim Bx) \tag{13}$$

instead of (8) to symbolize (3), we get a different result (because $\sim(P \ \& \sim Q)$ is not equivalent in $L_\aleph$ to $(P \supset Q)$). Since there will be elements of the domain assigned to "x" and "y" for which $|By| \approx .5$ and $|\sim Bx| \approx .5$ even though $|Mxy| = 1$, the value of (13) will be no higher than the neighborhood of .5; it cannot go lower either, since all values of "x" and "y" for which $|Mxy| = 1$ will make $|By|$ very close to $|Bx|$, with the result that as $|By|$ decreases below .5 $|\sim Bx|$ increases above .5, and values of "x" and "y" which do not make $|Mxy| = 1$ make $|Mxy| = 0$. On this reading of premise (3) the *sorites* argument is not nearly so plausible. This, I think, is as it should be, for (13) essentially says that it never happens that of two persons differing by just a hair it can be said that one is bald and the other isn't. Since it can be somewhat true as well as somewhat false that *one* individual is bald, when his hair is very sparse, it can naturally also be quite true that *two* individuals, roughly alike, are both bald to some extent and not bald to some extent. Hence, the low truth value of (13) which denies this can happen.

The $L_\aleph$ approach to the *sorites* argument taken earlier allows us to have just about everything we want and yet we escape the paradox: the inductive premise of the argument (premise (3)) is interpreted as being quite true, so it is no wonder it seems plausible. The argument form has some validity, and in fact preserves truth quite well for many steps when the initial premises are quite true, so it is not surprising the logic of the argument should appear acceptable. There is no one point in the argument chain at which we can say that we have completely lost the guarantee of truth all in one big jump. Our result is what the common man wants: he's convinced that such "slippery slope" arguments are fine if they're not carried too far. We can agree, because on the present view the truth guarantee for the conclusions in the chain of argument goes down rather slowly.

Let us check now to see how Tarski's convention (T) and *reductio ad absurdum* fare in $L_\aleph$. I take it that I have been saying that the predicate "is true" applies to various propositions in varying degrees, so that $|$"p" is true$| = |p|$ (semantic paradoxes aside). Symbolizing (T) as follows

$$T(P) \equiv P$$

yields the result then that Tarksi's convention (T) is *completely* true, for $|p \equiv q|$ in general = 1 when $|p| = |q|$ on our definition of "$\equiv$". Of course, in order to obtain this result I have interpreted the connective in (T) as "$\equiv$" in $L_\aleph$. But if $L_\aleph$ is the proper logical system for handling vagueness, that is surely appropriate, since "is true" is vague, as are many of the substitutions on "p" in (T).

A form of reductio can also be maintained in $L_\aleph$. In $L_\aleph$ a proposition of the form $p \,\&\, \sim p$ always has a value $\leq .5$. Hence, if the argument from the set of premises $S \cup \{Q\}$ to the conclusion $P \,\&\, \sim P$ is completely valid, on every assignment at least one proposition in $S \cup \{Q\}$ has value $\leq .5$. There are only two cases to consider, then: (1) $\min(|S_i|) \leq .5$, where the S_i are the members of S, and (2) $\min(|S_i|) > .5$. In the first case, we know nothing about $|Q|$, except that $0 \leq |Q| \leq 1$. But this is enough to ensure that $|\sim Q|$ can never fall more than .5 below $\min(|S_i|)$. In the second case, since $\min(|S_i|) > .5$, but $\min(|S_i|, |Q|) \leq .5$, we know $|Q| \leq .5$. Thus, in this case, $|\sim Q| \geq .5$, and once again $|\sim Q|$ can't fall more than .5 below $\min(|S_i|)$. Hence, consideration of the two cases shows that reductio is somewhat truth preserving. More precisely, if $S \cup \{Q\} \vdash_1 P \ \& \sim P$, then $S \vdash_5 \sim Q$, using an obvious extension of the notion of degreed implication discussed earlier. I.e., reductio is a "half-way valid" mode of inference in $L_\aleph$.

An additional result regarding reductio in $L_\aleph$ shows $L_\aleph$ to be consistent with the remarks made earlier in the discussion of Tarski's convention (T). If $S \cup \{Q\} \vdash_1 P \ \& \sim P$, and if $|P \ \& \sim P| = 0$, then we know $\min(|S_i|, |Q|) = 0$, since $\min(|S_i|, |Q|) \le |P \ \& \sim P|$. Then, if $\min(|S_i|) > 0$, we know $|Q| = 0$ and thus that $|\sim Q| = 1$. On the other hand if $\min(|S_i|) = 0$, we know only that $0 \le |Q| \le 1$. But in either case, we know $\min(|S_i|) \le |\sim Q|$. That is, $S \cup \{Q\} \vdash_1 P \ \& \sim P$ and $|P \ \& \sim P| = 0$, we know the inference from S to $\sim Q$ is *completely* truth-preserving. When a valid argument from $S \cup \{Q\}$ leads to an out-and-out contradiction, one may legitimately infer $\sim Q$ from S, which is just what was done in our earlier discussion of convention (T).

Finally, with respect to the philosophy of mathematics, a few remarks may be in order. Since the logic presented here is normal and since I assume precise propositions take on only classical truth values, nothing in the classical analysis of precise mathematical propositions is affected by my insistence on a peculiar logic. I have assumed classical logic is fine as far as it goes; if one is convinced otherwise, as are the intuitionists, my proposals in this paper will be seen as generalizations of the wrong logic. But in any case that is a separate issue—neither intuitionistic nor classical logic is designed to handle vague propositions. And if classical logic is indeed fine for precise propositions we may cheerfully go on using it in doing philosophy of mathematics so long as we restrict attention to precise mathematical propositions. The claims made in this paper become relevant only when the propositions of mathematics are subject to vagueness. However, there are important cases of potentially vague mathematical propositions worth mentioning here, I think. The principle of mathematical induction and the least number principle, to name two, can have vague instances if these principles are taken to apply for ordinary predicates. The former principle can be understood to claim that if any given predicate meets certain conditions, then it follows that predicate truthfully applies to all the natural numbers; the latter principle can mean that there is a least number that has a given predicate meeting certain conditions. If I am right, these principles, understood in the way just described, are completely true only when limited to precise predicates. If one allows the substitution of vague predicates into these hallowed principles, it turns out that versions of the *sorites* paradox will be generated, as Cargile (this volume) and Black (1963) have shown. In addition to difficulties with mathematical induction and the least number principle, vagueness may cause trouble in the application of mathematics to physics or everyday life. Investigation of such problems would be a worthy subject for further efforts in the study of vagueness.[16]

16 I am grateful for the careful comments of the referee—comments which provided useful suggestions, and which saved me from at least one major blunder

12 Further reflections on the sorites paradox

Crispin Wright

In two papers published just over a decade ago (Wright 1975; and Wright (I), this volume), I argued that the major premises—usually universally quantified conditionals[1]—which feature in sorites paradoxes owe their plausibility to an assumption which it then seemed appropriate, from the perspective of a philosopher of language in Oxford, to dub the "governing view". The governing view was a combination of two claims. The first was that a master of a language is someone who has, at some deep level, internalized a definite set of semantic and syntactic rules, definitive of the language. The second was something of a *pot pourri* of specific ideas about how such rules might be brought into the light or more fully characterized and understood. It included the admissibility of, for instance, considerations concerning speakers' known limitations (of memory or perceptual acuity, for example), standardly accepted criteria of (mis-)understanding, salient features of standard linguistic training, and the purposes and role which a particular distinction might have. The argument was that once the *relevance* of such considerations was granted, the major premises for sorites paradoxes could be seen as guaranteed by aspects of the semantic rules governing the relevant expressions (together with such general facts as the non-transitivity of indiscriminability). Since the other premises involved in such paradoxes, and the principles of inference which they utilize, seem incontestable, the conclusion suggested was that the governing view was responsible for them. That (at least some) sorites paradoxes are *genuine*—do no more than reflect features of the meanings of the affected expressions and aspects of the world, and so commit no identifiable fallacy nor involve any identifiable error—is a view which has been adopted by a number of writers, most notably by Dummett (this volume). My suggestion, in contrast, was that this is an illusion, generated by the governing view; specifically, that its second, epistemological ingredient is unacceptable, and that its first ingredient—the

From *Philosophical Topics* 15 (1987) pp. 227–290 © Board of Trustees, University of Arkansas Reprinted by permission, omitting Section V of the original paper

1 Though other forms of major premise will serve Overlooking this has caused problems for some writers—see the remarks about Putnam below, pp 228–29

overall conception of language-mastery which it embodies—needs, at the least, severe qualification.

Despite their antiquity, the sorites paradoxes had received comparatively little attention in the literature prior to 1975. Since then, there has been something of an explosion. One purpose of the present paper is to try to respond to various criticisms of my earlier efforts which have appeared, notably in Christopher Peacocke's very interesting (1981). I now wish to restrict the scope of my original proposal. Major premises for sorites paradoxes can actually be motivated in a number of quite different ways, which it is essential to distinguish. Only for a limited class of cases does it now seem to me that my earlier diagnosis is apt. The widespread conviction that the paradox afflicts all vague expressions (and hence virtually all our language) is best represented as the product of a different and, I believe, confused line of thought. And we have to reckon also with a third line of thought, leading to what I have called in this paper the *Tachometer paradox*. Moreover this threefold division is probably not exhaustive.

Even in the restricted class of cases in which I still wish to press my original proposal, I am no longer content with the kind of formulation which I offered. Where I earlier spoke, vaguely, of the inappositeness of the comparison of language with a game, and of the need for a more purely "behavioristic" conception of language-mastery, I now wish to offer something different. It is less that I think these formulations wrong than that they appeal to contrasts which may seem unclear and which are anyway very difficult to sharpen. A first statement of the particular moral which these formulations tried to capture would better proceed, it seems to me now, in somewhat different terms.

I have tried, so far as is possible, to write the present paper in a fashion which will not presuppose that a reader is familiar with my earlier two papers. But since my principal objective has been to improve on them, it is unavoidably, to that extent, a sequel.

1 The governing view and the sorites paradox

There is an idea about the kind of ability which mastery of a language (basically) is which would figure in virtually anyone's first philosophical thoughts on the topic. Suppose we had to teach somebody to play chess without any kind of verbal or written exchange. Could it be done? There seems no reason why not; no reason, that is, why an intelligent and receptive subject could not acquire a knowledge of the moves and of checkmate and stalemate, and so on, just by immersion in the practice of the game, suitably reinforced by nods and shakes of the head or punishment and reward. Such a subject might become an average or better than average chess player without ever learning any of the vocabulary which we use in description of the game. However once there was unmistakable evidence of mastery, we would not hesitate to attribute to the trainee the knowledge which *we* express by a statement of the rules and object of the game and also, if the trainee were an accomplished player, the knowledge which we can express by a description of certain strategies and of their rationale. We would think of the trainee as having this knowledge although unable—for the time being anyway—to talk chess-theory at all. Such knowledge would be viewed as *implicit*; but its content would coincide with that of the sort of explicit articulate knowledge which is normally acquired when someone learns to play chess.

This way of describing the example seems natural, almost inevitable, because the ability in question is par excellence a rational one, involving intelligence, insight and purpose. If recourse to rationalistic explanation—explanation involving attribution of beliefs, goals and intentions—were for some reason excluded, we simply should not know how to begin to describe the trainee's accomplishment. But beliefs, e.g., are contentful states; and we should be equally at a loss if none of the beliefs allowably attributable to the trainee could have a content which we would specify using the standard vocabulary of chess. So provided the eventual performance were good enough, the idea that the trainee possessed implicit knowledge of the rules of chess would be just as attractive if he or she mastered chess before acquiring *any* linguistic competence; or, indeed, if the trainee were a deaf mute whose prospects of ever understanding a language were slight.

The first philosophical thought about language-mastery to which I allude is, in effect, a large-scale analogue of the foregoing. Language-mastery, like mastery of chess, is apt to seem an exemplar of rational ability, differing only in that the set of rules—syntactic, semantic, and pragmatic—whose knowledge it involves are inordinately more complex than the rules of chess, and the purposes to which it is adapted far more various. Yet we perforce acquire language-mastery in much the manner of the fictional chess trainee, at least when learning a first language: we are immersed in the practice of those who can already "play", and explicit verbal instruction can be received only when enough of the language has already been grasped to enable an understanding of the terms in which it is couched. No doubt a good deal of the instruction *is* explicit—in typical school curricula a great deal is given in the way of exact definitions of terms, and precise characterizations of what is good grammar. But it remains true that the greater part of anyone's competence in their native language is not and could not be acquired that way.

In short: it comes naturally to think of someone with a good level of mastery of their native language as knowing a great deal more than they were ever explicitly taught; and it follows that there can be at best a contingent connection between the possession of this knowledge and the ability to articulate it. If the chess trainee's performance when playing the game is completely convincing, we shall not be any less inclined to credit him with knowledge of the rules of chess should it prove, when he acquires explicit chess vocabulary, that he finds it difficult to articulate them for himself. So too with language-mastery. The idea of implicit knowledge thus has just the same attractiveness, just the same seemingly inevitable part to play in the explanation of linguistic ability, that it should have in accounting for the performance of our fictional chess trainee.

The conclusion of this way of thinking about the matter, then, is that, as someone proceeds towards mastery of a first language, it must be true at certain stages, and may be true at any later stage, that some or all of the knowledge which they have acquired is implicit. But that, it seems, need pose no barrier to the possibility of an explicit description, either in a different language or in a larger fragment of the same language, of what is thereby implicitly known. On the contrary, since this "implicit knowledge" has been characterized from the outset as a contentful state, as in effect propositional knowledge, it must be possible in principle to specify the contents known by language learners, even if they themselves cannot yet do so or will never be able to do so. It would follow that there must be a formulable theory which stands to the competence of speakers of English rather as a complete codification of the rules of chess stands to the competence of someone whom we credit with a complete implicit knowledge of those rules but who is able to give, for whatever reason, at most a partial characterization of them. But there is a difference. Chess is a complex enough game, but it would nevertheless be surprising if, once introduced to the names of the pieces and other terms of art like "castling" and "checkmate", a subject whose knowledge of chess had originally been implicit did not prove to be able, on relatively brief reflection, to produce a passable statement of the rules of chess. In sharp contrast, it is obvious even on superficial reflection that the task of producing an explicit statement of the rules governing just the fragment of English concerned with literal statement making would be one of the greatest difficulty, even if we restricted our concern to legality, as it were, and prescinded from all consideration of what constituted "good play". We are as if in the situation of people who have all been taught, by directly practical methods and with a minimum of formal explanation, to play a game hugely more complex than chess, but now find that all the instructors—those who might have produced a written codification of the rules of the game if asked—have disappeared. We therefore confront, if we choose to rise to the challenge, an intriguing project: work out what the rules are. The result, if the task could be accomplished for an entire natural language, would be something that nobody has ever beheld: a complete explicit formulation of the knowledge which any master of the language knows but knows (mostly) only implicitly.

These ideas represent one possible route into sympathy with the modern philosophical project of a "theory of meaning". (They may, indeed, represent the only such route, though that is a nice question.[2]) I am not recommending them: I hope only to have made it intelligible, if there is anyone to whom they have never occurred, how they might nevertheless constitute an attractive vision. Their significance in the present context is that the sorites paradox, or so I have argued in my 1975 and in Wright (I), casts serious doubt on their acceptability in general. That is one claim which I wish to review in this paper. The claim is important; for the most fundamental task in the philosophy of language is the achievement, in the most general terms, of an understanding of the nature of language-mastery. It is here, if I am right, that the paradox has most to teach us.

If the tension is to be perceived, however, we have to ride the analogy a little bit harder. Consider the task of trying to draw up the rules of a game which we have all been able to play since childhood but of which there is no extant codification. How should we set about it? No doubt we should first need to invent some vocabulary to describe the materials and situations which are specific to the game; but then what? Recognition of one's own hitherto unformulated intentions is a peculiar business in any case; but the natural approach would be for a number of competent players to draw up severally as complete a description as they could by reflection, and then to compare notes. But when, as is likely, differences of opinion are revealed, how should they be resolved? The extent of the consensus on a particular point would be important, of course. But if somebody, e.g., listed a rule which no-one else had, that would not necessarily be decisive against that particular rule. If, for example, there was universal consensus that behavior in the course of the game which was in fact a breach of the putative rule would be regarded as outré and unacceptable, we would probably take that as strong prima facie evidence that the rule should be included and that the majority who did not list it had overlooked something. If, on the other hand, the putative rule seemed too complex, or incorporated

---

2　For some reflections on it, see Wright 1986d

distinctions too subtle to be remembered with any degree of surety, or relied on our ability to make contrasts which we felt that the direct, "immersive" training which we had received could not have possibly got across—if any consideration of that sort applied, there would be a strong case for discounting the rule.

Perhaps the most intriguing thing about sorites paradoxes is that an important class of them seem to arise very directly from the application of this sort of thinking to the rules of which implicit knowledge is supposed, on the other side of the analogy, to constitute our language-mastery. Once the content of those rules is supposed to be constrained by considerations like the limitations of the methods whereby we were trained in them, and our limitations, e.g., of memory, and the criteria for correct understanding of them which we now find intuitively satisfying, it is relatively straightforward to argue that they imply the unrestricted acceptability of the major premises—standardly, universally quantified conditionals—involved in sorites paradoxes.

The arguments to this effect developed in my 1975 and in Wright (I) were various and I shall give only the most general indication of them now. One thought was that it could not be part of understanding an expression to be able to make *unmemorable* distinctions if the learning and use of the expression standardly involves no reliance on external aids of any kind. Another was that distinctions too fine to be detected by casual observation could not be incorporated into the conditions of application of a predicate like "bald" or "heap" whose utility depends on being applicable on the basis of casual observation. A third was the thought that the conditions of application of an expression which, like "adult", is associated with substantial moral and social significance, cannot incorporate distinctions too refined to sustain that significance. A fourth was that the conditions of application of any ostensively teachable expression cannot incorporate distinctions—in particular the kind of distinction that may obtain between observationally indiscriminable items—not amenable to ostensive display. A fifth was that no distinction can mark a watershed in the conditions of application of an expression if treating it as such would standardly be taken to display a misunderstanding of that expression.

Typically, the major premises in plausible sorites paradoxes can be supported by considerations of more than one of these kinds. The paradox for "red", for example, may draw on any, or all, of the first, second, fourth and fifth. A paradox for "heartbeat of childhood" may draw on either the second or third. And so on. The exact manner in which the major premises are supposed to follow from such considerations will bear rather more careful scrutiny than I gave it before and we shall return to the question in section 6. But what seems beyond dispute is that if we accept that linguistic competence is constituted by sensitivity to the dictates of internalized rules, it is overwhelmingly natural to suppose that features of these rules may be discerned by reflection on our practical limitations, the ways the application of an expression would be defended if challenged, the interest which we attach to the classification effected by it, the way it is standardly taught, and the criteria for someone's misunderstanding it.

How we should respond to the situation depends, of course, on whether the specific arguments are truly watertight. But there is little at least in the literature with which I am familiar which tries to meet the problem head-on, to show that it is simply mistaken to think that relevant major premises can be validated in this way. For the present, let us continue to suppose that they can.

On that assumption, the position which we arrive at is as follows. Two separable claims have been made (together, they constitute the "governing view"). There is the general claim that our language-mastery is to be seen as the product of (mostly) implicit knowledge of rules; and there is the more specific claim that the enterprise of attempting to arrive at an explicit statement of these rules—or to enlarge on features of them which need not be reflected in such a statement, if we are doing semantics in the "homophonic" mould—is rightly seen as constrained by considerations of the seemingly platitudinous sort outlined. If both these claims are accepted, we are faced with the realization that sorites paradoxes (or at least some of them) merely serve to unravel certain features of the semantics of the expressions with which they deal, which must accordingly be viewed as at least *de facto* incoherent; that is, the rules for the use of those expressions, taken in conjunction with undisputed features of the world, enable flawless cases to be made for simultaneously withholding them from and applying them to certain situations.

There are then only three possible modes of response. The first is acceptance of both claims, with their consequence that our use of a large class of expressions is governed by incoherent rules. Second, we might essay to retain the first claim while jettisoning the second: the result would be to hold that while the implicit-knowledge conception of our language-mastery is fundamentally correct, the platitudinous-seeming constraints on the explicatory enterprise are not. Third, there is the apparently radical step of rejecting the first claim. How deep such a rejection would have to go would be a matter for determination, but, at the very least, it would be necessary to construct some alternative conception of our mastery of the use of sorites-susceptible expressions, to supplant the idea that it is comprised by implicit knowledge of the requirements of rules.

It is important to be clear that there cannot be any further alternative. (There is, of course, no possibility of retaining the second claim at the expense of the first.) Or rather: the only alternative is to disclose error in the supposition that the two claims, in conjunction with further undisputed premises (e.g., that indiscriminability is a non-transitive relation), inescapably generate sorites paradoxes. A fully satisfactory treatment of the problem must therefore accomplish one of two things: either it must demonstrate that the link between the two ingredient claims of the governing view and the major premises of sorites paradoxes can be broken—in which case it will need, in addition, to explain how exactly those premises fail of truth—, or it must explain why one of the three responses outlined is superior to the others and intuitively satisfying when properly fleshed out.[3]

2 Accepting the paradox

Towards the end of "Wang's paradox" (this volume), Dummett summarizes some conclusions as follows:

(1) Where non-discriminable difference is non-transitive, observational predicates are necessarily vague.

(2) Moreover, in this case, the use of such predicates is intrinsically inconsistent.

(3) Wang's paradox merely reflects this inconsistency. What is in error is not the principles of reasoning involved, nor, as on our earlier diagnosis, the induction step. The induction step is correct, according to the rules of use governing vague predicates such as "small": but these rules are themselves inconsistent, and hence the paradox .... (p. 115)

This is a clear enough example of the first kind of response. Why not this response? Why should it not be the case that the "language-game" is governed by (*de facto*) inconsistent rules? Clearly, appeal to our knowledge of such rules couldn't provide a completely satisfactory explanation of our actual linguistic practice—some supplementary account would be wanted of why we do not fall into confusion. But the idea of making some sort of successful enterprise out of an incoherently

---

3   In comparison with what is needed, it is not unduly harsh to say that much of the literature on this topic which has mushroomed over the last decade or so has amounted to little more than tinkering Writers have been content to devise more or less *ad hoc* semantics in whose terms the major premises fail of strict truth without doing anything to disclose *why* their plausibility is specious, still less confront the intuitively powerful arguments on their behalf. It should go without saying that the solution of a paradox requires more than designing wallpaper

codified practice is not in itself incoherent.[4] So what, if any, is the real objection to it here?

There are, it seems to me, three related objections. First it is open to question whether the idea of inconsistency can actually get any grip unless we are concerned with rules which have been *explicitly* codified. Suppose that we play an inconsistently formulated game, but never notice the inconsistency, sometimes going by one rule in a particular kind of situation and sometimes going by another which conflicts with it. If a third party, trying to find out the exact character of the rules of the game, was restricted to observation of play and *never allowed to see a written version of the rules*, what reason could they possibly have to suspect that the game was inconsistent rather than that at least two different courses of action were permissible in the situation in question? The analogy is not, indeed, accurate, since it is not as if we sometimes go along with the results of sorites reasoning but sometimes prefer the response which such reasoning can be made to contradict. But just for that reason a radical interpreter of our use of color vocabulary, for instance, would have even *less* reason to suspect an inconsistency than the observer of the game. If we say that there is an inconsistency nevertheless, with what right do we claim an insight into the character of the rules governing this vocabulary from which an observer of the way we use it is barred? The answer will be, presumably, that the methodology implicit in the second claim of the governing view already transcends the resources available to radical interpretation if the latter must prescind from consideration of our intellectual and sensory limitations, the kind of training which we receive, and so on. But then is not deliverance of so peculiar a conclusion some cause for disquiet with the richer methodology?

Second, what is actually responsible, on this view, for the large degree of coherence and communicative success which our use of color vocabulary enjoys? Indeed, what is the justification for continuing to think of the use of such expressions as governed by rule? Knowledge of appropriate rules was supposed to constitute linguistic competence. But it cannot do so if competent usage essentially has a coherence which, in Dummett's view, the rules lack. Dummett's response needs supplementing with an explanation of our communicative success with such vocabulary in which the idea of knowledge of inconsistent rules has an ineliminable part to play. For either such knowledge is still to be a basic ingredient in competence or we should drop the idea. But it is quite unclear, to me at least, how such an explanation should proceed.

---

4   A point Wittgenstein stresses repeatedly in the observations on consistency in *Remarks on the Foundations of Mathematics* (1978)

That brings us to the third, and, I think, a decisive objection to Dummett's response. I do not see how we can rest content with the idea that certain implicitly known semantic rules are incoherent when *nobody's* reaction, on being presented with the purported demonstration of the inconsistency, i.e., the paradox—even if they can find no fault with it—is to lose confidence in the unique propriety of the response— e.g., "That's orange"—which the demonstration seems to confound. Think of your reaction when, having received as explanation of the notion of class only the usual informal patter plus the axioms of naive set theory, you first confronted Russell's paradox. If, which is unlikely, you held any intuitive conviction about whether Russell's class was a member of itself, you will have been forced to recognize an exact parity in the opposing case; and the effect should have been to cause you to realize that there is just no view to take on the matter before some refinement of the notion of class has been made. But that is exactly *not* our response to the sorites paradox for "red". Our conviction of the correctness of the non-inferential ingredient in the contradiction is left *totally undisturbed*. So far from bringing us to recognize that, pending some refinement in the meaning of "red", there is just no such thing as justifiably describing something as "red" or not, our conviction is that no-one *ought* to be disturbed by the paradox—and this conviction is not based on certainty that we shall be able to disclose some simple fallacy. If the rules for the use of "red" really do sanction the paradox, why do we have absolutely no sense of disturbance, no sense that a *real case* has been made for the inferential ingredient at all? Are we so abjectly irrational that we cannot recognize our confusion even when it is completely explicit? A different account is called for.

3 Resolving the paradox by jettison of the first claim of the governing view

In Wright 1975 and Wright (I), I came down fairly strongly in favor of the third approach: that of rejecting the claim that understanding the relevant expressions should be seen as consisting in the implicit knowledge of semantic rules. This response need not involve total banishment of the concept of semantic rule from any satisfactory account of what it is to understand such an expression. Indeed, it would be a serious objection if banishment were involved since *some* sort of notion of rule would appear to be prerequisite for the very idea that such expressions have *meaning*, which we wish, presumably, to retain. So I am now inclined to acknowledge little real contrast between the third approach and the second—that of retaining the first part of the governing view while rejecting the patchwork epistemology of semantic rules mooted in its second part. What I had in mind in my earlier proposal was that we should, in any case, repudiate the idea that knowledge of the character of the rules governing sorites-affected expressions is to be construed as *propositional* knowledge, acquired by immersion, and largely implicit. That is the idea which sets up the project of rendering the purported content of this knowledge explicit, and which makes the second ingredient seem so natural and harmless. If we insist that, in these cases at least, there are *no* "contents" implicitly known—so, in only that sense, no rules—there is no space for an argument that the rules are incoherent. However, if it continues to be appropriate to think of correct use of the relevant expressions as subject to rule, in whatever appropriate sense, then it ought also to be harmless to continue to think of competent speakers as *knowing* the rules in question. Something like the letter of the first part of the governing view may accordingly yet be sustained. But, if we follow my former proposal, the knowledge which competent speakers have of the rules relating to the relevant expressions will not be implicit, propositional knowledge; it will be knowledge which—like the knowledge *how* which constitutes practical skills like ice-skating and balancing—calls for no content as its object.

This proposed response to the sorites may still seem frustratingly indefinite. If it can be worked into a satisfactory treatment of the problem, two matters, in particular, need extensive clarification. We need an account of the restricted class of cases, if any, in which it remains appropriate to think of understanding as constituted by implicit knowledge of the contents of rules. And we need a much fuller account of what positive conception of understanding should supplant the implicit knowledge conception in the problematic cases. If understanding "red", for instance, is to be thought of on the model of a practical skill, comparable to the ability to hit a good crosscourt backhand or ride a bicycle, we need both a sharp theoretical account of the distinction between those abilities in whose explanation it is legitimate and needful to invoke the idea of the agent's implicit propositional knowledge and the abilities, like those two examples, where we feel it is not; and also, ideally, independent reason to regard our understanding of sorites-affected expressions as constituted by abilities of the latter sort. Pending clarification of these matters, my earlier proposal offers, at most, a strategy for resolving the sorites paradox, and a pointer only to the general tenor of the lesson which it has to teach us.

Christopher Peacocke (1981) is unsanguine about the strategy, believing that it can be shown in advance that certain versions of the paradox will survive even if we abandon the conception that understanding is informed by (implicit) propositional knowledge of semantic rules. Peacocke invites consideration of a predicate, C, which is to apply to an object just in case the community will agree in calling that object "red". Suppose that some small difference, d, in the wavelength of light is not visually discriminable by any member of the community. And let light of wavelength k be definitely red. Then, according to Peacocke, we still have this paradox:

If a reflects light of wavelength k, then C(a).

If an object differs in the wavelength of light when it reflects by just d from something that is C, it too is C.

∴ All visible objects (reflecting pure light) are C.

Hence, "the paradox seems to arise even if we do not suppose that the use of these expressions is governed by rules." (Peacocke 1981, p. 122).

This may seem a rather puzzling thought. The example ought to be one, it seems, where a paradox arises for a predicate understanding which does not involve propositional knowledge of a rule. So how can a predicate *expressly defined* for the purpose, understanding which is thereby explicitly associated with knowing the content of a semantic rule, fit the bill?

Well, there are two different points to whose service Peacocke's example might be put. First, if C really is sorites-susceptible, there seems, for just the reason given—viz., that it is introduced by explicit statement of a rule—simply to be no space for the response recommended in my earlier papers. How can we possibly avoid bringing in the idea of propositional knowledge of the content of a rule if pressed to give an account of what it is to understand C? What Peacocke should claim, it seems, is not that the paradox arises in certain cases even after we have made the recommended response but that it arises in cases where the recommended response is not a possible option. But second, and more interesting, there is, in any case, reason to think that C is sorites-susceptible only if there is reason to think that communal consensus with "red" will be stable under indiscriminably small variations in light wavelength. Now of course, *one* reason for that thought would be if one supposed that "red" was governed by incoherent rules and that the community would stick by them. But if that were the only reason, dissolving the "red" paradox in the way I recommended would dissolve the C-paradox as well. So that cannot be Peacocke's reason. Rather, his thought is best interpreted as follows. Think, if you will, of competence with "red" as a practical skill, uninformed by propositional knowledge. The operation of the skill involves differential sensitivity to varying visual stimuli, but if—as is so—the stimuli permit variation too slight to be detected by our visual apparatus, the skill cannot involve discrimination exercised over differences of that order of magnitude. So if there is communal consensus that a patch of color is red, and if all that the participants in the consensus are responding to is the visual stimulus, it may seem quite unintelligible how the response can vary if the situation is changed only by altering the stimulus by an amount insufficient to be picked up by our visual systems.

That this way of looking at the matter really does prescind from the propositional knowledge conception is testified to by the fact that it now seems incidental to the example that it concerns subjects who are capable of grasping contents at all. Think instead of a digital tachometer on a car. All such a device goes on, all it is designed to respond to, are variations in electronic impulses. There will be limitations to its sensitivity—so sufficiently slight variations in the incoming impulse will not, presumably, provoke any variation in the reading. And now it is neither more nor less plausible than before to conclude that, provided we are careful at each stage not to vary the impulse too greatly, the reading will *never* vary over a series of steps, no matter how many.

It would, of course, be quite unphilosophical to take comfort in the thought that actual tachometers do not behave this way—it is only *because* they do not so behave that we have the appearance of paradox. So Peacocke should be granted that some apparent paradoxes of the sorites family are not amenable to the response I suggested. That, of course, completely disposes of the value of that suggestion only if we assume that the entire family must admit of a uniform solution. What, I suggest, Peacocke's example teaches us is that that is not so. In fact, when sorites paradoxes are individuated by reference to the type of ground adduced for their major premises, they fall, I believe, into at least three separate groups. One group involves support from the governing view; the C-paradox and the Tachometer paradox exemplify another group; and we shall be concerned with the third in section 5. (The groups are not, of course, individuated by the expressions which they concern: there is no reason a priori why one and the same expression should not be argued to be sorites-susceptible by reasoning of each of the three kinds.)

If it would be unphilosophical to take comfort in the fact, it remains that actual functioning tachometers cannot be stabilized through any number of uni-directional but sufficiently marginal changes in the incoming impulse: sooner or later they jump—and a good one will do so often enough, no matter how marginal the changes, to continue to serve as a practically reliable instrument. Therefore the premises of the Tachometer paradox are not true of actual tachometers; and the paradox must be resolved by explaining how exactly that is so. The obvious and presumably correct thought is nothing very exciting: the major premise, to the effect that if the instrument gives reading R in response to impulse i, it will also give R to any i' differing from i by no more than some specified amount, will turn out to be a misinterpretation of what is entailed by possession of a sensitivity threshold. Quite what the correct account will be will depend on the design of the particular instrument concerned. But one would expect it to be fairly typical that, within the continuous interval, $\langle i_1, ..., i_n \rangle$, there will be a finite subset of points, $\{b_1, ..., b_k\}$ such that in response to an impulse of any of these values, b_j, or lying within some margin, d, of b_j, the instrument will always respond with the reading f_j; while responses to other impulses with values in the interval, $\langle i_1, ..., i_n \rangle$, will depend additionally upon the prior state of the instrument.[5] One consequence, of course, is that such an instrument will, on different occasions, give different readings in response to the same impulse, depending on how that impulse is "approached"; but perhaps that is just what such instruments do.

The salient point is that it has to be consistent with the claims that a tachometer has a sensitivity threshold, and that its response is entirely to stimuli of a certain sort, to suppose that the major premise in the paradox is not everywhere true. Presumably, then, since communal consensus in the use of "red" does not extend all the way down to orange objects, the major premise in the C-paradox will be false on similar grounds. And the explanation of its falsity will be consistent with supposing that we all possess visual sensitivity thresholds and respond only to visual stimuli in our use of "red".

Peacocke is aware of the possibility of this kind of response to the C-paradox, and is dissatisfied with it. He writes

> ... any model for an application of vague observational predicates must provide analogues of three things involved in such application: there must be states which are the analogues of having experiences, there must be something analogous to the ... non-transitivity of non-discriminable difference, and there must be some analogue of the application of an observational predicate upon a particular occasion. (Peacocke 1981, p. 123)

Peacocke believes that it is impossible to provide for all three conditions in the sort of model illustrated by the tachometer. Suppose we assimilate the state of the instrument, induced by the reception of a particular

---

5 Pictorially

impulse, to the having of an experience; and the reading which it issues to the application of the predicate. What about the non-transitivity of indiscriminability? In the case illustrated, for instance, we can, by choosing a pair of values which are respectively within and just outside the d-margin of some b_1 elicit—at least sometimes—differential responses from the instrument *no matter how small* the difference between the two chosen values may be. How then can it be claimed that sufficiently small differences are indiscriminable for the instrument, so that—since larger ones are not—the relation, "... is not discriminable by the instrument from ...", behaves non-transitively?

But Peacocke is wrong about this. Or rather: he is right to think it essential that some analogue of non-transitive indiscriminability should be a feature of the model but wrong to suppose that one cannot be provided. The impression to the contrary requires that the instrument's *sometimes* issuing different responses to a pair of stimuli should be regarded as sufficient for its being able to discriminate between them. And the error in that supposition is easily demonstrated if, reverting once again to a case in which human beings are the instruments, we consider Michael Dummett's example of the slowly moving pointer (Dummett, p. 112). You observe a pointer which is initially at rest but then begins to move, too slowly however for you to see that it is moving. You are asked to give a signal—to raise your right hand, say—as soon as it seems to you to occupy a different position to the initial position; and—let us add to Dummett's example—to raise both hands as soon as it seems to you to have moved into another position again. Suppose that you raise one hand after four seconds, and both after eight. Are we to conclude that the position which the pointer seemed to you to occupy after the third second looked different to the position which it seemed to you to occupy after the fourth? The answer, of course, is that you cannot detect any difference between those positions—what you meant to indicate when you first raised one hand was only that the position now seemed to you to be different to the starting point.

As Dummett brings out, there are ways of describing the phenomenology of the situation which are threatened with incoherence—and perhaps none which are not. But it is legitimate to suppose, for the purposes of the analogy with the tachometer, that your permissible "signals" are restricted to the raising and lowering of hands. Suppose, then, that the actual positions of the pointer after each second are determined by some appropriately finely calibrated instrument. The situation will be that you sometimes will and sometimes won't respond to the sorts of changes involved from one second to the next by varying your signal; but that *asked* about any single such change, you will report the positions involved seem to you to be the same. More: if we imagine that, once you have raised both hands, the movement of the pointer is reversed, we would expect to find that when it regained the position originally occupied after three seconds, you would still have one hand raised. If we—as is permissible—suppose further that your signals for the positions occupied initially, after four seconds, and after eight seconds, are by-and-large respectively uniform, then your performance is now in all relevant respects assimilable to that of the hypothetical tachometer. And, crucially, the fact that you always (more or less) have a hand raised when the four-second position is presented, but only sometimes have a hand raised when the three-second position is presented is *no indication that those positions seem different to you*. On the contrary, if they did seem different, you would *always* give a different signal. So far, then, from its being a sufficient reason for regarding the tachometer as able to discriminate between a pair of impulses that it sometimes issues different readings in response to them, the fact that it does not *always* do so should be regarded as decisive for regarding the relation in which they stand to it as an analogue of *indiscriminability*. And the modelling of non-transitivity is then provided by the reflection that among three distinct impulses, the tachometer may *only sometimes* respond differentially with respect to the first and second, and *only sometimes* respond differentially with respect to the second and third, but *always* respond differentially with respect to the first and third.[6]

I conclude that this class of sorites paradoxes need not detain us. Their major premises are false, and false in a way which classical two-valued semantics is quite adequate to describe. The details of why they are false will, of course, depend upon the character of the particular "instruments" concerned; and I am not seriously suggesting that the tachometer provides a satisfactory model of all aspects of human competence with color vocabulary. My point is only that, once the first

---

6   It may occur to the reader that, as I have presented the example, the raising and lowering of hands will involve judgments in which an observational *relation*— "seems to be differently positioned from"—rather than an observational predicate is an ingredient I do not think this qualifies the force of the example, however First, the holding aloft of zero, one, or two hands—while undoubtedly "observational" responses in the sense which currently occupies us—would have to be encashed in terms somewhat like, "looks to be in the original position", "looks to be in the four second position", and "looks to be in the eight second position" respectively. It is not obvious that these are not properly regarded as observational predicates Second, the point that the example is being used to make—that a tendency sometimes to respond differentially to a pair of stimuli need imply no capacity to tell them apart—could be illustrated in lots of other ways in any case.

claim of the governing view is abandoned, the residual case which Peacocke thinks he sees for supposing C to be sorites-susceptible is perfectly matched by the Tachometer paradox; and the model solution sketched for the latter depends on no feature of the tachometer without an analogue in the "instrument" constituted by a human being responding to color. Accordingly, while different things might need to be said about why precisely the major premise in the C-paradox is false, we can at least understand why we shall not be committed to its truth simply by supposing that our descriptions of color are nothing but responses to visual stimuli among which our discriminations are not everywhere transitive.

4 Tolerance and observationality

Peacocke concludes his objection to the tachometer analogy with the complaint that, if it were apt,

> ... there would be no difficulty in the idea of an observational predicate ... definitely applying to one but not to the other of two objects which produce experiences which are not discriminably different in quality. But in fact we can make no sense of this idea. (Peacocke 1981, p. 124)

Undoubtedly, we can make no sense of it if observational predicates are governed by the *rule* that they apply to both, if to either, of any pair of observationally indistinguishable items. But that, I want to suggest, is just the misunderstanding of what an observational predicate is which the governing view encourages. The question is therefore, what should we replace it with?

Of course, the question whether *any* vocabulary is worth distinguishing as "observational" has been intensively debated by twentieth century philosophy of science; and the received wisdom has been in favor of a negative answer. Still, it is natural to feel, there *is* a class of predicates—those expressing colors, places, musical pitch, or perhaps any Lockean secondary quality—for which Peacocke's thought has prima facie force. Whether we style these predicates as observational or not, how exactly are they equipped to effect the sort of distinction, among qualitatively indistinguishable items, whose intelligibility Peacocke is questioning? We shall get an inkling about how an answer to this question might go by reflecting on what may seem a fairly obvious lacuna in the response to the sorites which I have been canvassing. The response claims, in essentials, that the *motivation* for the major premises in (a large class of) sorites paradoxes is misguided; that the pressure to assent to the major premises is generated only by the mistaken assumptions of the governing view. But can it suffice for a solution just to undercut the *motivation* for the major premise in, e.g., the sorites paradox for "red"? Do we not need, in addition, to disclose some *specific* fault with the major premise? If there is really no paradox, then that conditional *cannot be true*; and we cannot rest content until we have explained exactly why not, and, if necessary, have devised a semantic apparatus in terms of which the manner of its untruth can be properly described.

We are now in a position to see how at least the outline of such an account might run. Let us essay to see ourselves, in accordance with rejection (or, at least, severe qualification) of the first claim of the governing view, on the model of *signalling instruments* for qualities like red—albeit voluntary signallers. Then there ought to be the same kind of connection between an item's being red and the description to which we are prepared to assent, when appropriately placed and functioning normally in normal circumstances, as obtains between, say, an engine's operating at 4500 rpm and the reading issued by a number of correctly connected tachometers which are functioning properly and are free from external interference. This connection is actually such as to generate a *truth condition*: for a particular reading to be correct *is* for it to be the case that the mean value of the readings issued by sufficiently many appropriate instruments, which are appropriately situated, functioning properly, and free from external interference, will coincide with that reading. So, too, for red, or any quality of the kind which Peacocke's quoted thought seems plausible. For an object to be (definitely) red *is* for it to be the case that the opinion of each of a sufficient number of competent and attentive subjects who are appropriately situated to command a clear perception of the object, functioning normally, and free from interfering background beliefs—for instance, some doubt about their situational competence—would be that it was red.

What follows? Well, one thing we know—and, having disposed of the Tachometer paradox, can bring to bear with a clear conscience—is that if a sorites-series of indistinguishable color patches is run past a group of such subjects under the specified conditions, and they are agreed about the redness of the initial elements, there will be, as the series moves towards orange, a specific *first* patch over which the consensus fractures. The occurrence of the fracture need not raise any doubt about the continuing competence of the subjects or about the satisfaction of the specified conditions at that point; nor need any of the subjects be able to re-identify that patch if it is subsequently re-presented with its immediate predecessor in a different setting. So the upshot is simple. If observational qualities, whatever should be their proper characterization, essentially sustain the sort of equation which the tachometer analogy suggests—if their application is a function of what

competent observers, under suitable conditions, etc., will assent to—
then a predication of red, or any observational quality, fails of definite
truth as soon as the right hand side of the equation fails of truth. We
have therefore to acknowledge, surprising as it may seem, that a sorites
series of indistinguishable color patches *can* contain a last patch which
is definitely red: it will be a patch about whose redness there is a
consensus meeting the described conditions, and its immediate successor will be a patch about which the consensus breaks down in a way
that still observes those conditions.

It may be difficult or impossible to *identify* such a patch in a particular
case, either because it is difficult to verify that consensus has broken
down in a way which still observes the conditions, or because it is
known that one or more of the conditions is unsatisfied. But it remains
that there can be such a patch; that it *can* be identified under favorable
circumstances; and that, even in circumstances which are not favorable,
when the consensus has broken down for irrelevant reasons, it is legitimate to suppose that there is such a patch which could have been
identified had the conditions been different. No doubt, it would usually
be of absolutely no interest to effect such an identification. And it
should be noted that there is, a priori, no reason to suppose that "the
last definitely red patch" would turn out to have a stable reference; if it
did not, that would disclose an element of context-relativity in the
concept of red which we normally do not suspect.

Provided, then, that observational qualities indeed sustain the
relevant sort of equation, we can, more than undercut the motivation
for believing them to be true, explain how specifically the major
premises in sorites paradoxes for observational predicates fail of truth.
(The question remains how such explanations could proceed for other
kinds of sorites—I shall return to it below.) We can also make sense of
the idea of an observational predicate definitely applying only to one of
a pair of phenomenally indiscriminable objects, which Peacocke
claimed was unintelligible. What *is* unintelligible is how someone
might tell just by inspection of a pair of indiscriminable items that they
in fact mark the watershed, in a particular context, between what is
definitely red and what is not. But Peacocke's claim follows from that
only if we suppose that any observational predicate worth the title must
be such that this distinction can be drawn purely observationally. And
that is the mistake: the raising of an arm, in the example of the slowly
moving pointer, is a gesture made purely in response to how things
look—it is explicitly instructed that this is how it should be made—and
so may be regarded as analogous to the application of an expression
which is observational in the sense which Peacocke intends. The fact
remains that if we suppose that having a single arm in the air is *definitely*

an appropriate response only in situations when—supposing the satisfaction of all the relevant conditions—the subject *always* has a single arm raised, the observationality of the response is consistent with the existence of a sharp boundary to the cases where it is definitely appropriate.

On the account of observationality which figures in Dummett (this volume) and in my earlier papers, a predicate is observational if whether it applies to an object can invariably be determined just by (unaided) observation of that object. It seems to follow immediately that any such predicate must be applicable to both, if to either, of any pair of objects which (unaided) observation cannot tell apart; so that the account renders all observational predicates tolerant with respect to indiscriminable change and thus takes us straight over the precipice. But there is an unclarity here: is it intended that the distinction between definite cases of application and *all others* be observationally decidable,[7] or merely that between definite cases of application and those where the predicate definitely *fails* to apply? A little reflection suggests that what we really want is the second, weaker version. The observationality of "red", for instance, should entail only that something is red only if any suitable subject may, in appropriate circumstances, observe it to be so; and that something is not red only if any such subject may, likewise, in appropriate circumstances, observe it not to be red. A predicate's being observational in this sense need not entail that a distinction can always be drawn, just by observation of the objects concerned, between cases to which it definitely applies and cases of any other sort. Indeed there is something absurd about the idea that *that* distinction might be observationally decidable, since borderline cases of "red", for instance, are exactly cases about whose classification observation, even in appropriate circumstances, leaves at least some suitable subjects essentially *unsure*.

Let me pause to review the two principal suggestions of this section so far. The first is that it is not, contrary to Peacocke's claim, unintelligible how anything worth regarding as an observational predicate might definitely apply only to one of a pair of observationally indistinguishable items; on the contrary, the possibility is implicit in the consideration

---

7 Note that observational decidability, in the intended sense, does not preclude the intrusion of considerations from scientific theory into our conception of *when* "unaided observation" is to be able to deliver the correct verdict So "red" can count as observationally decidable consistently with the occurrence of red illusions associated, e g., with red shift and the Doppler effect on light traversing galactic distances Observational decidability, like all concepts of possibility, is a concept of what is possible *in appropriate circumstances*, but our idea of which circumstances are appropriate may well be theoretically informed

(to which we were led by consideration of the analogy with the tachometer but which stands independently) that it is a necessary condition for an observational predicate to apply to a particular item that any suitable subject who observes the item under appropriate circumstances will judge that it does so. The second is that it is an error to think that Peacocke's idea follows if we agree that anything worth regarding as an observational predicate must be such that whether or not it applies to an object can be determined, in appropriate circumstances, etc., just by observation of it. What that commits us to is only the second, weaker principle sketched in the preceding paragraph. To be sure, the governing view arguably provides grounds for thinking that "red" is observational in a sense which subserves the stronger, paradoxical principle. We shall review those grounds in section 6.

There is much more that needs to be said about the notion of an observational predicate. Here though, I can only briefly canvass two further suggestions. First, on the relation between the two thoughts just summarized. There is no objection, one would imagine, to interpreting the reference to "appropriate circumstances" in the weaker principle along exactly the lines featured in the biconditional for qualities like red to which consideration of the tachometer analogy led us. "Appropriate circumstances" are those where the subject is appropriately placed to observe the object concerned; "suitable subjects" are competent, attentive, perceptually normal subjects who are free of interfering background beliefs. So the weaker principle, so interpreted, has just the effect in its own right which the biconditional had: reason to doubt that competent, etc., subjects would, in appropriate circumstances, judge an object to be red—reason afforded, perhaps, by such subjects actually failing to do so—is reason to doubt that the object should be classified as red. Thus the weaker principle, so far from motivating acceptance of the major premises for sorites paradoxes involving observational predicates, actually subserves the form of rejection of such premises suggested by the analogy with the tachometer.

Note, therefore, the perspective in which the stronger principle is now placed. The stronger principle differs from the weaker only in its second clause. But the effect of the weaker principle just described is wholly owing to its first clause. So the stronger principle likewise has that effect: to endorse the principle is to be committed to treating a lack of consensus among competent, etc., subjects in appropriate circumstances as a sufficient reason for doubting that something is definitely red, even if the object in question is indistinguishable from one about which a consensus obtains. If therefore, as it seems, the stronger principle also entails that "definitely red" tolerates indiscriminable difference, the conclusion is forced that the ingredient clauses of the stronger principle are actually incoherent: collectively they entail that a difference must always be apparent to observation between anything which is definitely red and anything of any other sort; but the first clause also entails that different responses by competent, etc., subjects may suffice for such a difference even if the items in question are observationally indistinguishable. This is a quite different conclusion to anything that might be inferred from the role of the stronger principle in the generation of one kind of sorites paradox for "red". For one thing, that paradox depends, in addition, on assumption of the non-transitivity of indiscriminability; for another, the kind of semantic incoherence which the paradox has been thought—by Dummett, for instance—to disclose, must not be confused with the kind of incoherence just bruited. It is not inconsistent to suppose that there might be semantically incoherent predicates; but no predicate can be observational in a sense which subserves the stronger principle—at least if the foregoing is correct—since to be so would be to meet an inconsistent specification.[8]

Finally, let me sketch a possible connection with a proposal for the characterization of observational expressions which I have entertained elsewhere (Wright 1986c, especially pp. 276–80). Observational expressions are those which connect most intimately and immediately with our experience. The account of observationality given by Dummett, (and Peacocke's purported refinement—see note 8) both locate this intimate, immediate connection in the *conditions of application* of the expression. Observational expressions are to apply, or not, in virtue of how things appear. But an alternative would be to seek an account by

---

8 Peacocke's discussion takes a rather strange turn just after the passage quoted on p. 220, on which he proceeds to base a refinement of the idea of an observational predicate (See Peacocke 1981, pp. 127–28) According to the refinement, observational predicates are distinguished by their satisfaction of the condition that, with respect to any pair of indiscriminable items x and y, it cannot be the case that such a predicate definitely applies to x but does not definitely apply to y, formally,

$$Ixy \rightarrow (Def(Fx) \& \neg Def(Fy))$$

How exactly does this proposal prevent observational predicates from being generically sorites-susceptible? Peacocke's answer, in a familiar tradition, is that such predicates are predicates of degree. His own positive response to the paradox . is that the consequents of the conditionals which are instances of the major premise will typically be *slightly less* true, accordingly, than the antecedents He is thus able to maintain that the consequent of the above conditional may have a lower degree of truth than its antecedent consistently with the conditional's retaining its distinctive acceptability for observational expressions it will be so acceptable just in case whenever the antecedent is true, the consequent is *almost* true Now, the consequent will presumably, be almost true just in case the conjunction, $Def(Fx) \& \neg Def(Fy)$, is almost false, which, intuitively, should be the situation when one, or both of the

exploration, rather, of the *conditions of understanding*. To be sure, items qualified by an observational predicate ought, under appropriate circumstances, to present a distinctive appearance; and understanding the predicate ought to involve attaching a proper significance to the appearance, or range of appearances, associated in this way with it. But there are some expressions—a good example is a natural kind term like "banana"—which we would not wish to regard as observational because, e.g., they carry implications about constitution and origin, even though the things they qualify have distinctive enough appearances. And it is striking that somebody's use of an expression could be quite properly responsive to the kind of appearances associated with it and yet they might not understand it precisely because ignorant of such additional implications. A natural suggestion, then, is that observational expressions are marked off from this wider class precisely by the circumstance that, while anyone who understands such an expression must display an appropriate sensitivity to a certain distinctive range of appearances with which its application is standardly associated, there must in addition be no space for the possibility of their doing so yet failing to understand the expression. "Gene", "torque converter", and "pulsar" fail to qualify as observational because there is no particular kind of appearance possessed by the things to which they apply; "banana" and "human being" fail to qualify because someone who had no grasp of the kinds of thing which bananas and human beings respectively are might still be quite clear about the way they tend to look, and might show as much in their employment of "banana" and "human being".

This indicates, at most, merely the rough shape which a satisfactory

conjuncts are almost false, although neither is actually false Hence if *Def(Fx)* is true, ¬*Def(Fy)* will be almost false, so *Def(Fy)* will be almost true But that, on Peacocke's view, will be the most that can be inferred from the acceptability of the original conditional, the indiscriminability of *x* and *y*, and the truth of *Def(Fx)* So the paradox is obstructed (The reader will be able to see how similar remarks would apply to the attempt to work the paradox from right-to-left, as it were, taking as premise ¬*Def(Fy)*)

What immediately strikes one, however, is that, once Peacocke has a conditional which allows of almost-truth, there is no need for this reformulated account of observationality. For the mere *almost-truth* of the conditional

Ixy → (*Def(Fx)* → *Def(Fy)*)

would not subserve the sorites paradox either The way in which Peacocke makes his preferred account of observationality avoid paradox is equally open to the original, seemingly inevitably paradoxical version Still, that is just a quibble The substantive point remains that if we wish to avoid trafficking in degrees of truth, we owe a different kind of account of what observationality is—if not the sort outlined in the text, than another account of observationality might assume.[9] What is salient is that any expression which conforms to it is presumably going to sustain something very close to the clause which is common to the weaker and stronger principles which we have been discussing. If "φ" is such an expression, for instance, then it follows from the sketched account that anything which it qualifies will present, under appropriate circumstances, a distinctive kind of appearance to which anyone suitable who understands "φ" will be appropriately responsive; i.e., they will be prepared to judge that the item is so qualified provided other appropriate conditions are met.

Natural kind concepts, like "banana" and "human being", will likewise sustain such clauses, provided it really is essential that their instances have a certain sort of appearance. (If it is not, then they should be classified with "pulsar" and "torque converter" after all.) The question arises, therefore, whether the addition of a stipulation that such sensitivity is to suffice for understanding "φ", though not "banana",[10] somehow imports commitment to the tolerance of "φ" with respect to indiscriminable change. It is clear that the stipulation pre-empts the kind of explanation which can be given, in the case of natural kind predicates, of how they may distinguish between observationally indiscriminable items. An artefact—a "fool's banana", for instance—may be indistinguishable from an instance of natural kind; understanding "banana" involves grasping this possibility. Needless to say, pre-empting one kind of explanation need not be to foreclose on all, but the question is still outstanding: how might the corresponding explanation go in the case of predicates which conform to the proposed account?

---

9   This proposal is actually very close to the account of observationality offered by Peacocke himself in his 1983, chapter 4 Peacocke is there concerned not with the sorites but with the prevailing scepticism among philosophers of science concerning the very idea of an observational concept/statement I doubt if I should have conceived the present suggestion without the benefit of conversations and correspondence with Peacocke prior to the publication of his 1983 But the reader should be wary of assuming that Peacocke would endorse my suggestion; it contains, in particular, no explicit analogue of the play with *experience* which Peacocke's treatment involves.

10   The proposal that if someone's use of "red" manifests an appropriate sensitivity to color-appearances, that suffices for their understanding "red", leaves us free, of course, to ponder just what kind of sensitivity *is* appropriate. In particular, we are free to insist that the sensitivity be informed by the conception that red is a property of the object of predication, and so to require, e g , that the subject acknowledge certain a priori principles which evince this conception—for instance, that red things retain their color when unperceived Analogues of all such principles may be expected to hold for natural kind terms also, so there is no threat here of compromise of the contrast drawn in the text

How could the "appropriate kind of responsiveness" operate selectively among indiscriminabilia? If I am right that the kind of account of observationality mooted will entail that observational expressions comply with the first clause of the stronger (and weaker) principle, then what is asked for is, in effect, an explanation of why the mooted account does not entail their compliance with the second clause of the stronger principle—the clause whose inclusion makes it impossibly strong. I shall revert to the matter in section 6.

5 Higher-order vagueness and the No Sharp Boundaries paradox

It was remarked earlier that in addition to the lines of reasoning which the governing view encourages, major premises for sorites paradoxes may be motivated in (at least) two further, quite different ways. One such is the train of thought that generates the Tachometer and C-paradoxes. But it is another which seems to make the connection between vagueness and sorites-susceptibility most explicit and most intimate. Surely, this train of thought proceeds, the very vagueness of φ must entail that in a series of appropriately gradually changing objects, φ at one end but not at the other, there will be no n-th element which is φ while the $n + 1^{st}$ is not; for if there were, the cut-off between φ and not-φ would be sharp, contrary to hypothesis. Accordingly, the vagueness of φ over such a series must always be reflected in a truth of the form:

(i) $\neg(\exists x)(\varphi x \,\&\, \neg\varphi x')$

That, of course, is a classical equivalent of the universally quantified conditional which is the major premise in standard formulations of the sorites paradox—a thought which has prompted Putnam[11] to suggest that a shift to intuitionistic logic might be of value in the treatment of the paradox. So indeed it might. But it will not be enough; for intuitionistic logic will yield a paradox direct from the negative existential premise (as will any logic with the standard $\exists$- and &-Introduction rules plus *reductio ad absurdum*).[12] This form of the paradox—the *No Sharp Boundaries paradox*—thus appears to constitute a proof that (one kind of) vagueness is *eo ipso* a form of semantic incoherence.

---

11. Putnam 1983, especially pp 284–86. Intuitionistically, $\neg(\exists x)(\varphi x \,\&\, \neg\varphi x')$ is equivalent to $(\forall x)(\varphi x \to \neg\neg\varphi x')$, but not to $(\forall x)(\varphi x \to \varphi x')$ unless φ is effectively decidable, for non-effectively-decidable φ, the last may consistently be denied without commitment to $(\exists x)(\varphi x \,\&\, \neg\varphi x')$

12 See Read and Wright 1985 Putnam 1985 has since protested that he never intended to recommend *denial* of $(\exists x)(\varphi x \,\&\, \neg\varphi x')$; his point was only that, intuitionistically, we could accept $\neg(\forall x)(\varphi x \to \varphi x')$—as the paradox seems to force us to—without commitment to the fictitious boundary imported by asserting $(\exists x)(\varphi x \,\&\, \neg\varphi x')$ But Read and I said nothing to the contrary Our point was that bringing the

Only "appears" though. What the No Sharp Boundaries paradox brings out is that, when dealing with vague expressions, it is essential to have the expressive resources afforded by an operator expressing *definiteness* or *determinacy*. I have heard it argued that the introduction of such an operator can serve no point since there is no apparent way whereby a statement could be true without being definitely so. That is undeniable, but it is only to say that—in terms of Dummett's distinction (1981, pp. 446–47)—the *content senses* of "*p*" and "Definitely *p*" coincide; whereas the important thing, for our purposes, is that their *ingredient senses* differ, the vital difference concerning the behavior of the two statement forms when embedded in negation. Equipped with an appropriate such operator, we can see that a proper expression of the vagueness of φ with respect to the relevant sort of series of objects is not provided by the above negative existential but rather requires a statement to the effect that no definitely φ element is immediately succeeded by one which is definitely not φ; formally.

(ii) $\neg(\exists x)[Def(\varphi x) \,\&\, Def(\neg\varphi x')]$

This principle generates no paradox. The worst we can get from it, with or without classical logic, is the means for proving, for successive x', that

(iii) $Def(\neg\varphi x') \rightarrow \neg Def(\varphi x)$.

And nothing untoward follows from that.

A believer in higher-order vagueness[13] may want to reply that this

---

distinctions of intuitionist logic to bear on vague statements—for which, Putnam acknowledges, the semantic motivation must be quite unlike that appealed to in the mathematical case—won't stop the sorites paradox We have, independently, to find something wrong with the impression that $\neg(\exists x)(\varphi x \,\&\, \neg\varphi x')$ is a satisfactory expression of the vagueness of φ in the relevant series of objects

In Read and Wright 1985, we remarked that there would still be a place for at least one intuitionistic ploy—rejection of the inference from $\neg\neg(\exists x)(\varphi x \,\&\, \neg\varphi x')$ to $(\exists x)(\varphi x \,\&\, \neg\varphi x')$ Putnam acknowledges this, but in fact the argument to "unmotivate" $\neg(\exists x)(\varphi x \,\&\, \neg\varphi x')$ about to be developed in the text shows that even this is wrong: $\neg\neg(\exists x)(\varphi x \,\&\, \neg\varphi x')$ is as bad an expression of the proposition of which the paradox is a legitimate proof by *reductio* as $\neg(\exists x)(\varphi x \,\&\, \neg\varphi x')$ is of φ's vagueness in the relevant series

13 A nice example of succumbing to the allure of the idea is provided by Dummett (1978, p 182).

. the vagueness of a vague predicate is ineradicable Thus "hill" is a vague predicate, in that there is no definite line between hills and mountains But we could not eliminate this vagueness by introducing a new predicate, say "eminence", to apply to those things which are neither definitely hills nor definitely mountains, since there would still remain things which were neither definitely hills nor definitely eminences, and so *ad infinitum* [sic]

A sophisticated discussion of the topic is Fine's (this volume) section 5

merely postpones the difficulty. If, for example, the distinction between things which are φ and borderline cases of φ is itself vague, then assent to

(iv) $\neg(\exists x)[Def(\varphi x)\ \&\ \neg Def(\varphi x')]$

would seem to be compelled even if assent to (i) is not. Someone who sympathized with the drift of section 4 will want to dispute that predicates like "red" do indeed possess higher-order vagueness—the truth is merely that the distinction between the last definitely φ item and the first case where some measure of indefiniteness enters is not to be placed just by looking. For present purposes, though, let us suppose that the phenomenon is real. Then once again the materials for paradox seem to be at hand, each ingredient move taking the form, for instance, of a transition from $\neg Def(\varphi k')$ to $\neg Def(\varphi k)$.

I believe that this thought, that higher-order vagueness is *per se* a source of paradox, may quite possibly be correct. But some complication is needed. For the following is the immediate reply. Of *any* pair of concepts which share a blurred boundary, we shall want to affirm

(v) $\neg(\exists x)[Def(\varphi x)\ \&\ Def(\psi x')]$

when x ranges over the elements of an appropriate series in which the blurred boundary between φ and ψ is crossed. The original problem occurred when, with ¬φ in place of ψ, we overlooked the necessary role of the definiteness operator. And now we are guilty of the same oversight again; it is merely that this time ψ has been replaced by $\neg Def(\varphi)$. As soon as the inclusion of the definiteness operator is insisted on, all that emerges is

(vi) $\neg(\exists x)[Def(Def(\varphi x))\ \&\ Def(\neg Def(\varphi x'))]$

which yields nothing more than the harmless

(vii) $Def(\neg Def(\varphi k')) \to \neg Def(Def(\varphi k))$

Evidently the strategy will generalize; we need never, it seems, be at a loss for a way of formulating φ's possession of vagueness, of whatever order, in a way that avoids paradox.

But this is too quick. We are able to be confident that the sort of formulation illustrated avoids paradox only because we have so far no semantics for the definiteness operator, and are treating it as logically inert. Without considering what form a semantics for it might take, the crucial question is whether it would be correct to require validation for this principle:

(DEF) $\dfrac{\Gamma \vdash P}{\Gamma \vdash Def(P)}$; provided Γ consists of propositions, all of which are prefixed by "*Def*".

For, in the presence of DEF, and assuming that the corrected formulation, (vi) above, of what it is for the borderline between φ and its first-order borderline cases to be itself blurred, is itself *definitely* correct, the harmless (vii) gives way to

(viii) $Def(\neg Def(\varphi k')) \rightarrow Def(\neg Def(\varphi k))$,

a generalization of which will enable us to prove that φ has no definite instances if it has definite borderline cases of the first order.[14]

DEF has this effect because it sanctions the inference from $Def(\varphi k)$ to $Def(Def(\varphi k))$. More generally, assuming that what is definitely true is true, DEF yields the biconditional theorem,

(IT) $\vdash Def(A) \leftrightarrow Def(Def(A))$.

If, as was supposed, A and $Def(A)$ may have differing ingredient senses, this may seem obviously unacceptable. But matters are not so straight-forward. The question is whether the difference is one to which the context, "$Def(\ )$", is, like "$Not(\ )$", itself sensitive. Suppose, for instance, we had a semantics which accounted $Def(A)$ *false* when A was anything other than definitely true, and Not-A as borderline when A was border-line. Not-$Def(A)$ would then, presumably, be true when A was border-line—diverging, as it intuitively should, from Not-A; but $Def(A)$ and $Def(Def(A))$ would both be false. An approach having these features would not, I suppose, be a non-starter—the idea has some appeal that if A is on any sort of borderline, the claim that it is anything else is false. But unless we found more to say, there would be no evident objection to DEF.

There *is* more to say, of course. To take higher-order vagueness seriously is just to allow that cases may arise where it is indeterminate whether a statement is true or borderline. To say that its definitization was *false* in such a case would be, in effect, to rule that the original was borderline—to ignore its leanings, as it were, towards truth. So the sort of semantics adumbrated which promises to validate DEF is anyway guilty of failing to take higher-order vagueness seriously: to repeat, taking higher-order vagueness seriously involves allowing that $Def(A)$ may itself, on occasion, be borderline.

So to allow, however, will make no difference as far as IT is concerned unless, when $Def(A)$ is borderline, $Def(Def(A))$ may either be false or, at any rate, of an inferior degree of truth to that of $Def(A)$. But the idea that $Def(Def(A))$ may be false when $Def(A)$ is borderline can hardly be separated from the corresponding claim about $Def(A)$ and A respec-tively—the claim just accused of failing to take higher-order vagueness seriously. So a defender of higher-order vagueness should prefer the second type of proposal: when a statement is borderline, so should its definitization be, but not in such a way as to sustain IT, left-to-right.

14　A derivation is given on p 233 below.

How might this proposal be elaborated? Let us pretend for a moment that we really do understand the idea of an indefinite hierarchy of orders of vagueness, along the following lines:

Level $-\omega$:   statements which are false

⋮

Level -2:   statements which are neither definitely false nor definitely at level -1

Level -1:   statements which are neither definitely false nor definitely at level 0

Level 0:   statements which are neither definitely true nor definitely false

Level 1:   statements which are neither definitely true nor definitely at level 0

Level 2:   statements which are neither definitely true nor definitely at level 1

⋮

Level ω: statements which are true

where it is understood that each statement of finite positive level is closer to truth than any statement which is definitely of level 0; and each statement of finite negative level is closer to falsity. Then a relatively straightforward proposal would be that, for any statement of level k, its definitization is of level $k-1$, if k is finite or 0, but otherwise is also of level k. So if A is definitely true, or false, so is $Def(A)$; but if A is on some sort of borderline, $Def(A)$ lies on the immediately inferior borderline. And A $\leftrightarrow$ B will hold only if A and B are of the same level.

But the problem with this is evident enough. Any statement, A, of finite level k, > 0, is part-characterized as one which is not definitely true. So the statement of which that part-characterization is the negation ought to be *false*—and that statement ought to be $Def(A)$. It is accordingly impossible to marry the sense given to "*Def*" by the proposal with our intuitive understanding of "definitely".

The point is a general one. We cannot intelligibly characterize higher-orders of vagueness in terms which invoke statements' failure to be definitely true, yet simultaneously require definitization to generate falsity only when applied to false statements. We could, of course, drop the latter requirement without reverting to the original idea that $Def(A)$ *always* polarizes to truth or falsity. A (somewhat messy) compromise would be that $Def(A)$ continues to drop a level on A just in case A occupies some finite negative level, but polarizes to falsity if A occupies any finite positive level or 0. But, as will be apparent if we now construct an explicit derivation, this compromise does nothing to obstruct the relevant version of the No Sharp Boundaries paradox:

1	(1)	$Def(\neg(\exists x)[Def(Def(\varphi x)) \ \& \ Def(\neg Def(\varphi x'))])$	Ass.
2	(2)	$Def(\neg Def(\varphi x'))$	Ass.
3	(3)	$Def(\varphi x)$	Ass.
3	(4)	$Def(Def(\varphi x))$	IT
2,3	(5)	$(\exists x)[Def(Def(\varphi x)) \ \& \ Def(\neg Def(\varphi x'))]$	2,4, $\exists$-intro.
1	(6)	$\neg(\exists x)[Def(Def(\varphi x)) \ \& \ Def(\neg Def(\varphi x'))]$	1, *Def*-elim.
1,2	(7)	$\neg Def(\varphi x)$	3,5,6, RAA
1,2	(8)	$Def(\neg Def(\varphi x))$	7, DEF
1	(9)	$Def(\neg Def(\varphi x')) \to Def(\neg Def(\varphi x))$	2,8 CP

Clearly IT and DEF do not survive the mooted compromise without restrictions: $Def(A)$ will fail of equivalence to $Def(Def(A))$ for any A of finite negative level; and $Def(A)$ will be of level lower than A for A of any finite level, negative or positive. But remember that each φx or $\varphi x'$ with which we are concerned in this version of the paradox is of level 0 or greater—we start with an x' which is a definite borderline case of φ and "work left", so to speak. So the compromise poses no obstacle to the application of IT at line (4): $Def(\varphi x)$ and $Def(Def(\varphi x))$ will both be false for every germane φx. Similarly, the compromise offers no objection to the application of DEF at line (8): if φx is of level 0 or greater finite level, $\neg Def(\varphi x)$ and $Def(\neg Def(\varphi x))$ will both be true, and if φx is of level ω (in which case why doesn't it mark a sharp boundary?), $\neg Def(\varphi x)$ and $Def(\neg Def(\varphi x))$ will both be false. And, to stress: every φx at which we arrive by "working left" is in one of those two cases.

I am under no illusion that these sketchy remarks constitute a treatment of the topic. But they do suggest that the No Sharp Boundaries paradox may have something to teach us, not about vagueness generally but about the idea of an indefinite hierarchy of orders of vagueness. The idea, which has smitten some writers,[15] that lack of sharp boundaries is *per se* paradoxical is merely retribution for working with too crude a formulation of what lack of sharp boundaries is. It is essential to have the expressive resources of a definiteness operator. But the case for thinking that higher-order vagueness—always a difficult and vertiginous-seeming idea—may be *per se* paradoxical still needs an answer.

There is a further, very important point to which the introduction of a definiteness operator into our formulations gives rise. Earlier, in section 4, the complaint was briefly considered that it could not suffice to resolve a sorites paradox simply to undermine any motivation for believing the major premise. For there is a paradox in any case unless

---

15 The most notorious case, I suppose, is Peter Unger A typical example of his use of the sorites is his 1979a.

the major premise, motivated or not, is *untrue*—the paradox is, indeed, a *reductio* of the major premise—and an account is therefore owing of *how*, specifically, it is untrue. Such an account is provided, for expressions like "red", by the considerations—if sound—which were advanced in section 4 to support the idea that such expressions can have determinate thresholds of application in the appropriate kind of series. But, correct or not, would nothing less than such an account, or, e.g., an account along Peacocke's lines, suffice to discharge the obligation?

The doubt whether such an account is necessary arises because—obviously enough—the presence of vague expressions may divest complex sentences of determinate truth value no less than simple predications. So it is plausible to insist that we have other options open besides affirmation or denial of the major premise in a sorites—the premise may itself lack any determinate status. Once that is recognized, the point about the insufficiency of responses which do no more than undercut the motivation for the major premises is likely to seem less compelling. Perhaps we will have said enough about the "manner of untruth" of the major premises when we have shown that they may reasonably be regarded as lacking any determinate truth status. And showing that there is no good reason to regard them as true would accomplish just that—provided that there is also no good reason to regard them as false.

Well, the evident problem with this is that a sorites, as remarked, itself appears to constitute a *reductio* of its major premise, and so to exclude the response that the premise may be viewed as indeterminate. As a result, the challenge to explain how specifically the major premise is false—does one of the ingredient conditionals, e.g., cross a threshold, or are they all marginally false, or what?—is apt to seem compelling. Perhaps it could be resisted—it is a suggestive thought, for instance, that a conjunction of indeterminate conjuncts may have determinately false consequences. But with definiteness operators in our weaponry, we can now see, once again, that the challenge need not arise. What, we should claim, a sorites establishes as false is the claim that the major premise is *definitely* true. The attempt to express the major premise without recourse to the definiteness operator is a source of needless difficulty no less than the corresponding attempt with the expression of lack of sharp boundaries. The paradox establishes only the negation of the definitization of the major premise—a conclusion quite consistent with its indeterminacy. In contrast, the challenge presupposes, illegitimately, that what is established is the definitization of the negation.[16]

---

16 Refer to footnote 12, concluding remarks.

The suggestion demands, of course, sufficient of a semantical account for the definiteness operator to sustain the intuitively plausible idea that what is really up for *reductio* is the definitization of the major premise—that it is somehow improper to put it forward undefinitized. But it does not seem far-fetched to suppose that such an account can be provided. If it can, then undercutting the motivation for the major premises can be enough, provided it is acceptable methodology to regard compound statements involving vague expressions as indeterminate in truth-status if no evidence is available to the contrary. If so, one corollary is that the way adopted with observational expressions in section 4 involved biting off more than it was strictly necessary to chew. (That is not to say that the conclusions there drawn are not good in any case.) Another, more general, is that the problem of explaining *how* the transition from F-ness to non-F-ness is effected in a sorites series can be dismissed as spurious. It *may* be that there is, after all, some kind of sharp boundary, and it *may* be, in particular cases, that diminutions of degree are uniformly involved. But we are under no obligation to provide an account—there may be nothing determinately correct to say about the matter.

6 The governing view and the major premises

I now revert to the various types of ground, briefly canvassed in section 1, which the governing view provides for the major premises in sorites paradoxes. Such grounds involve reference to a number of factors including (i) standard criteria for understanding and misunderstanding an expression, (ii) the way the use of the expression is standardly explained, (iii) what is known about relevant cognitive limitations of ours—of visual acuity, or memory, for instance—, (iv) the way the applicability of the expression can standardly be determined—by casual observation, for instance—, and (v) our understanding of the point or significance—the practical consequences—of its applying. These are all considerations of a kind which, once it is accepted that our use of an expression is governed by implicitly known semantic rules, must at least be *relevant* to determining the character of the content which those rules have. But it's a different question how convincing in detail are the applications which were made of them in my 1975 and in Wright (I).

There is, to begin with, some doubt about the use there is made of the first. It is one thing to claim that standard criteria for misunderstanding "red" should have implications for the character of the rules which govern the use of that predicate; quite another to argue, as I did, that a subject who was prepared to describe one but not the other of a pair of indiscriminable color patches as "red" would invariably give cause to think that he misunderstood the predicate (Wright (I), p. 161). Certainly, that would very *often* be so; it would, I suggest, always be so if the pair was presented to the subject in isolation and in a context in which he had no reason to suspect any abnormality of lighting, etc. But it is not obviously so precisely in the context that interests us, namely that of a sorites series: here we should want to recognize the right of the subject to "switch off" at some point—and since that *is* our response to the case, an argument for saying that his doing so would nevertheless be in contravention of the rules for "red" would better draw on considerations of a different sort.

There are also reservations about the way the line of thought, which appealed to the moral and explanatory significance of terms like "adult" and "child", was supposed to support the major premise for the "heartbeats of childhood" paradox (Wright (I), p. 158–59). It is of course true that giving these concepts mutually sharp boundaries would bring it about that important differences concerning rights and responsibilities would come to be associated, in certain cases, with no substantial change in the subject, and useful lay-psychological and lay-sociological generalizations, would be placed in jeopardy. But the fact is that, in order for a certain distinction—say that between "adolescent" and "adult"—to serve such purposes and carry such consequences, it is not necessary that absolutely *every* instance of the distinction be able to do so. If we troubled to have an absolutely sharp distinction between adolescence and adulthood, it would still be true that most adolescents would differ sufficiently from most adults to justify the sort of differential treatment and expectations visited upon them. So the absence of a sharp boundary cannot be imposed on us by the wish to have these concepts associated with their standard moral and explanatory significance. Only if the association had to be unfailing would there seem to be such an imposition. But it would be quite good enough if it were merely usual; or so it could be plausibly argued.

At this point, however, it becomes urgent to inquire how *exactly* the kinds of consideration canvassed are supposed to yield the major premises in sorites paradoxes. The point just considered, for example, would seem to have been whether *mutual precision* in the "child", "adolescent", "adult" family of predicates would be consistent with certain important features of their use. But surely, even if we decided that it would not, the most that could follow—on the standpoint of the governing view—would be that the semantic rules for these expressions prescribed that there should be *no sharp cut-offs*; and that conclusion would foster paradox only if lack of sharp boundaries was thought to be tantamount to sorites-susceptibility—a thought which, unqualified, is just an endorsement of the No Sharp Boundaries paradox, to which an outline solution was offered in the previous section. Presenting considerations which, under the aegis of the governing view, deepen our understanding of the vagueness of certain expressions is absolutely not to the point unless it is supposed (that one who endorses the governing view must hold) that to be vague *is* to be sorites-prone.

I was, I think, alive to this consideration in my previous discussions (Wright 1975, pp. 334–35; Wright (I), p. 157). But how exactly do the arguments advanced negotiate the pitfall? The second, third and fourth types of consideration—those concerning standard explanation, cognitive limitations of users, and methods for assessing application of an expression—can each, it seems, be made to furnish a case for the quantified conditional

$(\forall x)$(it is not the case that the rules for "red" prescribe its application to x' → it is not the case that the rules for "red" prescribe its application to x).

where x, as usual, ranges over the members of an appropriate series of color patches and x' is the successor of x therein. We proceed by putting forward for *reductio* the suggestion that there is a last case in the series to which the rules prescribe application of "red". That is distinct, of course, from the suggestion that a case to which the rules prescribe application of "red" is immediately followed by one to which they prescribe that "red" does not apply. The argument, whether we bring the second, third or fourth kind of consideration to bear, is very straightforward. Mastery of a set of rules involves knowledge not just of what they require, permit and prohibit, but also of their limits: if the rules for "red" do not prescribe application of the predicate to certain kinds of case to which they also do not prescribe its non-application, then one who has mastered those rules ought to know this and have the capacity, other things being equal, to recognize such a case if presented. So much will be part of understanding "red". Suppose, then, that all the distinctions which such an understanding empowers one to draw can be drawn by someone with normal limitations of memory without reliance on external aids; that nearby surveyable objects which are red can, in normal circumstances, be recognized to be so just by casual observation; and that a full understanding of red can be bestowed by ostensive training. Each of these suppositions is plausible and, apparently, inconsistent with the hypothesis. If the hypothesis were true, a k to which the rules prescribed application of "red" would be followed by a k' to which they did not. Someone who fully understood "red" ought therefore to be able to recognize the pair as such. But doing so would require reliance upon a distinction—that exemplified by k and its successor—which was unmemorably fine, undetectable by casual observation, and—in the case where adjacent patches are indiscrim-inable—incapable of ostensive display. So, on the stated suppositions, the hypothesis is false for arbitrary choice of k'; and the quantified conditional is thereby established.

One response to these considerations would be to wonder whether appropriate interpolation within the argument of occurrences of the definiteness operator might make some material difference. Someone who fully understands the rules for the use of "red" ought indeed to be empowered to recognize any k and k' such as the rules definitely prescribe applications of "red" to k and definitely do not prescribe its application to k'. But that is to say that understanding bestows grasp of the distinction between things which are definitely red and things which are definitely something else—either definitely not-red or definitely borderline. Can anything weaker be so much as coherently formulated? In Wright 1975 (p. 242) I spoke of the distinction between things which are definitely red and things of "any other sort". But it seems reasonable to insist that any distinction to which understanding demands sensitivity must be one between items of *determinate* status—otherwise it cannot be determinate that there *is* any relevant distinction between them, and of no response in particular can it therefore be correct to say that it is what understanding requires.

Well and good. What follows is that all we may legitimately put up for reductio is the supposition of a sharp threshold between the definite reds and the definite borderline cases. And no problem will be presented if this is expressed by straightforward definitization of what we had above. "The rules prescribe applications of 'red' to k'" and "The rules do not prescribe application of 'red' to k'" respectively. For the worst that will then be forthcoming is

(Definitely: it is not the case that: the rules prescribe application of "red" to k') $\rightarrow$ (It is not the case that: definitely: the rules prescribe application of "red" to k).

However, the supposition of sharp threshold would be as well captured by conjoint assumption of

Definitely: it is not the case that: definitely: the rules prescribe application of "red" to k';

and

Definitely: the rules prescribe application of "red" to k.

And a *reductio* of this assumption does afford a conditional of paradoxical potential—one of uniform antecedent and consequent—provided, as we know, the definiteness operator may be manipulated in accordance with DEF.

The position, then, is that, in the presence of DEF and assuming the (definite) correctness of the suppositions about memorability, casual observability and ostensive teaching which were made, there is a good case for thinking that "red" and its ilk are subject to the higher-order version of the No Sharp Boundaries paradox. That is not, indeed, the conclusion drawn in my 1975 and in Wright (I), that the governing view constrains us to regard such predicates as tolerant with respect to indiscriminable (or unmemorable) degrees of change (Wright 1975, pp. 333–34; Wright (I), p. 156). But it is no more comfortable a conclusion for one who wants to hold the governing view.[17]

What room is there for maneuver? DEF can be challenged, of course, though the prospects do not seem encouraging. A more plausible response, at least at first sight, is to claim that the background suppositions are at fault. The claim, for instance, that the whole meaning of "red" may be taught by ostensive means is open to the same reproach as that earlier directed against Dummett's account of observationality: if it were right, there would be no space for a distinction between looking red and really being so. For that distinction cannot, presumably, be ostensively explained—(or, if it can, it is no longer evident why ostensive teaching could not encompass an explanation of how only one of a pair of indiscriminable items could be red.) The same consideration, indeed, seems to disarm the other suppositions as well. If we

---

17. It is not clear, however, that the argument about "child, "adult", etc , based on considerations about moral and explanatory role, can be similarly reconstructed Even if—contrary to the suggestion in the text above—*every* instance of the adolescent/adult distinction has to involve substantial difference if the moral and explanatory role of these expressions is not to be compromised, the corresponding claim about the adolescent/definite-borderline-case-of-adolescence distinction is rather less plausible The trouble is that whereas each of

If x is in adolescent, there are certain moral demands which it would not be reasonable to make on x but which it would be reasonable to make, *ceteris paribus*, on an adult·

and

If x is an adult, there are no moral demands which it would not be reasonable to make on x but which it would be reasonable to make, *ceteris paribus*, on an adult,

is unexceptionable, no such conditional beginning

If x is definitely on the adult/adolescent borderline,

is clearly correct And some such conditional is going to be needed in order to reconstruct the argument, since it will have to be argued that a sharp distinction between adolescence and definite-borderline status would be associated with disproportionate moral/explanatory significance But I leave the reader to ponder the matter

allow that a *k* which is definitely red can be indiscriminable, or only just barely discriminable from a *k'* which is definitely borderline, the memorability is thereby jeopardized of the distinction between things which are definitely red and things which are not only if that distinction has to be drawn by reference solely to appearances. But to recognize the contrast between looking red and being red—and a corresponding contrast, presumably, between looking a borderline case of red and being one—is to recognize that appearance need not be the whole basis of that distinction. Likewise, it is possible to tell that something is red by casually observing it only insofar as its appearance is, in the circumstances, a good guide to its color; for the appearance is all that, to a casual observer, is apparent. There is therefore no requirement that every distinction in real color status be one to which casual observation can be sensitive.

This response does not, however, take us very far. Even if "red" could be saved by such appeals to the "is red"—"looks red" contrast, no parallel hope seems to be proffered for the other contrasted term. Surely the distinction between what definitely looks red and what does not is one which it must be possible to make salient by ostensive means;[18] and surely it is a distinction which the competent can draw just by casual observation and without reliance upon external aids. These suppositions remain vividly plausible for "looks red" even if they do not hold for "red", and the problem remains, even if restricted in scope. Moreover, it is not even clear that the scope of the problem *has* been restricted. For to be red *is* to look red in circumstances of observation which leave nothing to be desired—however exactly that condition should be explicated. So if there is still a sorites paradox to solve for "looks red", then, relative to the assumption that such are the prevailing circumstances of observation, there is still a sorites paradox for "red". Looking red suffices for being red when other things are equal, and for being justifiably assertible to be red if there is no reason to doubt that other things are equal. It is as well, of course, to pay proper heed to the

---

18 That is not the same as saying that "looks red" is ostensively definable The claim in the text would still hold if "looks more than six feet tall" were substituted for "looks red" So the question of ostensive definability turns on whether "looks red" is genuinely semantically structured, with "red" a significant component in that structure A bad reason for an affirmative answer would be based on confusing "looks red" with "looks as if it is red" or "looks the way red things look", since in special circumstances it may be necessary, in order to look the way red things look, to look, e g , brown (if, say, bathed in green light). To be sure, it is a priori that looking red is looking the way red things look in good lighting, etc But that does not entail that understanding "looks red" involves grasp of this a priori truth For a sophisticated discussion of such matters, see Peacocke 1984

distinction between looking and being red; but doing so gets us no further forward in the present context.

Whether it is correct to suppose that "looks red" is ostensively definable or not (see note 18), it is certain that competence with that predicate is practised by subjects who have only quite ordinary powers of observation and rely on nothing but casual exercise of those powers, eschewing in particular any use of the kind of external aids—color charts, or whatever—which could compensate for limitations of memory. So the escape route *has* to involve finding a way of avoiding drawing paradoxical conclusions from this undeniable fact. But how— if we say that competence consists in knowing certain rules and their limits? For it then seems inescapable that both every distinction prescribed by the rules, and the distinction between cases where the rules have something to say and cases where they do not, can be based only on contrasts which may be detected by casual exercise of ordinary powers of observation, without reliance on external aids; and, hence, that no such distinction can be exemplified by items which conjointly exhibit no such contrast. So the conclusion still looks good: competence with expressions of the class which "looks red" typifies *cannot* consist in knowledge of the requirements of certain rules and of their limits.

There is still the possibility of making trouble for DEF, without which the particular version of the sorites which threatens is not, apparently, obtainable. But once we concentrate on "looks red" and its ilk, the route to paradox outlined is anyway needlessly indirect. The *best* argument afforded by the governing view for a major premise for "looks red" is [this]. If items are visually indiscriminable, they look the same. So visual indiscriminability is necessarily a congruence relation for any predicate whose rules of application take account only of how things look. Our conception of the role and purpose of "looks red", "looks orange", etc., is, unquestionably, that we use them purely to record public appearances. So if, as the governing view permits, we may legitimately base upon this conception conclusions which concern the character of the rules governing such predicates' application, those rules must have the feature, it seems, of relating only to appearance, of prescribing application of such predicates only and purely on the basis of appearance. But then they must prescribe application of such a predicate to both members, if either, of any pair of items whose appearances are the same.

Now there is terribly little room for maneuver. It would suffice if we could somehow drive indistinguishability and sameness of appearance apart—if, while granting that the rules for "looks red" relate only to appearance, we could provide some principled basis for denying that indistinguishability suffices for sameness of appearance. But I do not see any hopeful direction for such an attempt to take. I mention it only by way of noting one formal alternative to the response which I want to recommend. This, as the reader will anticipate, is to drop the idea that the harmless truism that we use predicates like "looks red" to record how things appear to us has any bearing on the character of the putative semantic rules which govern their use. Since—so it seems to me—the truism could hardly fail to have the very direct bearing illustrated so long as there *are* governing semantic rules for such expressions at all, the recommendation is that we drop that assumption, and adopt, as the matter was expressed in Wright (I), a "more purely behavioristic" conception of what competence with such expressions involves.

But what does that mean? A way to provide at least the beginnings of a proper account of the contrast is to enquire what connection there is between the obtaining of an instance of the type of state of affairs which confers truth on a token of the sentence "*x* looks red", and our willingness to assent to that token. It should not be controversial, I think, that each is necessary and sufficient for the other so long as certain provisos are met which are distinctive of this class of expression; that is, for no other class of expressions do exactly these provisos subserve such a biconditional dependence. The provisos are that the judging subject understands "looks red", that his perceptual faculties are functioning normally, that he is otherwise in good cognitive order, that *x* is presented to him in clear view, and that he is attentive to *x*.[19] Subject to these provisos, assent and truth necessarily coincide. We have, that is,

> Necessarily: if the subject and the circumstances are as required by the provisos, then "*x* looks red" is true if and only if the subject assents to "*x* looks red".

Now, two quite different broad perspectives on this principle—the *proviso biconditional*—are possible. One—required by the governing view—will hold that the circumstance that "looks red" applies to *x* is settled, independently of any subject's response to *x*, by the semantic rules which govern the use of "looks red" in English and by how, objectively, *x* appears. The role of the provisos, on this view, is to ensure the subject's ability to "track", or detect this independent state of affairs: thus, his understanding of "looks red" and his being in "good cognitive order" ensure his sensitivity to the requirements of the relevant semantic rules; and his normal perceptual function and attentiveness to *x*, and the clear presentation of *x* to him, ensure his sensitivity to *x*'s objective

---

19 The corresponding provisos for "*x* is red" would include not merely that *x* be presented in clear view but that the circumstances of presentation be normal, or appropriate

appearance. On this view, then, appeal to the idea of how a subject will or would respond to the utterance when the provisos are satisfied, should play no essential part in an account of its truth-conditions. Such an account need consider nothing but the semantics of the utterance and the characteristics of *x*. What the provisos do is to foreclose on every possible explanation of fracture between the fact of the matter and a subject's response.

The reason why this perspective is required by the governing view is not that the latter *platonizes* semantic rules, as it were—writes us out of the story altogether—but rather that we are allowed to feature only in a limited way. To be sure, it is by reference to *our* cognitive limitations, what *we* can casually observe, *our* conception of the function of a certain class of predicates, etc., that conclusions are to be drawn about the content of semantic rules. But conclusions are, apparently, *not* to be drawn by reference to the character of our response to a predication of "looks red" when, *by ordinary criteria*, all the provisos are fulfilled. And in order for this exclusion to be legitimate, the dictates of the semantic rules for "looks red" have to be thought of as constituted independently of such responses. The point is, indeed, quite general and simple. In order for there to be a sorites paradox of this kind, our actual classificatory responses have to be out of accord with the requirements of the relevant semantic rules. So to think you have such a paradox, you have to be working with an epistemology of semantic rules which allows firm conclusions to be drawn about their character independently—or anyway, in a manner sufficiently inattentive to—the shape which those responses are disposed to assume. Such a view need nevertheless pose no barrier to recognizing the proviso-biconditional. Whatever epistemology is utilized, it will contain the resources for a declaration that where responses are not in accord with the rules as it construes them, subjects are, for instance, muddled or inconstant in their apprehension of the requirements of those rules and so, to that extent, out of good cognitive order.

That is the first broad perspective. But the alternative perspective turns it all around. Now the proviso-biconditional is seen, instead, as itself supplying the canonical form of a statement of the truth-conditions of "*x* looks red". The provisos are no longer seen as serving to describe the conditions under which a subject succeeds in tracking an independent fact; rather, for *x* to look red just *is* for subjects to be willing to assent to that judgment when the provisos are met. Whatever else we want to say about the meaning of such expressions, and about the epistemology of their meaning, it is all answerable to this point. Hence, there is no possibility of such an epistemology teaching us that the provisos are in fact not satisfied in circumstances where, by normal criteria, we should have been satisfied that they are. It is the other way about: if we are tempted to opinions about the meanings of such expressions which force us to draw such a conclusion, it is those opinions which are at fault. There is no ulterior fact which meeting the provisos ensures that we can detect, so no possibility—by reference to independent criteria for the existence or non-existence of such a fact—of surprising conclusions about when the provisos really are not met, notwithstanding the satisfaction of ordinary criteria for saying that they are.

What does this distinction do for us?[20] Well, suppose a group of subjects, are agreed that "looks red" applies to the first color patch in a sorites-series in circumstances when the provisos are met. As the series is run from apparently red to apparently orange patches, a point will be reached where, despite its indiscriminability from the immediately preceding patch, a consensus in subjects' responses breaks down for the first time. That is undeniable. It is also undeniable that, when that happens, no single subject in the group need, by ordinary criteria, have fallen out of accord with any of the provisos. (Borderline cases are exactly cases about which competent subjects are allowed to differ.) The second perspective on the proviso-biconditional gives us the right to treat such a circumstance as raising a doubt about the predicability of "looks red".[21] The first perspective, by contrast, leads to the cancellation of that right.

Someone who succumbs to the arresting, apparently simple thought that "looks red" must be applicable to both, if to either, of any pair of indiscriminable items, is likely to be taking it in one of two ways. Taken one way, it is the central move in the Tachometer paradox: how can a signalling device, even a properly functioning signalling device, discriminate among stimuli whose difference is smaller than its sensitivity threshold? We now know, I hope, how to respond to that question. But the second and, I think, more natural way of taking the thought conceals, in effect, a presupposition of the first perspective on the proviso-biconditional. You have to forget that we do not, or would not so apply the predicate in every case and fall in, instead, with the idea that something can be discerned about its *proper* conditions of application just by intuitive reflection upon the kind of content which it overtly seems to have. If there were facts about the proper application of such predicates which were constituted independently of our best

---

20 This very important form of distinction was utilized by Mark Johnston in classes on ethics in Princeton in the spring of 1986 It is further discussed in Wright 1988; and put to work in Wright 1987b

21 Because A → (B ↔ C) entails B → (A → C)

responses—the responses we would have when, by ordinary criteria, all the provisos were met—what else could they be but the offspring of rules which correlated their proper use with *appearances*? And how, when following such rules, could it ever be justifiable, in consequence, to assign to identical appearances distinct responses? The reply should be that competence with such predicates is nothing to do with the capacity to fit one's usage to the dictates of rules of that kind. Indeed, it is not a matter of compliance with rules at all, if that is taken to imply the propriety of a "detective" direction of interpretation of the proviso-biconditional. What it is correct to say using such a predicate is a function only of what we are actually inclined to say when there is no reason to doubt that the provisos are met.

The distinction, between these two perspectives on the proviso-biconditional would undoubtedly benefit from further work. But it is, I hope, tolerably clear. It unravels the most important strand in what my 1975 and Wright (I) were attempting to say. The "behavioristic" conception of meaning advocated towards the conclusion of the latter is just the non-detective reading of the proviso-biconditional which lets us take "best behavior" seriously. It is, indeed, the belief in the conception of meaning which sustains a detective reading of proviso-biconditionals that constitutes the real essence of the governing view, of which its involvement with the idea of *implicit knowledge* of semantic rules is merely a corollary. For, as noted, the separation, effected by the detective reading, between on the one hand what *constitutes* the correctness of a particular response with "looks red", for instance, and on the other the fact that the response observes the provisos, enjoins viewing the provisos as collectively ensuring a subject's ability to keep cognitive track of the independent, constitutive fact. So there has to be substantial knowledge of the ingredients of that fact, including the requirements of the relevant semantic rules. Since the subject's response will usually come to him involuntarily and unreflectively, it would appear that the relevant cognitive processes must usually be implicit. One does not need to be wary of the notion of implicit knowledge in general to reject this way of involving it in the theory of linguistic understanding. The rules to which competent use of "looks red" conforms—if indeed we wish to continue to think in terms of semantic rules for such expressions at all—are not rules knowledge of whose content, at some deep level, makes competence possible; rather their content is given by the course assumed by competent use.

It remains to respond to a question outstanding from the end of section 4. An observational expression, it was there suggested, should be characterized as, inter alia, one which a subject could not fail to understand if his use of it displayed an appropriate sensitivity to a certain distinctive range of appearances. The question was whether the presence of this condition in an account of observationality could be seen to spare observational expressions the tolerance which Dummett's account, for instance, would lumber them with. "How could the *appropriate* kind of sensitivity operate selectively among indiscriminabilia?" (see above, p. 228). If what I have been saving has any force, it should now seem as if this question has rather disappeared. "Looks red" ought certainly to qualify as observational on this count. But the kind of sensitivity to appearance which someone who understands "looks red" (and is normally-sighted) must have just *does* operate selectively among items which, in respect of apparent color, cannot be told apart. If, for instance, we present a subject with each of the elements of a sorites series of indistinguishable color patches but *out of sequence*, such selectivity will have to be manifest in the collation of his or her responses the question, "Does this look red?", so long as we are to be satisfied that the provisos have been met in every case. The suggestion that there is some kind of tension between such selectivity of response and its being the sort of response appropriate in the case of an observational predicate, depends on the thought that it cannot then be purely in response to appearance—either it is unprincipled or else it is a principled response to *more* than the appearances. But "unprincipled" here just means: not guided by rules correlating responses with appearances. So we should embrace the first alternative: such responses are indeed unprincipled, and no less appropriate or less purely "to" appearances on that account.

7 Conclusion

We have covered a lot of ground, and a substantial proportion of our findings have been negative. But a number of positive points have emerged which, if I am right about them, are worthy of emphasis. First, it is a mistake to think of the sorites as a *single* paradox, which admits of a large variety of illustrations. Rather, we have here a family of different paradoxes, formally similar but distinct when identified by reference to the type of ground which supports their major premises. By this criterion, the Tachometer paradox, the No Sharp Boundaries paradox, and the various sorites paradoxes which are the progeny of the governing view, all need to be distinguished and treated differently. A further important group are constituted by the sorites paradoxes which affect predicates of practical intellectual possibility—like "intelligible" when applied to expressions, "memorable' when applied to patterns, "surveyable" when applied to proofs, and so on. The proper response to paradoxes in this last group is a matter of great consequence for finitism in the philosophy of mathematics, but I have no space to engage the issues here.[22]

Second, the distinctions among the sorites family correspond to a variety of lessons which the broad lines of solution to these paradoxes contain for us. The Tachometer paradox is perhaps the least interesting in this respect. The positive lesson from it is only the very local point that what it is for an instrument or human subject to have a threshold of sensitivity is something which needs careful description if incoherence is to be avoided. That is a point which it is as well to know, but it hardly trembles the foundations of the subject. Still, as recently noted, the paradox represents one way of being seduced by the thought that phenomenal predicates like "looks red" apply to both, if to either, of any pair of indiscriminable items, so it needs a proper resolution. And pursuit of the signalling instrument analogy which arose in the course of our discussion of the paradox led us indirectly towards what, I would contend, is the germ of a good account of the distinguishing features of *observational* vocabulary. The essence of the No Sharp Boundaries paradox, on the other hand, is the thought that vagueness is *per se* sorites-generating, and hence that the paradox afflicts almost the entirety of our language. This thought is defective, or so I argued, but points up the need for definiteness-operators in any coherent philosophical treatment of vagueness, and for a proper account, in turn, of the semantics and logical behavior of such operators. Even so, the question was left unresolved whether paradox might not be inherent in higher-order vagueness at least. Since, as noted, at least two important writers on vagueness have taken the view that higher-order vagueness is essential to a large class of vague expressions, this is an issue on which further work is much needed.

Third, we have found ourselves taking a somewhat unexpected route to one of the central concerns of Wittgenstein's later philosophy of language, mathematics and mind: the issues to do with what I have elsewhere called the *objectivity of meaning* (Wright 1986b, Introduction, pp. 3–8 and 26–29; and 1986c) which seem to me to be the principal focus of his discussions of rule-following in the *Investigations* and *Remarks on the Foundations of Mathematics*.[23] One who accepts the objectivity of meaning thinks of understanding an expression in quasi-contractual terms: there is, for instance, when one confronts the question whether

---

22 Some preliminary discussion may be found in my 1982, especially pp. 262–69.

23. One is more wary of quoting Wittgenstein in support of a particular interpretation of his writings than virtually any other philosopher But a sceptical reader should be reminded of these passages from *Philosophical Investigations*: §§188, 218, 219. Likewise consider from the *Remarks on the Foundations of Mathematics*: IV 44, 48; VII 42.

or not to classify a particular object in a particular way, a response to which one is *obligated* if one is to keep faith with the meaning of the relevant expressions as they were taught to one (and pay due heed to the relevant worldly facts).[24] Less metaphorically, finite, over-and-done-with episodes of explanation and other forms of linguistic behavior may succeed in fully determining the meaning of a so far unmade utterance in a fashion independent of any reaction which we will or would have to it: there is only the question of whether our reaction, if one is forthcoming, is in line with the meaning so independently constituted. Wittgenstein's discussion has tempted many commentators to conclude that he is advocating scepticism about the very notions of meaning and of correct or incorrect linguistic practice.[25] But that is as much a misreading as the opposite tendency which finds in Wittgenstein's discussion only a corrective to a crudely phenomenalistic conception of understanding, intention, and other cognate notions.[26] What is at issue is the conception of our relationship with the meaning of a novel utterance as being *purely cognitive*, of its meaning as something which, with any necessary help from the world, can determine the utterance's truth value quite independently of any contributive reaction from us. There is and can be no such independence. We are ceaselessly actively involved in the determination of meaning. This is not to say that a reference to "us" or to the "community" is somehow implicit in a full account of the truth-conditions of any sentence,— still less that truth is what we take to be the truth, or anything of that sort.[27] Wittgenstein, like anyone else, was aware that whole communities can be in error. The point is rather that failure to keep track of independently constituted meanings is not intelligible as a separate source of such error, alongside factual ignorance, misperception, illusion, prejudice, forgetfulness and the like. The platitude, that the truth-value of an utterance is a function only of its meaning and of the context and prevailing states of affairs, is not in question either. What is in question is the idea that the meaning of the utterance is something which is as much constituted independently of our response to it as are the germane features of the context and prevailing states of affairs, and

---

24. The point of Wittgenstein's concentration upon simple arithmetical series is that it enables him to drop this part of the proviso

25. See most notably Kripke 1982

26 A criticism which could be levelled at the otherwise useful contributions of Budd 1984 and McGinn 1984

27 The matter is so widely misunderstood that it is still worth emphasizing Wittgenstein's explicit denials at *Philosophical Investigations* §241, *Remarks on the Foundations of Mathematics* VII, 40, and elsewhere

no less something which, in appraising the utterance's truth-value, we have to cognize.

As Wittgenstein saw, the conception of meaning as objective in this way is prerequisite for the sort of platonism in mathematics which views mathematical activity as the exploration of our conceptual constructs. It is also prerequisite for the thought—essential to the "private linguist"—that just by a personal ostensive definition, or by otherwise going through the motions of forming an intention to use an expression in a certain way, it is possible to generate facts about the correct use of that expression on subsequent occasions which are independent of our reaction on reaching them, and supply, at least in principle, the standard which those reactions have to meet.[28] It is the objectivity of meaning which is at the heart of the governing view and which sustains the detective reading of the sort of proviso-biconditional discussed in the last section. The principal lesson of that discussion is thus that, more than being deeply problematical for the reasons which Wittgenstein's deliberations bring out, the objectivity of meaning is actually a source of paradox.

The third species of sorites paradoxes—those issuing from the governing view—thus bring us up against absolutely basic questions in the philosophy of language. But how general is the challenge to the objectivity of meaning which they uncover? It is not confined to "looks red" and its ilk since, as noted above, being red *is* looking red when other things are equal. So both secondary quality predicates and, when they are distinct, what we might term their phenomenalizations—the corresponding "looks", "sounds", etc., predicates—come within range. Also in range are all predicates of the sort, "is justifiably characterizable as ..." for whose correct application looking, or sounding, etc., so-and-so suffices, *ceteris paribus*. This is a wide class but hardly a comprehensive one. While it is possible to argue for a global rejection of the objectivity of meaning on the basis of its failure for this class (see Wright 1986c, pp. 292–94), I do not know of any such argument which does not draw on considerations quite different to those with which we have been occupied here. In my earlier papers I rather tended to write as though the governing view paradoxes show us a route to rejection of the objectivity of meaning which is quite different to anything to be found in Wittgenstein's writings but of no less generality. But that now seems to be an over-statement. The best paradoxes of the kind—par excellence

---

28 That is not to say that "private language" falls with objective meaning It has still to be shown that there is no other way of establishing content for the "seems right" / "is right" contrast which the private language has to have For an attempt to show just that (and to explain why the contrast is necessary), see my 1986a.

that for "looks red" on which we have concentrated—depend on quite special considerations, and no global extension seems to be in prospect.[29]

29. Versions of parts of this material were presented at colloquia at M. I. T., Johns Hopkins University, and the University of Michigan at Ann Arbor in Spring 1986 I am grateful to those who participated for a number of useful comments and questions.

13   Concepts without boundaries

R. M. Sainsbury

Philosophers have been interested in vagueness for centuries. One reason is the fascination, and threat, posed by the so-called sorites paradoxes. If someone is not bald, then he does not become bald by losing just a single hair. But then, it seems, however many hairs he loses, he can never become bald. No hair's loss marks the transition; so, it seems, there can be no transition. We know that the conclusion is false. The problem is to say how it can be avoided.

Vagueness is of interest independently of the paradoxes. It seems to be an extremely pervasive phenomenon, invading almost every area of thought, and banished from scientific work, if at all, only by constant vigilance. What is its origin? Does it correspond to a feature of the world? Or is it we, perhaps through our deficiencies, who are responsible? And is it obvious that it is a Bad Thing, given the extent to which the throbbing centres of our lives appear to be describable only in vague terms?

A more preliminary question is: what is vagueness? The standard definition is that a vague word is one which admits borderline cases. I agree that if a word is vague, then there are or could be borderline cases; but I deny the converse: non-vague expressions, too, can have borderline cases, so we do not yet have a grasp of the essence of vagueness. That essence is to be found in the idea that vague concepts are concepts without boundaries.

1   Some concepts classify by setting boundaries but some do not. In the philosophical tradition, the former have received all the attention, and have lent a distinctive character to attempts to study classificatory concepts and their linguistic correlates. Within what I shall call the "classical picture", a picture which dominates most thinking about thought and language, there is no room for the thesis I wish to put forward: that concepts can classify without setting boundaries.

According to this classical picture, the job of classificatory concepts is to sort or segregate things into *classes* by providing a system of pigeon-holes, by placing a grid over reality, by demarcating areas of logical space. Boundaries are what count, for a concept must use a boundary to

From *Concepts without boundaries*, an Inaugural Lecture, given at King's College London, 6 November 1990. © R M Sainsbury. Reprinted by permission.

segregate the things which fall under it from the things which do not. This intuitive view receives definitive expression in classical semantic theories. A predicate, linguistic vehicle of a concept, is thought of as having a meaning which fixes its extension, the set of things of which it is true. A semantic theory will provide an at least partial characterization of a predicate's meaning by specifying this set in some appropriately revealing fashion. In the light of such specifications, one can model the logical features of the language in which the predicate occurs by generalizing over the sets which predicates do, or can, determine.

Thus the classical picture, informed by a connection between concepts and sets present in the very word "classify", sees the theoretical resources of set theory as the proper instruments for describing language and thought.

Classes, and sets, have sharp boundaries. Hence, at least *prima facie*, a description of concepts or predicates in terms of what sets they determine is a description of them as boundary-drawers. This mode of description, and the picture which underlies it, thus makes no room for concepts without boundaries, those which are not boundary-drawers. We have a choice: we could take the classical picture as exhausting the ways classificatory concepts can be, and conclude that there are no concepts without boundaries; or else, convinced that there are such concepts, we could reject the comprehensiveness of the classical picture. What I suggest is that almost all concepts lack boundaries, so that the classical picture is of very little use to us.

The concepts which classify without setting boundaries include the ones traditionally counted as vague: *red, heap, child, bald*, to take some famous examples. The first stage in showing that these are boundaryless concepts involves showing that there is no set of which they are true: they do not classify at all, if the only way to classify is to assign things to classes or sets.

2 Sets have sharp boundaries, or, if you prefer, are sharp objects: for any set, and any object, either the object quite definitely belongs to the set or else it quite definitely does not. Suppose there were a set of things of which "red" is true: it would be the set of red things. However, "red" is vague: there are objects of which it is neither the case that "red" is (definitely) true nor the case that "red" is (definitely) not true. Such an object would neither definitely belong to the set of red things nor definitely fail to belong to this set. But this is impossible, by the very nature of sets. Hence there is no set of red things.

This seems to me as certain as anything in philosophy, yet it can often be a bitter pill to swallow, by non-philosophers and by philosophers alike. In some debates about abortion, one can feel a real sense of shock at the realization that there is no set of persons: the concept *person* is vague at just the relevant point. The difficulty is that moral concepts are often boundary-drawing (especially so the more naive the morality), and legal concepts typically have to be. Trying to tie the application of a boundary-drawing concept (as *may legitimately be aborted* is supposed to be) with a boundaryless one like *is a person* poses a problem which is simply not soluble in the straightforward terms in which it is often posed. A quite general reflection on boundaries, their absence and presence, should reshape what one could expect to emerge from a discussion of abortion and the law.

Philosophers, too, are attracted by the classical picture, even when not engaged upon formal semantic projects. To take one example from a million, when Peter Strawson some time ago considered whether "Socrates is human" is equivalent to "Socrates belongs to the set of humans" his many interesting observations did not include the point that the equivalence must fail since there is no set of humans.

If vague predicates and vague concepts do not have "extensions"— sets of things of which they are true—they do not draw boundaries, at least not in any simple sense. For a boundary should divide things into two sets, those which fall on one side and those which fall on the other. So if vague predicates do not effect a division into sets, they draw no boundaries.

But, it may be objected, this is too simple. For may not a vague predicate draw an unsharp boundary? May not an unsharp boundary work without dividing into two? May there not be things whose status is unresolved by the boundary?

When one says that a vague predicate does not draw *sharp* boundaries, "sharp", I believe, does no work, for there is only one kind of boundary. Hence we cannot regard vague predicates as drawers of boundaries, but ones which are unsharp. I shall establish this by the following route. Anything worthy of the name *boundary* will effect set-theoretically describable divisions, even if more complex ones than the simple twofold division envisaged just now. But any such division, however complex, will misdescribe the functioning of a vague predicate.

3 I shall start with a general reason for thinking that there is no adequate set-theoretic description of vague predicates. It is that a set-theoretic description of a language typically ends up identifying a set of truths. (More exactly, it specifies for each sentence a condition upon which the sentence will belong to this set, or to the set of truths-upon-S, for a relativization to some structure, S.) But the argument which showed that there was no set of red things shows also that there is no set of truths in a language which contains the predicate "red". For

consider a sentence ascribing *red* to a borderline case. This sentence will neither (definitely) belong nor (definitely) fail to belong to the set of such truths; which is another way of saying that there is no such set.

But surely (one may object) this simple thought does not do justice to all the cunning twists and turns which set-theorists have made in their attempts to describe vagueness. What about fuzzy logic? What about supervaluation theory?

I believe that the simple minded point of a moment back—that there is no set of truths—does ultimately carry the day against such theories. But I recognize that to convince an opponent involves more detail.

The preliminary claim I need to make is that one cannot do justice to the phenomena of vagueness, in particular to phenomena called "higher order vagueness", simply by increasing the number of sets of individuals associated with a predicate. A set-theoretic description might start by associating a vague predicate not with two sets but with three: the set of things of which the predicate is (definitely) true, the set of things of which it is (definitely) false, and the remainder, the set of borderline cases. So far, so good: a sharp predicate has two extensions, a positive extension, and a negative one (its complement within the domain) whereas a vague predicate has three, a positive one, a negative one, and a penumbral one (the complement within the domain of the union of the other two).

But a predicate which effects such a threefold partition is not vague. This fact, which shows why one cannot characterize vagueness merely in terms of borderline cases, follows from the fact that the partition does identify a set of truths, which we have seen to be inconsistent with vagueness. Once again more detail will reinforce the point. Consider a child developing into adulthood. We cannot associate "child" with a twofold division because there is no set of children (at a time). There is no such set because of the borderline cases. Thus far, some encouragement for a threefold partition, which explicitly allows for borderlines. However, essentially the very point which scuppers a twofold partition also scuppers a threefold one: the latter posits a set of children, or at least a set of definite children. Yet it would be as absurd to suppose that a heartbeat could make the difference between membership of this set, and consignment to the set of borderline cases, as it would be to suppose that a heartbeat could make the difference between belonging to the set of children and belonging to the set of non-children. Childhood, even definite childhood, fades gradually away, and does not come to a sudden end. This is not to deny that we can by convention stipulate a sharp boundary; it is only to say that our concept *child* does not supply one.

A proponent of set-theoretic divisions might seek to meet this point by making more divisions. He might say that a predicate is sharp, that is, not vague at all, or as I shall say is vague$_0$, just on condition that it draws a single boundary, thus partitioning the domain into two sets; that a predicate possesses the lowest level of vagueness, is vague$_1$, just on condition that it draws two boundaries, partitioning the domain into three sets. If it is unacceptable to suppose that "child" or "red" does this (on account of the unacceptability of supposing that there is a last heartbeat of one's childhood, or of one's definite childhood), then the correct description of such a predicate must look further up the hierarchy: perhaps it draws four or forty boundaries, making correspondingly many partitions of the domain.

The generalization of this set-theoretic approach is that a predicate is vague$_n$ iff it draws 2^n boundaries, thus partitioning the domain into $2^n + 1$ sets. A predicate is sharp iff it is vague$_0$; is vague iff it is vague$_n$ for some positive n; is higher order vague iff it is vague$_n$ for some $n > 1$, and is radically vague iff it is vague$_n$ for no n. The phenomena mentioned a moment back—such facts, now agreed by the set-theorist, as that there is no sharp division between children and borderline cases of children—are to be described, on the envisaged approach, by going higher in the hierarchy of higher order vagueness. If the set-theoretic description assigns a cut-off where none can be found in the actual use of the predicates, then the description has not set the level of vagueness high enough. The hope is that the unlimited upwards mobility is enough to enable one to get on top of all the phenomena.

This hope, however, is groundless. Indeed, its very structure should be unappealing: you do not improve a bad idea by iterating it. In more detail, suppose we have a finished account of a predicate, associating it with some possibly infinite number of boundaries, and some possibly infinite number of sets. Given the aims of the description, we must be able to organize the sets in the following threefold way: one of them is the set supposedly corresponding to the things of which the predicate is absolutely definitely and unimpugnably true, the things to which the predicate's application is untainted by the shadow of vagueness; one of them is the set supposedly corresponding to the things of which the predicate is absolutely definitely and unimpugnably false, the things to which the predicate's non-application is untainted by the shadow of vagueness; the union of the remaining sets would supposedly correspond to one or another kind of borderline case. So the old problem re-emerges: no sharp cut-off to the shadow of vagueness is marked in our linguistic practice, so to attribute it to the predicate is to misdescribe it.

4   In effect, this same point is what scuppers the set-theoretic descriptions of vague languages offered by fuzzy logicians and by supervaluations theorists.

The fuzzy logic I envisage associates with each predicate not a set whose only members are individuals, the individuals of which the predicate is true, but what Goguen calls a "J-set": a function from each object in the domain of discourse to a real number in the closed interval [0,1]. The number, as value to the function, represents the degree to which the predicate is true of the object which is argument to the function. The real numbers are continuous, so surely now we have a mode of description apt for vagueness, one which does not necessitate sharp boundaries? Yet a fuzzy set is a genuine set, a completely sharp object.

The reason for thinking this approach cannot succeed is essentially the same as that given earlier: the fuzzy logician, too, will (whether he likes it or not) be committed to a threefold partition: the sentences which are true to degree 1, those true to degree 0, and the remainder. But to what in our actual use of language does this division correspond? It looks as if, as before, it should correspond to the sentences true beyond the shadow of vagueness, those in some kind of borderline position, and those false beyond the shadow. But, as several times noted, we do not know, cannot know, and do not need to know these supposed boundaries to use language correctly. Hence they cannot be included in a correct description of our language.

Fuzzy logic does, indeed, describe a feature of our use of many vague predicates: that, and how, they are associated with a dimension of comparison. Our use of "red" is properly regarded as regulated by such principles as that anything redder than a red thing is red. The "redder than" relation is tracked by fuzzy logic's numerical ordering, which in turn bears straightforwardly on the applicability of "red". For many predicates, things are more complex: many relations are relevant to applicability. Childhood is affected by age, but also by many other factors as well, so that two individuals of the same age may differ in point of how much of a child they are. Yet, plainly, fuzzy logic could be supplied with the resources to describe the nature and weights of a whole complex of applicability-determining relations. Could we not somehow reap these benefits without succumbing to fuzzy logic's threefold partitioning?

Here is one possible line of thought. One can expect the empirical data for fuzzy logic to be quite messy. One might run trials in which one asked people to do two kinds of thing: order all the objects in terms of their strength as candidates for application of the predicate; and identify the definite cases and the definite non-cases. The results would be variable, both intra- and inter-personally. Let us say that an *admissible* J-set for a predicate is one which matches some trial for that predicate both in point of order and in point of definite cases. That is to say, if in the trial the subject treats α as a better case of the predicate than β, then the J-value for α must exceed that for β; if the subject identifies an object as a definite case for the predicate, the J-value for that object must be 1; if the subject identifies an object as a definite non-case for the predicate, the J-value for that object must be 0. When it comes to specifying truth, the theorist could adopt a vague definition, for example he could say that an atom $\phi\alpha$ is true iff the object denoted by α has J-value 1 for almost all J-sets admissible for ϕ.

The general idea behind the strategy is to take the set-theoretic description as a kind of basis, and exploit it in a vague way to deliver an account of whatever one takes to be the central semantic notion.

The idea is not unattractive, but it does not fall within the scope of the approach I wish to attack. For what is envisaged is that the real work of describing the functioning of a predicate is done not by fuzzy logic itself, but in terms of some *vaguely* specified semantic notion. The proposal, then, ends up as not one in which a predicate is described by being associated with an extension or with boundaries.

A similar series of moves can be made in connection with supervaluations. The supervaluational theory, too, will end up making a threefold partition: the set of sentences true-upon-all-sharpenings, the set of sentences false-upon-all-sharpenings, and the remainder. An attempt to do justice to "higher order" vagueness by acknowledging vagueness in the notion of a sharpening would force one outside the set theoretic language in which the theory is supposed to be couched, and would mean that the real work of semantic description was being done in a vague language, rather than in a set-assigning one.

5 A vague concept is boundaryless in that no boundary marks the things which fall under it from the things which do not, and no boundary marks the things which definitely fall under it from those which do not definitely do so; and so on. Manifestations are the unwillingness of knowing subjects to draw any such boundaries, the cognitive impossibility of identifying such boundaries, and the needlessness and even disutility of such boundaries.

To characterize a vague concept as boundaryless is an improvement on characterizing it as one which permits borderline cases, since a non-vague concept may admit borderline cases. If "child*" is defined as true of just those people whose hearts have beat less than a million times, false of those whose hearts have beaten more than a million and fifty times, and borderline with respect to the remaining people, it has borderline cases but behaves quite unlike our paradigms of vagueness.

A boundaryless concept cannot be described in set-theoretic terms. How can it have a classificatory role? How is it to be described, either semantically or in terms of cognitive processing? How are the paradoxes of vagueness to be avoided?

Scepticism about whether boundaryless classification is possible can be set to rest, I believe, by contemplating a very familiar case: the colour spectrum, as displayed, for example, in an illustration in a book on colour. Looking carefully, we can discern no boundaries between the different colours: they stand out as clearly different, yet there are no sharp divisions. There are bands, but no bounds. This does nothing to impede the classificatory process: the spectrum is a paradigm of classification.

The image of pigeon-holes is powerful. Is there a comparable one which would represent how boundaryless concepts classify? We could, perhaps, think of such concepts as like magnetic poles exerting various degrees of influence: some objects cluster firmly to one pole, some to another, and some, though sensitive to the forces, join no cluster.

At least one aspect of this image deserves more literal statement. Boundaryless concepts tend to come in systems of contraries: opposed pairs like child/adult, hot/cold, weak/strong, true/false, and the more complex systems exemplified by our colour terms. This is a natural upshot of boundarylessness, as we can see by reflecting on what is involved in grasping a concept.

Such a grasp, it must be agreed on all sides, involves knowing how something would have to be for the concept to apply to it, and how something would have to be for the concept not to apply. A distinctive feature of the classical picture is that it takes this latter fact as primitive. Grasping what a concept excludes is part of grasping the concept, and is achieved through the mediation of no other non-logical concept. Hence it is very natural to see the division between what a concept includes and what it excludes in terms of a boundary. Certainly, perception of a boundary would be enough; but the proponent of boundarylessness will insist that it is not the only way.

On the alternative picture, what a concept excludes is graspable in a positive way, mediated by other contrary concepts. A grasp of *red* attains grasp of what is not red at a derivative level, via a grasp of *yellow, green, blue* and so on. A system of such concepts is grasped as a whole, as can be seen in the way paradigms are used in learning. There are paradigms of red, but nothing is non-derivatively classifiable as a paradigm of not-red. Any paradigm of another colour will serve as a paradigm of how not to be red, but only in virtue of its positive classification as another colour.

Not just any clear case of the non-applicability of a concept will serve to help a learner see what the concept excludes. Television sets, mountains and French horns are all absolutely definite cases of non-children; but only the contrast with *adult* will help the learner grasp what *child* excludes. So it is no accident that boundaryless concepts come in groups of contraries. Correlatively, the image of attracting poles, replacing the classical image of pigeon-holes, is not without value.

It also serves to record some empirical data. For example, subjects asked to classify a range of test objects using just "young" and "old" make different assignments to these words from those they make to them when asked to classify using, in addition, "middle-aged". The introduction of a third magnetic pole can attract some of the things only loosely attached to two existing ones, without diminishing the forces the existing ones exert.

6   Let me now turn to the question about paradox, which might take a more aggressive form: does not the very notion of boundarylessness make the paradoxes unavoidable? For the absence of a boundary has been treated as the impossibility of very similar things differing in point of the applicability of a predicate. But then it seems that we can form a sorites series of objects, adjacent pairs being too similar to merit a difference in applicability, but remote pairs being sufficiently dissimilar to require a difference. Starting with a clear case of red, we assemble closely resembling patches in a series through which the colour shifts gradually towards yellow. The boundarylessness of red is supposed to ensure that there is no adjacent pair of which the first is red and the second not. The first member, by hypothesis, is red. Hence, by boundarylessness, the one adjacent to it is also red; and so on. So does not familiar reasoning lead inexorably to the intolerable conclusion that all members of the series are red, even the yellow ones?

This worry can take a form which can only be assuaged by a technical and formal semantic theory, and nothing of that kind is on offer here. However, let me make a simple observation which should establish that the present picture of vagueness as boundarylessness is no less well placed than any other to come to terms with sorites reasoning.

The classical picture has a totalitarian aspect: there is no difference between its being not mandatory to apply a concept and its being mandatory not to apply it. If the very nature of the concept *prime*, together with the nature of some number, say eight, does not require you to apply the concept to it, then the very nature of the concept, together with the nature of the number, requires you not to apply the concept to it. For a rational and fully informed thinker, there is no freedom.

By contrast, vagueness offers freedom. It can be permissible to draw a line even where it is not mandatory to do so. No one can criticize an art materials shop for organizing its tubes of paints on various shelves, including one labelled "red" and another "yellow", even though there is a barely detectable, or perhaps even in normal circumstances undetectable, difference between the reddest paint on the shelf marked "yellow" and the yellowest paint on the shelf marked "red". Hence one can consistently combine the following: *red* draws no boundaries, that is, there is no adjacent pair in the series of tubes of paint such that the nature of the concept, together with the colour in the tube, requires one to apply *red* to one member of the pair but withhold it from the other; yet one can draw a boundary to the reds, that is, one may behave consistently with the nature of the concept in drawing a line between adjacent pairs.

The envisaged attack on boundarylessness can be set out as the following argument, which makes plain how the recent observation addresses it. A boundaryless concept is one which, for closely similar pairs, never makes it mandatory to apply the concept to one member of the pair, and withhold it from the other; hence, the argument runs, a boundaryless concept is one which, for closely similar pairs, makes it mandatory never to apply the concept to one member of the pair, and withhold it from the other. The inference depends upon the move from something being not mandatory to its being forbidden; a move legitimate within the totalitarianism of boundary-drawing concepts, but not within the liberality of boundarylessness.

I do not suggest that this simple observation puts an end to the lure of sorites reasoning, which, like a virus, will tend to evolve a resistant strain. Must there not be an outer limit to the things to which it is mandatory to apply "red", and a first member of the sorites series with respect to which we have licence to withhold? The answer is "No: 'mandatory', too, is boundaryless"; though I shall not now stop to show how this answer can be justified. It is enough for the moment to have shown that boundarylessness should give no special encouragement to paradoxical sorites-style reasoning.

7 If standard set-theoretic descriptions are incorrect for boundaryless concepts, what kind of semantics are appropriate? A generalization of the considerations so far suggests that there is no precise description of vagueness. So what kind of description should be offered? More pointedly, I hear a certain kind of objector say: we can't even tell what boundarylessness is until you give us your semantics.

If driven in this way, I would urge an idea of Donald Davidson's. A semantic theory can quite legitimately be *homophonic*, that is, can reuse in the metalanguage the very expressions whose object-language behaviour it is attempting to characterize. Asked how a boundaryless predicate like "red" works, my first response would be: "red" is true of something iff that thing is red.

Whether or not vagueness is at stake, this Davidsonian idea has met with resistance. No one could claim that such remarks are untrue, but they have been held to be trivial or unilluminating. Many such objections are confused, or are based on a misunderstanding of what, by Davidson's lights, a semantic theory should aim to achieve. In his view it should enable us to understand how some expression conspires with others to fix a truth condition, an understanding which would answer the question: "what are these familiar words doing here?"; and it should supply an account of what it would be enough for a speaker to know, in order to understand a language. Homophony impedes neither aim. On the contrary, it can provide a check upon their successful accomplishment. But a homophonic semantics for vague expressions could lead to two more specific objections, one misguided, but one sound and important.

The misguided one is that homophonic semantics will fail to make explicit which predicates are vague. In fuzzy logic, for example, the distinction will emerge in the structure of J-sets. Those associated with vague predicates will, for some or many objects as arguments, deliver numbers intermediate between 0 and 1 as values; whereas a sharp predicate's J-set will have 0 or 1 as the only values, whatever objects are arguments. In a homophonic theory the information is in a way present, but is inexplicit. It is present, because in specifying the applicability of, say, "bald" homophonically, you specify it vaguely and so *as* vague. But it is inexplicit, since there is no rule, usable by one who did not yet know which predicates are vague, on the basis of which, together with the semantic theory, he could pick out the vague ones.

However I know of no reason why this fact in itself counts against the homophonic approach. First, I know no reason for thinking that all such information must be made explicit, if the mentioned aims of semantics are to be achieved. Secondly, even if the mentioned aims, or others, did require that the information be made explicit, I know of no argument to establish that this cannot be achieved simply by means of a list, and thus consistently with homophony.

The sound and important objection is that the homophonic approach fails us in connection with logic. Davidson himself envisages a first-order metalanguage, and thus a metalanguage of which classical model theory is true, and thus a metalanguage in which predicates are associated with sets as their extensions. Thus envisaged, the project succeeds in fixing a logic for the object language, namely, classical first order logic; but it fixes it while at the same time mischaracterizing the semantics of the object language. For, despite syntactic homophony, if the metalanguage is first order, its predicates will be boundary-drawing, and so will misrepresent the object language predicates as also being boundary-drawing.

This first order feature of Davidson's proposals is, as he says, inessential. Abandoning it makes possible serious homophony: an account of the object language predicates in which they are not merely reused in point of their sounds or shapes, but also in point of their meaning. The problem then, however, is to say something worthwhile about the logic of the object language. There are two obstacles. First, we do not know what our actual logic, which would be reapplied homophonically, is. We do not know, for example, whether every instance of *P or not-P* is counted true in our language and thought, and one pertinent reason for this doubt stems from vagueness. Secondly, even if we knew what our actual logic is, we could not uncritically reuse it in a semantic project, for the existence of sorites reasoning casts doubt upon whether we are right to subscribe to the logic to which we actually subscribe.

The logic of vagueness, characterized as boundarylessness, thus remains to be described. I believe that the way forward involves taking the notion of a vague object as basic; but this is a suggestion I shall not pursue here.

8 If the semantic description of a vague concept is to have all the thinness of homophony, can we not achieve a richer description in other ways, perhaps in terms of the psychological mechanisms whereby a vague concept is acquired or applied?

For example, it seems that very often a boundaryless concept is acquired on the basis of paradigms. We acquire the concept from the inside, working outwards from central cases, and locating the central cases of contrary concepts, rather than from the outside, identifying boundaries and moving inwards. Can this thought be used to say anything illuminating about the nature of boundaryless concepts?

If it can, I am not sure how. Perhaps we should try to specify a boundaryless concept's relation to the world in terms of a paradigm—an object, α, to which it quite definitely applies, and which might therefore be an appropriate example to use in a teaching situation—together with a relation of similarity. Then we might say, non-homophonically, that the concept is true of something iff that thing is sufficiently similar to α.

But the suggestion has many vices. For one, it presupposes, without any justification, that every boundaryless concept must be instantiated. For another, the condition will not state anything which users of the concept have to know, since there may be more than one paradigm, and so one could master the concept just as well without knowing anything of α. Thirdly, anything which might have worried one about boundarylessness, for example any problems about the sorites paradox, naturally remain just as they were, though now attaching to the similarity relation.

Surely, however, I should take note of, and perhaps make use of, psychologists who have, it might be thought, investigated essentially this phenomenon under the name of prototype theory. Eleanor Rosch, for example, has suggested that the notion of a prototype helps us to understand vagueness since prototypicality is a property of degree, and vague predicates are associated with such properties. However, it turns out that prototypicality, in this sense, is orthogonal to vagueness, as demonstrated by the fact that an absolutely definite case may have low prototypicality (as penguins do relative to their classification as birds). Indeed, even boundary-drawing concepts induce prototypicality scales. Thus 2 is highly prototypical for *even number*, but it is no surprise to learn that there are plenty of even numbers which have a very low prototypicality rating for this concept: many even numbers are extremely unlikely to be chosen in teaching or exemplifying the concept.

A more promising alternative source of understanding boundarylessness is the parallel distributed processing (PDP) model of the material basis of cognitive activities. Crucial to such a model is another notion of a prototype: an object which has played a causal role as a positive instance in so adjusting the weights of the hidden elements of the network as to help tune it to its recognitional task. This might turn out to correspond more closely to what, a moment ago, I called a paradigm.

Any attempt to describe boundarylessness in such psychological or neurophysiological terms will, however, miss the normative features. We might explain confident application of, say, "red" as the organism's response to a high level of activation of the output of the red-recognizing network, and a reduction in confidence by a combination of a reduction of the level of this output and an increase in the level of output from the yellow-recognizing network. There may also be explanations in neurophysiological terms of the tendency to include more colours in the reds if you start from reds and move gradually to the yellows than if you reverse the direction of application. But no such facts will begin to capture such aspects of the use of the word "red" as the mandatoriness of its application in some central cases, the freedom available for borderlines, and such rules as that anything at least as red as a red thing is not merely likely to be called "red" but ought to be so called.

The general point is that the vagueness of a vague expression need not, and perhaps should not, feature in a psychological account of how it is used. This account may describe the dispositions-at-a-time to use the expression in terms of a probability function, and may describe a more enduring state in terms of a range of such functions. But the psychologist's task would be made no harder if he resisted anything homophonic in describing the inputs to the functions. Thus he might describe the input to a person's function relating to the ascription of "red" not in our colour vocabulary but in terms of the physical constitution of the light striking the eye. So while one should expect harmony between the semantic fact of boundarylessness and such psychological descriptions, the latter can never exhaust the former.

9 Let us take stock. Vagueness should be characterized as boundary-lessness, not merely in terms of borderlines. Boundarylessness cannot be described sharply, for example set-theoretically; so, whatever insight psychological descriptions may offer, the only semantic description which appears plausible is vague, for example homophonic. We must reject the classical picture of classification by pigeon-holes, and think in other terms: classifying can be, and often is, clustering round paradigms.

Just how widespread vagueness is can be underestimated. Let me draw attention to an area sometimes wrongly thought to be free of it: biological species. Even in quite recent philosophy, there is a tendency to suppose that species come in the "eternal and fixed forms" beloved, according to John Locke, of the Port Royal logicians. It may seem that *strawberry* draws boundaries, since there are no borderline cases. But this is just an accident. There could very well be, and no doubt with the advent of genetic engineering soon will be, a series of plants between strawberries and raspberries, many of them borderline for both concepts. Such concepts do not impose boundaries, but constitute one of the largest and most impressive systems of contrary boundaryless concepts. Locke was right to draw attention to the lack of boundaries by reminding us of boundary-defying "monsters".

One practical application of work on vagueness is in cognitive science, where a possible goal is to implement in machinery the vague-ness of our concepts. Another application has already been mentioned. The law must rule a boundary between legitimate and illegitimate acts. Here, boundarylessness would be out of place. Yet such rulings must often traverse territory spanned by a boundaryless concept, like that of being a person. Given the nature of boundarylessness, semantics give freedom. There is some number of minutes such that the nature of the concept of a person, together with the nature of the world, makes it neither mandatory nor impermissible to apply the concept to a foetus of that age in minutes. Hence arguments that use the vague concept to establish or overthrow a sharp ruling are alike inadequate. We can no more argue that aborting a foetus of this age is right because it is not a person than we can argue that it is wrong because it is a person, if *person* is vague at the crucial point. In general, only a pragmatic justification could be found for drawing a legal line in an area where there are no relevant boundaries.

I mention this merely as an example of a possible application whose details remain to be worked out. It proleptically exemplifies my hope that work in the philosophy of vagueness will enable us better to under-stand how the demands of law and morality should be tailored to the boundaryless fabric of most of our thought and talk.

14   Vagueness and ignorance

Timothy Williamson

No one knows whether I'm thin. I'm not clearly thin; I'm not clearly not thin. The word "thin" is too vague to enable "TW is thin" to be recognized as true or as false, however accurately my waist is measured and the result compared with vital statistics for the rest of the population. Is this ignorance? Most work on vagueness has taken for granted the answer "No". According to it, there is nothing here to be known. I am just a borderline case of thinness; "TW is thin" is neither true nor false. Doubt will be cast on the coherence of this view. There are standard objections to the alternative that "TW is thin" is either unknowably true or unknowably false. Doubt will be cast on them too. For all we know, vagueness is a kind of ignorance.

1   Why doubt the majority view? Well, suppose that "TW is thin" is neither true nor false. If I were thin, "TW is thin" would be true; since it isn't, I'm not. But if I'm not thin, "TW is not thin" is true, and so "TW is thin" false. The supposition seems to contradict itself. Yet on the majority view it is true.

   To generalize the argument, consider a language L with negation ($\sim$), disjunction ($\vee$), conjunction ($\&$) and a biconditional ($\leftrightarrow$). Extend L to a metalanguage for L by adding a truth predicate (T) for sentences of L and quotation marks ("...") for naming them. The falsity of a sentence of L is identified with the truth of its negation. Thus the supposition at issue, the denial of bivalence for a sentence of L, is equivalent to the denial that either it or its negation is true:

   (1) $\sim[T("P") \vee T("\sim P")]$

Two instances of Tarski's disquotational schema for truth are:

   (2a) $T("P") \leftrightarrow P$

   (2b) $T("\sim P") \leftrightarrow \sim P$

The argument uses (2a) and (2b) to substitute their right-hand sides for their left-hand sides in (1):

   (3) $\sim[P \vee \sim P]$

From *Proceedings of the Aristotelian Society, Supp. Vol* 66 (1992) pp. 145–62. © The Aristotelian Society Reprinted by permission

It then applies one of De Morgan's laws to (3), giving

(4) $\sim P$ & $\sim\sim P$

This is a contradiction, whether or not the double negation is eliminated. Thus (1) reduces to absurdity. In effect, one uses Tarski's schema to equate bivalence $(T("P") \vee T("\sim P"))$ with the law of excluded middle $(P \vee \sim P)$, and then argues from the incoherence of denying the latter to the incoherence of denying the former.[1]

The argument does not purport to show that bivalence must be asserted, only that it must not be denied. Whether bivalence must be asserted will depend on whether the law of excluded middle must be asserted, an issue which has not been addressed. Even so, the argument may seem to prove too much. Can every denial of bivalence be reduced to absurdity? However, the argument applies not whenever bivalence is denied, but only when it is denied of a particular sentence. It does not touch intuitionism in mathematics, for example. Although intuitionists deny the general principle of bivalence, they are forbidden to give particular counterexamples, just because the inference from (1) to (4) is intuitionistically valid.[2] They sometimes refrain from asserting the bivalence of a particular sentence, but they never deny it. This does not undermine their denial of the general principle, for "Not every sentence is bivalent" does not intuitionistically entail "Some sentence is not bivalent". Vagueness is a different matter. Vague sentences are supposed to be obviously not bivalent in borderline cases, and the usual way of evoking this sense of obviousness is by vivid descriptions of particular examples. If it is obvious that not all vague sentences are bivalent, it is obvious that "TW is thin" is not bivalent. So if one must not deny the bivalence of "TW is thin", does vagueness give any reason to deny bivalence in general?[3]

The core of the argument is its use of Tarski's disquotational schema for truth; everything else is relatively uncontroversial.[4] At first sight, it

---

1   Tarski derives bivalence (which he calls "the principle of excluded middle") from his definition of truth (rather than the disquotational schema) as Theorem 2 of his 1931 (see Tarski 1956, p 197) The proof uses the law of excluded middle (in the present sense)

2   The intuitionist is assumed here to equate "true" with "provable" rather than with "proved".

3   The sorites paradox might move some to deny that all sentences of the form "n grains make a heap" are bivalent, but not to deny bivalence for any particular n (although for some n they would refrain from asserting it) If the argument in the text is sound, the supposedly obvious assumptions which might drive one to this view are false

4.   A general setting for the argument is as follows. There is a partial ordering $\leq$ of the semantic values assigned to sentences (e g. truth values) under which they form

looks vulnerable to an obvious objection. If P is neither true nor false, should not T("P") be simply false? But then the left-hand sides of (2a) and (2b) but not their right-hand sides would be false; on a strong reading of the biconditional this would make (2a) and (2b) not true. This is just what one might say in the case of reference failure. Consider, for example, a context where "this dagger" fails to pick anything out. One might hold that no sentence in which "this dagger" is used is true in the context. Thus neither "This dagger is sharp" nor "This dagger is not sharp" is true, so "This dagger is sharp" is neither true nor false. By the same principle, the Tarskian biconditional "'This dagger is sharp' is true if and only if this dagger is sharp" would not be true in the context, for it uses as well as mentions "this dagger". The argument has no force in the case of reference failure; why should it have any force in the case of vagueness?

On the suggested treatment of reference failure, "This dagger is sharp" says nothing that could have been true or false, and even counterfactuals such as "If the servants had been assiduous, this dagger would have been sharp" are neither true nor false (of course, the sentence type "This dagger is sharp" could have been used in a different context to say something true or false). According to the parallel treatment of a vague sentence in a borderline case, "TW is thin" says nothing that could have been true or false, and even counterfactuals such as "If he had dieted, TW would have been thin" are neither true nor false.[5] Such consequences are unwelcome. Unlike "This dagger is sharp", "TW is thin" could have said something true without saying

---

a lattice, i e each pair of values has a greatest lower bound (glb) and a least upper bound (lub), greater values being thought of as "truer" If $|P|$ is the semantic value assigned to P, $|P \& Q| = \text{glb}\{|P|, |Q|\}$, $|P \vee Q| = \text{lub}\{|P|, |Q|\}$ and if $|P| \leq |Q|$ then $|\sim Q| \leq |\sim P|$ These assumptions are met by standard classical, supervaluational, intuitionist and many-valued treatments and others Now suppose that $|P| = |T("P")|$ and $|\sim P| = |T("\sim P")|$. Then $|P| = |T("P")| \leq \text{lub}\{|T("P")|, |T("\sim P")|\}$ $= |T("P") \vee T("\sim P")|$; similarly, $|T("\sim P")| \leq |T("P") \vee T("\sim P")|$ Thus $|\sim[T("P") \vee T("\sim P")]| \leq |\sim P|$ and $|\sim[T("P") \vee T("\sim P")]| \leq |\sim\sim P|$, so $|(1)| \leq \text{glb}\{|\sim P|, |\sim\sim P|\} = |(4)|$. Thus what is needed is a defence of Tarski's schema which assigns the same semantic value to each side of the biconditional, this is supplied in the text. Two further assumptions are that P has a negation whose falsity is equivalent to the truth of P and that a contradiction is indeed absurd. The former is clearly correct for "TW is thin", which is enough for the argument. As for the latter, if the denial of bivalence for vague sentences is obviously correct, it does not involve a contradiction (someone might answer the question "Is TW thin?" with "He is and he isn't", but it would take a bold man to revise logic on the basis of that idiom)

5. A standard analysis of "If he had dieted, TW would have been thin" is assumed, on which it results from feeding "He [or TW] dieted" and "TW is thin" into a counterfactual conditional.

something different. Most simply, "TW is thin" means that TW is thin; on the suggested treatment, "'This dagger is sharp' means that this dagger is sharp" is neither true nor false, for "this dagger" is used, not mentioned, on its second occurrence. But since "TW is thin" means that TW is thin, what it is for "TW is thin" to be true is just for TW to be thin. Similarly, since "TW is not thin" means that TW is not thin, what it is for "TW is not thin" to be true, and so for "TW is thin" to be false, is just for TW not to be thin.[6] The difference between reference failure (as treated above) and vagueness favours the Tarskian biconditionals in the latter case.[7] In doing so, it undermines the thought that "TW is thin" is neither true nor false, i.e. (1), by vindicating the argument from it to (4).

We can consistently deny bivalence of a sentence with reference failure precisely because in doing so we abjure the use, embedded or unembedded, of that sentence in that context. If we are not willing to abjure the use, embedded or unembedded, of a vague sentence in the context of borderline cases, we cannot consistently deny its bivalence. According to a sceptical view, rigour demands that we should abjure such uses because vagueness is itself a kind of reference failure. Adjectives refer, if at all, to sharply defined properties, but a vague one like "thin" fails to single out such a property and so fails to refer; sentences of the form "*a* is thin" say, strictly, nothing, whether or not *a* is a borderline case. Since almost all our utterances involve vague terms, this view

---

6. A homophonic truth theory is thus not essential to the argument; the translatability of P and $\sim P$ into the metalanguage is enough, as Tarski noted Incidentally, it is not claimed that a Tarskian theory tells the whole truth about truth, just that it tells an essential part of the truth Without a disquotational schema, it is doubtful that one has a truth predicate at all

7. The supervaluational treatment of vagueness, most systematically expounded by Kit Fine (this volume), may seem an obvious counterexample to the argument in the text from failure of bivalence to failure of excluded middle However, Fine allows a Tarskian truth predicate "true$_T$"; he argues that it is conceptually prior to the ordinary truth predicate "true", because "x is true" is to be defined by "Definitely (x is true$_T$)"; "true" is not subject to the Tarskian schema (pp. 148–49, compare Kripke 1975, p. 715). Since Fine's account validates the law of excluded middle, it validates bivalence for the primary notions of truth and falsity Where the present approach differs is in its claim that the ordinary notion of truth is subject to the Tarskian schema and is therefore not to be defined in Fine's way The "definitely" operator is discussed in section 2 In *The Logical Basis of Metaphysics*, Michael Dummett argues that the ordinary notion of truth for a vague language is the non-Tarskian one because only it is "objective" in the sense that "every sentence determinately either does or does not possess it" (Dummett 1991, p 74) This condition is not self-evident, not least because it is inconsistent with second-order vagueness The disquotational schema is endorsed for a vague language by Machina (this volume, p 201), Peacocke 1981, pp. 136–7 (both within theories of degrees of truth), Sainsbury (this volume)

makes almost all of them mere noise. They are not even failed attempts to express thoughts, since parallel considerations would suggest that almost all our concepts are equally contentless.[8] The only consistent expression of such a view is in silence.[9]

Once we are permitted to use "thin", we can argue that "TW is thin" says something that would have been true in various circumstances, because I would have been thin. Then "'TW is thin' is true if and only if TW is thin" says something too. But if it says anything, it is true. For, given that "TW is thin" means that TW is thin, what more could it take for "TW is thin" to be true than for TW to be thin?

To deny bivalence for vague sentences while continuing to use them is to adopt an unstable position. The denial of bivalence amounts to a rejection of the practice of using them. One is rejecting the practice while continuing to engage in it. Rapid alternation between perspectives inside and outside the practice can disguise, but not avoid, this hypocrisy.

2 If one cannot deny bivalence for vague sentences, can one deny something like it? There is a standard move at this point. Instead of saying that "TW is thin" is neither true nor false, one says that it is neither *definitely* true nor *definitely* false. Definite truth does not itself obey the disquotational schema, otherwise nothing would have been gained. It takes less for "TW is thin" not to be definitely true than for TW not to be thin. Since it does not take less for "TW is thin" not to be true than for TW not to be thin, truth is not the same thing as definite truth. On pain of the argument in section 1, this new position does not involve a denial of bivalence. Indeed, the principle of bivalence does not mention definiteness; it merely says that a sentence is either true or false. On the face of it, the claim that a sentence is neither definitely true nor definitely false has no more to do with bivalence than the claim that it is neither necessarily true nor necessarily false, or that it is neither obviously true nor obviously false.[10] To pursue indirect connections would be premature.

Before one can assess the claim that vague sentences are neither definitely true nor definitely false in borderline cases, one needs to know what it means. That the adverb "definitely" has been given a clear

---

8   Even the intention to express some thought or other harbours vagueness.

9   The classic expression of a sceptical view is section 56 of Frege 1903 The more limited sceptical view that observational predicates are vague in such a way as to be incoherent is discussed in my 1990a, pp 88–103, in effect section 6 below explains how the incoherent principle "If x and y are indiscriminable by the naked eye, x is thin if and only if y is thin" could look true while being false.

10. For a contrary view see Dummett 1991, pp. 74–82

relevant sense is less than obvious. If "definitely true" were just a circumlocution for "true", no problem would arise, but the view under consideration requires the two expressions to have quite different senses. Can "definitely" be explained in other terms, or are we supposed to grasp it as primitive? No doubt "TW is thin" is definitely true if and only if TW is definitely thin, but what is the difference between being thin and being definitely thin? Is it like the difference between being thin and being very thin? Again, "TW is thin" is presumably not definitely true if and only if TW is not definitely thin; what is the difference between not being thin and not being definitely thin?[11]

Let it be obvious that "TW is thin" is neither definitely true nor definitely false. In reporting this obvious truth, the philosopher has no right to stipulate a theoretical sense for "definitely". Rather, it must be used in a sense expressive of what is obvious. Yet what is *obvious* is just that vague sentences are sometimes neither knowably true nor knowably false. The simplest hypothesis is that this is the *only* sense in which the vague sentences are neither definitely true nor definitely false. Bivalence and classical logic hold. Either I'm thin and "TW is thin" is true or I'm not thin and "TW is thin" is false; we have no way of knowing which. Although this is not at all the standard view of what "definitely" means, the obscurity of the standard view gives us reason to explore alternatives. The epistemic view is usually held to be inconsistent with obvious facts, but the leading candidate for such a fact—the failure of bivalence—has already disappeared. The rest of the paper explores the epistemic view.[12]

3 Many descriptions of vagueness rule out the epistemic view from the start. A term is said to be vague only if it can have a borderline case, and a case is said to be borderline only if our inability to decide it does not depend on ignorance. But to assume that the cases ordinarily called "borderline" are borderline in this technical sense is just to beg the

---

11. There are views on which "definitely" makes a difference only in the scope of negation and in similar contexts. I also assume that the reference of "TW" is unproblematic

12. The epistemic view probably goes back to the Stoic logician Chrysippus, a man with some claim to have discovered the classical propositional calculus; see Barnes 1982 and Burnyeat 1982 More recently, it has been defended in Cargile (this volume), Campbell 1974, Sorensen 1988, pp 217–52; Horwich 1990, pp. 81–87, Williamson 1990a, pp 103–8 It is critically discussed in Heller 1990, pp 89–106 Sperber and Wilson 1986 retains classical logic and semantics while explaining vague utterances in pragmatic terms, "He is bald", said of a man with just one hair on his head, being false but relevantly informative, a generalization of this view from "bald" to "heap" might need to postulate ignorance

question against the epistemic view. For example, "TW is thin" would ordinarily be called a "borderline" case, but one should not assume without argument that our inability to decide the matter does not depend on ignorance. Of what fact could we be ignorant? There is an obvious answer: we are ignorant either of the fact that TW is thin or of the fact that TW is not thin (our ignorance prevents us from knowing which). If that is a bad answer, it has yet to be explained why. That it uses the word "thin" is just what one would expect in the light of section 1. There is no general requirement that vague words be definable in other terms.

Those wholly predictable opening moves against the epistemic view mismanage a deeper objection. It can be made using the idea that vague facts *supervene* on precise ones. If two possible situations are identical in all precise respects, they are identical in all vague respects too. For example, if x and y have exactly the same physical measurements, x is thin if and only if y is thin. More generally:

(*) If x has exactly the same physical measurements in a possible situation s as y has in a possible situation t, x is thin in s if and only if y is thin in t.[13]

The objection to the epistemic view can now be formulated. Let my exact physical measurements be m. According to the epistemic view, I am either thin or not thin. By (*), if I am thin, necessarily anyone with physical measurements m is thin. Similarly, if I am not thin, necessarily no one with physical measurements m is thin. Thus either being thin is a necessary consequence of having physical measurements m, or not being thin is. Suppose that I find out, as I can, what my physical measurements are. I would then seem to be in a position either to deduce that I am thin or to deduce that I am not thin. But it has already been conceded that no amount of measuring will enable me to decide whether I am thin.[14]

The basis of this objection to the epistemic view is not that one can know all the relevant facts in a case ordinarily classified as "borderline" but that one can know a set of facts on which all the relevant facts supervene, without being able to decide the case. Unlike the first claim, the second does not beg the question against the epistemic view. The epistemic theorist has as much reason as anyone else to accept supervenience claims like (*). However, the objection commits a subtler fallacy.

---

13 More accurately, one's thinness may depend on the physical measurements of one's comparison class as well as on one's own This does not affect the point about to be made

14 Exercise how does this argument fare against the supervaluational approach?

The kind of possibility and necessity at issue in supervenience claims like (*) is metaphysical. There *could not be* two situations differing vaguely but not precisely. Suppose that I am in fact thin. By (*), it is metaphysically necessary that anyone with physical measurements *m* is thin. If I know that I have physical measurements *m*, in order to deduce that I am thin I must *know* that anyone with physical measurements *m* is thin. The plausibility of the objection to the epistemic view thus depends on something like the inference that since the supervenience generalizations are metaphysically necessary, they can be known *a priori*. The inference from metaphysical necessity to *a priori* knowability may be a tempting one: but, as Kripke has emphasized, it is fallacious. Indeed, metaphysical necessities cannot be assumed to be knowable in any way at all, otherwise all mathematical truths could be assumed knowable. It is integral to the epistemic view that metaphysically necessary claims like "Anyone with physical measurements *m* is thin" can be as unknowable as physically contingent ones like "TW is thin".

One should not be surprised that the known supervenience of *A*-facts on *B*-facts does not provide a route from knowledge of *B*-facts to knowledge of *A*-facts. A more familiar case is the supervenience of mental facts on physical facts. Suppose, for the sake of illustration, that bravery is known to supervene on the state of the brain. Then if *s* is a maximally specific brain state (described in physical terms) of brave Jones, it is metaphysically necessary that anyone in brain state *s* is brave. Clearly, however, there is no presumption that one could have found out that Jones was brave simply by measuring his brain state and invoking supervenience. "Anyone in brain state *s* is brave" cannot be known *a priori*. Perhaps one can know it *a posteriori*, because one can find out that someone is brave by observing his behaviour, then combine this knowledge with knowledge of his brain state and of the supervenience of mental states on brain states. "Anyone with physical measurements *m* is thin" cannot be known *a posteriori* in a parallel way, for no route to independent knowledge of someone with physical measurements *m* that he is thin corresponds to the observation of brave behaviour.

The epistemic view of vagueness is consistent with the supervenience of vague facts on precise ones. The next section considers a different objection to the epistemic view, and makes another application of the concept of supervenience.

4   A common complaint against the epistemic view of vagueness is that it severs a necessary connection between meaning and use. Words mean what they do because we use them as we do; to postulate a fact of the matter in borderline cases is to suppose, incoherently, that the

meanings of our words draw lines where our use of them does not. The point is perhaps better put at the level of complete speech acts, in terms of sentences rather than single words. The meaning of a declarative sentence may provisionally be identified with its truth conditions, and its use with our dispositions to assent to and dissent from it. The complaint is that the epistemic view of vagueness sets truth conditions floating unacceptably free of our dispositions to assent and dissent.

So far, the complaint is too general to be convincing. If our dispositions to assent to or to dissent from the sentence "That is water" do not discriminate between H_2O and XYZ, it does not follow that the truth conditions of the sentence are equally undiscriminating. What needs to be emphasized is that there is no sharp natural division for the truth conditions of "He is thin" to follow corresponding to the sharp natural division between H_2O and XYZ followed by the truth conditions of "That is water". The idea is that if nature does not draw a line for us, a line is drawn only if we draw it ourselves, by our use. So there is no line, for our use leaves not a line but a smear.

Before we allow the revised complaint to persuade us, we should probe its conception of drawing a line. On the face of it, "drawing" is just a metaphor for "determining". To say that use determines meaning is just to say that meaning *supervenes* on use. That is: same use entails same meaning, so no difference in meaning without a difference in use. More formally:

(#) If an expression e is used in a possible situation s in the same way as an expression f is used in a possible situation t, e has the same meaning in s as f has in t.

There are various problems with (#), such as its neglect of the environment as a constitutive factor in meaning and its crude notion of "used in the same way". However, some refinement of (#) will be assumed for the sake of argument to be correct. For the epistemic view of vagueness is quite consistent with (#) and its refinements. Although the view does not permit simple-minded reductions of meaning to use, it in no way entails the possibility of a difference in meaning without any corresponding difference in use. Had "TW is thin" had different truth conditions, our dispositions to assent to and dissent from it would have been different too.

Our use determines many lines. Of these one of the least interesting is the line at which assent becomes more probable than dissent. It is no more plausible a candidate for the line between truth and falsity than is the line at which assent becomes unanimous. The study of vagueness has regrettably served as the last refuge of the consensus theory of truth; the theory is no more tenable for vague sentences than it is for precise ones. We can be wrong even about whether someone is thin, for we can be wrong both about that person's shape and size and about normal shapes and sizes in the relevant comparison class. These errors may be systematic; some people may characteristically look thinner or less thin than they actually are, and there may be characteristic misconceptions about the prevalence of various shapes and sizes. To invoke perfect information or epistemically ideal situations at this point is merely to swamp normal speakers of English with more measurements and statistics than they can handle. Perhaps an epistemically ideal speaker of English would be an infallible guide to thinness, but then such a speaker might know the truth value of "TW is thin". If one sticks to actual speakers of English, there is no prospect of reducing the truth conditions of vague sentences to the statistics of assent and dissent, whether or not one accepts the epistemic view of vagueness.

The failure of simple-minded reductions is quite consistent with supervenience. There may be a subtler connection, perhaps of a causal kind, between the property of thinness and our use of "thin". Even if everything has or lacks the property, the reliability of our mechanism for recognizing it may depend on its giving neither a positive nor a negative response in marginal cases. The cost of having the mechanism answer in such cases would be many wrong answers. It is safer to have a mechanism that often gives no answer than one that often gives the wrong answer. From such a mechanism, one might be able to work back to the property, through the question "Which property does this mechanism best register?".[15]

It might be objected that if a mechanism sometimes gives no response, there will be distinct properties p and q such that both are present when it responds positively, both are absent when it responds negatively, but sometimes one is present and the other absent when it does not respond, and that since it is equally good at registering p and q, and no better at registering any other property, the question "Which property does this mechanism best register?" has no unique answer. This objection ignores the statistical nature of reliability. The mechanism cannot be expected to register any distal property infallibly; since its functioning depends on the state of the subject as well as on the state of the environment, no distal property will be present whenever there is a positive response and absent whenever there is a negative one.[16]

---

15 A more teleological question would be "Which property did this mechanism evolve to register?". Considerations like those in the text would still apply

16 Why consider distal properties rather than proximal ones? This is a general but not unanswerable question for causal theories of reference, it is not a special problem for the epistemic view of vagueness

Reliability is a matter of minimizing a non-zero probability of error; for all that has been shown, just one property may do that.[17]

A subject whose primary access to a property is through a recognitional mechanism may not be helped to detect it by extra information of a kind which cannot be processed by that mechanism, even if the new information is in fact a reliable indicator of the presence of the property —for the subject may not know that. My exact measurements may in fact be a sufficient condition for thinness, and knowledge of the former still not enable us to derive knowledge of the latter; for all that, thinness may be the property best registered by our perceptual recognitional capacity for thinness.

The foregoing speculations should not mislead one into supposing that a causal theory of reference is essential to an epistemic view of vagueness. They illustrate only one way in which our use of a vague expression might determine a sharp property. A comprehensive account of the connection between meaning and use would no doubt be very different. Since no one knows what such an account would be like, the epistemic view of vagueness should not be singled out for its failure to provide one. No reason has emerged to think that it makes such an account harder to provide. At the worst, there may be no account to be had, beyond a few vague salutory remarks. Meaning may supervene on use in an unsurveyably chaotic way.

5 The charge against the epistemic view of vagueness might be revised. If the view does not force what we mean to transcend what we *do*, perhaps it forces what we mean to transcend what we *know*. The new charge is as obscure as the old one, but may be worth exploring.

A cautious answer is that the epistemic view of vagueness allows us to know what we mean. No gap need open between what we mean and what we think we mean, for both are determined in the same way, perhaps that described in section 4. We know that "TW is tall" as we use it means that, and is true if and only if, TW is tall. If we cannot know whether TW is tall, who but the verificationist thought that actual knowledge of truth conditions requires possible knowledge of truth value?

It may be replied that the epistemic view makes us ignorant of the sense of a vague term, not just of its reference. Of course we do not know where all the thin things are in physical space; the point is that we should not even know where they all are in conceptual space. We should be using a term that does in fact determine a line in conceptual

---

17 If several properties tie for first place, the obvious candidate is their conjunction (even if it is not itself one of them)

space without being able to locate that line. We should understand it partially, as one partially understands a word one has heard used once or twice. But in the latter case the word's meaning is backed by other speakers' full understanding, whereas no one is allowed full understanding of the vague term. The objection to the epistemic view is that it attributes partial understanding to the speech community as a whole. It is not entitled to say that we know what we mean. It attributes to the community incomplete knowledge of a complete meaning; would it not be more reasonable to attribute complete knowledge of an incomplete meaning?

The objection is based on the Fregean model of the sense of a term as a region in conceptual space: to grasp a sense is to know where its boundary runs. Individual points in this space are located by means of precise descriptions such as "having exact physical measurements m". Thus the demand that one know which points are in the region marked off by a vague term such as "thin" is simply the demand that one know truths such as "Anyone having exact physical measurements m is thin" or "No one having exact physical measurements m is thin". The unreasonableness of that demand was already noted in section 3; the metaphysical necessity of such truths does not justify the demand to know them. The metaphor of conceptual space adds no force to the demand. Rather, its function is illicitly to collapse distinctions between concepts whose equivalence is metaphysically necessary but not *a priori*. If a proposition is identified with a region in a space of possible worlds, cognitively significant distinctions are lost in a familiar way; exactly the same happens when the objection identifies a sense with a region in conceptual space.

On the epistemic view, our understanding of vague terms is not partial. The measure of full understanding is not possession of a complete set of metaphysically necessary truths but complete induction into a practice. When I have heard a word used only once or twice, my understanding is partial because there is more to the community's use of it than I yet know. I have not got fully inside the practice; I am to some extent still an outsider. It does not follow that if we had all understood the term in the vague way I do, all our understandings would have been partial, though they would still have determined complete intensions.[18] In that counterfactual situation, we should all have been insiders. To know what a word means is to be completely inducted into a practice that does in fact determine a complete intension.

---

18 My deference to speakers with fuller understanding may be excluded from the counterfactual situation. Think of an intension as a function from possible worlds to extensions.

That rather minimalist answer to the objection is enough. However, a more speculative line of thought may be mentioned. If meaning supervenes on use, might it also supervene on knowledge? The idea can be developed. Let the *verification conditions* of a sentence be those in which its truth conditions knowably obtain, and its *falsification conditions* be those in which its truth conditions knowably fail to obtain. A kind of supervenience claim quite consistent with the epistemic view of vagueness is:

> (@) If two sentences have the same verification conditions and the same falsification conditions, they have the same truth conditions.

(@) claims a supervenience of truth conditions on verification and falsification conditions. It no more identifies truth conditions with verification conditions than it identifies them with falsification conditions. In general, (@) is probably too strong. For example, there may be a sentence whose truth conditions cannot be known to obtain and cannot be known not to obtain; it would have the same verification conditions and falsification conditions as its negation, but not the same truth conditions. However, ordinary vague sentences are not like that. (@) might hold for them. In fact a formal version of (@) can be proved for a simple modal logic in which "necessity" is interpreted as knowability, truth does not entail knowability, and the underlying propositional logic is classical.[19]

(@) will not satisfy reductionist aspirations, for the truth conditions are used in characterizing the verification and falsification conditions. But that is a problem for the reductionist aspirations, not for the epistemic view of vagueness. What the consistency of (@) with the epistemic view shows is that the latter does not force what we mean to transcend what we know, if the purport of the charge is that the epistemic view would not allow truth conditions to supervene on the conditions in which they can be known to obtain or not to obtain.

6 Little has been said to explain our ignorance in borderline cases. Of course, ignorance might be taken as the normal state: perhaps we should think of knowledge as impossible unless special circumstances make it possible, rather than as possible unless special circumstances make it impossible. However, we may be able to do better than that in the case at hand.

Consider again the supervenience of meaning on use, at least for a fixed contribution from the environment. For any difference in meaning,

---

19 See my 1990b The result is consistent with the doubt expressed about (@), since it cannot automatically be lifted to extensions of the language

there is a difference in use. The converse does not always hold. The meaning of a word may be stabilized by natural divisions, so that a small difference in use would make no difference in meaning. A slightly increased propensity to call fool's gold "gold" would not change the meaning of the word "gold". But the meaning of a vague word is not stabilized by natural divisions in this way. A slight shift in our dispositions to call things "thin" would slightly shift the meaning of "thin". On the epistemic view, the boundary of "thin" is sharp but unstable. Suppose that I am on the "thin" side of the boundary, but only just. If our use of "thin" had been very slightly different, as it easily could have been, I would have been on the "not thin" side. The sentence "TW is thin" is true, but could easily have been false.[20] Moreover, someone who utters it assertively could easily have done so falsely, for the decision to utter it was not sensitive to all the slight shifts in the use of "thin" that would make the utterance false.

The point is not confined to public language. Even idiolects are vague. You may have no settled disposition to assent to or dissent from "TW is thin". If you were forced to go one way or the other, which way you went would depend on your circumstances and mood. If you assented, that would not automatically make the sentence true in your idiolect; if you dissented, that would not automatically make it false. What you mean by "thin" does not change with every change in your circumstances and mood. The extension of a term in your idiolect depends on the whole pattern of your use in a variety of circumstances and moods; you have no way of making each part of your use perfectly sensitive to the whole, for you have no way of surveying the whole. To imagine away this sprawling quality of your use is to imagine away its vagueness.[21]

An utterance of "TW is thin" is not the outcome of a disposition to be reliably right; it is right by luck. It can therefore hardly be an expression of knowledge. Contrapositively, an utterance of "TW is thin" is an expression of knowledge only if I am some way from the boundary of "thin", that is, only if anyone with physical measurements very close to mine is also thin. More generally, for a given way of measuring difference in physical measurements there will be a small but non-zero constant c such that:

(!)   If x and y differ in physical measurements by less than c and x is known to be thin, y is thin.

---

20 The point is not that I might easily not have been thin In the relevant counterfactual situations, my physical measurements are just what they actually are, but "thin" means something slightly different from what it actually means.

21 What goes for words in your idiolect also goes for your concepts.

Similar principles can be formulated for other vague terms. Vague knowledge requires a margin for error.

Given (!), one cannot know a conjunction of the form "x is thin and y is not thin" when x and y differ in physical measurements by less than c. To know the conjunction, one would have to know its first conjunct; but then by (!) its second conjunct would be false, making the whole conjunction false and therefore unknown. Since such conjunctions cannot be known, the unwary may suppose that they cannot be true. "Thin" will then look as though it is governed by a tolerance principle of the form: if x and y differ in physical measurements by less than c and x is thin, y is thin. One can now construct a sorites paradox by considering a series of men, the first very thin, the last very fat, and each differing from the next in physical measurements by less than c: by repeated applications of the tolerance principle, since the first man is thin, so is the last man. Fortunately, "thin" is not governed by the tolerance principle; it is governed by the margin for error principle (!), which generates no sorites paradox.[22]

The plausibility of (!) does not depend on the epistemic view of vagueness. Its rationale is that reliable truth is a necessary (perhaps not sufficient) condition of knowledge, and that a vague judgement is reliably true only if it is true in sufficiently similar cases. This point does not require the judgement to be true or false in every case. But once our uncertainty has been explained in terms of the independently plausible principle (!), it no longer provides a reason for not asserting bivalence, for bivalence is quite compatible with (!).

7   The most obvious argument for the epistemic view of vagueness has so far not been mentioned. The epistemic view involves no revision of classical logic and semantics; its rivals do involve such revisions. Classical logic and semantics are vastly superior to the alternatives in simplicity, power, past success, and integration with theories in other domains. In these circumstances it would be sensible to adopt the epistemic view in order to retain classical logic and semantics even if it were subject to philosophical criticisms in which we could locate no

---

22   (!) might be thought to generate a sorites paradox not for "thin" but for "known to be thin", given that (!) is known, that each man in the series is known to differ from the next in physical measurements by less than c, and that the very thin man is known to be thin However, analysis of the argument shows it to require the KK principle that what is known is known to be known But since "known to be thin" is itself vague, it too obeys a margin for error principle, which in turn implies that one can know x to be thin without being in a position to know that one knows that x is thin. Thus the KK principle fails The failure of the KK principle (i.e. the S4 axiom) in the modal logic KT is essential to the result cited at n 19.

fallacy; not every anomaly falsifies a theory.[23] Although that second line of defence exists, there is no need to occupy it if the argument of this paper is correct, for we can locate the fallacies in philosophical criticisms of the epistemic view of vagueness.[24]

---

23. For another argument for the epistemic view see my 1990a, p 107

24 Some of the material on which this paper is based has been presented in talks at the universities of Oxford, London (University College), Dundee, Stirling, A N.U , New England (Armidale), Queensland, Monash, Bradford, Lisbon, and Bristol More people have helped with good questions than I can name

15   Sorites paradoxes and the semantics of vagueness

Michael Tye

It is sometimes supposed that sorites paradoxes are an inevitable consequence of the very nature of vagueness. Take, for example, the term "bald". If "bald" is vague then it lacks precise boundaries. So

(1)   There is a definite number, N, such that a man with N hairs on his head is bald and a man with $N+1$ hairs on his head is not

is false. But intuitively the denial of (1) is equivalent to the assertion of

(2)   For any definite number, N, if a man with N hairs on his head is bald then a man with $N+1$ hairs on his head is also bald.

And (2), together with the obvious truth

(3)   A man with no hairs on his head is bald

entails the obvious falsehood

(4)   A man with a million hairs on his head is bald

via a million applications of modus ponens and universal instantiation. To treat this line of reasoning as a *reductio* of the denial of (1) is to concede that "bald" is not vague, and hence, in the general case, to concede that no predicates are vague. This conclusion is, of course, itself paradoxical. What, then, has gone wrong?

In this paper I want to present a novel semantics of vagueness which is, I maintain, invulnerable to sorites paradoxes such as the one above. On the approach I favor, there are three truth-values: true, false, and neither true nor false (or indefinite). The third value here is, strictly speaking, not a truth-value at all but rather a truth-value gap. In my view, there are gaps due to failure of reference or presupposition and gaps due to vagueness.[1] Corresponding to the two-valued connectives

From *Philosophical Perspectives 8. Logic and Language*, ed. James E Tomberlin (1994), pp 189–206. Atascadero, CA Ridgeview Publishing Co This selection omits §1 of the original paper © Ridgeview Publishing Co. Reprinted by permission

1   Where a gap is due to vagueness, I maintain that something is said which is neither true nor false. I deny, however, that anything is said in the case where a gap is due to failure of reference I am inclined to extend the latter view to gaps due to failure of presupposition.

~, &, ∨, ⊃, and ≡ are the three-valued connectives ┌, ∧, ∨, →, and ↔. These connectives have the following tables:

P	┌P
T	F
I	I
F	T

P＼Q		P∧Q			P∨Q			P→Q			P↔Q	
	T	I	F	T	I	F	T	I	F	T	I	F
T	T	I	F	T	I	F	T	I	F	T	I	F
I	I	I	F	T	T	T	T	I	F	T	I	F
F	F	F	F	T	I	I	T	I	I	I	I	I
				T	I	F	T	T	T	F	I	T

The guiding principles in the construction of these tables are easily explained.[2] (1) The negation of a statement of given truth-value is its opposite in truth-value. (2) A conjunction is true if both its conjuncts are true and false if either conjunct is false. Otherwise it is indefinite. (3) A disjunction is true if either disjunct is true and false if both disjuncts are false. Otherwise it is indefinite. (4) The truth-value of $P \to Q$ is to be the same as that of $┌P \vee Q$. (5) The truth-value of $P \leftrightarrow Q$ is to be the same as that of $(P \to Q) \wedge (Q \to P)$.

The tables presented above agree with the usual two-valued ones when only Ts and Fs are involved. However, there are no three-valued tautologies, since two-valued tautologies can take the value I in the three-valued case. For example the Law of Excluded Middle, that is, $p \vee ┌p$, takes on the value I when p does so. Let us say that a statement form is a quasi-tautology just in case it has no false substitution instances. Then the Law of Excluded Middle and all other two-valued tautologies are quasi-tautologies in the above system.

It may perhaps be charged that the proposed truth-tables yield some implausible truth-value assignments in connection with certain compound sentences having indefinite components. In particular, if A is indefinite, then $A \to A$ is indefinite as is $A \wedge ┌A$. I concede that the tables would certainly be mistaken, if they permitted $A \to A$ to be false and $A \wedge ┌A$ to be true. But they do no such thing. $A \to A$ is a quasi-tautology and $A \wedge ┌A$ is a quasi-contradiction. So, while the former statement cannot be false and the latter cannot be true, both can be indefinite. This seems to me entirely palatable. After all, it is surely reasonable to require that sentences of the form $P \to Q$ be equivalent to sentences of the form $┌P \vee Q$ and also that $P \wedge ┌P$ be equivalent to $┌(P \vee ┌P)$. As I urged earlier, it is also surely reasonable to deny that sentences of the form $P \vee ┌P$ must always be true, given the existence of borderline cases. There is, then, good reason to deny that $A \to A$ must

---

2. The tables are due to S C Kleene (although Kleene himself did not apply them to vague statements). See his 1952, pp. 332–40 For an application of Kleene's approach to the paradox of the Liar, see Kripke 1975.

be true and also good reason to deny that $A \wedge \neg A$ must be false.[3]

Turning next to predicates, I suggest that for the purposes of formal semantics the following treatment suffices for any extensionally vague monadic predicate F: given a non-empty domain D, F is assigned an extension S and a counterextension S'. S is the set of objects of which F is true; S' is the set of objects of which F is false. S and S' are not classical sets, however.[4] Nor even are they sets of the sort countenanced by the degrees of truth theorist (i.e., sets having precise identity conditions and members to precise degrees). Rather it is crucial to a proper understanding of the semantics of vagueness that they be taken to be genuinely vague items. This needs a little explanation.

Consider the set of tall men. Men who are over 6 feet 6 inches are certainly members of this set and men who are under 5 feet 6 inches are certainty not. Intuitively, however, some men are borderline members: there is no determinate, objective fact of the matter about whether they are in the set or outside it.[5] Are there any remaining men? To suppose that it is true that this is the case is to postulate more categories of men than are demanded by our ordinary, non-philosophical conception of the set of tall men and hence to involve ourselves in gratuitous metaphysical complications. It is also to create the need to face a potentially, endless series of such questions one after the other as new categories of men are admitted. On the other hand, to suppose that it is false that there are any remaining men is to admit that every single man fits cleanly into one of the three categories so that there are sharp partitions between the men in the set, the men on the border, so to speak, and the men outside. And intuitively, pre-theoretically it is not true that there are any sharp partitions here. What, I think, we should say, then, is that it is objectively indeterminate as to whether there are any remaining men. In the ways I have just described, the set of tall men is, I maintain, a vague set.

I propose to generalize from this example. Let us hold that something x is a borderline F just in case x is such that there is no determinate fact

---

3 The claim that $A \rightarrow A$ is sometimes indefinite is, of course, compatible with the claim that A is a logical consequence of A, since one sentence will be a logical consequence of another so long as it is cannot be true that the first is anything other than true when the latter is true. Within the above framework, then, the deduction theorem no longer holds

4. Some philosophers might respond here, "Well, they aren't *sets* at all then " This response is given from a particular theoretical perspective It forgets that the term "set" is a perfectly ordinary one and that in its ordinary usage it is *not* reserved for sharp entities See below for an example of a common or garden vague set.

5. I might add that I do not deny that some borderline tall men are closer to being tall than other borderline tall men.

of the matter about whether x is an F. Then I classify a set S as vague (in the ordinary robust sense in which the set of tall men is vague) if, and only if, (a) it has borderline members and (b) there is no determinate fact of the matter about whether there are objects that are neither members, borderline members, nor non-members. This characterization of vague sets may seem to entail that one of the basic axioms of set theory, namely the Axiom of Extensionality, is false. But in reality it does no such thing. I shall elaborate upon this point later.

I hope that I have now managed to provide an informal clarification of my use of the term "vague" in application to sets. I might add here that I do not wish to deny that other kinds of objects may properly be classified as vague. The property of baldness, for example, is, in my view, a vague object. It is neither clearly a feature of some people nor clearly not a feature of those people. Baldness, moreover, would have remained vague, even if there had been only very hairy or wholly hairless people. In general I take a property P to be vague (in the ordinary, robust sense in which baldness is vague) only if (a) it *could* have borderline instances, and (b) there is no determinate fact of the matter about whether there *could* be objects that are neither instances, borderline instances, nor non-instances.[6] I include clause (b) here for essentially the same reasons as those I gave in connection with the earlier (b) clause for sets.

One further point: once properties are acknowledged that could have borderline instances, no conceptual barrier exists to the admission of properties which are such that there is no determinate fact of the matter about whether they could have borderline instances. Such properties, some of which will concern us later, might be called "vaguely vague" or "indefinitely vague".[7] And what goes here for properties goes *mutatis mutandis* for sets.

Returning now to the formal semantics, with the introduction of vague sets in connection with extensionally vague predicates, we may state truth conditions for vague singular sentences as follows. For any

---

6. For an explanation of why these conditions are not both necessary and sufficient for property vagueness together with a statement of some more complex conditions that are, see Tye 1990.

7. There also seems to be no immediate conceptual barrier to the admission of properties that are such that (a) they could have borderline instances and borderline borderline instances, and (b) there is no determinate fact of the matter about whether there could be objects that are neither instances, borderline instances, borderline borderline instances, nor non-instances These properties might be called "second level vague" Still higher levels of vagueness may be intelligible However, I can think of no clear common or garden examples of properties exhibiting even second level vagueness.

individual constant c, let i_c be the object in D assigned to c. Then Fc is true iff i_c belongs to S; Fc is false iff i_c belongs to S'; and Fc is indefinite iff there is no determinate fact of the matter about whether i_c belongs to S (or to S').[8] The generalization to n-place predicates is straight-forward.

It may be objected that my use of the locution "there is no determinate fact of the matter about whether" introduces a vicious circularity into the above truth-conditions. But I deny that this is really the case. The truth conditions state conditions for the application of the *predicates* "is true", "is false", and "is indefinite". By contrast, the words "there is no determinate fact of the matter about whether" form a *sentence operator*. This sentence operator cannot be analyzed as, nor is it equivalent to, the predicate "is indefinite" or "is neither true nor false". For one thing, a sentence such as "Everything James says is indefinite" may be true but "There is no determinate fact of the matter about whether everything James says" is unintelligible. For another, it seems to me no more plausible to classify assertions of the type "There is no determinate fact of the matter as to whether p" as covertly meta-linguistic than it is to classify assertions of the type "It is not the case that p" in like manner. Finally and relatedly, on my view, it makes good sense to say that a given singular sentence is indefinite because there is no determinate fact of the matter about whether the appropriate individual belongs to the appropriate set but not to say that the converse is the case.[9] So, I reject the above charge of vicious circularity.

Turning now to the quantifiers, we may introduce $(\exists x)$ and (x) as follows: $(\exists x)Fx$ is to be true if Fx is true for some assignment of an object of D to x; false if Fx is false for all assignments; and indefinite otherwise. $(x)Fx$ is to be true if Fx is true for all assignments of objects of D to x; false if Fx is false for some assignments; and indefinite otherwise.

---

8   The term "iff", as it is used in these truth-conditions, is not to be understood classically One possible interpretation is in terms of ↔ Under this interpretation, the biconditionals in the text have the status of quasi-(necessary truths) See below. I might add that corresponding points apply to the term "if", as it is used in the statements of various truth-conditions elsewhere in the text

9   The only worthwhile equivalence I can provide for sentences of the type "There is no determinate fact of the matter about whether p" is "It is not the case that it is determinate that p and it is not the case that it is determinate that not-p". This equivalence doesn't constitute a reductive analysis, since it introduces another comparable sentence operator, namely "it is determinate that" or, abbreviated, *Det* Truth-conditions for *Det* may be stated as follows: *Det* p is true if p is true, and false if p is false or indefinite. These truth-conditions do not analyze the meaning of *Det* any more than the truth-conditions for $\vee$ or $(\exists x)$ analyze the meanings of "or" or "some" See here my comments on truth-conditions on p 287.

Given these definitions, we can see why my claim that some sets are vague does not entail that the Axiom of Extensionality is false. What the Axiom asserts is this: where S and S' are any sets, S is identical with S' if and only if, for any object, x, x belongs to S if, and only if, x belongs to S'. Trouble for the Axiom lies with the case where S and S' are vague sets which are identical (or which differ only with respect to their borderline members). Here, the statement schema—call it "A"—that x belongs to S if, and only if, x belongs to S' has assignments under which it is not true, since there are objects that are borderline members of S and S'. However, A is not false under these assignments. Rather, by the truth-table for $\leftrightarrow$, it is neither true nor false. So, the universally quantified statement $(x)Ax$ is neither true nor false. So, the statement, $S = S' \leftrightarrow (x)Ax$, has an indefinite right hand side in the above case. So, the Axiom of Extensionality comes out as *indefinite* under the proposed semantics.

Just as the Axiom of Extensionality is not false, on my view, so too are none of the other axioms of classical set theory. Moreover, it is not merely a contingent fact that the Axiom of Extensionality is not false. Rather it is necessary. My position here with respect to the Axiom of Extensionality is parallel to the one taken above with respect to two-valued tautologies. In the three valued case, these tautologies become quasi-tautologies. Likewise, the Axiom of Extensionality becomes a quasi-(necessary truth). Of course, if the Axiom is qualified by a clause which restricts S and S' to precise sets then it remains a full blooded necessary truth.

If, as I am claiming, the Axiom of Extensionality is neither true nor false, it cannot be used to demonstrate that two sets that differ only with respect to their borderline members are not identical. This need not concern us, however. For the sets can be distinguished by means of Leibniz' Law: one set has a property that the other lacks, namely having such-and-such an object as a borderline member.[10]

At this stage, it might be objected that there is another problem of circularity with my proposal. Vague sets are essentially governed by the logic I have presented. So, the concept of a vague set cannot be understood unless the logic itself is already understood. But the logic makes reference to vague sets. So the concept of a vague set cannot really be understood at all.

The claim that I reject here is the claim that the concept of a vague set cannot be understood unless the logic is already understood. Consider

---

10 I might add that the two occurrences of "if and only if" in the Axiom of Extensionality do not *have* to be taken as instances of the connective $\leftrightarrow$. Other non-classical interpretations are possible. See here my *Vagueness and Reality*, in preparation.

a parallel. The concept of disjunction is essentially governed by the logic of disjunctive sentences. But this logic uses the concept of disjunction: "*p* or *q*" is true just in case "*p*" is true or "*q*" is true. So, understanding the logic cannot be a precondition for understanding the concept. It is, then, a mistake to suppose that the truth-conditions for disjunctive sentences analyze the meaning of the term "or". Rather it is because "or" means what it does that the truth-conditions obtain. One who understands the concept will use it in accordance with the logic but a full grasp of the metalinguistic sentences which utilize the concept in the logic is no part of that understanding.

What is true here for disjunction is true, on my view, for the concept of a vague set. This concept can be explained in an intuitive, pre-theoretical way, as I did earlier. Grasping this explanation does not itself presuppose a full understanding of the metalinguistic sentences specifying the conditions of application of the truth-value predicates for vague sentences—unless, of course, the operator "there is no determinate fact of the matter about whether" is to be analyzed in terms of the metalinguistic predicate "is indefinite", a position I have already rejected. So again I deny that there is any troublesome circularity.

This brings me to a general point. It seems to me that if sorites paradoxes are to be satisfactorily handled, it is crucial that the truth conditions for vague sentences not be stated in a language that is governed by classical logic. The purpose of formal semantics, in my view, is not to give reductive explanations or analyses of the meanings of various sorts of sentences in vague terms (or in any other terms for that matter). One who lacks the concept *all*, for example, will not come to understand it by being shown the truth conditions for universally quantified sentences. Likewise, one who has no grasp of the concept *possibility* will not be enlightened by being given truth conditions for modal sentences that employ modal primitives.[11] Rather the purpose of a formal statement of truth conditions is, or should be, to explain rigorously how the truth-value predicates are to be applied, and to do so in a way that is compatible with our prior, ordinary, understanding of the relevant concepts and sentences.

We are now ready to take up the sorites paradoxes. Let us begin with the paradox from the opening paragraph of the paper. I have three objections to this sorites. First, since premise (3) is true and the conclusion, (4), false, what follows, on my view, is that it is not true that premise (2) is true, and *not* that it is false as the classical reasoning supposes. Secondly, (2) is, in fact, indefinite in truth-value. Let me explain. It is not true that there is any assignment of numbers to the

---

11. For one such semantics, see Plantinga 1974

statement schema

    (5) If a man with N hairs on his head is bald then a man with $N + 1$ hairs on his head is bald

under which it is false. However, there are assignments under which both its antecedent and its consequent are indefinite, since there are borderline bald men who would not cease to be borderline bald by gaining a hair. So, there are assignments under which (5) is indefinite. So, the universally quantified statement, (2), is itself indefinite. Thirdly, if (2) is indefinite then the statement

    (6) It is not the case that there is a number N such that a man with N hairs is bald and a man with $N + 1$ hairs is not,

which is equivalent to (2), must also be indefinite. So (1) is indefinite. So it has not been shown that it is true that there is an N such that a man with N hairs is bald and a man with $N + 1$ hairs is not.[12] So the argument certainly does not show that "bald" is precise.

Before I turn to the sorites which is based on a sequence of conditionals, I want to discuss another sorites which may seem to create difficulties for my position at the meta-linguistic level. Consider the list of statements whose members are of the form

    (7) A man with N hairs on his head is bald,

where N ranges from 0 to 1,000,000. Call these statements M_0, M_1, ..., $M_{1000000}$. Surely, it may be said, it can be demonstrated that, on my view, there is some statement, M_k, such that M_k is true and M_{k+1} is not true. For suppose that there is no such statement. Then it follows that for any statement, M_k, if M_k is true then M_{k+1} is true. And from this, given that M_0 is true, by repeated applications of universal instantiation and modus ponens it may be inferred that $M_{1000000}$ is true. But $M_{1000000}$ is false. So, there is a sharp transition from the true statements in the sequence to the indefinite ones. This claim is no more plausible, however, than the already rejected claim that the addition of a single hair changes a bald man into a man who is not bald.

What this argument shows, I maintain, is that the statement

    (8) It is not the case that, for some k, there is a statement M_k such that M_k is true and M_{k+1} is not true

is not true. But this does not entail that

    (9) For some k, there is a statement M_k such that M_k is true and M_{k+1} is not true

---

12. On my view, then, what follows from "bald"'s being vague is that (1) is not true, and not that (1) is false, as the sorites argument supposes

is true, since (8) may be indefinite. And, in fact, in my view, both (8) and (9) are indefinite. My defense of this classification is as follows: in the sequence of statements $M_0, M_1, ..., M_{1000000}$ there are initially true statements, then later there are indefinite statements, and then finally there are false statements. It seems clear that competent language users will not agree upon precisely where the boundaries are to be drawn in the sequence between the true, the indefinite, and the false statements. Of course, this is not to say that such people will not specify precise points if they are *forced* to assign either "true" or "false" or "neither" to each of the statements $M_0, M_1, ..., M_{1000000}$ one after another.[13] Still it seems highly unlikely that even one and the same person will pick exactly the same points on different occasions. It is not true, then, that the transitions from true to indefinite statements and from indefinite to false statements are sharp. Consider now the sequence of statements "M_0 is true", "M_1 is true", ..., "$M_{1000000}$ is true". Given that it is not true that there is a sharp transition from true to indefinite statements in the object language, I maintain that it is not true that any conjunction of the type "M_n is true $\wedge$ M_{n+1} is not true" is itself true. So, it is not true that (9) is true. Equally, however, it is not true that every conjunct of the above type is false. For that would entail that the millionth statement is true, given that the first is. So (9) must be classified as indefinite, as must (8).

It may be objected that (9) cannot be indefinite unless some statements of the form "M_n is true" are themselves, indefinite. And, on my account, it is false that some such statements are indefinite. For if any given statement M_i is true then "M_i is true" is certainly true; and if M_i is either false or indefinite then it is false that M_i is true. Either way, then, "M_i is true" is not indefinite.

My response to this objection is twofold. First, what my position commits me to is the claim that there is no determinate fact of the matter about whether there are any statements of the form "M_n is true" that are indefinite and not to the claim that it is false that there are such statements. To see this, suppose that there is a statement "M_j is true" that is indefinite. Then it cannot be true that M_j itself is either true or false or indefinite. So it is not true that there is a statement "M_j is true" that is

---

13 Indeed, one can imagine people changing their views within the space of a few seconds. Consider, for example, the following imaginary exchange. "You said that M_{130} is true. Now that you've classified M_{131} as neither true nor false, do you still think that M_{130} is true?" "Well, I guess not." "So, M_{130} is neither true nor false then?" "I suppose so." "What of M_{129}? Is that neither true nor false too or is it true as you held before?" "Oh, I just don't know what to say." "But if you don't know how to classify M_{129}, do you still want to classify M_{130} as neither true nor false?" "Yes. No. I'm befuddled."

indefinite. But neither is it false that there is such a statement. For then every statement of the type "M_n is true" would be either true or false, with the result that there would be a sharp transition from the true statements of the type "M_n is true" to the false ones. Intuitively, it is not true that there are such transitions. So it is, I maintain, indeterminate whether there are statements of the type "M_n is true" that are indefinite.

Secondly, nothing in the earlier semantics requires that an existentially quantified sentence, $(\exists x)Fx$, be indefinite only if Fx comes out as indefinite under some assignments. If there is no determinate fact about whether Fx is indefinite under some assignments then it will not be true that Fx is false under all assignments. So if it is also not true that Fx is true under some assignments, $(\exists x)Fx$ will count as indefinite.[14] So (9) can be indefinite without it being true that some statements of the form "M_n is true" are indefinite.

In claiming that it is not true that there are sharp transitions between the true and the indefinite statements and the indefinite and the false statements in sequences like $M_0, M_1, ..., M_{1000000}$ I am not thereby claiming that the predicates "is true", "is indefinite", and "is false" are extensionally vague. For if "is true" is extensionally vague then it follows that the set of true sentences has borderline members. This requires that there be sentences which are such that it is neither true nor false that they are true. And this, in turn, requires that there be sentences that are neither true nor false nor indefinite. I maintain that it is not true that there are such sentences. So I do not accept that "is true" is extensionally vague. And the same goes *mutatis mutandis* for "is false" and "is indefinite". Of course, in taking this view I am not committing myself to the position that these predicates are precise. Indeed, it is crucial to my account that they *not* be classified as precise. For if they were then every sentence would be either true or false or indefinite, and that would not only generate sorites difficulties of its own (as we shall shortly see) but also run counter to my claim that it is indefinite whether no statement of the form "M_n is true" is indefinite. Rather my view on the truth-value predicates is that they are vaguely vague: there simply is no determinate fact of the matter about whether the properties they express have or could have any borderline instances. So, it is indefinite whether there are any sentences that are neither true nor false nor indefinite.

Given my position on "true" and the other truth-value predicates in the first meta-language, what should be said about the truth-value

---

14 The understanding expressed here of the "otherwise" clause in the truth conditions for $(\exists x)Fx$ extends *mutatis mutandis* to the "otherwise" clauses appearing elsewhere in truth conditions in this paper This understanding guarantees that it is not true that there are any further alternatives

transitions in the higher meta-languages? The answer must be that in the higher level sequences it is *never* true that such transitions are sharp. Let me explain. Consider again the sequence of statements, "M_0 is true", "M_1 is true", ..., "$M_{1000000}$ is true". Suppose that for some n there is a statement of the form "M_n is true" which is true and which is such that "M_{n+1} is true" is not true. If any statement of the form "M_n is true" is true then the corresponding object language statement of the form M_n is true. Also if any statement of the form "M_{n+1} is true" is not true then the corresponding statement of the form M_{n+1} is not true. For obviously if, for any given n, M_{n+1} is true then it is true that M_{n+1} is true and hence that "M_{n+1} is true" is true. So if the initial supposition is true, then there is a statement of the form M_n which is true and which is followed by a statement of the form M_{n+1} which is not true. But the consequent here is not true, according to my view earlier. So, it is not true that the initial supposition is true. So, it is not true that the transition from "true" to "not true" in the second level sequence is sharp. Clearly, this argument may be generalized to show that it is not true that the transitions from "true" to "indefinite" and from "indefinite" to "false" are sharp in any of the higher level meta-linguistic sequences.

I come finally to the sorites based on the conditionals:

(10) A man with zero hairs on his head is bald.

(11a) If a man with zero hairs on his head is bald then a man with one hair on his head is bald.

(11b) If a man with one hair on his head is bald then a man with two hairs on his head is bald.

...

(11k) If a man with 999,999 hairs on his head is bald then a man with a million hairs on his head is bald.

Therefore, by a million applications of modus ponens

(12) A man with a million hairs on his head is bald.

My response to this sorites should not be difficult to anticipate: given that (12) is false, we must accept that it is not true that all of (11a)–(11k) are true. But we need not hold that there is a first conditional in the sequence that is not true. Instead, given the proposed semantics, we should hold that it is neither true nor false that there is a first conditional that is not true. Thus, there are true conditionals initially, and indefinite conditionals later, but it is not true that there is a sharp transition from the former to the latter.

It may seem that there is a difficulty lurking here that I have not fully put to rest. Since there are indefinite conditionals in the sequence, (11a)–(11k), not all of the conditionals are true. So, either (11a) is not true or (11b) or some later conditional is not true. Surely then at some point in the sequence there must be a pair of adjacent conditionals such that the first is true and the second is not.

There is an unstated assumption in this argument, namely that each conditional in the sequence is either true or not true. Without this assumption, the reasoning is invalid. To see why, consider how the argument must go. (11a) is true. So (11b) or some later conditional is not true. Suppose (11b) is true. Then either the next conditional is not true or the one after that is not true or .... On the other hand, suppose (11b) is not true. Then (11a) and (11b) differ in truth-value and there is a pair of conditionals such that the first is true and the second is not. It is obvious that repeating this style of argument an appropriate number of times will not generate the overall conclusion unless we assume

(13)   Every conditional in the sequence is either true or not true
       (i.e., false or indefinite.)[15]

I refuse to accept this assumption. On my view, (13) is indefinite. Let me explain.

According to what I said earlier, given a nonempty domain D, $(x)Fx$ is true if Fx is true for all assignments of objects of D to x; false if Fx is false for some assignments; and indefinite otherwise. Now, the truth value predicates, I claim, are vaguely vague. So, there is no determinate fact of the matter about whether the schema

(14)   If x is a conditional in the sequence then x is either true or not
       true

is indefinite under any assignments. So, it is not true that (14) is true under all assignments. Nor is it true that (14) is false under some assignments. For there is no determinate fact of the matter about whether there are *any* assignments under which (14) has a true antecedent and a false consequent. So, (13) must be classified as indefinite. The point to note, then, is that, on the stated semantics, $(x)Fx$ can be indefinite even if it is not true that Fx has any indefinite assignments. This point parallels the point I made earlier about $(\exists x)Fx$ in response to an objection to my classification of (9) as indefinite.[16]

15 It should be noted that for a finite sequence the claim that each conditional is either true or not true is equivalent to a conjunction, the first member of which is that (11a) is true or not true This conjunction is indefinite even though, on my view, it is not true that there is an indefinite conjunct No problem arises here in connection with the earlier truth-tables, since the principle I stated for the case of conjunction was as follows a conjunction is true if both (all) conjuncts are true, false if at least one conjunct is false, and indefinite *otherwise*.

16. I want to mention here a complication which arises in connection with what I earlier called (in footnote 7) "second-level" vague entities If there can be such entities then the semantics I have sketched will not apply to them To see this, suppose

I conclude that sorites paradoxes present no real difficulty for my semantics. This is, I maintain, largely because, unlike other prominent semantics, it concedes that the world is, in certain respects, intrinsically, robustly vague; and it avoids, at all levels, a commitment to sharp dividing lines. This position is, I suggest, consonant with both our ordinary, common-sense view of what there is and our pre-theoretical intuitions about vagueness.[17]

---

that Q is a second-level vague property and that a is one of its borderline borderline instances Then the statement that a has Q will be such that it is neither true nor false that it is neither true nor false. So there will be a statement that cannot be assigned one of the three truth values true, false, indefinite For an account of how the semantics I have presented can be extended to the higher-level vague, see my 1990, pp 554–55.

17 An earlier version of this paper was read at a symposium on vagueness at the American Philosophical Association, Pacific Division, March, 1991.

Horgan 1994 presents a direct challenge to both the metaphysical position I have elaborated and the associated logic Consider a sorites sequence of baldness statements, $B(0)$–$B(10^7)$, beginning with $B(0)$ and its right hand neighbour, $B(1)$ Either $B(1)$ has the same truth-value as $B(0)$, or else $B(1)$ and $B(0)$ differ in truth-value. But if $B(1)$ and $B(0)$ differ in truth-value, then there is a sharp boundary (contrary to my view). So, given that $B(0)$ is true, $B(1)$ must be true Consider next $B(1)$ and $B(2)$ A structurally identical argument for $B(1)$ and $B(2)$ establishes that $B(2)$ must be true Ten million such arguments eventually establish that $B(10^7)$ must be true But $B(10^7)$ is not true. So, Horgan concludes, there can be no sorites sequence with true statements at the beginning and false statements at the end, but no sharp transitions anywhere in between

My reply, in brief, is that the overall argument here is sound only if each sub-argument is sound; but the claim that each sub-argument is sound is indefinite. This does not require, of course, that there be some particular sub-argument which is such that it is indeterminate whether it is sound It suffices that it be indeterminate whether there is a sub-argument which is not sound

Horgan assumes in a further development of the above sorites that it is legitimate to force the defender of my semantics to face a question of the form "Are $B(n)$ and $B(n + 1)$ alike in truth-value?" for *every* pair of adjacent statements in the sorites sequence, one after the other. But this can be legitimate only if *each* such question has an answer And, in my view, it is simply not true that each question has an answer. As before, and in parallel ways, this assertion is indefinite This follows directly from the position I have elaborated (To suppose that each question has an answer is effectively to suppose either that all the statements in the sequence are alike in truth-value or that there are sharp boundaries) So, the full question and answer game Horgan describes is one which an astute defender of the semantics must, by the very principles of the semantics, refuse to play.

This is not to say, of course, that if I am asked only whether $B(0)$ and $B(1)$, say, have the same truth-value, it is incorrect for me to say "Yes". Nor is it to claim that this reply is not to be taken at face value. The point is rather that if I am a cogent defender of the position, I should not allow myself to be drawn into answering questions about *every* member of a sorites sequence.

16 Vagueness by degrees

Dorothy Edgington

There are lessons to be learned about deductive reasoning in vague languages—the languages we speak—by comparison with deduction from beliefs which are less than certain. A pitfall the latter must avoid, the lottery paradox, is analogous to a pitfall the former must avoid—the sorites paradox. A well-known framework for theorizing about uncertainty yields a plausible account of deduction from uncertain premises. I shall defend a structurally similar framework for vagueness. What will emerge is a degree-theoretic treatment of vagueness less open to objection, I think, than others. Degree theorists took the right track, I believe, but then took a couple of wrong turns.

The theory I develop is conservative. Classical logic, the principle of bivalence, the equivalence principle about truth, all survive. They may not be sacrosanct, but vagueness need not throw them into doubt. There is something which is a little hard to swallow, which I do my best to make palatable.

A structural analogy might seem a recipe for reduction: support for the conclusion that vagueness *is* epistemic uncertainty. I shall argue, against the reduction, that the phenomena are distinct.

1 The analogy

Subsections labelled (U*n*), on uncertainty, could be read continuously, and are, I think, relatively uncontentious. They are interwoven with subsections labelled (V*n*), on vagueness.

(U1) One way of thinking about epistemic attitudes (call it the A-way: "A" for absolute) treats belief as an all-or-nothing category. Faced with a proposition, on this scheme, there are three possibilities: you believe it, you neither believe nor disbelieve it, you disbelieve it. Now belief as it is ordinarily understood, outside and inside philosophy, does not entail certainty. Some uncertainty is compatible with belief. How much? Context will help determine how cautious you need be in counting or professing a proposition something you believe. Fixing the context, there will still be vagueness: unclarity about the point at which you switch from agnosticism to belief, or vice versa, as evidence, or doubt, mounts up. Even granting context-dependence and vagueness,

First published in this volume, this paper is a development of Edgington 1992
© Dorothy Edgington

for some purposes this classification of epistemic attitudes is too crude. To explain differences in behavior, for instance, we may need finer discriminations. Not only your beliefs (together with your desires, etc.) but the *strengths* of your beliefs are relevant. A and B each believe there won't be a storm at sea. There is no relevant difference in their other beliefs, desires, attitudes or situation. Yet A takes out his boat, B refrains from taking out his. Why? Because A is virtually certain that there will not be a storm, while B's belief is distant enough from certain to keep him on dry land.

Also, the lottery paradox and its kin are troublesome for an all-or-nothing conception of belief. It seems compelling that a belief that A and a belief that B justify a belief that A & B. But iteration of this principle leads to paradox. For each n which is the number of a ticket, I believe that ticket n won't win. But I do not believe the conjunction of all those propositions.

The lottery case has a beautifully transparent structure, but for some it may not be the most persuasive example of its genre. Perhaps it can be denied that you do believe that ticket 1 won't win, etc.—the possibility of error (however tiny) is staring you in the face. This is incidental to the example. The paradox of the preface will do as well: the author who acknowledges that almost certainly not everything said in her book is true. Each statement commands her assent. Yet she does not believe that they are all correct—an error is almost bound to have crept in somewhere. More generally: who would be so rash as to claim that he has no false beliefs?

For some purposes, we do better to adopt a different classification of epistemic attitudes (call it the D-way), as admitting of degree. Faced with a proposition p, there is a spectrum of epistemic attitudes, ranging from one extreme—certainty that p, to the other—certainty that ¬p, and of varying degrees of distance from these two poles. Some propositions are closer to certain than others. p can be *much* nearer certain than q, q *only a little* more certain than r, etc.

This thread will be continued. Now let me introduce a second theme.

(V1) One way of thinking about predication, and hence truth for simple sentences (call it the A-way) treats it as an all-or-nothing matter whether a predicate applies to an object, and hence whether a simple sentence is true. There are just two boxes into which a predication can go: the true and the false. For many judgements this is unproblematic. But for any empirical predicate which we are capable of applying, we can at least conceive of borderline cases, which would not fit neatly into either box. And for hosts of predicates—red, tall, bald, heap, intelligent, wicked, a case for such-and-such medical treatment or legal verdict, ...—we face actual borderline cases. Context may help reduce the indeterminacy but won't eliminate it: fix the context, and there is still no sharp boundary.

This creates problems. I am casting for a play, and need a tall man for a part. It is hard to deny that if x will do for height, and y is one millimeter shorter, then y will do for height. But iteration of that thought leads to paradox. The paradox is not just a philosopher's puzzle, but something which affects our lives. There's the "mañana paradox": the unwelcome task which needs to be done, but it's always a matter of indifference whether it's done today or tomorrow; the dieter's paradox: I don't care at all about the difference to my weight one chocolate will make. The machine is in a dangerous state if some variables like pressure and temperature are too high, and should be switched off. How high is too high? If we try to state precise values, they will usually be arbitrary. A machine does not normally switch from safe to dangerous as a result of a *minute* change. And the degree of danger of one variable may depend on the values of others. We can be criticized for being too cautious, and for being too rash, but it is often not easy to see *how* good judgements are to be made.

When borderline cases are an issue, another way of classifying may be superior, call it the D-way. Think of the color spectrum. You can identify the different colors. But the very idea of a line which divides one color from the next can seem misguided: there is just a gradual shading off. What purpose would a line serve? The difference between a true and a false judgement is meant to be a difference which *matters*. Yet for any putative line, there will be no significant difference—no difference which matters—between things just either side of it. In Mark Sainsbury's phrase (this volume, p. 258; 1991, p. 182), perhaps we should think of concepts as "like magnetic poles exerting various degrees of influence". There are clearly red things, and clearly orange things. In between, there are things which are closer to or further from the red pole. Perhaps, instead of a cut-off point, we should think in terms of varying degrees of closeness to clear cases.[1]

Back to our first theme.

(U2) We may idealize by representing the degree to which someone is close to certain that p by a number, between 1 (for certainty that p) and 0 (for certainty that $\neg p$). Doing so is of great instrumental value, for it gives access to arithmetical operations in exhibiting the logical structure of degrees of uncertainty. Of course, it *is* an idealization: our

---

1   A neater exploration of the analogy would consider 2-fold, 3-fold and many-fold classifications on both sides But on the belief side, there is nothing to be said for a 2-fold classification On the vagueness side, I do not think a 3-fold "true/false/neither" classification is helpful, but do not argue for that opinion here See Williamson 1994, pp. 102–13.

degrees of closeness to certainty are not really that precise (except perhaps in a minority of especially simple cases). The relation between the representation and the reality is still vague: there need be no fact of the matter about exactly what number to assign. Worthwhile results generated by the idealization must be robust enough to be independent of small numerical differences, which may be without real significance. Frank Ramsey, a pioneer of the D-way with epistemic attitudes, recognized this inexactness: "I only claim for what follows approximate truth ... which like Newtonian mechanics can, I think, still be profitably used" (1926, p. 173); and again, on a possible complication, "This would be like working out to 7 decimal places a result valid only to 2" (p. 180).

(V2) We may likewise idealize by representing the degree to which something is close to a clear case of "red", or the degree to which a judgement is close to clearly true, by a number, between 1 (for clear cases, clear truths) and 0 (for clear non-cases, clear falsehoods). Likewise, this is of instrumental value; likewise, we must not forget that it is an idealization. The proposal does not eliminate vagueness.[2] The numbers serve a purpose as a theoretical tool, even if there is no perfect mapping between them and the phenomena; they give us a way of representing significant and insignificant differences, and the logical structure of combinations of these.

This use of the real numbers as a theoretical tool, whether or not they are isomorphic with the phenomenon they represent, is common scientific practice. Perhaps, over sufficiently small distances, tables have fuzzy edges and shade off into their surroundings as red shades off into orange, so there is no such thing as the *exact* length of a table, even at a time. This does not impugn our use of numbers to give approximate lengths of tables. Perhaps space itself has a peculiar micro-structure. It is common to use the real numbers to theorize about quantities which are really discrete, and not to worry that mathematical operations, including the infinitesimal calculus, valid only for continuous quantities, may give results which could not possibly be exactly correct. The results may still be approximately correct.

(U3) One manifestation of this imprecision is that it may be unclear whether 1 or $1 - \varepsilon$ should be assigned. Where certainty leaves off and something very close to it begins is context-dependent, and fixing the context, still vague. We shall therefore want, in our use of this structure, little to depend on the distinction between certainty and its near neighbors.

---

2 Michael Tye (1995, p. 14) says of the degree-theoretic approach "One serious objection is that it replaces vagueness by the most refined and incredible precision" The theory I advocate is not open to this objection

(V3) Similarly, even fixing the context, it is unclear where clear truth leaves off and something very close to it begins: whether 1 or $1-\varepsilon$ should be assigned. Again, the use we make of the framework should not be sensitive to that distinction. We should aim to solve problems raised by the vagueness of (e.g.) "red" while allowing that "clearly red" is itself vague.

(U4) Another symptom of the vagueness of the relation between the numbers and the phenomena is that comparisons cannot be made arbitrarily finely. Suppose I am trying to calibrate your opinion that it will rain tomorrow, by comparing it to your opinion that the needle of the fair spinner will come to rest in area A, a section of the spinner which can be adjusted in size. You can choose the condition under which you win $10: rain tomorrow, or the spinner's landing in area A. (To play fair, you won't know the outcome of either until tomorrow.) By repeating the offer, I narrow down your opinion about rain to a certain range. But within a range, your choice may well be arbitrary: you cannot compare that finely. Approximate equalities are all we can hope for.

(V4) The imprecision of comparisons is also manifest with vague predicates. Which is closer to clearly red, this purplish patch or this orange-ish patch? There may be a clear answer, but over a certain range there will not be. For "intelligent", "wicked", "left-wing (politically)", etc., the same applies. We must make do with judgements of rough equality, in cases where no clear comparative judgement can be made.

(U5) What should we call these epistemic attitudes which come by degree? "Degree of closeness to certainty" is a mouthful. "Degree of belief" is Ramsey's term (1926). But it is not ideal, given that "belief" is already used as an all-or-nothing term, the A-way. Pseudo-problems, or apparent contradictions, may arise if we try to use a term in the all-or-nothing way, and the more-or-less way, at the same time. Take something you definitely believe$_A$ (in a context)—not a borderline case of belief$_A$—yet you are less than certain of it. Do you fully believe it? On the A-way, it is natural to answer that you do; degrees don't come into it. Prescinding from the vagueness of the border, which is not at issue, belief *is* full belief. On the D-way, it is natural to answer that you don't: you only (say) 95% believe it—you have what Ramsey called a partial belief. Take something you definitely disbelieve, yet are not certain that it is false. You do have some partial degree of belief$_D$ that it is true. I have already resorted to subscripts to avoid this purely terminological problem; henceforth, I shall follow David Lewis (1980) in adopting a different term, "credence", for your degree of closeness to certainty that A, $c(A)$.

(V5) "Degree of closeness to clear truth" is a mouthful. "Degree of truth" is subject to dangers similar to those of "degree of belief". Using an all-or-nothing term of the A-way, as a more-or-less term of the D-way, invites confusion. Suppose "*a* is red" is definitely borderline: neither clearly true nor clearly false. It would not be definitely wrong to call it true$_A$; but it would be definitely wrong to give it a "degree of truth" of 1. Therefore, true$_A$ is not to be identified with a "degree of truth" of 1. To avoid mixing the disparate demands of the two schemes, it is safer to adopt a new technical term for "degree of closeness to clear truth", a sister for credence. I shall call this the *verity* of a judgement, and write it $v(A)$. (The neologism serves to emphasize that I do not see verity as disturbing or displacing the concept of truth.)

(U6) There is no general precise mapping of the A-categories onto the D-categories, although credence of 1 is a sufficient condition for belief, credence of 0 is sufficient for disbelief. We have two ways of classifying the same phenomena, each vague, and only vaguely related to each other. The A-way is simpler, and adequate for some purposes. For some purposes, the D-way is needed. It yields a more fine-grained account of rational decision. And, we shall see, it enables us to solve the lottery paradox, in the context of a general account of reasoning from uncertain premisses.

(V6) A sufficient condition for the truth of A is that $v(A) = 1$; a sufficient condition for the falsity of A is that $v(A) = 0$. Beyond that, there is no precise mapping. Here too, we have two ways of classifying the same phenomena, each vague, and only vaguely related to each other. The A-way is simple, adequate when vagueness is not at issue, and too basic to be tampered with. The D-way is needed when vagueness is in focus: it enables us, we shall see, to solve the sorites paradox, in the context of a general theory of reasoning from vague premisses.

(U7) Rational credences, idealized as precise, would have the logical structure of probabilities; to the extent that they approximate numerical precision, they should approximate this structure. This is to claim that your credences in a set of exclusive and exhaustive propositions should sum to one. From this, all the usual probabilistic laws follow. I do not attempt to defend that thesis here.[3]

(V7) The logical structure of verities will be investigated in Section 3.

2 Validity

(U8) By a valid argument, throughout this paper, I mean an argument such that it is impossible that all its premises are true and its conclusion

---

3 I show this in Edgington 1995 A *locus classicus* is Ramsey 1926

false.[4] Here is a Scare Story. The lottery paradox casts doubt on the *use* of valid arguments, in our inferential practice, when we make deductions from premises which are less than certain. Many applications of "&-introduction" take us from premises each of which is close to certain, to a conclusion which is certainly false. Even one application of &-introduction yields a conclusion less certain than either premise: "Neither T_1 nor T_2 will win" is less certain than "T_1 won't win", and less certain than "T_2 won't win". In this sense, validity does not preserve rational credence. Moral: valid arguments furnish good methods of belief-formation only when the premises are certain; they are not to be relied upon in making inferences from more than one uncertain belief.

This is a radical restriction on the use of deduction. We gain information from different sources, by testimony and perception. We retain it in memory. We know that these sources of information are not guaranteed to be error-free. The value of deduction, in contingent matters, lies in the putting together of distinct pieces of information. It is announced that the meeting will be chaired by either the Principal or the Vice-Principal. It is of some importance to you which. Later, you read in the newspaper that the Principal is to be lecturing elsewhere at the time. Should you refrain from concluding that the Vice-Principal will take the chair, because your sources are not infallible?

A further disadvantage of the Scare Story is that it founds a sharp change in inferential practice on a vague distinction. We have many beliefs in the region of certainty, of which we would be hard-pressed to say whether they are strictly certain, or merely very close. It is unfortunate if a huge difference in the inferential potential of our beliefs should rest upon this unclear difference.

We could not afford such a loss of inferential power. Fortunately, a nice result shows that the Scare Story is an over-reaction to the lottery paradox. I state the result in terms of probability.

Let $p(A)$ be the probability of A. $p(\neg A) = 1 - p(A)$. Call $p(\neg A)$ the improbability of A, $i(A)$. Take any valid argument. Any consistent assignment of probabilities to its premises and conclusion has this property: *the improbability of the conclusion does not exceed the sum of the improbabilities of the premises.* Call this property the *constraining property.*

Example, about a forthcoming test:

---

4. I shall be concerned only with paradigm cases of arguments which recognizably have this property When I say "*A* entails *B*" I mean that there is a valid argument from *A* to *B* (For reasons which do not bear on this paper, this conception of validity is, in my view, too narrow, applying as it does only to truth-bearers See Edgington 1992, section 2)

A: Ann will get a higher mark than Bob.
B: Bob will get a higher mark than Carl.
C: Ann will get a higher mark than Carl.

Let $p(A) = 0.9$ and $p(B) = 0.9$. What can we say about $p(C)$? As $A \& B$ entails C, $\neg C$ entails $(\neg A \vee \neg B)$. So $p(\neg C)$ cannot be greater than $p(\neg A \vee \neg B)$.[5] But with $p(\neg A) = 0.1$ and $p(\neg B) = 0.1$, $p(\neg A \vee \neg B)$ cannot exceed 0.2. (It will equal 0.2 if $p(\neg A \& \neg B) = 0$; otherwise it will be less than 0.2.[6]) So if $i(A) = 0.1$ and $i(B) = 0.1$, $i(C) \leq 0.2$, $p(C) \geq 0.8$. (The example is easily generalized to any probabilities and any number of premises.)

Conversely, if an argument is invalid (i.e. there is a possible situation in which its premises are true and its conclusion false) then there is an assignment of probabilities, consistent with the laws of probability, which give its premises probability 1 and its conclusion probability 0. So it does not have the constraining property. (Example, about a forth-coming tennis tournament in which everyone plays everyone, A': Ann will beat Bill; B': Bill will beat Carl; C': Ann will beat Carl. The argument from A' and B' to C' is invalid; there is no inconsistency in ascribing arbitrarily high probabilities to A' and to B', and an arbitrarily low probability to C'. Maybe Ann is the best player, but always goes to pieces against Carl.) An argument has the constraining property if and only if it is valid.[7]

Credence, idealized as precise, is similarly constrained. Substitute $c(A)$ for $p(A)$, and $u(A)$ [the uncertainty of A] for $i(A)$. The uncertainty of the conclusion of a valid argument cannot exceed the sum of the uncertainties of the premises. The result vindicates forming beliefs on the basis of deduction from uncertain premises, provided that there are not too many such premises, and provided that they are sufficiently close to certain. Given a valid argument from two premises each at least 99% certain, the conclusion must be at least 98% certain. Do not expect much, though, from a valid argument with 100 premises each of which is 99% certain. The trouble with the lottery paradox and its kin is that a huge number of tiny uncertainties mount up; the conclusion, in the worst case, inherits uncertainty from each premiss, and hence the sum of the

---

5. If D entails E, $p(D \& \neg E) = 0$. It is a theorem of probability theory that if $p(D \& \neg E) = 0$, $p(D) \leq p(E)$ [If $p(D \& \neg E) = 0$, $p(D) = p(D \& E)$ $p(E) = p(D \& E) + p(\neg D \& E) = p(D) + p(\neg D \& E) \geq p(D)$]

6   This is an application of the law $p(D \vee E) = p(D) + p(E) - p(D \& E)$

7   The result was first noticed by Ernest Adams (1966). See also Adams 1975 and Adams and Levine 1975. Adams usually states the constraining property a different way· for all and only valid arguments, the following is true Choose any probability p for the conclusion, then there is some probability p' such that, if each of the premises have at least p', the conclusion must have at least p.

uncertainties of the premises. Consider a series of "&-introductions" each adding an almost-certain belief. No single step makes a significant difference. But enough steps can take you a long way downhill.

The principle "A belief that A and a belief that B justify a belief that $A \& B$" is true when the beliefs are certainties; and it is approximately true when the beliefs are approximate certainties: if $c(A)$ and $c(B)$ each exceed $1 - \varepsilon$ then $c(A \& B)$ must, if consistent, exceed $1 - 2\varepsilon$. We needn't worry, in shortish deductions, about the fact that our premises are not *quite* certain, or that the line between certainty and its near neighbors is unclear; near enough is good enough. (The result nicely illustrates the essential use of numbers to state and derive a property of valid arguments which, when understood, has qualitative significance.)

(V8) We have, say, 101 patches of color, ranging from red at one end, to orange at the other, and changing only very gradually. a_0 is red; a_{100} is not red. The conditionals "If a_n is red, a_{n+1} is red" are all at least very close to clearly true.[8] 100 steps of modus ponens, with these conditionals and the premiss that a_0 is red, yield the clear falsehood that a_{100} is red. A typical step will permit valuations like the following: $v(a_{10}$ is red$) = 0.9$; $v($If a_{10} is red, a_{11} is red$) = 0.99$; $v(a_{11}$ is red$) = 0.89$.

Degree-theoretic accounts of the sorites have usually gone for the analogue of the Scare Story:[9] modus ponens can't be legitimately applied to premises which are not clearly true, for the conclusion can be further than either premiss from clear truth. This, I submit, is not a useful criterion. It is an over-reaction to the sorites. It rejects good reasoning along with bad. And it makes a sharp distinction between permissible and impermissible inferential practice rest on a vague distinction between the clearly true and the not clearly true.

A better alternative is to treat the sorites like the lottery paradox. We should aim for the following. Call the "unverity"[10] of a proposition, one minus its verity. An argument is valid if and only if it has the verity-constraining property: the unverity of the conclusion cannot exceed the sum of the unverities of its premises. Modus ponens is valid. Applied to clear truths, it generates clear truth. If the verities of the premises each exceed $1 - \varepsilon$, the verity of the conclusion exceeds $1 - 2\varepsilon$. We needn't worry, in shortish deductions, that our premises may not quite be clear truths;

---

8 We have yet to see how to justify this, but it is intuitively correct, and common ground among degree-theories

9 Peacocke 1981, p 127, Forbes 1985, pp. 169–71, Sainsbury 1988, pp 42–43, Williamson 1994, pp. 123–24 (Williamson is expounding, not defending, a degree-theoretic account)

10 This is not a new word The *OED* records its use in 1574, in a *Life of the 70th Archbishop of Canterbury* (in the expression of deplorable sentiments about Catholics)

and we needn't worry that the line between clear truth and its near neighbors is itself unclear; near enough is good enough. The trouble with the sorites is not modus ponens, but the fact that a huge number of tiny unverities mount up; the conclusion, in the worst case, inherits the unverity of each premiss, and hence the sum of the unverities of the premisses. No single step makes a significant difference, but enough steps take you all the way down. In Section 4 I derive these results.

Familiarity with clear cases (and clear counterfoils) will play a large part in our mastery of a vague term. The cases we meet will often differ relevantly, to some extent, from the clear cases, and our best judgements may be of the form: this is at least close to a clear case of *F*. For instance, a doctor or a judge will meet cases relevantly different from clear textbook cases for a given treatment or verdict. A judge who argues "Jones is a case for verdict *V*; if Jones is a case for verdict *V*, so is Smith; so Smith is a case for verdict *V*", has a conclusion pretty close to clear truth if his premisses are close to clear truth. He would be unwise to iterate this reasoning many times: each iteration allows the conclusion to be a little further from clear truth than the previous conclusion. But a single application of modus ponens may be the best inference available. To reject it as "invalid" in the presence of vagueness (as degree-theorists have done) is to lump it together with a bloomer like "Jones broke the law and anyone deserving a life sentence broke the law so Jones deserves a life sentence".

On the better alternative, we can normally afford to be casual about where clear truth ends: we use the same reasoning, whether it has ended or not, with approximately the same results. We are easily fooled by the sorites: each premiss is as near to clearly true as, in normal contexts, makes no difference. But the sheer number of tiny steps leads us astray. The worse alternative, on the other hand, licenses modus ponens on clearly true premisses, and licenses nothing on not-clearly-true premisses. It is unable to specify exactly where we should change our inferential habits. And it leaves us inferentially impotent, in the presence of vagueness.

3 Verity and the logical constants

To vindicate the better alternative—to demonstrate that valid arguments have the verity-constraining property, and that this yields a natural explanation of the sorites—we need first to investigate how verities interact with the logical constants. Degree theorists have favored the following generalizations (due to Łukasiewicz[11]) of the two-valued

---

11 See Łukasiewicz and Tarski in Tarski 1983, pp. 30–59, Williamson 1994, pp 114–20

truth functions, for determining the verity ("degree of truth") of negations, conjunctions, disjunctions and conditionals:

(¬) $v(¬A) = 1 − v(A)$
(∨) $v(A ∨ B) = \text{Max}[v(A), v(B)]$
(&) $v(A \& B) = \text{Min}[v(A), v(B)]$
(⊃) $v(A ⊃ B) = 1$ if $v(A) ≤ v(B)$, $1 − [v(A) − v(B)]$ otherwise.

These are not the only generalizations of the truth tables. But they have
some claim to be the most plausible among *degree-functional* generalizations—those such that the verity of the compound sentence is determined by the verities of its parts (see Williamson 1994, pp. 114–17, for
some plausible constraints singling out these rules).

I accept (¬). The others are dubious, and I shall argue against them,
and against degree-functionality *tout court* for connectives other than
"¬". (This is important. These rules have come to be closely identified
with "Fuzzy Logic", and much advertised as *the* way forward in
degree-theoretic thinking.)

Suppose we have a collection of balls of various sizes and colors.
These are independent variables: how close a ball is to a clear case of
"small" (in the context) is unaffected by its color; and how close it is to
a clear case of "red" is unaffected by its size. Let *Ra*, *Rb* and *Rc* be the
statements that balls *a*, *b* and *c* are red, respectively, and *Sa*, *Sb* and *Sc* be
the statements that they are small. Suppose:

$v(Ra) = 1, v(Sa) = 0.5$
$v(Rb) = 0.5, v(Sb) = 0.5$
$v(Rc) = 0.5, v(Sc) = 0.$

(1) According to (&), $v(Ra \& Sa) = v(Rb \& Sb) = 0.5$. But it is plausible
that *a* is a better case for "red and small" than *b*: both are borderline in
size, and *a* is clearly red while *b* is not. "Bring me a ball which is red and
small; if you can't find a clear case, bring the closest you can find".
Would not *a*—perfectly red and arguably small—be a better choice
than *b*?

(2) According to (∨), $v(Rb ∨ Sb) = v(Rc ∨ Sc) = 0.5$. But it is plausible
that *b* is a better case of "red or small" than *c* is. "Bring me a ball which
is either red or small (or whatever comes closest to this specification)".
Would not *b* be a better choice than *c*? Both are borderline on color; *b* is
borderline on size, while *c* is huge.

(3) An argument against degree-functionality for "&", this time with
conjuncts which are not independent: let $v(Re) = 0.5$ and $v(Rd)$ be a little
less than 0.5, say 0.4. What is $v(Rd \& Re)$? Here (&) gives a plausible
answer: 0.4, the minimum of the two. But note: $v(¬Re)$ is also 0.5. By (&),
$v(Rd \& ¬Re)$ is also 0.4. This is immensely implausible. *e* is redder than

d. How could it be other than completely wrong, in any circumstance, to say "*d* is red and *e* is not"? $v(Rd \& \neg Re)$ should be zero. This refutes degree-functionality, for the values of the conjuncts are the same in $(Rd \& Re)$ as in $(Rd \& \neg Re)$.

(4) This example spells trouble for the degree-functional conditional. Once more let $v(Re) = 0.5$ and $v(Rd) = 0.4$. By ($\supset$), $v(Rd \supset Re) = 1$. That seems right. But note: $v(Rd \supset \neg Re) = 1$ also. That seems crazy. *e* is redder than *d*. How can it be clearly true that if *d* is red, *e* is not red? Note also: by ($\supset$), we have above two *clearly* true conditionals with the same antecedent and contradictory consequents. At the very least, we should expect to be able to derive from them that the antecedent is clearly false. But no: $v(Rd) = 0.4$. Note further: although $v(Rd \supset Re) = 1$, by (&), $v(Rd \& \neg Re) = 0.4$. The clear truth of "$A \supset B$" does not guarantee the clear falsity of ($A \& \neg B$). Things have gone awry. (Even a defender of the two-valued truth-functional conditional should be disturbed.)

(5) The last two cases are arguments against degree-functionality *tout court* for "&" and "if". The first two were arguments against only the particular degree-functional rules (&) and ($\vee$). Is there a general argument against degree-functionality for "$\vee$"? Well, some consequences of ($\vee$) are no doubt correct. Here are two which should, on my view, survive: (i) $v(A \vee A) = v(A)$; (ii) if $v(A) = 0$, $v(A \vee B) = v(B)$. By (ii), $v(Rc \vee Sc) = 0.5$. If the thought in (2) above is correct, then $v(Rb \vee Sb) > 0.5$. But by (i), $v(Rb \vee Rb) = 0.5$. Yet $v(Rb) = v(Sb) = 0.5$: the verity of a disjunction is not determined by the verity of the disjuncts.

To abandon degree-functionality is not to give up on a systematic treatment of the logical constants. To see this, turn to our old friend, probability theory. Let the following propositions each have probability 0.5: heads on toss #1 (H_1); tails on toss #1 (T_1); not tails on toss #1 ($\neg T_1$); and heads on toss #2 (H_2); yet $p(H_1 \& T_1) = 0$; $p(H_1 \& \neg T_1) = 0.5$; $p(H_1 \& H_2) = 0.25$.

The difference in the values of these conjunctions, for the same values of the conjuncts, is explained by different relations of positive and negative dependence, or independence, between the conjuncts. The probability of T_1, given that H_1, is zero; the probability of $\neg T_1$, given that H_1, is 1; and the probability of H_2, given that H_1, is 0.5. Early probability theorists discovered this key to the probability of a conjunction. In the words of Thomas Bayes (1763, p. 378), "The probability that two events will both happen, is the probability of the first, [multiplied by] the probability of the second on the supposition that the first happens". That is,

$$p(A \& B) = p(A) \times p(B \text{ given } A).$$

(When *A* and *B* are independent, supposing that *A* makes no difference to the probability of B, $p(B$ given $A) = p(B)$. In this special case, we do have degree-functionality: $p(A \& B) = p(A) \times p(B)$.)

Return to case (3) above: $v(Re) = v(\neg Re) = 0.5$ and $v(Rd) = 0.4$. A natural explanation is forthcoming of the difference between $v(Rd \& Re)$ and $v(Rd \& \neg Re)$, if we employ an analogue of the notion of conditional probability to exhibit the non-independence of the conjuncts. $v(Re$ given $Rd) = 1$; $v(\neg Re$ given $Rd) = 0$. So (if the analogy holds) $v(Rd \& Re)$ $= v(Rd) \times 1$, $v(Rd \& \neg Re) = v(Rd) \times 0$.

Conditional verity may be explained thus. Borderline cases of a vague term, e.g. "red", with verities between 1 and 0, are cases which it would not be definitely wrong to count as red. We can hypothetically decide to count such a case as above the borderline—as definitely red— and see what consequences this hypothetical decision has for other propositions. $v(B$ given $A)$, the conditional verity of B given A, is the value to be assigned to B on the hypothetical decision to count A as definitely true.[12] Two features: (i) if A entails B, then $v(B$ given $A) = 1$; deciding that A is definitely true, commits one to the definite truth of the logical consequences of A. (ii) Whatever value B gets under the assumption that A is true, $\neg B$ gets one minus that value: $v(\neg B$ given $A) = 1 - v(B$ given $A)$; the negation rule still holds under the assumption that A is true.

Let us examine the conjecture that verities of conjunctions and disjunctions satisfy the probabilistic structure:

$$v(A \& B) = v(A) \times v(B \text{ given } A)$$
$$[\text{unless } v(A) = 0, \text{ in which case } v(A \& B) = 0]$$
$$v(A \vee B) = v(A) + v(B) - v(A \& B).$$

These, too, are generalizations of the ordinary two-valued truth-tables for "&" and "∨": when the verities of A and B are restricted to 1 and 0, we get the right values for conjunctions and disjunctions. They are not degree-functional generalizations, although some special cases are degree-functional. We do have $v(A) = v(A \& A) = v(A \vee A)$; if $v(A) = 1$, $v(A \& B) = v(B)$; if $v(A) = 0$, $v(A \vee B) = v(B)$. If A and B are independent, $v(B$ given $A) = v(B)$, so $v(A \& B) = v(A) \times v(B)$, $v(A \vee B) = v(A) + v(B) - (v(A) \times v(B))$. Applying these results to cases (1) and (2) above, we do get $v(Ra \& Sa) > v(Rb \& Sb)$, and $v(Rb \vee Sb) > v(Rc \vee Sc)$.

$v(A \& B) \leq v(A)$; and, assuming $v(A \& B) = v(B \& A)$, $v(A \& B) \leq v(B)$; so, in place of (&) and (∨), inequalities survive: $v(A \& B) \leq \text{Min}[v(A), v(B)]$—a conjunction cannot have verity greater than its lowest conjunct; and $v(A \vee B) \geq \text{Max}[v(A), v(B)]$—a disjunction cannot have verity less than its highest disjunct.

---

12 If A is definitely true, the hypothetical decision that it is so is vacuous if $v(A) = 1$, then for any B, $v(B$ given $A) = v(B)$. If A is definitely false, $v(B$ given $A)$ is undefined

I shall set aside, in this paper, the question of the correct treatment of vague conditionals[13] (tempting as it is to identify v(If A, B) with $v(B$ given A)). Consider the material conditional, $A \supset B$, as simply an abbreviation for $\neg(A \,\&\, \neg B)$. $A \supset B$ is the weakest conditional, the weakest statement for which modus ponens is valid. It is strong enough to generate the sorites paradox. It is important to have a solution for the version of the paradox with the weakest premises, and it is this version which I address below.

I have not *proved* that verities have probabilistic structure. I have argued against degree-functionality for conjunctions and disjunctions, and hypothesized that their verities satisfy the best-known non-degree-functional generalization of the two-valued truth tables, a structure which already has more than one application. The hypothesis fits the cases which create difficulties for degree-functionality. I turn now to its consequences for reasoning from vague premises.

4 Delivering the goods

I shall prove that valid arguments have the verity-constraining property: the unverity of the conclusion cannot exceed the sum of the unverities of the premises. (Recall that the unverity of a proposition is one minus its verity, i.e. the verity of its negation.) There are four stages:

(i) If A entails B, $v(A) \leq v(B)$. Proof: (a) trivially, if $v(A) = 0$ and A entails B, then $v(A) \leq v(B)$. (b) Suppose $v(A) > 0$ and A entails B. Then $v(B$ given $A) = 1$: hypothetically deciding that A is definitely true, commits one to the definite truth of the logical consequences of A. So $v(A \,\&\, B) = v(A) \times v(B$ given $A) = v(A)$. But $v(A \,\&\, B) \leq v(B)$. Therefore $v(A) \leq v(B)$.

(ii) The two-disjunct case: $v(A \vee B) \leq v(A) + v(B)$. [This follows immediately from the rule for disjunction: $v(A \vee B) = v(A) + v(B) - v(A \,\&\, B)$.]

(iii) The many disjunct case. We want to prove that $v(A_1 \vee \ldots \vee A_m) \leq v(A_1) + \ldots + v(A_m)$. By (ii), it holds for $m = 2$. If we can prove that whenever it holds for $m = n$, it holds for $m = n + 1$, we're home: it holds for all n. So here is the required step.

Suppose $v(A_1 \vee \ldots \vee A_n) \leq v(A_1) + \ldots + v(A_n)$. Adding $v(A_{n+1})$ to each side preserves the inequality: $v(A_1 \vee \ldots \vee A_n) + v(A_{n+1}) \leq v(A_1) + \ldots + v(A_n) + v(A_{n+1})$. But, by (ii), $v((A_1 \vee \ldots \vee A_n) \vee A_{n+1}) \leq v(A_1 \vee \ldots \vee A_n) + v(A_{n+1})$. By the transitivity of $\leq$, we get $v((A_1 \vee \ldots \vee A_n) \vee A_{n+1}) \leq v(A_1) + \ldots + v(A_{n+1})$.

(iv) Suppose $A_1 \ldots A_n$ entail C; then $\neg C$ entails $\neg A_1 \vee \ldots \vee \neg A_n$. So $v(\neg C) \leq v(\neg A_1 \vee \ldots \vee \neg A_n)$ [by (i)], and so $\leq v(\neg A_1) + \ldots + v(\neg A_n)$ [by (iii)].

---

13. On a good account of vague conditionals, strengthening should fail: let a be only slightly redder than c, "If a is red, c is red" gets a high value; let b be intermediate in redness between a and c, "If a is red and b is not red, c is red" should get zero.

The unverity of the conclusion cannot exceed the sum of the unverities of the premises.

(Conversely, if an argument is invalid, there is no inconsistency in an assignment of verities of 1 to the premises, and 0 to the conclusion. The constraining property does not hold. An argument has the verity-constraining property if and only if it is valid.)

This vindicates the "better alternative" of Section 2 (p. 302). Small departures from clear truth among the premises of valid arguments may safely be ignored, provided that there are not too many such premises. Let us turn to the sorites.

Consider a series for "red" (R). Suppose a is redder than b, $v(Ra) = r$, $v(Rb) = r - \varepsilon$. I shall prove that $v(Ra \;\&\; \neg Rb) = \varepsilon$; so $v(\neg(Ra \;\&\; \neg Rb)) = 1 - \varepsilon$; so the latter is indeed close to 1 when ε is small.

We need to evaluate $v(Rb$ given $Ra)$. Now, under the hypothetical decision that a is red, anything redder than a is red, but borderline cases less red than a remain borderline cases. The hypothesis reduces the borderline to the cases between 0 and r, and leaves the relative values of these cases unchanged. So the hypothesis induces a re-scaling of those

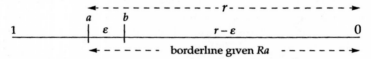

cases with values between 0 and r: under the hypothesis that a is red, their values are between 0 and 1. $v(Rb) = r - \varepsilon$; $v(Rb$ given $Ra) = (r - \varepsilon)/r$. So $v(\neg Rb$ given $Ra) = 1 - v(Rb$ given $Ra) = \varepsilon/r$. $v(Ra \;\&\; \neg Rb) = v(Ra) \times v(\neg Rb$ given $Ra) = r \times (\varepsilon/r) = \varepsilon$. Therefore $v(\neg(Ra \;\&\; \neg Rb)) = 1 - \varepsilon$.

Take any sorites series of length > 100, 100 of whose steps each descend by one hundredth. Let P_n be $\neg(Ra_n \;\&\; \neg Ra_{n+1})$. If $v(Ra_{n+1}) = 1$, $v(P_n) = 1$ (we have not yet begun the descent from clear truth). If $v(Ra_n) = 0$, $v(P_n) = 1$ (we have already reached rock bottom). The difference between adjacent pairs in the descending part of the sequence is, ex hypothesi, 0.01, so, by our previous result, if P_n contains propositions in the descending part, $v(P_n) = 1 - 0.01 = 0.99$.[14]

Of course, this is just a precise mathematical model of an imprecise phenomenon. There are no exactly correct numbers to assign. There is no precise point where 1 ends, or 0 begins. But it gives, modulo that imprecision, the structure of the phenomenon. The demand for an exact account of a vague phenomenon is unrealistic. The demand for an

---

14 The degree-functional rule (&) gives a less happy result for this sorites according to (&), if $v(Ra_n)$ is close to 1 or close to 0, $v(P_n)$ is close to 1, but if $v(Ra_n)$ is close to 0 5, $v(P_n)$ is close to 0 5. See Wright 1987a, pp 251–52.

account which is precise enough to exhibit its important and puzzling features is not. I do not deny that there is higher-order vagueness—that a sorites can be run on "clearly red". But I am urging that we can get a good enough understanding of what is going on in a sorites on "red", while ignoring higher-order vagueness.

Theorizing about uncertainty in terms of probabilistic structure similarly uses an idealized precise structure to yield insights about an imprecise phenomenon. If this is acceptable for uncertainty, why not for vagueness? Vagueness has not been eliminated, but a framework provided which exhibits the distinction between significant and insignificant difference, how this distinction interacts with the logical constants, and how it should affect our inferential practices.[15]

5 Should we accept the package?

The word "definitely" occurs a lot in this section. It is meant to be a theoretically innocent operator, understandable by anyone who concedes (and who can deny?) that vagueness exists, whatever the right account of it. Vagueness is about borderline cases. a is a borderline case of F iff a is not definitely F, and a is not definitely not F. A proposition is a borderline case of truth, iff it is not definitely true, and not definitely false. Hence "definitely" denies that what it operates on is a borderline case. Abbreviating "definitely" to "*Def*", I accept the following: $Def(A)$ iff $v(A) = 1$. But this is an explanation of the right-hand side, not the left. (I actually used "clearly", "clear cases", when introducing verities; "clearly", "definitely" and "determinately" I use interchangeably.) Both sides of the above equivalence are, of course, themselves vague.

---

15 There is one putative sorites paradox which I would treat differently. that which uses phenomenal predicates like "looks red" We can arrange a series of color patches, starting with one which clearly looks red, such that when we look at any two adjacent patches, they look *exactly* the same. So if a looks red, b looks red. . . Crispin Wright (1975, pp. 348–51, this volume, pp. 164–66, 1987a, pp 258–61) uses this fact against degree-theories. This threat of paradox can be resisted by appeal to the context-sensitivity of looks· it is incontrovertible that things look different when seen against different backgrounds, etc. Looking just at a and b, you detect no difference, similarly for b and c, but looking at a and c, they are distinguishable in shade Now look at a and b against a background of the larger patch c Focus on all three parts of this array Something has to change Perhaps a and b are now distinguishable, for the background shows up against a, but not against b, or b and c are now distinguishable, for the background shows up against both a and b, or the patches no longer look uniform in color; or the way they look oscillates unstably with slight changes in focus; or … There is a hidden parameter in this putative sorites· a looks the same as b in context C; b looks the same as c in context C'; …. No vicious conclusion follows. See Jackson 1977, p. 113 ff

"Sibling" means the same as "brother or sister".[16] There are sex changes; and they are not instantaneous. Therefore, at times, while someone is definitely a sibling, it is indeterminate whether they are a brother, or a sister. Therefore, someone can be definitely a brother or a sister, without being definitely a brother, or definitely a sister: a disjunction can be definitely true without either disjunct being definitely true. $v(A \vee B)$ can be 1 while $v(A) \neq 1$ and $v(B) \neq 1$.

The phenomenon is more commonplace than the example. A library book can be such that it is not clear whether it should be classified as Philosophy of Language or Philosophy of Logic; but if we have a joint category for books of either kind, it clearly belongs there. It is not unusual for a term in one language to require a disjunctive translation in another. Suppose a language trivially different from English which has one word, "bleen", for "blue or green". Something can be definitely bleen, but neither definitely blue nor definitely green. Therefore, something can be definitely blue or green, while neither definitely blue, nor definitely green.

If these examples are acceptable, there cannot be any general objection to "A or not A" being definitely true when neither disjunct is definitely true. Indeed, instances of this law could be derived from some of our examples. "x is a sister" entails "x is not a brother". So the definite truth of "x is a brother or a sister" entails the definite truth of "x is a brother or not a brother", even if it is not definite which.

There is no reason to deny the equivalence of "It is true that A" and "A", or of "It is false that A" and "¬A". If $v(A) = 0.5$, v(It is true that A) = 0.5. As $v(A$ or not $A) = 1$,[17] so v(It is true that A or it is false that A) = 1, even if each disjunct gets 0.5. Parallel claims can be made if we prefer to treat "true" as a metalinguistic predicate. There is no obstacle to giving homophonic truth conditions for vague sentences in a vague metalanguage.

A principle which is stronger than bivalence is rejected: the principle that every proposition is either definitely true, or definitely false, that every proposition has verity of 1 or 0. We saw earlier: a disjunction can be definitely true, without either disjunct being definitely true.

Existential quantification goes with disjunction. In a finite domain of

---

16. On a very fine view of meaning, no structurally complex expression has the same meaning as a simple one Nothing nearly so fine is needed for this argument. Extensional equivalence would suffice

17 A proof of the Law of Excluded Middle for vague propositions, 1 e that $v(A \vee \neg A) = 1$ our rule of disjunction gives us $v(A \vee \neg A) = v(A) + v(\neg A) - v(A \& \neg A)$ As $v(A) + v(\neg A) = 1$, we need to prove that $v(A \& \neg A) = 0$ If the verity of either conjunct is 0, $v(A \& \neg A) = 0$. Suppose the verity of neither conjunct is 0 $v(A \& \neg A) = v(A) \times v(\neg A$ given A) $v(\neg A$ given A) = $1 - v(A$ given A) = $1 - 1 = 0$ So $v(A \& \neg A) = v(A) \times 0 = 0$

objects, it is immaterial whether I say "*a* is *F* or *b* is *F* or … " or "Something is *F*". It accords with what has gone before that we can have "Definitely something is *F*" while no object in the domain is definitely *F*: not definitely *Fa*, not definitely *Fb*, …. The analogue of "*Def*($A \lor B$) & ¬*Def*(*A*) & ¬*Def*(*B*)" is "*Def*($\exists x$)(*Fx*) & ¬($\exists x$)*Def*(*Fx*)". That is, we can have $v((\exists x)(Fx)) = 1$ while for no object in the domain, *a*, is $v(Fa) = 1$.

Now here is a part of the package that still has to be sold. We have a perfect solution to the "long sorites" with its many premises, each with verity $1 - \varepsilon$. But suppose we gather up these many premises to a single premiss, equivalent to a long conjunction: $(\forall x)(Fx \supset Fx')$ (where x' is the successor of *x*), or equivalently, ¬($\exists x$)(*Fx* & ¬*Fx'*). This must be clearly false, its negation,

(∗) $(\exists x)(Fx \,\&\, \neg Fx')$,

clearly true. Consider the "short sorites":

(1) Fa_0; (2) ¬($\exists x$)(*Fx* & ¬*Fx'*); therefore (3) Fa_{100};

(1) is clearly true; (3) is clearly false; the argument is valid; so (2) is clearly false.

We need to defuse the air of paradox regained. Recall that the definite truth of (∗) does not require the truth of

(+) $(\exists x)Def(Fx \,\&\, \neg Fx')$,

though the inference in the other direction is valid. (+) is one possible basis for (∗); but it is not the actual basis—not what makes (∗) true. Rather, what makes (∗) true is what makes its negation (2) false, viz., the small departure from clear truth of each of sufficiently many instances of ($Fx \supset Fx'$), that is of ¬(*Fx* & ¬*Fx'*). If there are 100 descending cases, any one has verity 0.99; the conjunction of any two has verity 0.98, and so on; the conjunction of 100 has verity 0. Its negation has verity 1. (It is important to remember that the sorites is a *finite* descending series. Proofs have finitely many steps.)

With vagueness in the picture, there are more ways a proposition can be clearly false, or clearly true, than without it. "*A* & ¬*A*" is clearly false, even if neither conjunct is; "*A* ∨ ¬*A*" is clearly true, even if neither disjunct is (let $v(A) = v(\neg A) = 0.5$). With the major premiss of the short sorites, and its negation (∗), we have a pathological case of this phenomenon. (∗) is true because each of the many instances of which it is the disjunction departs minimally from clear falsity. The major premiss is false because each of its many instances departs minimally from clear truth. Of course this is puzzling: such small departures are, in most circumstances, insignificantly different from no departure at all.

The long sorites has to be seen as the basic form. The universally quantified statement in the short version has to be understood via the relatively basic, relatively less complex statements which are its grounds. The short version is puzzling because we wrongly identify what features of reality make the major premiss false. "No single grain makes the difference between a heap and a non-heap." If this means: no single grain makes a decisive difference—takes you from a clear heap to a clear non-heap—it is true. If it means: no single grain makes any difference at all to heapdom, it is false, though easily mistaken for a truth, because the difference any single grain makes is so small.

6 Why verity is not credence

Some philosophers (e.g. Williamson 1994) hold that vagueness is a species of epistemic uncertainty: there is a precise line which divides the red from the non-red, etc., but it is epistemically inaccessible to us. Were this true, verity would be a kind of credence: the credence that a person with no relevant ignorance other than about the precise line, would give to a statement like "that's red". If a is redder than b, but neither is clearly (certainly) red, then one must, if rational, be more confident that a is red than that b is: a is more likely to be above the mystery line than b is. The nearer to clearly red is the nearer to certainly red. Credence and verity, I argued, have the same logical structure. This could be interpreted as grist for the epistemicist's mill. What better explanation of the analogy I have developed, than that verity is credence, and so vagueness a kind of epistemic uncertainty?

Distinct concepts can have the same logical structure. Some tense logics and modal logics are isomorphic. Closer to home, credence and objective chance each have probabilistic structure, but they are not the same thing (see Lewis 1980). I shall argue that credence and verity are also distinct. Credence helps explain and justify behavior, by interacting with preferences in certain specific ways. Credence *is* what plays that role. Verity, I shall argue, does not play that role, so does not deserve the name "credence". So vagueness is not epistemic uncertainty.

I shall focus on one simple case. You substantially prefer X to Y. You have a choice between three alternative courses of action. You are almost certain that if you do a_1 you will get X, and that if you do a_3 you will get Y. You think that if you do a_2 you may get either X or Y: your credence divides roughly equally between these two possible outcomes. There are no other relevant considerations bearing on your choice. How should you rank these alternative actions?[18] Obviously, a_1

---

18 (a) There are those who think no "should" comes into it unless your credences are themselves rationally based Then suppose that they are rationally based (b) There may be some situations in which it is of paramount value to know the outcome now, so the worse outcome with certainty is better than a good chance of the better outcome I stipulate that this is not one of them

is better than a_2, which is better than a_3. The following is sound practical reasoning:

> (S) X is better than Y; so (ceteris paribus), X for certain is better than X or Y each equally uncertain [$c(X) = c(Y) = 0.5$], which is better than Y for certain.

A simple example: I want a cup of coffee; tea would do as second best. My cupboard is bare. I shall call on a colleague. C will almost certainly give me coffee; it's about 50–50 whether D will give me coffee or tea; and E will almost certainly only have tea. There are no other relevant considerations governing my choice. C, unfortunately, is out. I make for D's office.

Now let us change the story about D. D, the archetypal absent-minded genius, has curious ways of making hot drinks. He is liable to ignore the difference between teapots and coffee pots, to use either regardless of previous use, and to top up old concoctions with new. You get a cup of something from D, and it is genuinely indeterminate whether the word "coffee" can be properly applied, or the word "tea": it is a borderline case.

Perhaps I find D's hot drinks refreshing novelties. Perhaps I don't: despite preferring coffee to tea, I prefer something which is tea with verity 1, to something which is coffee and tea each with verity 0.5.

Substitute verity for credence in (S), "X is better than Y; so (ceteris paribus) $v(X) = 1$ is better than $v(X) = v(Y) = 0.5$, which is better than $v(Y) = 1$", and it is no longer sound. (Sometimes the verity version will have a true premiss and conclusion, but *per accidens*.) Verities do have a role to play in a more refined account of decision, in giving, when relevant, a more fine-grained specification of the possible states of affairs over which our preferences and credences range. But there is as little rational constraint on your preferences among verities as there is on your preference for coffee over tea.[19] In caricature: there's the extremist, who prefers clear cases, and the Aristotelian, who goes for the golden mean. "I like living in cities, and I like living in the country, but I hate the suburbs—neither one thing nor the other". For others, the suburbs are the "best of both worlds". "It would be best to match the curtains; if we can't, we'll go for a contrast; a near match would be the worst choice". "I think a slightly different shade of blue would be lovely". Californian fruit-growers have developed the pepple—a cross between a pear and an apple; there are all sorts of pepple, ranging from almost-pears to almost-apples. That you prefer pears to apples does not determine whether you will prefer pepples to pears, or apples to

---

19. I don't mean to deny that there might be objective values, including values of borderline cases I am talking about personal preferences.

pepples, or the more pear-like to the more apple-like of pepples.

Verity doesn't play the role of credence, I have claimed. The epistemicist might object that I am ignoring the difference it makes to my preferences whether something is knowably F, or unknowably F. What my first example shows is that I may prefer knowable coffee, to knowable tea, to unknowable coffee-or-tea. This is consistent with preferring coffee to tea: preferring X to Y does not entail ranking every possible X-outcome above every possible Y-outcome; it is the result of a weighted average over evaluations of different possible Xs and Ys. It can matter to know what you're drinking.

This won't do as a general reply. I can rerun the coffee example with all outcomes unknowable. Las Vegas drinks machines produce at random, on receipt of a coin, coffee, tea, and sometimes borderline cases. One can't tell which by looking. My taste buds have been anesthetized. There is no one else around. I am thirsty. I would prefer coffee because I believe the extra caffeine would do me good. I would least prefer the borderline, because I have read that this mixture is bad for you. Regulations require that machines display figures giving the chances of the different outcomes. I scan the figures, and decide this machine is a good bet (though neither I nor anyone else will ever know the outcome). Well, the outcomes may not be in the strictest sense unknow*able*. But no stricter unknowability has any effect on my preferences.

Suppose the truth of A is not a matter of indifference. You might prefer that, if true, it is not known to be true: you might prefer $A \& \neg KA$ to $A \& KA$. Or you might have the opposite preference. Mr Grump, who likes to moan, is often put out by good news. Ms Rosy has a remarkable ability to avoid knowing bad things. It is arguable that (K): with things that matter, good or bad, if true, it is normally better to know that they are true. *All this is orthogonal to vagueness.* Accepting (K) does not predispose one to an antipathy towards borderline cases, nor does rejecting (K) go with a penchant for them. Preferences between clear and borderline cases have nothing to do with preferences between knowability and the lack of it.

The ceteris paribus clause in (S) means that exceptions need special explanation. (Exceptions are common enough: other things being equal, I'd prefer coffee to tea; but I detest a brand of coffee Bill often buys; so I'd better ask for tea.) If the epistemicist can't explain in a principled way why, when the uncertainty in (S) is due to vagueness, *cetera* are not *paria*, verity isn't credence. If he *can* explain this, he is not out of trouble: judgements that something is a borderline case, contentiously characterized as judgements of epistemic uncertainty, will have been shown *systematically* to provide exceptions to principles like (S) which are central to epistemic uncertainty—which give it its point.

My arguments that verity and credence have the same structure should not, then, be taken as support for an epistemic view of vagueness. Why, then, the structural isomorphism? Does the range of phenomena to which probabilistic structure applies have anything interesting in common, besides coming in degrees between 0 and 1? There is perhaps a very general sense of uncertainty, such that one thing may be (more or less) uncertain, relative to something else. A is uncertain relative to what I take myself to know (epistemic case). Whether this will happen is uncertain relative to what has already happened and the laws (objective chance). The instantiation of this property is uncertain relative to the instantiation of that one (actual frequency). Given the way this concept applies to the world, it's just uncertain whether it applies in this case (vagueness).

We don't know how to eliminate vague concepts. (Six-foot-two-talk is less vague than tall-talk, but, interpreting the former in a sense in which we can apply it, still vague.) Nor would it be obviously desirable to eliminate them if we could. Even in a world where an exact description of a situation is always possible, the ability to recognize vague patterns *as well* could be a conceptual bonus. (Here I have in mind something like the difference between the ways computers and humans play chess.[20])

Although we can't eliminate vagueness, an adequate set of concepts keeps it to tolerable proportions. If borderline cases of a concept become too prevalent and intrusive, they become instances of a new concept. (Most people live in the suburbs.) Over-use of this strategy is too costly in terms of economy, utility, and other competing virtues of a classificatory scheme.

Finally, let me mention the relation between the theory presented here and a supervaluational approach to vagueness, which uses the notion of a permissible sharpening of a vague predicate (Fine, this volume). If you start with a supervaluational account, you can introduce degrees of closeness to clear truth, as the proportion of sharpenings on which a proposition comes out true (or a weighted proportion of sharpenings —I leave that sophistication aside). This is discussed by Lewis (1970, pp. 228–29) and by Hans Kamp (1975). Proportions satisfy probabilistic structure. From my point of view, this proves a useful heuristic device, for (e.g.) figuring out the workings of the logical constants. The conditional verity of *B* given *A* becomes the proportion of those sharpenings which make *A* true, which make *B* true. But I do not want to rely upon sharpenings as more than a heuristic device, as a philosophically illuminating

---

20 Daniel Dennett 1991 is persuasive on the utility of vague descriptions in a chequer-board world.

account of the phenomenon. (Compare: undeniably, possible-worlds apparatus is an aid to grasping subtle modal points, whether or not it is the best philosophical account of modality. Undeniably, subtle probabilistic arguments are most easily grasped by thinking in terms of plain proportions of cases, whether or not there is a philosophical reduction here.) First, I have tried to explain the most puzzling feature, the falsity of the major premiss in the short sorites, in terms of the small departure from clear truth of enough of its instances (Section 5. p. 311), not in terms of its being false on all sharpenings. Second, I have left plain (vague) truth alone, and not equated it with truth on all sharpenings (still vague, though less so). Third, supervaluationists explain vague languages in terms of sharp languages. Vagueness is presented as a relatively superficial phenomenon, eliminable in principle. It is far from obvious that this is so.[21]

_____

21 I am very grateful to Tod Hodson, Rosanna Keefe, Peter Smith, Scott Sturgeon, Ruth Weintraub, Alan Weir and an anonymous referee, for helpful comments and discussion

17 Can there be vague objects?

Gareth Evans

It is sometimes said that the world might itself *be* vague. Rather than vagueness being a deficiency in our mode of describing the world, it would then be a necessary feature of any true description of it. It is also said that amongst the statements which may not have a determinate truth value as a result of their vagueness are identity statements. Combining these two views we would arrive at the idea that the world might contain certain objects about which it is a *fact* that they have fuzzy boundaries. But is this idea coherent?

Let "a" and "b" be singular terms such that the sentence "$a = b$" is of indeterminate truth value, and let us allow for the expression of the idea of indeterminacy by the sentential operator "∇".

Then we have:

(1) $\nabla(a = b)$.

(1) reports a fact about b which we may express by ascribing to it the property "$\hat{x}[\nabla(x = a)]$":

(2) $\hat{x}[\nabla(x = a)]b$.

But we have:

(3) $\sim\nabla(a = a)$

and hence:

(4) $\sim\hat{x}[\nabla(x = a)]a$.

But by Leibniz's Law, we may derive from (2) and (4):

(5) $\sim(a = b)$

contradicting the assumption, with which we began, that the identity statement "$a = b$" is of indeterminate truth value.

If "Indefinitely" and its dual, "Definitely" ("Δ") generate a modal logic as strong as S5, (1)–(4) and, presumably, Leibniz's Law, may each be strengthened with a "Definitely" prefix, enabling us to derive

(5') $\Delta\sim(a = b)$

which is straightforwardly inconsistent with (1).

From *Analysis* 38 (1978) p. 208 © Antonia Phillips. Reprinted by permission.

18 Vague identity: Evans misunderstood

David Lewis

Gareth Evans's article "Can there be vague objects?" is over-brief, cryptic, and often misunderstood.[1] As misunderstood, Evans is a pitiful figure: a "technical philosopher" out of control of his technicalities, taken in by a fallacious proof of an absurd conclusion. Rightly understood, Evans endorses neither the bad proof nor the bad conclusion. Instead he is making a good argument in favour of a very different conclusion. To honour his memory, and to make his point more clearly available, it is worth setting the record straight.

Evans discusses a purported proof that there can be no such thing as a vague identity statement. There are two problems about this proof. One problem is that its conclusion is plainly false. There are vague identity statements. Example: "Princeton = Princeton Borough". (It is unsettled whether the name "Princeton" denotes just the Borough, the Borough plus the surrounding Township, or one of countless somewhat larger regions.) The other problem is that if we understand vagueness as semantic indeterminacy, a deficiency in our language, we can diagnose a fallacy. The proof twice invokes an alleged equivalence between statements of the forms (1) and (2):

(1) it is vague whether ... a ...,
    symbolized as $\nabla(\ldots a \ldots)$,

(2) a is such that it is vague whether ... it ...,
    symbolized as $\hat{x}\nabla(\ldots x \ldots)a$.

If vagueness is semantic indeterminacy, then wherever we have vague statements, we have several alternative precisifications of the vague language involved, all with equal claim to being "intended". These alternative precisifications play a role analogous to alternative worlds in modal logic. The operator "it is vague whether ..." is analogous to an operator of contingency, and means "it is true on some but not all of the precisifications that ...". A term like "Princeton" that denotes different

From *Analysis* 48 (1988) pp 128–30. © David Lewis Reprinted by permission

1 The misunderstanding I have in mind can be found in about half of the published discussions of "Can there be vague objects?" known to me, though never, I think, in the pages of *Analysis*

things on different precisifications is, analogically speaking, non-rigid. When *a* is non-rigid, the alleged equivalence between (1) and (2) is fallacious. It is analogous to the fallacious modal equivalence between "It is contingent whether the number of planets is nine" (true) and "The number of planets is such that it is contingent whether it is nine" (false), or between "It is contingent whether the number of planets is the number of planets" (false) and "The number of planets is such that it is contingent whether it is the number of planets" (true). For a fuller discussion see Thomason 1982.

The misunderstanding is that Evans overlooks the fallacy, endorses the proof, and embraces the absurd conclusion that there can be no vague identity statements. Besides ascribing folly to a man who was no fool, this interpretation makes nonsense of the title and first paragraph of Evans's article:

> *Can there be vague objects?* It is sometimes said that the world might itself *be* vague. Rather than vagueness being a deficiency in our mode of describing the world, it would then be a necessary feature of any true description of it. It is also said that amongst the statements which may not have a determinate truth value as a result of their vagueness are identity statements. Combining these two views we would arrive at the idea that the world might contain certain objects about which it is a *fact* that they have fuzzy boundaries. But is this idea coherent?

How could Evans think that the purported proof—which occupies the rest of the article—addresses his question whether vagueness is due to vague objects, as opposed to vagueness in our mode of describing? A proof that there cannot be vague identity statements would be trouble for the vagueness-in-describing view, no less than for vague objects.

The correct interpretation is that Evans trusts the reader— unwisely!—to join him in taking for granted that there are vague identity statements, that a proof to the contrary cannot be right, and that the vagueness-in-describing view affords a diagnosis of the fallacy. His point is that the vague-objects view cannot accept this diagnosis, because it says that a name like "Princeton" rigidly denotes a certain vague object. In fact, the vague-objects view does not afford *any* diagnosis of the fallacy, so it is stuck with the unwelcome proof of an absurd conclusion, so it is in bad trouble. (Or better, what is in trouble is the vague-objects view combined with the view that vague identity yields identity statements with indeterminate truth value.) On this interpretation, every bit of what Evans says fits into place. However, he has left some important things unsaid.

You might think that charity can be overdone and the textual evidence is inconclusive. One way, Evans comes out saying too much; the other way, too little. What's to choose?

Therefore I end by reporting an exchange of letters in 1978 that ought to settle the matter. A friend sent me a draft taking Evans to task for overlooking the fallacy, endorsing the proof, and embracing the conclusion. I wrote back, hesitantly proposing the interpretation that I have here called correct; and I sent a copy (with my friend's name blanked out) to Evans. Evans replied: "Exactly! Just so! Yes, Yes, Yes! I am covered with relief that you see so clearly what I was doing ... and that you were able to ward off the misunderstanding of Anonymous so effectively."[2]

---

2 I thank Antonia Phillips for her kind permission to quote this passage

19 Worldly indeterminacy of identity

Terence Parsons and Peter Woodruff

1 Background

The past fifteen years have seen extensive discussion of whether the identity of objects can itself be indeterminate or vague. That is, whether identity statements can lack truth value not because of a deficiency in language but because there is genuine indeterminacy of identity in the world. Many think that the answer is no—indeed, that the answer *must* be no. The arguments for this are virtually all versions of Gareth Evans' one-page 1978 article on this topic.[1] We maintain that genuine worldly indeterminacy of identity is perfectly coherent, and is immune to these arguments. Whether there actually is genuine indeterminacy of identity is something that we think is presently not settled. We will not try to argue in favour of its truth; we will focus on the preliminary task of defending its coherency, and its usefulness in settling certain longstanding metaphysical problems.[2]

The hypothesis of indeterminacy of identity arises naturally as a plausible explanation of why identity questions sometimes seem to have no answers. Examples in the literature fall into three classes. First, there is a simple question of identity over time when there is a disruption of some kind. For example, a person receives a new brain having the old memories, or a new set of memories in an existing brain, or ... The question then arises as to whether person *a* (the person before the disruption) is identical with person *b* (the person after the disruption)? Cleverly designed cases will undermine any simple plausible answer to

From *Proceedings of the Aristotelian Society* 95 (1995) pp 171–91 © The Aristotelian Society Reprinted by permission.

1 Cook 1986, Evans (this volume), Higginbotham (personal communication, 1988), Lewis (this volume), Noonan 1982, 1984, 1990, Pelletier 1989, Salmon 1981, all argue against the possibility of indeterminacy of identity in the world. These arguments are criticized by Broome 1984, Garrett 1988, Johnsen 1989, Parsons 1987, Sainsbury 1989, among others.

2 There are two popular ways of conceiving of the world. One is as totally independent of us. On this conception, indeterminacy is an objective matter that cannot be presumed either to hold or not to hold. So it's an option that needs to be taken seriously. The other conception is that the world is dependent on us, either because we have a hand in creating it, or because it's a theoretical construct based on our verification procedures. On this conception, indeterminacy is extremely plausible. So we really do have to take it seriously

the question, and we hypothesize that this is because the world leaves the answer indeterminate.

Additional complexities arise in cases of splitting across time. If a ship is repaired by having its parts replaced one at a time, and if the original parts are reassembled, is the repaired ship b identical to the original ship a, or is the reassembled ship c identical to a? Here we have a non-identity to complicate the picture:

$$b \neq c \ \& \ a \ ?\!\!\!= \ b \ \& \ a \ ?\!\!\!= \ c.$$

Again, there is the option that the question marks do not indicate uncertainty about a definite answer, but rather the lack of an answer, and again not because of any deficiency in language, but rather because of indeterminacy in the world.

A third popular sort of case arises at-a-time. Cats have indeterminate boundaries, and there may be no answer to the question whether a molecule loosely attached to the tip of a hair that is midway in the process of being shed is a part of the cat or not. Consider a cat, and consider the various cat-like objects that overlap it and that have determinate boundaries. (E.g. a catlike thing that definitely includes the molecule, a catlike thing that definitely excludes it, a catlike thing that includes that molecule but excludes a certain other one, and so on.) Call these *p-cats*. Then the p-cats are definitely distinct from one another, but there may be no answer to the question of whether the cat itself is identical with p-cat number 9, and so on for all the others. In this case the pattern is:

$$p_1 \neq p_2 \ \& \ p_1 \neq p_3 \ \& \ \ldots \ \& \ cat \ ?\!\!\!= \ p_1 \ \& \ cat \ ?\!\!\!= \ p_2 \ \& \ \ldots$$

These three sorts of puzzles arise from different motivations; what they have in common is the possibility that identity claims may have no answer. We will address what they have in common, by exploring the view that the questionable identities are ordinary identities that are not made determinate by the world.

What would it be like for there to be genuine indeterminacies in the world that are not just due to indeterminacy of how our language relates to the world? Here is a statement of the view.

> The world consists of some objects, and some properties and relations, with the objects possessing (or not possessing) properties and standing in (or not standing in) relations. Call these possessings and standings-in *states of affairs*. Then the world determines that certain of them hold, and that certain of them do not hold, but leaves the rest undetermined.

On this view it is *states of affairs* that are indeterminate. To blame the indeterminacy of states of affairs either on objects or on their properties yields a more specific theory, but one that is hard to test. For this reason we do not describe this view as pertaining to vague *objects*.[3]

Given an object x, and a property P, x may have P, or x may lack P, or the world may not determine either of these. Exactly one of these must hold:

$$Px, \neg Px, \nabla(Px)$$

where "∇" means "it is indeterminate whether".[4] (Similar remarks apply to pairs of objects standing in a relation R.)

Now what about identity? We get the clearest picture of things if we accept the traditional definition of identity between a and b as indistinguishability of a from b in terms of the actual properties and relations that they have or stand in. *Not* in terms of the interchangeability of names of a and b in some language, for this is language dependent, and clearly wrong in many cases: sometimes names of a and b are not interchangeable because of how the language works (it may contain "non-extensional" contexts) even when a is b, and sometimes names of distinct entities a and b are interchangeable in a language because the language fails to contain vocabulary for the properties or relations in which a and b differ. Tests for identity phrased in terms of language alone will not be conclusive for real identity in the world.[5] That test is whether a and b share all the same properties and stand in all the same relations. Whether this holds in a particular case may be undetermined

---

3 We also avoid the term "vague object" since it suggests objects that have fuzzy spatio-temporal boundaries We are not concerned with the issue of whether an object can have fuzzy spatio-temporal boundaries, that view is logically independent of whether it can be indeterminate whether an object a is identical with some object b Cf Burgess 1989, Cook 1986, Johnsen 1989, Noonan 1982, Sainsbury 1989

4 We understand "∇" in such a way that if "∇S" is true then "S" is neither true nor false. This accords with most discussion in the literature. Wiggins 1986 understands it differently, for him, "S" might be true but not determinately true, so "∇S" would also be true We assume that Wiggins does not mean the same by "∇" as we do.

5 We thus take exception to Noonan 1982, 1984, and 1990, who insists that identity be defined in terms of *predicates* (1984, p. 118) Noonan suggests (same page) that if identity is defined in terms of properties, and if satisfying a predicate does not necessarily count as a property, then one is speaking merely of "a kind of *relative identity* a relation which ensures indiscernibility of its terms in some, but not all, respects—in particular, not in respects only expressible by predicates containing "∇" or synonyms of such predicates " This is an important charge In fact, the notion of identity that we are discussing validates Leibniz's Law· if a and b are identical for us, then their names are interchangeable in all extensional contexts. We agree that if this principle does not hold (for extensional contexts) then true identity is not under discussion. Leibniz's Law holds for the identity we discuss (Its contrapositive is another matter; see discussion below.)

by the facts. If so, *a* and *b* will actually be neither determinately identical nor determinately distinct. This will be a case of indeterminacy of identity. The framework of properties and relations sketched above is neutral about whether this ever actually happens. It will happen if there are objects *a* and *b* where there is no property that one of these (definitely) has and the other (definitely) lacks, but there is some property that *a* definitely has or definitely lacks and it is indeterminate whether *b* has it (or vice versa).

Any discussion of indeterminacy proceeds within a framework in which some sentences may lack truth value. A major theme of this paper is that most of the implausibility that people feel toward indeterminate identity has another source, which is the unintuitive nature of the reasoning that results when lack of truth value is taken seriously. Some ordinary principles of argument (such as contraposition of valid argument) no longer hold, and this is disconcerting. If this is kept clearly in mind, then much of the resistance to indeterminate identity vanishes. Or so we claim.

At some point in this discussion we need a convention about assertability of sentences. We adopt what we think is the most natural convention, which is that if you assert *S*, then you are presenting *S as true*, so that if *S* is indeterminate and you assert it you are wrong.[6] When we make an assertion without special qualification, we present its content as something true.

2   Abstracts and the Evans argument (and its successors)

Any theory that allows for indeterminacy in the world places constraints on how language might relate to the world. Suppose that our language has (at least) the syntax of the predicate calculus with identity, and that it contains some predicates that stand for properties, and some names that stand for objects. Suppose further that an atomic sentence of the form *Fa* is true if what *a* stands for definitely has the property that *F* stands for, false if what *a* stands for definitely lacks the property that *F* stands for, and otherwise indeterminate.

Now suppose, in addition, that we have in this language some lambda abstracts that form complex predicates, such as "$\lambda x[Ax \ \& \ Bx]$", i.e. the predicate of "being both *A* and *B*". If the language is sufficiently rich then we cannot assume that *any* such abstract refers to a property whose application to objects is perfectly characterized in the usual way by lambda abstraction, the principle that "$\Phi(a)$" is interchangeable with

---

6   You *can* put forth statements merely as nonfalse, so that if you assert *S* in this manner and *S* is indeterminate you are right. Woodruff 1970 calls this "hedged assertion"

"λx[Φ(x)](a)" in all extensional contexts. Such a powerful assumption leads to paradoxes (like the Russell paradox) whenever the language is sufficiently rich. Such constraints are well-known, and people are used to restricting either the abstraction axiom or quantification over properties to avoid such paradoxes.

Here is a less familiar constraint. Suppose our language contains an indeterminacy operator "∇", which obeys these laws:

> ∇(S) is true iff S is lacking in truth-value.
> ∇(S) is false iff S is true or is false.

Then one *cannot* take for granted that lambda abstracts that bind variables in contexts governed by "∇" stand for properties *and also* fully satisfy lambda abstraction. This may seem to be a dry technicality, but it is a crucial one. This is because Evans' 1978 argument and all arguments similar to it (that is, virtually all arguments on this matter in the literature) beg the question by ignoring this point—by assuming without argument that such abstracts automatically stand for properties and that they simultaneously satisfy the abstraction principle. We are not in a position here to find fallacies in arguments for these joint assumptions, for such arguments are never given. But we can say with some confidence that the assumption that arbitrary abstracts both stand for properties and satisfy lambda abstraction cannot be proved from the assumptions stated two paragraphs above. It is an additional assumption, and one that must be rejected by any proponent of indeterminate identity. Indeed, Evans' argument proves this.

To get clear on this, consider the Evans argument. It is a proof that if there were a case of indeterminacy of identity, the supposed indeterminate identity could be shown to be a determinate *non*-identity. That is, from the claim that there are objects *a* and *b* such that it is indeterminate whether *a* is *b* one can prove that *a* is not *b*:

1.	∇(a = b)	Hypothesis
2.	λx[∇(x = b)](a)	From 1 by abstraction
3.	¬∇(b = b)	(Definite) truth of self-identity
4.	¬λx[∇(x = b)](b)	From 3 by abstraction
5.	(∃P)[P(a) & ¬P(b)]	Conjoin 2 and 4 and existentially generalize
6.	¬(a = b)	From 5 together with the definition of identity

Thus from the assumption that it is not determinate whether *a* is *b*, we prove that *a* is not *b*.

Several authors point out that the argument as stated is too strong; surely identity statements can lack truth values if there is linguistic vagueness in the singular terms.[7] We agree with most commentators that Evans intended his argument to prove that *if* the singular terms are not themselves vague, then there can be no truth-valueless identity statements. If the only escape from the argument is to hold that the terms are linguistically vague, then the argument successfully disproves the possibility of indeterminate identity in the world.

Since one *can* coherently maintain that it is indeterminate whether *a* is *b*, we regard this proof as establishing instead that the fault lies elsewhere, in particular, either in the abstraction steps or in the existential generalization in 5. We cannot assume that there is a genuine property ("not being determinately identical to *b*") that behaves in accordance with the full abstraction principle. To avoid assuming this, we have two options. One is to assume that the principle of abstraction always holds for predicates, but to leave it open whether the resulting predicates stand for properties. If we do this, the above argument begs the question at step 5. The other option is to take for granted that abstracts stand for properties, but reject the principle of abstraction as always providing the conditions under which such properties hold of objects. Then the abstraction steps 2 and 4 may be unjustified.

Recall what is at issue. It is not whether all property abstracts are meaningful; that is a conceptual point, and says nothing about what there is. The issue is whether for every such abstract there is a *property in the world* for which the abstract stands. In the case of identity, the issue of how identity behaves *in the world* is not a conceptual matter, it is an ontological one. It is characterized in terms of properties and relations, not in terms of concepts or meanings. And so assuming that a property abstract is *meaningful* does not mean that it stands for a property. The abstract used above does not stand for a property, or it stands for a property that is not fully equivalent with the subformula in the abstract.

Evans' own argument appears to avoid these considerations, since that argument does not quantify over properties at all. Evans apparently bypasses any appeal to properties by moving directly from lines 2 and 4 to line 6, citing Leibniz's Law:

> From $a = b$
> and $... a ...$
> infer $... b ...$

If one of your premises is "$a = b$", then you are assuming that "$a = b$" is true. But if it is true, it is determinately true, and a determinately true identity should sanction interchangeability of its terms (assuming that there are no non-extensional contexts at issue). We agree completely,

---

7   Broome 1984, Cook 1986, Burgess 1989, Garrett 1988, Noonan 1982, 1984, Rasmussen 1986, Thomason 1982

and we note that the metaphysical account of identity sketched above sanctions this version of Leibniz's Law. But Evans does *not* appeal to Leibniz's Law; he appeals to its contrapositive. In classical logic without truth-value gaps a principle and its contrapositive are equivalent. But if there is a possibility of truth-value gaps, a principle and its contrapositive are not necessarily equivalent, and presuming that they are equivalent begs a question of logic that arises independent of any question about identity.[8] For example, the following argument is valid for any sentence A:

$$\frac{A}{\therefore \; \neg \nabla A}$$

but its contrapositive is clearly not valid:[9]

$$\frac{\nabla A}{\therefore \; \neg A}$$

This is how the Evans argument as stated begs the question: it cites a good principle (Leibniz's Law) but uses its contrapositive instead. In the argument given above, we have broken down that step into two, so as to more clearly identify what is needed to bridge the gap. It is no surprise that on the metaphysical account of identity given earlier, the gap cannot be bridged, for what Evans is trying to prove does not hold on that account.

3 Describing the theory

It is one thing to find logical lapses in refutations of a view; it is another to defend its coherency in the face of genuine doubt about its coherency. Many people sincerely doubt the cogency of indeterminate identity. And stating the view literally does not help. People are bothered because the very statement of the view seems to presuppose the coherence of indeterminate identity; if this notion seems incoherent, then a literal statement of it seems incoherent too.

There are different ways to defend a view whose coherence is at issue.

---

8. This point is made in connection with Evans' argument by Broome 1984, Garrett 1988, Parsons 1987, among others, and, in slightly different terms by Johnsen 1989 Many authors (such as Johnsen) express their point in terms of the logical behavior of conditional statements in three-valued logic We avoid these because the Evans argument does not use conditionals, and the discussion of conditionals adds complexity without raising essentially different considerations

9   We call a principle "valid" if it is guaranteed to preserve truth. Call a principle "ultra-valid" if it also preserves non-falsehood We ignore ultra-validity because in the Evans argument and in all of the arguments we will examine simple validity is what is at issue.

One way is to describe the view in its own terms, and to produce sufficient discussion of problem cases from this point of view that it begins to become clear that the view suffers from no internal incoherence. This is frustrating to those who genuinely have difficulty in comprehending it. Another way is to provide a modelling of the view in neutral terms. Below, we give a way to do this for indeterminate identity: to model indeterminate identity from within a classical, bivalent conceptual scheme that makes no use of indeterminate identity, just as a possible worlds modelling of modal logic can be stated in language containing no modalities. This modelling shows that the proposed view is coherent, because it can be coherently modelled by the classical view; incoherencies in the view under discussion, if they existed, would show up as inconsistencies in the modelling. In addition, the modelling provides one intuitive picture of what is being claimed, and this should assist everyone in formulating both objections and replies.

This modelling can *not* be used to automatically prove that there is no real indeterminacy after all, since we are "really" talking in terms of the modelling. This does not follow, any more than correlating numbers with physical objects proves the truth of pythagoreanism. I am not a number, even if you and I can be modelled by numbers.

A classical modelling. Here is the modelling. Suppose that we have a domain of objects, where each object consists of a *set* of things—call them "ontons". These are the "logical constituents" of objects. They are purely artificial, much as possible worlds are purely artificial in modal model theory. Positing ontons allows us to use diagrams (similar to Venn diagrams) to picture objects and their properties.[10]

Objects will turn out to be identical if they consist of the same ontons, distinct if they share no ontons, and their identity will be indeterminate if they share some ontons but do not share some others. The picture is:

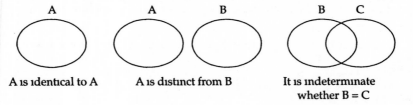

A	A B	B C
A is identical to A	A is distinct from B	It is indeterminate whether B = C

---

10 Our goal here is similar to that of van Inwagen 1988. We find our modelling more pictorial and easier to work with. Our modelling is equivalent in certain ways to what you get by modifying van Inwagen's system by adding a domain of properties and relations, and adopting condition R of Cowles 1994 (but, unlike Cowles, interpreting the condition as applying only to formulas that express properties), as well as certain other conditions. For discussion, see Woodruff (in progress)

We assume that no objects lie hidden within others; that is, every object contains some ontons (at least two) that are not in any other object. Such ontons constitute the *core* of the object.

No objects are complete inside others

We assume that each property has a figurative extension, which is a set of ontons, and each relation has a figurative extension which is a set of pairs of ontons. An object *o has* a property *p* iff every onton in *o* is in the figurative extension of *p*. An object *o lacks* a property *p* iff no onton in *o* is in the figurative extension of *p*. And an object *o* neither has nor lacks a property *p* iff some of its ontons are in the figurative extension of *p* and some are not. (Similar conditions apply to pairs of objects and relations.)

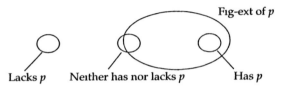

Lacks *p*   Neither has nor lacks *p*   Has *p*

Some sets of ontons picture objects. We assume that *every* set of ontons is the figurative extension of some property. The theory can get along with weaker versions of this assumption, but things are simplest if we make it. The following version of Leibniz's account of identity then follows from the assumptions we have made:

> *a* is (definitely) identical to *b* iff *a* and *b* both have and lack the same properties;
>
> *a* (definitely) differs from *b* iff *a* has some property that *b* lacks, or vice versa;
>
> it is indeterminate whether *a* is identical to *b* iff there is no property such that *a* has it and *b* lacks it (or *vice versa*), and there is some property that one of them has or lacks and such that the other is indeterminate with respect to having it.

4 Semantics

In discussing a metaphysical thesis about identity it is important to distinguish issues about language from issues about the world. There is no way around discussing both. And so here is a sample semantics that takes account of the worldly indeterminacy of states of affairs, including states of affairs concerning identity. Most of the semantics is stated in terms that do not appeal to our modelling at all; so much of it makes sense on any account of indeterminate identity.

1. We assume that each atomic predicate is true of certain objects, and is false of certain other objects, and is thus neither true nor false of the remainder. An atomic predicate may or may not express a property. If it expresses a property, then it must be true of exactly those objects that have the property and false of exactly those objects that lack the property. (Similarly for relations.)

2. Satisfaction:

(i) An object o satisfies "Px" if "P" is true of o; o dissatisfies "Px" if "P" is false of o, and otherwise o neither satisfies nor dissatisfies "Px".

(ii) "$x = y$" is satisfied by a pair of objects if they both have and lack the same properties, dissatisfied if one of them has a property that the other lacks; otherwise it is neither satisfied nor dissatisfied by that pair of objects.

3. We have to make some arbitrary choices about how our connectives and quantifiers work, in order to have any logical terminology at all. We use the commonest ones, which are these:

$\neg A$ is true if A is false, false if A is true, and truthvalueless if A lacks truth value.

$A \& B$ is true if A and B are both true, false if either A or B is false, and otherwise lacks truth value.

$(\exists x)A$ is true if A is satisfied by at least one object, false if A is dissatisfied by every object, and otherwise neither true nor false.

∇A is true if A lacks truth value, and is otherwise false.

Many different conditional connectives can be defined in this framework; we ignore conditionals entirely because controversies about the naturalness of how to construe "if ... then ..." distract from the metaphysical issues we are discussing.

Our modelling fleshes out the above conditions by positing that objects are sets of ontons, that properties (and relations) have figurative extensions based on these sets, and that an object's having or lacking a property is characterizable in terms of being included in or disjoint from that figurative extension. The coincidence of identity (defined in terms of sharing properties) with overlap of objects is a consequence of these assumptions.

Lastly, in order to address the issues raised by the Evans argument, we need to consider abstracts used to make complex predicates. We have two options. One is to insure that abstracts stand for properties, thereby abandoning full abstraction principles (as proved above); the other is to hold onto the full abstraction principles but without assuming that abstracts always stand for properties. Call the first "ontological abstraction," since such abstracts are guaranteed by the semantics to stand for properties, and call the second "conceptual abstraction," since these abstracts are guaranteed to reproduce the conceptual content of the formulas from which they are generated. Both can be added to the language.

4. Ontological abstraction is symbolized by $\lambda^*x[\Phi x]$, where the asterisk on the λ indicates the ontological loading. Ontological abstraction is interpreted as follows:

> $\lambda^*x[\Phi x]$ stands for a property whose figurative extension contains all ontons that are in objects that (definitely) satisfy Φx plus some but not all ontons in the core of each object that neither satisfies nor dissatisfies Φx.[11]

5. Conceptual abstraction (using a "*c*" for "conceptual") produces complex predicates that work as follows:

> $\lambda^c x[\Phi x]$ is a predicate that is true of an object *o* iff *o* satisfies Φx, and is false of *o* iff *o* dissatisfies Φx.

Now how do these abstracts work? We need to make some distinctions that are not needed in a classical setting. First, there is the question of the validity of the ordinary abstraction inferences:

Abstract Introduction:
$$\frac{\Phi a}{\therefore \lambda x[\Phi x](a)}$$

Abstract Elimination:
$$\frac{\lambda x[\Phi x](a)}{\therefore \Phi a}$$

These principles are valid without restriction for either sort of abstract even if Φ contains instances of the indeterminacy operator. That is, in any such case, if the premise is true, so is the conclusion. Thus all of our abstracts are minimally well-behaved.

But in a non-classical setting, we can ask another question: must the

---

11 Such a figurative extension will always exist, the "some but not all" condition is satisfiable because of the assumption above that every object has a core with at least two ontons It is possible for more than one figurative extension to meet the condition given in this clause for ontological abstracts, but when this happens the distinct figurative extensions completely include and completely exclude exactly the same objects.

conclusions of the above arguments be indeterminate (or true) if the premises are indeterminate? And the answer here is *yes* for conceptual abstracts for both inferences, *yes* for abstract introduction for ontological abstracts, but *no* for abstract elimination for ontological abstracts. If the abstracts are conceptual, then the conclusions must have exactly the same status as the premises. But if the abstracts are ontological, the premise for abstract elimination might be indeterminate and the conclusion false. This means that the contrapositive of ontological abstract elimination:

$$\frac{\neg \Phi a}{\therefore \ \neg \lambda x^*[\Phi x](a)}$$

is not valid.

The Evans argument can either be taken to appeal to conceptual abstracts or to ontological ones. If the abstracts are conceptual, they do not necessarily stand for properties, and the fallacy lies in assuming that they do (step 5). If the abstracts are ontological, the fallacy lies in assuming that the contrapositive of abstract elimination is valid (step 4).

5 How many cats are there?

We illustrate the modelling given above with a popular application. Consider a cat on a table. Cats have imprecise boundaries. Suppose that given any reasonable way of making the cat's boundaries precise throughout its life it is indeterminate whether the cat has exactly those boundaries. But those boundaries are filled with matter. So suppose that each such continuous matter-filled boundary determines a physical object—one that has precisely those boundaries. Call such an object a p-cat. Then one can wonder about the relations of the p-cats to each other and to the cat. It is plausible that the p-cats are all definitely distinct from one another, since they all have definitely distinct boundaries.[12] But are any of the p-cats identical to the cat?

We make the commonsense assumption that there is exactly one cat on the table. The p-cats are distinct from one another, by dint of having determinate distinct boundaries. None of the p-cats can (definitely) be the cat, since otherwise (by Leibniz's Law) the cat would have definite boundaries. This leaves open two possibilities: that the p-cats are definitely distinct from the cat, and that it is indeterminate whether each p-cat is or is not identical to the cat. Both are consistent views, and the former wins by default if identity cannot be indeterminate. But this

---

12. This presupposes that having such and such a boundary is a genuine property, this might be questioned.

view leads to a kind of ontological explosion; in addition to there being a physical object corresponding to every filled region of space-time, there are additional physical objects, objects that are contained in the region exhausted by the others, yet distinct from all the others. We see no way to disprove this,[13] but it is at least worth exploring the other option: for every p-cat p it is indeterminate whether p is the cat.

The term "p-cat" is taken from Lewis 1993, who calls these "precisifications" of the cat. But this is misleading. It is true that the cat is imprecise, because it is indeterminate whether the cat has such and such a boundary. But each p-cat is also imprecise, because it is indeterminate whether it is a cat.[14] (If each p-cat is definitely not a cat, then they are all distinct from the cat, which is the option that we are *not* exploring; if all of the p-cats are cats, then we must abandon the commonsense view that there is only one cat.) So the p-cats are not privileged with respect to determinacy of properties; they are only privileged with respect to determinacy of locational properties.

On our modelling the p-cats are represented by disjoint sets of ontons, each of which properly overlaps the cat:

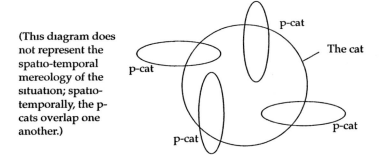

(This diagram does not represent the spatio-temporal mereology of the situation; spatio-temporally, the p-cats overlap one another.)

---

13 In other cases this sort of solution has consequences that are slightly different in terms of the mereology For example, in the case of the person before and after a disruption, this view holds that there is a person-like thing that survives the disruption and also an early person-like thing that does not and a later person-like thing that is created at the time of the disruption. Unlike the p-cats, these person-like things have whatever boundaries the person has, except that they either definitely do or definitely do not have cutoffs at the time of the disruption. Then at any given time before the disruption there are two distinct person-like things (the "long" one and the early "short" one) located *exactly* where the person is located at that time Disconcerting questions then arise as to whether these several person-like things fall down, walk, eat, talk, think, .., and how many of them I am married to

14. This is typical; when it is indeterminate whether a is b, then a has some property such that it is indeterminate whether b has it. This is validated by our model

The figurative extension of "cat" contains the ontons in the cat, and contains none of the ontons in the p-cats outside of the cat. The figurative extension of "on the table" includes the cat and all the p-cats. The figurative extension of "cat on the table" then coincides exactly with the cat; the cat is definitely a cat on the table, and each p-cat is indeterminately a cat on the table.

It is clear that we have a modelling in which every p-cat is determinately distinct from every other p-cat, and in which it is indeterminate whether any given p-cat is the cat. But how many cats are there according to the modelling? Lewis argues that there are many, since each p-cat is a cat. This seems to be the wrong answer, one that he is driven to. But are we any better off?

Skipping technicalities, the answer is that on our modelling there is exactly one cat on the table.[15]

In the case of a person undergoing a disruption, the modelling says that it is false that there is no person in the room during the time in question, it is indeterminate whether there is one, and indeterminate whether there are two, but false that there are three or more. So a framework that allows for indeterminacy of identity is consistent with the normal judgments that we make about how many things of various kinds there are.

6 Indeterminate naming

Several writers[16] have suggested that there is no genuine indeterminacy of identity; there is just indeterminacy in what certain names or definite descriptions denote. Apparent indeterminacy of identity comes from the lack of truth value of certain identity statements, but this lack of truth value is due entirely to the fact that it is indeterminate which

---

15 The technicality is that there are two natural ways to formulate a question of how many Φ's there are Each way uses the familiar logical analysis of cardinalities in terms of quantifiers and identities, but they differ with regard to the question of definiteness We can ask how many *definite* cats there are or how many perhaps indefinite ones there are In a classical framework, definiteness is taken for granted, and these formulations are equivalent In a framework allowing for indefiniteness, adding "definitely" is not redundant, and it is needed to get the intended answers To say "x is definitely a cat" is to say "x is a cat and $\neg \nabla(x$ is a cat)". The natural representation of the claim that there is exactly one (definite) cat on the table is then (using Φ for "is a cat and is on the table")·

$$(\exists x)[\Phi x \& \neg \nabla \Phi x] \& \neg (\exists x)(\exists y)[\Phi x \& \Phi y \& \neg \nabla \Phi x \& \neg \nabla \Phi y \& x \neq y]$$

It is then easy to verify from the modelling proposed above and the semantics based on it that there is exactly one (definite) cat on the table

16. This seems to be the view of Evans (this volume), Lewis (this volume), Noonan 1982, 1984, 1990, Thomason 1982, and, we suspect, of many others as well

object or objects the singular terms denote.

We cannot refute this claim. Perhaps all indeterminacy in truth value is due to deficiencies of language. But we do dispute that every case of apparent indeterminacy of identity *must automatically* be a case of indeterminacy in denotation. The bare bones argument for thinking that indeterminacy of identity is automatically indeterminacy of denotation is simple:

> If a name *n* denotes *a*, and if it is indeterminate whether *a* is *b*, then it *must* be indeterminate whether *n* denotes *b*. So there could never be a case of indeterminacy in the world without there being indeterminacy of denotation.

This view is important, for if there is never a *need* for indeterminacy of identity to explain anything at all, one might reject it on instrumental grounds.[17]

The argument can be expressed in the object language itself. Suppose that "denotes" is a predicate of the object language.[18] And suppose that "*a*" and "*b*" are names of names, and that the names that they name denote objects whose identity is indeterminate, so this is true:

$$(\exists x)(\exists y)(\nabla x = y \text{ \& } a \text{ denotes } x \text{ \& } b \text{ denotes } y)$$

To make this even stronger, also assume:

> *a denotes exactly one thing* & *b denotes exactly one thing.*

Then the modelling shows that these assumptions are consistent, and it does not follow that the names in question indefinitely denote anything; this does not follow:

$$(\exists x)(\nabla a \text{ denotes } x).$$

Indeterminacy of identity does not automatically entail indeterminacy in denotation. If there is such an entailment, it must employ further substantive assumptions that have not been spelled out.

We consider one final challenge. Perhaps one can never prove that denoting an "indefinite object" entails indefinite denotation, but one might suspect that whenever there is denotation of an indefinite object according to one account there is automatically an equally good account that explains the same facts and that involves indefinite denoting rather than indefinite identity. We think this too may not be true.

---

17 Van Inwagen 1988 settles the matter by definition, he defines indefinite denotation as denotation in which there is something indefinitely identical to what is denoted. But there is a substantive issue here that cannot be settled so easily

18. There is nothing to prevent "denotes" from being a predicate of the object language if we don't assume that it stands for a relation and if (to avoid semantic paradoxes) it does not apply to locutions containing the very word "denotation" itself, or other semantical terms.

There are too many alternatives to survey here, so we need to focus on one. We will examine a view that admits that there is indeterminacy in the world, but denies that this extends to identity. We will not try to survey views that deny any worldly indeterminacy at all.

The alternative view holds that lack of truth value can have two sources. If a name n denotes an object that is indeterminately P, then the sentence Pn lacks truth value. So indeterminacy in the world is one source of lack of truth value. The other source is indeterminacy in what a name denotes. Suppose that n denotes any of $o_1, ..., o_n$ but that there is no fact of the matter which of the o_i's are denoted. Then Pn is true if all of the o_i's are definitely P, false if all of them are definitely not P, and otherwise lacking in truth value. The view under examination holds that identity sentences can have only the latter cause of lack of truth value, though predications can have either.

This view has objectionable consequences. Suppose that n is a name that definitely denotes exactly one object o which is indefinitely P. So "Pn" lacks truth value. Suppose also that the sentence "$a = n$" lacks truth value. Since this is an identity sentence, the only way for it to lack truth value is for one or both of the names in it to lack definite denotation. Since we are assuming that n has a unique definite denotation, it follows that a must have more than one potential referent. If none of a's potential referents were the object o, then "$a = n$" would be false no matter what a refers to (recall that we are assuming that identity in the world is never indefinite), and "$a = n$" would be false. But "$a = n$" lacks truth value, so one of a's potential referents must be o. But then not all of a's potential referents are definitely P, and not all of them are definitely not P, and so the sentence "Pa" must lack truth value.

Summarizing, what we have shown is that the view in question commits us to the following pattern:

> If "n" definitely denotes a unique object,
> and if "Pn" lacks truth value,
> and if "$a = n$" lacks truth value,
> then "Pa" lacks truth value.

If this pattern is objectionable, so is the view that all indeterminacy in truth value of identity sentences is due to indefiniteness in denotation. And it is objectionable. Suppose that n denotes one of the p-cats, and let "P" be "is a cat on the table". Then "Pn" lacks truth value (see discussion in the last section). Suppose that "a" is "*the cat on the table*". Then "$a = n$" lacks truth value, and we conclude by the above pattern that it is indeterminate whether the cat on the table is a cat on the table. Clearly this is wrong.

There is a possible loophole in the above reasoning: we assumed for purposes of argument that it is possible to determinately denote one of the p-cats. And this might be challenged. After all, our conceptual resources for identifying specific p-cats depend on our resources for identifying specific locations, and the identification of these depends in turn on our abilities to identify familiar objects, such as cats. So perhaps we can't really pick out any specific p-cat to denote. We then escape the objection.

But the reasoning can be extended. Find a molecule such that it is indeterminate whether it is part of the cat, and so it is determinately part of some p-cats and not of others. This time let "*n*" name the cat and let "*a*" name a p-cat that contains the molecule. That is, take your super-sci-fi microscope, examine the cat throughout its existence, and do your best to list the exact ingredients of one of the p-cats. Any one will do, so long as it contains the molecule in question. There is no reason why we should not succeed, in which case we have filled in the loophole in the previous argument. But suppose we have not succeeded, and so we are not certain that "*a*" is a *completely* precise denoter. Then reapply the pattern above, letting "*P*" be "contains the molecule". We then have the inference:

> "*the cat*" definitely denotes a unique object
> "*the cat contains the molecule*" lacks truth value
> "*the cat = a*" lacks truth value
> Therefore, "*a contains the molecule*" lacks truth value,

and we reach an unacceptable conclusion again. Even if we are not certain that "*a*" is a precise denoter, we are sure that whatever p-cats it denotes contain the molecule in question. Now the loophole is the assumption that we can definitely denote the cat. But if we give this up too, then we are maintaining that we cannot definitely denote either p-cats or cats. But then similar applications of the inference pattern make it appear that *no* object can be definitely denoted. Thus the apparently conservative view that there is some indeterminacy in the world, though never indeterminacy in identity, leads to a much deeper skepticism than it would appear at first sight.[19] To our minds this increases interest in the (coherent) possibility that there is genuine indeterminacy of identity.[20]

---

19. Recall that this reasoning has presumed the option that identity statements between the cat and any given p-cat lack truth-value It ignores the "ontological explosion" option of the previous section according to which we have definite answers already the cat is definitely distinct from each p-cat So we could reword our conclusion as follows the view that there is indeterminacy in the world, but never indeterminacy of identity, is committed to the ignored option of the previous section.

20 We wish to thank several people for critical comments on early parts of this project Graeme Forbes, James Higginbotham, Nathan Salmon, and others for critical comments on later parts Jeff Barrett, Penelope Maddy, and Ruth Marcus

References

The references listed here are for the citations in this volume. For another bibliography on vagueness, see Williamson 1994.

Adams, E. W. 1966. "Probability and the logic of conditionals." In *Aspects of Inductive Logic*, eds. J. Hintikka and P. Suppes, 265–316. Amsterdam: North Holland.

Adams, E. W. 1975. *The Logic of Conditionals*. Dordrecht: Reidel.

Adams, E. W. and H. P. Levine. 1975. "On the uncertainties transmitted from premises to conclusions in deductive inferences." *Synthese* 30: 429–60.

Alston, W. P 1964. *Philosophy of Language*. Englewood Cliffs, N.J.: Prentice-Hall

Åqvist, L. 1962. "Reflections on the logic of nonsense." *Theoria* 28: 138–57.

Barnes, J. 1982. "Medicine, experience and logic." In *Science and Speculation*, eds. J. Barnes, J. Brunschwig, M. F Burnyeat, and M. Schofield, 24–68. Cambridge: Cambridge University Press.

Bayes, T. 1763. "An essay towards solving a problem in the doctrine of chances." *Philosophical Transactions of the Royal Society of London* 53: 370–418. Reprinted in *Biometrika* 45 (1958): 296–315.

Bernays, P. 1935. "On platonism in mathematics." In *Philosophy of Mathematics*, eds. P. Benacerraf and H. Putnam, 274–86 Cambridge. Cambridge University Press, 1964

Black, M. 1937. "Vagueness: an exercise in logical analysis." *Philosophy of Science* 4: 427–55. Reprinted (with omissions) in this volume: 69–81.

Black, M. 1963. "Reasoning with loose concepts." *Dialogue* 2: 1–12. Reprinted in his *Margins of Precision*, 1–13. Ithaca: Cornell University Press, 1970.

Broome, J. 1984. "Indefiniteness in identity." *Analysis* 44: 6–12.

Budd, M. 1984. "Wittgenstein on meaning, interpretation and rules." *Synthese* 58: 303–23.

Burgess, J. A. 1989. "Vague identity: Evans misrepresented." *Analysis* 49: 112–19.

Burgess, J. A. 1990a. "The sorites paradox and higher-order vagueness." *Synthese* 85. 417–74.

Burgess, J. A. 1990b. "Vague objects and indefinite identity." *Philosophical Studies* 59: 263–87.

Burgess, J. A. and I. L. Humberstone. 1987. "Natural deduction rules for a logic of vagueness." *Erkenntnis* 27: 197–229.

Burns, L. C. 1991. *Vagueness: An Investigation into Natural Languages and the Sorites Paradox*. Dordrecht: Kluwer.

Burns, L. C. 1995. "Something to do with vagueness." *Southern Journal of Philosophy* 33 (Supplement): 23–47.

Burnyeat, M. F. 1982. "Gods and heaps." In *Language and Logos*, eds. M. Schofield and M. C. Nussbaum, 315–38. Cambridge: Cambridge University Press.

Campbell, N. R. 1928. *An Account of the Principles of Measurement and Calculation* New York: Longmans, Green & Co.

Campbell, R 1974. "The sorites paradox." *Philosophical Studies* 26· 175–91.

Cargile, J. 1969. "The sorites paradox." *British Journal for the Philosophy of Science* 20: 193–202. Reprinted in this volume: 89–98.

Carnap, R. 1935. *Philosophy and Logical Syntax*. London: Kegan Paul.

Carnap, R. 1937 *The Logical Syntax of Language*. London: Kegan Paul

Carnap, R. 1939. "Foundations of logic and mathematics." In *International Encyclopedia of Unified Science, Vol. 1, No. 3*. Chicago: University of Chicago Press.

Carnap, R. 1950. *The Logical Foundations of Probability.* Chicago· University of Chicago Press.

Carnap, R. 1952. "Meaning postulates." *Philosophical Studies* 3: 65–73.

Chisholm, R. M. 1971. "Problems of identity." In *Identity and Individuation*, ed. M. K. Munitz, 3–30 New York: New York University Press.

Cohen, P. J. 1966. *Set Theory and the Continuum Hypothesis*. New York: W. A. Benjamin.

Cook, M. 1986. "Indeterminacy of identity." *Analysis* 46: 179–86.

Copeland, B. J. 1995. "On vague objects, fuzzy logic and fractal boundaries." *Southern Journal of Philosophy* 33 (Supplement): 83–96.

Cowles, D. W. 1994. "On van Inwagen's defense of vague identity." In *Philosophical Perspectives, 8. Logic and Language*, ed. J. E. Tomberlin, 137–58. Atascadero, CA: Ridgeview.

Cowles, D W. and M. J. White. 1991 "Vague objects for those who want them " *Philosophical Studies* 63: 203–16

Dennett, D. C 1991. "Real patterns." *Journal of Philosophy* 88: 27–51.

Duhem, P 1906. *La Théorie Physique: Son Object et Sa Structure*. Paris: Chevalier et Rivière. Translated by P. P. Wiener as *The Aim and Structure of Physical Theory.* Princeton: Princeton University Press, 1954.

Dummett, M. 1959. "Wittgenstein's philosophy of mathematics." *Philosophical Review* 68: 324–48.

Dummett, M. 1975. "Wang's paradox." *Synthese* 30: 301–24. Reprinted in this volume: 99–118.

Dummett, M. 1981. *Frege: Philosophy of Language*. 2nd ed., London: Duckworth.

Dummett, M. 1991. *The Logical Basis of Metaphysics*. London: Duckworth.

Edgington, D. 1992. "Validity, uncertainty and vagueness." *Analysis* 52: 193–204.

Edgington, D 1993. "Wright and Sainsbury on higher-order vagueness." *Analysis* 53: 193–200.

Edgington, D. 1995. "The logic of uncertainty" *Critica* 27 27–54.

Edgington, D. 1997 "Vagueness by degrees " This volume: 294–316.

Einstein, A. 1922. "Geometry and Experience." In his *Sidelights of Relativity,* 25–56. London: Methuen.

Essenin-Volpin, A. S. 1961. "Le programme ultra-intuitioniste des fondements des mathématiques." In *Infinitistic Methods*, ed. A. Mostowski, 201–23. Warsaw and Oxford: Pergamon Press.

Evans, G. 1978. "Can there be vague objects?" *Analysis* 38: 208 Reprinted in this volume: 317.

Field, H. 1973. "Theory change and the indeterminacy of reference." *Journal of Philosophy* 70: 462–81.

Fine, K. 1975. "Vagueness, truth and logic." *Synthese* 30: 265–300. Reprinted in this volume. 119–50.

Fitting, M. C. 1969. *Intuitionistic Logic, Model Theory and Forcing.* Amsterdam: North Holland.

Forbes, G. 1983. "Thisness and vagueness." *Synthese* 54: 235–59

Forbes, G. 1985. *The Metaphysics of Modality.* Oxford: Clarendon Press.

Frege, G 1903. *Grundgesetze der Arithmetik, Begriffsschriftlich Abgeleitet, Volume II.* Jena: Hermann Pohle.

Frege, G. 1952. *Translations from the Philosophical Writings of Gottlob Frege,* eds P. T. Geach and M. Black. Oxford: Basil Blackwell.

Garrett, B. J. 1988. "Vagueness and identity." *Analysis* 48: 130–34.

Garrett, B J. 1991. "Vague identity and vague objects." *Noûs* 25: 341–51.

Geach, P. T. 1980. *Reference and Generality.* 3rd ed., Ithaca: Cornell University Press.

Gibbins, P. F. 1982. "The strange modal logic of indeterminacy." *Logique et Analyse* 25· 443–46.

Goguen, J. A. 1969. "The logic of inexact concepts." *Synthese* 19: 325–73.

Goldstein, L. 1988. "The sorites as a lesson in semantics." *Mind* 97. 447–55.

Grim, P 1982 "What won't escape sorites arguments." *Analysis* 42: 38–43.

Haack, S. 1974. *Deviant Logic.* Cambridge: Cambridge University Press.

Haack, S. 1978. *Philosophy of Logics.* Cambridge: Cambridge University Press.

Haack, S. 1979. "Do we need 'fuzzy logic'?" *International Journal of Man–Machine Studies* 11: 437–45.

Haack, S 1980. "Is truth flat or bumpy?" In *Prospects for Pragmatism,* ed. D. H. Mellor, 1–20. Cambridge: Cambridge University Press.

Halldén, S. 1949 *The Logic of Nonsense* Uppsala: Uppsala Universitets Årsskrift.

Heck, R. G., Jr. 1993. "A note on the logic of (higher-order) vagueness." *Analysis* 53: 201–8.

Heller, M. 1988. "Vagueness and the standard ontology." *Noûs* 22: 109–31.

Heller, M. 1990. *The Ontology of Physical Objects: Four-Dimensional Hunks of Matter.* Cambridge: Cambridge University Press.

Hempel, C. G. 1939. "Vagueness and logic." *Philosophy of Science* 6: 163–80. Reprinted in part in this volume: 82–84.

Horgan, T. 1994. "Robust vagueness and the forced-march sorites paradox." In *Philosophical Perspectives, 8: Logic and Language,* ed. J. E. Tomberlin, 159–88 Atascadero, CA: Ridgeview.

Horwich, P. 1990. *Truth.* Oxford: Blackwell

Hughes, G E. and M. J. Cresswell. 1996. *A New Introduction to Modal Logic.* London: Routledge.

Jackson, F. 1977. *Perception.* Cambridge: Cambridge University Press.

Jeffrey, R. C. 1967. *Formal Logic: Its Scope and Limits* New York: McGraw-Hill.

Johnsen, B. 1989. "Is vague identity incoherent?" *Analysis* 49: 103–12.

Kamp, J. A. W. 1975. "Two theories about adjectives." In *Formal Semantics of Natural Language,* ed. E. L Keenan, 123–55. Cambridge: Cambridge University Press.

Kamp, J. A. W. 1981 "The paradox of the heap." In *Aspects of Philosophical Logic,* ed. U. Monnich, 225–77. Dordrecht: Reidel.

Kaplan, D. 1979. "On the logic of demonstratives." *Journal of Philosophical Logic* 8: 81–98.

Keefe, R. 1995. "Contingent identity and vague identity." *Analysis* 55: 183–90.

Keefe, R. and P. Smith. 1997 "Theories of vagueness." This volume: 1–57.

King, J. L. 1979. "Bivalence and the sorites paradox." *American Philosophical Quarterly* 16: 17–25.

Kleene, S C. 1952. *Introduction to Metamathematics* Amsterdam: North Holland.

Korner, S. 1960. *The Philosophy of Mathematics* London: Hutchinson.

Korner, S. 1966 *Experience and Theory.* London: Routledge and Kegan Paul.

Kripke, S A. 1965. "Semantical analysis of intuitionistic logic I " In *Formal Systems and Recursive Functions*, eds. J. N Crossley and M. Dummett, 92–130. Amsterdam: North-Holland.

Kripke, S. A. 1972. "Naming and necessity." In *Semantics of Natural Language*, eds D. Davidson and G. Harman, 254–355 Dordrecht: Reidel.

Kripke, S. A. 1975. "Outline of a theory of truth." *Journal of Philosophy* 72: 690–716.

Kripke, S. A. 1982. *Wittgenstein on Rules and Private Language.* Oxford: Blackwell.

Lakoff, G. 1973. "Hedges: a study in meaning criteria and the logic of fuzzy concepts." *Journal of Philosophical Logic* 2: 458–508.

Lee, R. C. T. and C.-L. Chang 1971. "Some properties of fuzzy logic." *Information and Control* 19: 417–31.

Lewis, D. K. 1969. *Convention.* Cambridge: Harvard University Press

Lewis, D. K. 1970. "General semantics." *Synthese* 22: 18–67. Reprinted in Lewis 1983b, 189–229.

Lewis, D. K. 1975 "Language and languages." In *Minnesota Studies in the Philosophy of Science, Vol. VII*, ed. K Gunderson, 3–35. Minneapolis: University of Minnesota Press. Reprinted in Lewis 1983b, 163–88.

Lewis, D. K. 1979. "Scorekeeping in a language game." *Journal of Philosophical Logic* 8: 339–59. Reprinted in Lewis 1983b, 233–49.

Lewis, D. K. 1980. "A subjectivist's guide to objective chance." In *Studies in Inductive Logic and Probability, Vol. 2*, ed. R. C. Jeffrey, 263–93. Berkeley: University of California Press. Reprinted in his *Philosophical Papers, Vol. II*, 83–113. New York: Oxford University Press, 1986

Lewis, D. K. 1983a. "New work for a theory of universals " *Australasian Journal of Philosophy* 61. 343–77.

Lewis, D. K. 1983b. *Philosophical Papers, Vol. I.* New York: Oxford University Press.

Lewis, D. K. 1986. *On the Plurality of Worlds.* Oxford: Basil Blackwell.

Lewis, D. K. 1988. "Vague identity: Evans misunderstood." *Analysis* 48: 128–30. Reprinted in this volume: 318–20.

Lewis, D. K. 1993. "Many, but almost one." In *Ontology, Causality and Mind: Essays in honour of D. M. Armstrong*, eds. J. Bacon, K. Campbell, and L Reinhardt, 23–38. Cambridge. Cambridge University Press.

Long, A. A. and D N Sedley, eds. 1987. *The Hellenistic Philosophers.* Cambridge: Cambridge University Press.

Lowe, E. J. 1994 "Vague identity and quantum indeterminacy" *Analysis* 54: 110–14.

Łukasiewicz, J. and A. Tarski 1930. "Investigations into the sentential calculus." In Tarski 1956, 38–59.

Machina, K. F. 1972. "Vague predicates." *American Philosophical Quarterly* 9: 225–33.

Machina, K. F. 1976. "Truth, belief and vagueness." *Journal of Philosophical Logic* 5: 47–78. Reprinted in this volume: 174–203.

McGee, V. 1991. *Truth, Vagueness, and Paradox: An Essay on the Logic of Truth.* Indianapolis: Hackett Publishing Company.

McGee, V. and B. McLaughlin. 1995. "Distinctions without a difference." *Southern Journal of Philosophy* 33 (Supplement): 203–51.

McGinn, C. 1984. *Wittgenstein on Meaning.* Oxford: Blackwell.

Mehlberg, H. 1958. *The Reach of Science.* Toronto: University of Toronto Press. Excerpt reprinted in this volume: 85–88.

Morris, C. W. 1938. "Foundations of the theory of signs." In *International Encyclopedia of Unified Science, Vol. 1, No. 2.* Chicago: University of Chicago Press.

Noonan, H. W 1982. "Vague objects." *Analysis* 42: 3–6.

Noonan, H. W. 1984. "Indefinite identity: a reply to Broome." *Analysis* 44: 117–21.

Noonan, H. W 1990. "Vague identity yet again." *Analysis* 50: 157–62.

Over, D. E. 1989. "Vague objects and identity." *Analysis* 49: 97–99.

Parsons, T. 1987. "Entities without identity." In *Philosophical Perspectives, 1: Metaphysics,* ed. J. E. Tomberlin, 1–19 Atascadero, CA: Ridgeview.

Parsons, T and P. Woodruff. 1995. "Worldly indeterminacy of identity." *Proceedings of the Aristotelian Society* 95: 171–91. Reprinted in this volume: 321–37.

Peacocke, C. 1981. "Are vague predicates incoherent?" *Synthese* 46: 121–41.

Peacocke, C. 1983 *Sense and Content.* Oxford: Clarendon Press.

Peacocke, C. 1984. "Colour concepts and colour experience." *Synthese* 58: 365–81.

Peirce, C. S. 1902. "Vague." In *Dictionary of Philosophy and Psychology,* ed. J. M. Baldwin, 748. New York: Macmillan.

Pelletier, F. J 1989. "Another argument against vague objects " *Journal of Philosophy* 86: 481–92.

Plantinga, A. 1974. *The Nature of Necessity.* Oxford: Clarendon Press.

Priest, G. and R. Routley. 1989. "Applications of paraconsistent logic." In *Paraconsistent Logic: Essays on the Inconsistent.,* eds. G Priest, R Routley, and J. Norman, 367–93. Munich: Philosophia Verlag.

Prior, A. N. 1968. "'Now'." *Noûs* 2: 101–19.

Przełecki, M. 1969. *The Logic of Empirical Theories.* London: Routledge and Kegan Paul.

Przełecki, M. 1976. "Fuzziness as multiplicity." *Erkenntnis* 10: 371–80.

Putnam, H. 1983. "Vagueness and alternative logic." *Erkenntnis* 19· 297–314.

Putnam, H. 1985. "A quick Read is a wrong Wright " *Analysis* 45· 203

Quine, W. V. 1981. "What price bivalence?" *Journal of Philosophy* 78: 90–95.

Raffman, D. 1994. "Vagueness without paradox." *Philosophical Review* 103: 41–74.

Ramsey, F. P. 1926. "Truth and Probability." In *The Foundations of Mathematics and Other Essays,* ed. R. B. Braithwaite, 156–98. London: Kegan Paul, 1931.

Rasmussen, S. A. 1986. "Vague identity." *Mind* 95: 81–91.

Read, S. and C. Wright. 1985. "Hairier than Putnam thought " *Analysis* 45: 56–58.

Rescher, N. 1969. *Many-valued Logic* New York: McGraw-Hill

Rolf, B. 1980. "A theory of vagueness." *Journal of Philosophical Logic* 9: 315–25.

Rolf, B. 1981 *Topics on Vagueness* Lund, Sweden: Studentlitteratur.

Rolf, B. 1984. "Sorites " *Synthese* 58: 219–50.

Russell, B. 1919. *Introduction to Mathematical Philosophy.* London: Allen & Unwin.

Russell, B. 1920. *The Analysis of Mind.* London: Allen & Unwin.

Russell, B 1923. "Vagueness " *Australasian Journal of Philosophy and Psychology* 1: 84–92. Reprinted in this volume: 61–68.

Sainsbury, R. M. 1986. "Degrees of belief and degrees of truth." *Philosophical Papers* 15: 97–106.

Sainsbury, R. M. 1988. *Paradoxes.* Cambridge: Cambridge University Press.

Sainsbury, R. M. 1989. "What is a vague object?" *Analysis* 49: 99–103.

Sainsbury, R. M. 1990. "Concepts without boundaries." Inaugural lecture published by the King's College London Department of Philosophy. Reprinted in this volume· 251–64.

Sainsbury, R. M. 1991. "Is there higher-order vagueness?" *Philosophical Quarterly* 41: 167–82.

Sainsbury, R. M. 1995. "Vagueness, ignorance and margin for error." *British Journal for the Philosophy of Science* 46: 589–601.

Salmon, N. 1981. *Reference and Essence.* Princeton: Princeton University Press.

Salomaa, A. 1959. "On many-valued systems of logic." *Ajatus* 22: 115–59.

Sanford, D. H. 1975. "Borderline logic." *American Philosophical Quarterly* 12: 29–39.

Sanford, D. H. 1976. "Competing semantics of vagueness: many values versus super-truth " *Synthese* 33: 195–210.

Sanford, D. H. 1979. "Nostalgia for the ordinary: comments on papers by Unger and Wheeler." *Synthese* 41: 175–84.

Sanford, D. H 1993. "The problem of the many, many composition questions, and naive mereology." *Noûs* 27. 219–28.

Simons, P. 1992. "Vagueness and ignorance." *Proceedings of the Aristotelian Society, Supplementary Volume* 66: 163–77.

Sorensen, R. A. 1988. *Blindspots.* Oxford: Clarendon Press.

Sorensen, R. A. 1994. "A thousand clones." *Mind* 103: 47–54.

Sorensen, R. A. 1995. "Commentary: the epistemic conception of vagueness." *Southern Journal of Philosophy* 33 (Supplement): 161–70.

Sperber, D and D. Wilson. 1985-6. "Loose talk." *Proceedings of the Aristotelian Society* 86: 153–71.

Stalnaker, R. 1988. "Vague identity." In *Philosophical Analysis: A Defense by Example*, ed. D. F. Austin, 349–60. Dordrecht: Kluwer.

Stout, G. F. 1898. *A Manual of Psychology.* London: University Correspondence College Press.

Tappenden, J. 1993. "The liar and sorites paradoxes: toward a unified treatment." *Journal of Philosophy* 90: 551–77.

Tappenden, J. 1995. "Some remarks on vagueness and a dynamic conception of language." *Southern Journal of Philosophy* 33 (Supplement)· 193–201.

Tarski, A. 1935 "The concept of truth in formalized languages." In Tarski 1956, 152–278.

Tarski, A. 1956. *Logic, Semantics, Metamathematics.* Translated by J. H. Woodger. Oxford: Clarendon Press.

Thomason, R. H. 1982. "Identity and vagueness " *Philosophical Studies* 42: 329–32.

Tye, M. 1989. "Supervaluationism and the law of excluded middle." *Analysis* 49: 141–43.

Tye, M. 1990. "Vague objects." *Mind* 99: 535–57.

Tye, M. 1994. "Sorites paradoxes and the semantics of vagueness." In *Philosophical Perspectives, 8: Logic and Language*, ed. J. E. Tomberlin, 189–206. Atascadero, CA: Ridgeview. Reprinted (with omissions) in this volume: 281–93.

Tye, M. 1995 "Vagueness· welcome to the quicksand." *Southern Journal of Philosophy* 33 (Supplement): 1–22.

Unger, P. 1979a. "I do not exist." In *Perception and Identity,* ed. G F. Macdonald, 235–51. London: Macmillan.

Unger, P. 1979b. "There are no ordinary things." *Synthese* 41. 117–54

Unger, P. 1980. "The problem of the many" In *Midwest Studies in Philosophy, Vol. 5,* eds. P A French, T. E. Uehling, and H K Wettstein, 411–69. Minneapolis: University of Minnesota Press.

van Fraassen, B C. 1966. "Singular terms, truth-value gaps, and free logic." *Journal of Philosophy* 63. 481–95.

van Fraassen, B. C. 1968. "Presupposition, implication, and self-reference." *Journal of Philosophy* 65: 136–52.

van Fraassen, B. C. 1969. "Presuppositions, supervaluations and free logic." In *The Logical Way of Doing Things*, ed. K. Lambert, 67–91. New Haven: Yale University Press.

van Inwagen, P. 1988 "How to reason about vague objects." *Philosophical Topics* 16: 255–84.

Waismann, F. 1945. "Verifiability." *Proceedings of the Aristotelian Society, Supplementary Volume* 19: 119–50

Walton, D N. 1992. *Slippery Slope Arguments*. Oxford. Clarendon Press.

Walzer, R. 1944. *Galen, On Medical Experience*. Oxford: Oxford University Press.

Wells, H. G. 1908 *First and Last Things* London: Constable.

Wheeler, S. C 1975 "Reference and vagueness." *Synthese* 30: 367–79.

Wheeler, S C. 1979. "On that which is not." *Synthese* 41: 155–73.

Wiggins, D. 1986. "On singling out an object determinately." In *Subject, Thought, and Context*, eds. P. Pettit and J. McDowell, 169–80. Oxford: Oxford University Press.

Williams, B. 1995. "Which slopes are slippery?" In his *Making Sense of Humanity,* 213–23. Cambridge: Cambridge University Press.

Williamson, T. 1990a. *Identity and Discrimination*. Oxford: Blackwell.

Williamson, T 1990b. "Verification, falsification and cancellation in KT." *Notre Dame Journal of Formal Logic* 31: 286–90.

Williamson, T 1992a. "Inexact knowledge." *Mind* 101: 217–42.

Williamson, T. 1992b. "Vagueness and ignorance." *Proceedings of the Aristotelian Society, Supplementary Volume* 66: 145–62. Reprinted in this volume· 265–80.

Williamson, T. 1994. *Vagueness*. London: Routledge.

Williamson, T. 1996a. "Putnam on the sorites paradox." *Philosophical Papers* 25: 47–56

Williamson, T. 1996b. "Wright on the epistemic conception of vagueness." *Analysis* 56. 39–45

Wittgenstein, L. 1953. *Philosophical Investigations*. Translated by G. E. M. Anscombe. Oxford: Blackwell.

Wittgenstein, L. 1978. *Remarks on the Foundations of Mathematics* 3rd ed. Translated by G. E. M. Anscombe Oxford: Basil Blackwell.

Woodruff, P. 1970. "Logic and truth value gaps." In *Philosophical Problems in Logic*, ed. K. Lambert, 121–42 Dordrecht: Reidel.

Wright, C. 1975. "On the coherence of vague predicates " *Synthese* 30: 325–65.

Wright, C. 1976. "Language-mastery and the sorites paradox." In *Truth and Meaning. Essays In Semantics*, eds. G Evans and J. McDowell, 223–47. Oxford: Clarendon Press. Reprinted in this volume: 151–73.

Wright, C. 1982. "Strict finitism." *Synthese* 51. 203–82

Wright, C. 1986a. "Does *Philosophical Investigations* I. 258–260 suggest a cogent argument against Private Language?" In *Subject, Thought, and Context*, eds. P Pettit and J. McDowell, 209–66. Oxford: Oxford University Press.

Wright, C. 1986b. *Realism, Meaning and Truth*. Oxford· Basil Blackwell.

Wright, C. 1986c. "Rule-following, meaning and constructivism." In *Meaning and Interpretation*, ed. C. Travis, 271–97. Oxford: Basil Blackwell.

Wright, C. 1986d. "Theories of meaning and speakers' knowledge." In *Philosophy in Britain Today*, ed. S. G. Shanker, 267–307. London: Croom Helm. Reprinted in Wright 1986b, 204–38.

Wright, C. 1987a "Further reflections on the sorites paradox." *Philosophical Topics* 15: 227–90. Reprinted (with omissions) in this volume· 204–250

Wright, C. 1987b. "On making up one's mind: Wittgenstein on intention." In *Logic, Philosophy of Science and Epistemology*, eds. P Weingartner and G. Schultz, 266–79. University of Minnesota Press.

Wright, C. 1988. "Realism, anti-realism, irrealism, quasi-realism." In *Midwest Studies in Philosophy, Vol. 12*, eds. P A. French, T. E. Uehling, and H. K Wettstein, 25–49. Minneapolis: University of Minnesota Press.

Wright, C. 1992 "Is higher order vagueness coherent?" *Analysis* 52: 129–39.

Wright, C. 1995. "The epistemic conception of vagueness " *Southern Journal of Philosophy* 33 (Supplement): 133–59.

Zadeh, L. A. 1965. "Fuzzy sets." *Information and Control* 8: 338–53. Reprinted in *Fuzzy Sets and Applications: Selected Papers by L. A. Zadeh*, eds. R. R. Yager et. al., 29–44 New York· John Wiley, 1987.

Zadeh, L. A. 1975. "Fuzzy logic and approximate reasoning " *Synthese* 30: 407–28.

Zemach, E. M. 1991. "Vague objects." *Noûs* 25: 323–40.

Index